Criminal Interrogation and Confessions Third Edition

Criminal Interrogation and Confessions Third Edition

Fred E. Inbau,
The John Henry Wigmore Professor of Law Emeritus,
Northwestern University,
and a Former Director of the Chicago Police
Scientific Crime Detection Laboratory
Chicago, Illinois

John E. Reid,
Late President, John E. Reid and Associates,
and a Former Staff Member of the Chicago Police
Scientific Crime Detection Laboratory
Chicago, Illinois

Joseph P. Buckley,
President, John E. Reid and Associates,
Chicago, Illinois

WILLIAMS & WILKINS
Baltimore • London • Los Angeles • Sydney

Editor: John Gardner
Associate Editor: Carol Eckhart
Copy Editor: Shelly Hyatt Blankman
Design: Bob Och
Production: Anne G. Seitz

First Edition, 1962
Second Edition, 1967
    Reprinted 1970, 1971, 1972, 1973, 1974, 1977, 1979, 1980, 1981
Japanese Edition, 1962

Library of Congress Cataloging in Publication Data

Inbau, Fred Edward.
    Criminal interrogation and confessions.
    Includes index.
    1. Police questioning—United States. 2. Confession (Law)—United States. I. Title.
KF9664.Z9I5   1985   363.2′54   84-21989
ISBN 0-683-04305-6

87 88 89 90   10 9 8 7 6 5 4 3

Preface

This third edition of *Criminal Interrogation and Confessions* is basically an entirely new book. The art of interrogation since the 1967 date of the preceding edition has been vastly improved. Moreover, the law governing interrogation and confessions has also experienced considerable changes. The present publication is reflective of both sets of developments.

New interrogation tactics and techniques have been added, and a number of the earlier published ones have been revised and rearranged to blend into the format of the nine steps toward effective interrogation that constitute the core of Part I of the the present edition. These developments are due primarily to the skill and ingenuity of my now deceased co-author, John E. Reid.

Reid was actively engaged in the professional specialty of criminal interrogation for almost 40 years, and he personally trained many persons to become excellent interrogators. Numerous others received the benefit of his skill through the medium of the interrogation seminars, conducted over a long period of time throughout the country by the staff of John E. Reid and Associates. He also participated in the planning of the present publication and in the preparation of some of the manuscript of Part I until his affliction with a cardiovascular illness, which ultimately resulted in his death on January 11, 1982.

Fortunately, Joseph P. Buckley, who was trained by Reid, and who has been a member of the staff of John E. Reid and Associates for 14 years and is now its president, was willing to work with me toward the completion of the book. Without the availability of his combination of the required skills, and his unstinting devotion to the project over a period of several years, the book would have taken a much longer time to complete, and it would have lacked the quality that I believe it possesses.

I am very grateful, and this gratitude is shared by my co-author Buckley, to the following members of the staff of John E. Reid and Associates for their general suggestions and enhancement of the concepts discussed herein: Louis C. Senese, James J. Bobal, William P. Schrieber and particularly to Daniel S. Malloy and Brian C. Jayne for specific recommendations regarding the semifinal draft of Part I of the manuscript, and to the latter for his preparation of the Appendix containing his analysis of the psychological principles underlying many of the book's interrogation techniques. An expression of appreciation is also due to a former member of the Reid staff who is now a Chicago lawyer, Philip A. Mullenix, for his very helpful suggestions regarding the Part I semifinal manuscript copy.

During the lengthy time spent on the preparation of Part II of the book, which deals with the law on interrogation and confessions, I received the help of a number of Northwestern University law student research assistants, to all of whom I am grateful.

Fred E. Inbau

NOTICE

Part 1 of this book contains materials relating to the method developed and used by John E. Reid and Associates, Inc. in teaching a course on Criminal Interrogation and Behavioral Analysis Interviews to law enforcement officers and others involved in security investigations. A description of such method, as taught in such course, has been included herein with the written consent of John E. Reid and Associates, Inc. and may be used by the reader in his or her work as an investigator. However, John E. Reid and Associates, Inc. has retained all property rights to teaching such method in its course and no part of such method may be used by others, for commercial purposes, in teaching similar courses without a written license from John E. Reid and Associates, Inc.

Inbau, Reid and Buckley: Criminal Interrogation and Confessions, Third Edition, Williams & Wilkins, 1986

Due to the special nature of this book, with its discourse between interrogator and suspect, the words *he* and *him* are used generically in order to avoid redundance.

Contents

Introduction

This text is presented in two parts. Part I deals with the tactics and techniques of criminal interrogation, which are listed in the Table of Contents of this text. Part II presents the law governing interrogations and certain aspects of the admissibility of confessions as evidence in criminal cases, which are also listed in the Table of Contents.

The first section of Part II—"Interrogation Law"—discusses the law as it pertains directly to the conduct of law enforcement officers and private security personnel who have the responsibility of interrogating criminal suspects. It is presented in such a way as to be understandable to the nonlawyer. Only the most important legal decisions are discussed in any detail, whereas others of lesser significance are merely footnoted.

The second section of Part II—"Confession Law"—is intended primarily for prosecuting attorneys, who will find in it concise discussions, accompanied by authoritative references, regarding the legal problems most frequently encountered with respect to a confession's admissibility as evidence.

It is suggested that both sections of Part II may be of further value to lawyers and other persons who are called upon to offer instruction to police or private security personnel regarding the law governing their functions as interrogators. Moreover, the entire book may be used as a text in an appropriate course within the curriculum of a criminal justice school.

In this introduction to the book, we have deemed it advisable to present the following discussion of the practical need for interrogation as an investigatory process. Although the discussion is obviously not required for persons who are directly involved in or well acquainted with the practicalities of law enforcement or private security investigations, it deals with certain aspects of interrogation that should alleviate some of the reservations, or even the strong negative feelings, that some persons and groups have about the criminal interrogation process in general.

There is a gross misconception, generated and perpetuated by fiction writers, movies, and TV, that if criminal investigators carefully examine a crime scene, they will almost always find a clue that will lead them to the offender; and that, furthermore, once the criminal is located, he will readily confess or otherwise reveal guilt, as by attempting to escape. This, however, is pure fiction. As a matter of fact, the art and science of criminal investigation have not developed to a point where the search for and the examination of physical evidence will always, or even in most cases, reveal a clue to the identity of the perpetrator or provide the necessary legal proof of guilt. In criminal investigations, even the most efficient type, there are many, many instances where physical clues are entirely absent, and the only approach to a possible solution of the crime is the interrogation of the criminal suspect himself, as well as of others who may possess significant information. Moreover, in most instances, these interrogations, particularly of the suspect, must be conducted under conditions of privacy and for a reasonable period of time. They also frequently require the use of psychological tactics and techniques that could well be classified as "unethical," if we are to evaluate them in terms of ordinary, everyday social behavior.

To protect ourselves from being misunderstood, we want to make it unmistakably clear that we are unalterably opposed to the so-called "third degree," even on suspects whose guilt seems absolutely certain and who remain steadfast in their denials. Moreover, we are opposed to the use of *any* interrogation tactic or technique that is apt to make an innocent person confess. We are opposed, therefore, to the use of force, threats of force, or promises of leniency—any one of which might well induce an innocent person to confess. We do approve, however, of such psychological tactics and techniques as trickery and deceit that are not only helpful but frequently indispensable in order to secure incriminating information from the guilty, or to obtain investigative leads from otherwise uncooperative witnesses or informants.

Private security officers frequently are confronted with the same type of problems encountered by the police. Commercial enterprises sustain enormous losses due to thievery on the part of employees, and to thieving by others, although to a much lesser extent. A large percentage of those losses can only be resolved by the interrogation of suspected persons.

Our position, then, may be presented in the form of three separate points, each accompanied by case illustrations:

1. *Many Criminal Cases, Even When Investigated by the Best Qualified Police Departments, Are Capable of Solution Only by Means of an Admission or Confession from the Guilty Individual or upon the Basis of Information Obtained from the Questioning of Other Criminal Suspects.*

As to the validity of the forgoing statement, we suggest that consideration be given to the situations presented by cases such as the following ones. A man is hit on the head while walking home late at night. He does not see his assailant, nor does anyone else. A careful and thorough search of the crime scene reveals no physical clues. Or, a woman is grabbed on the street at night and dragged into an alley and raped. Here, too, the assailant was unaccommodating enough to avoid leaving his wallet or other means of identification at the crime scene, and there are no physical clues. All the police have to work on is the description of the assailant given by the victim herself. She describes him as about 6 feet tall, white, and wearing a dark suit. Or consider this case, an actual one in Illinois. Three women are vacationing in a wooded resort area. They are found dead, the result of physical violence, alongside a foot trail, and no physical clues are present.

In cases of this kind—and they all typify the difficult investigation problem that the police frequently encounter—how else can they be solved, if at all, except by means of the interrogation of suspects or of others who may possess significant information?

There are times, too, when a police interrogation may result not only in the apprehension and conviction of the guilty, but also in the release of the innocent from well-warranted suspicion. Here is one such actual case within our own professional experience.

The dead body of a woman was found in her home. Her skull had been crushed, apparently with some blunt instrument. A careful police investigation of the premises did not reveal any clues to the identity of the killer. No fingerprints or other significant evidence were located; not even the lethal instrument itself could be found. None of the neighbors could give any helpful information. Although there was some evidence of a slight struggle in the room where the body lay, there were no indications of a forcible entry into the home. The deceased's young daughter was the only other resident of the home, and she had been away in school at the time of the crime. The daughter could not give the police any idea of what, if any, money or property had disappeared from the home.

For several reasons, the police considered the victim's husband a likely suspect. He was being sued for divorce; he knew his wife had planned on leaving the state and taking their daughter with her; and the neighbors reported that the couple had been having heated arguments, and that the husband was of a violent temper. He also lived conveniently near—in a garage adjoining the home. The police interrogated him and although his alibi was not conclusive, his general behavior and the manner in which he answered the interrogator's questions satisfied the police of his innocence. Further investigation then revealed that the deceased's brother-in-law had been financially indebted to the deceased; that he was a frequent gambler; that at a number of social gatherings that he had attended, money disappeared from some of the women's purses; that at his place of employment there had been a series of purse thefts; and that on the day of the killing, he had been absent from work. The police apprehended and questioned him. As the result of a few hours of competent interrogation—unattended by any abusive methods, but yet conducted during a period of delay in presenting the suspect before a committing magistrate—the suspect confessed to the murder. He told of going to the victim's home for the purpose of selling her a radio, which she accused him of stealing. An argument ensued and he hit her over the head with a mechanic's wrench he was carrying in his coat pocket. He thereupon located and took some money he found in the home and also a diamond ring. After fleeing from the scene, he threw the wrench into a river, changed his clothes, and disposed of the ones he had worn at the time of the killing by throwing them away in various parts of the city. He had hidden the ring in the attic of his mother's home, where it was found by the police after his confession had disclosed its presence there. Much of the stolen money was also recovered or else accounted for by the payment of an overdue loan.

Without an opportunity for interrogation the police could not have solved this case. The perpetrator of the offense would have remained at liberty, perhaps to repeat his criminal conduct.

2. *Criminal Offenders, Except, of Course, Those Caught in the Commission of Their Crimes, Ordinarily Will Not Admit Their Guilt unless Questioned under Conditions of Privacy, and for a Period of Perhaps Several Hours.*

This point is one that should be readily apparent not only to any person with the least amount of criminal investigative experience, but also to anyone who will reflect momentarily upon the behavior of ordinary law-abiding persons when suspected or accused of nothing more than simple social indiscretions. Self-condemnation and self-destruction not being normal behavior characteristics, human beings ordinarily do not utter unsolicited, spontaneous confessions. They must first be questioned regarding the offense. In some instances, a little bit of information inadvertently given to a competent interrogator by the suspect may suffice to start a line of investigation that might ultimately establish guilt. On other occasions, a full confession, with a revelation of details regarding a body, loot, or instruments used in the crime, may be required to prove the case; but whatever the possible consequences may be, it is impractical to expect any but a very few confessions to result from a guilty conscience unprovoked by an interrogation. It is also impractical to expect admissions or confessions to be obtained under circumstances other than privacy. Here again, recourse to our everyday experience will support the basic validity of this requirement. For instance, in asking a personal friend to divulge a secret, or embarrassing information, we carefully avoid making the request in the presence of other persons, and seek a time and place when the matter can be discussed in private. The very same psychological factors are involved in a criminal interrogation, and even to a greater extent. For related psychological considerations, if an interrogation is to be had at all, it must be one based upon an unhurried interview, the necessary length of which will in many instances extend to several hours, depending upon various factors, such as the nature of the case situation and the personality of the suspect.

3. *In Dealing with Criminal Offenders, and Consequently Also with Criminal Suspects Who May Actually Be Innocent, the Interrogator Must of Necessity Employ Less Refined Methods Than Are Considered Appropriate for the Transaction of Ordinary, Everyday Affairs by and between Law-Abiding Citizens.*

To illustrate this point, let us revert to the previously discussed case of the woman who was murdered by her brother-in-law. His confession was obtained largely by the interrogator's adoption of a friendly attitude in questioning the suspect, when concededly no such genuine feeling existed; by a pretense of sympathizing with the suspect because of his difficult financial situation; by suggesting that perhaps the victim had done or said something which aroused the suspect's anger and which would have aroused the anger of anyone else similarly situated to such an extent as to provoke a violent reaction; and by a resort to other similar expressions, or even overtures of friendliness and sympathy, such as a pat on the suspect's shoulder. In all of this, of course, the interrogation was "unethical" according to the standards usually set for professional, business, and social conduct, but the pertinent issue in this case was no ordinary, lawful, professional, business, or social matter. It involved the taking of a human life by one who abided by no code of fair play toward his fellow human beings. The killer would not have been moved one bit toward a confession by being subjected to a reading or lecture regarding the morality of his conduct. It would have been futile merely to give him a pencil and paper and trust that his conscience would impel him to confess. Something more was required—something that was in its essence an "unethical" practice on the part of the interrogator; but, under the circumstances involved in this case, how else would the murderer's guilt have been established? Moreover, let us bear this thought in mind: From the criminal's point of view, any interrogation is unappealing and undesirable. To him it may be a "dirty trick" to encourage him to confess, for surely it is not being done for his benefit. Consequently, any interrogation might be labeled as deceitful or unethical, unless the suspect is first advised of its real purpose.

Of necessity, therefore, interrogators must deal with criminal suspects on a somewhat lower moral plane than that upon which ethical, law-abiding citizens are expected to conduct their everyday affairs. That plane, in the interest of innocent suspects, need only be subject to the following restriction: Although both "fair" and "unfair" interrogation practices are permissible, nothing shall be done or said to the suspect that will be apt to make an innocent person confess.

There are other ways to guard against abuses by criminal interrogators short of taking the privilege away from them or by establishing unrealistic, unwarranted rules that render their task almost totally ineffective. Moreover, we could no more afford to do that than we could stand the effects of a law requiring automobile manufacturers to place governors on all cars so that, in order to make the highways safer, no one could go faster than 20 miles an hour.

PART I

INTERROGATION TACTICS
AND TECHNIQUES

CHAPTER ONE

Preliminary Preparations

DETAILS OF OFFENSE—INVESTIGATION EFFORTS AND RESULTS

How To Prepare for the Interrogation of a Suspect

Prior to the interrogation, and preferably before any contact with the suspect, become thoroughly familiar with all the known facts and circumstances of the offense. This information should be obtained from the most reliable available sources because any inaccuracies will seriously interfere with the effectiveness of the interrogation. If, for example, the interrogator is misguided by an investigator's preconceived theory, or by an erroneous piece of information procured during the course of the investigation, the use of such information may place the interrogator at a considerable disadvantage because the suspect who is guilty and realizes the inaccuracy of the interrogator's information will be more confident about lying; if the suspect is innocent, he will feel insecure because of a lack of confidence in the interrogator.

The following example demonstrates the difficulty that can result when an interrogator receives inadequate factual information or misconceived impressions from investigators: A triple murder occurred one winter some years ago in a state park. The three victims were married women, each about 50 years of age, who were vacationing together and staying at the park's lodge. They had gone for a walk along a pathway not frequently used at that particular time of year. When all three were found dead, their bodies bore evidence of severe beatings, their hands were tied in "chain" fashion (a hand of each victim tied to a hand of another one), and their underclothing was torn, with consequent exposure of the genital areas.

As a result of the absence of any observable evidence indicative of possible robbery, the investigators settled upon a sex motivation as the only plausible explanation. However, after a 6-month lapse and no solution to the crime, a different law enforcement agency began its own investigation. Only then was it discovered that among the clothing discarded at the scene was a glove that had been worn by one of the victims. Inside the

3

glove were two rings, one an engagement ring and the other a wedding ring. This finding gave rise to the probability of a robbery rather than sex-motivated offense because it revealed that one victim probably had attempted to save her rings by pulling them off along with her gloves to demonstrate to the robber that she had no jewelry on her person.

A 20-year-old dishwasher in the park's lodge had originally been questioned but was dismissed as a suspect primarily because of age — he was much younger than the victims and therefore presumably unlikely to be interested sexually in them. Once the motivation for the crime was shifted from sex to robbery, the dishwasher was interrogated again. This time, he confessed the triple murders, confirming that the motive was robbery. He said he had killed the lodge guests to avoid being identified and had torn their clothing to simulate evidence of sexual molestation, for which he thought he would not be considered a suspect. This decoy proved to be successful temporarily, as demonstrated by the erroneous surmise of the original investigators.

Another example of the difficulty experienced by interrogators because of a misinterpretation of certain evidence is a case where the murder victim's body was found with his trousers and underwear below his knees. The assumption of sexual motivation was dispelled when the offender confessed that he had killed the victim as a result of an argument in a car, and then had dragged the body through a field to the place where it was discovered. During the dragging process, the pants and underwear had become dislodged. There had been no sexual involvement.

Obtain whatever information is available about the suspect and, in certain types of cases, about the victim as well. A person equipped with such information will be in a much better position to ask the kind of probing questions required for an effective interrogation.

Do not rely upon a physician's estimate of the time of death of the victim or of the time when the fatal wound was inflicted. All too frequently, such reliance leads to a futile interrogation of a suspect. Even the most competent of trained forensic pathologists report that it is very difficult, and even impossible in many instances, to estimate accurately the time of death or of the infliction of the fatal wound. Unfortunately, the ordinary physician who has not received specialized training in this field is the one who usually indulges in unwarranted speculations. In one case, for example, a physician who worked part time on a coroner's staff estimated that an elderly woman found murdered in an alley behind her home had been killed between 11:00 p.m. and midnight. Since persons who knew her reported that she never would have been out alone at that time of night and because her son, who lived in the victim's residence, was at home during that time period, the son became a prime suspect and was questioned persistently, without success, by a series of police investigators. Finally, an experienced interrogator who was called into the case became convinced that the son was innocent. The interrogator suggested that the investigators consider the possibility that death had occurred at an earlier time and that they should look for other suspects. Eventually the perpetrator was discovered and he made a confession, which was thoroughly verified by the details of the occurrence that would have been known only by the killer himself. The crime had occurred hours before the physician's estimate.

Remember that when circumstantial evidence points toward a particular person, that person is usually the one who committed the offense. This may become difficult for some investigators and interrogators to appreciate when circumstantial evidence points to someone they consider highly unlikely to be the type of person who would commit such an offense, for example, a clergyman who is circumstantially implicated in a sexually-motivated murder. By reason of his exalted position, he may be interrogated only casually or perhaps not at all, and yet it is an established fact that some clergymen do commit such offenses.

An additional illustration of the unfavorable consequence of assuming that a person of a certain status or good repute "could not do such a thing" is the case of the wife of a business executive who had accepted a job as a part-time bank teller and who, for various reasons, seemed to be the one most likely to have embezzled $6,500 from a customer's bank account. It seemed incongruous to the investigators that a person with her personal financial assets, including $10,000 in her own savings account at the same bank, would have committed such an act. Nevertheless, an experienced, effective interrogator elicited a confession from her in which she revealed a very unusual explanation. Her mother, whom her husband despised, needed money for surgery. Under no circumstances would the husband have allowed a contribution to be made to assist her. If his wife had withdrawn the necessary money from her own account, that fact would have come to the husband's attention. As an alternative source, she diverted $6,500 from the bank account of a depositor, who was a friend of hers and whose savings account could well stand a withdrawal of that amount without it being discovered soon or even noticed at all. As the forgoing case demonstrates, no one should be eliminated from suspicion solely because of professional status, social status, or any other comparable consideration when there exists strong circumstantial evidence of guilt.

After obtaining information from an investigator, consider the possibility that the investigator may have become so convinced of the suspect's guilt and so anxious to obtain a confession himself, that he prematurely may have confronted the suspect with an accusation or may have indulged in some verbal abuse. These actions can, of course, severely hinder a subsequent interrogation by a competent interrogator, particularly in a case situation where an impulsive investigator already had threatened physical abuse of the suspect.

Consider that an investigator may have worked so many hours or days on a case that, without any malicious intent, he may have withheld relevant information or even may have supplied unfounded information to the interrogator.

Consider the possibility of rivalry between two or more investigative agencies — for example, a local police department and a sheriff's office. In such cases, the interrogator should conduct separate interviews with the case investigators affiliated with each agency. In this way, there is more likely to be a full disclosure of relevant details. The same may be true on occasions where two or more of a single agency's investigators on the same case have been working more or less independently of each other. Understandably, there is an ego factor that may discourage a full exchange of information between the two investigative units or between individual investigators.

While listening to an investigator's report of the incident in question, jot down notes regarding dates, time, and nicknames of participants or witnesses, and fill in the complete details later rather than interrupt the investigator who is giving the report. Otherwise, an interruption may result in a break in the continuity of the investigator's thoughts or memory, and he may inadvertently fail to disclose some significant information.

In appropriate situations, encourage the person relating the details of a case to sketch the place of the occurrence and to note on it any relevant points. If crime-scene photographs are available, they, of course, can be used, along with a freehand sketch, to trace the sequence of events. Usually, a sketch that is supplemented with notations is better for the interrogator's purpose than photographs alone, even though the sketch may be drawn crudely. Photographs, unaccompanied by a full explanation from the investigator, may be inadequate or even misleading because usually they cannot, by themselves, fully portray a situation or event.

When interviewing the person regarding the facts of a case, ask what he believes may have happened, whom he believes to be the chief suspect, and why. He, of course, is much closer to the details than the interrogator. In one case, for example, an investigator made the following observation that proved to be of considerable value: "Jim was in love with Amy and Joe was fooling around with her and that's why I think Jim shot Joe." In another case, an interrogator's inquiry of this nature drew the following response from an investigator: "The word on the street is that Frank did it because he flashed a lot of money around right after the robbery." In still another case, an investigator said: "That guy Mike was so damn nervous he couldn't stand still!" referring to the suspect's behavior soon after the crime. In each of these cases, the information obtained proved to be very helpful to the interrogators in formulating their interrogation tactics and techniques.

Give serious consideration to the reliability of information submitted by a paid informer. There are times when the information is based only upon the informer's conclusions rather than upon actual facts or observations. Then, too, on many known occasions, false information is deliberately furnished by an informant in order to obtain payment or to receive favorable consideration regarding his or her own criminal activities. Most certainly, many informers do reveal accurate and reliable information. However, the authors merely wish to urge a cautious evaluation.

View with suspicion any anonymous report implicating a person in a criminal offense. This is particularly true in instances where a reporter has experienced a personal problem, such as having been jilted or deserted by her spouse. Such a person might send the police an anonymous letter suggesting that the man who offended her committed a certain crime. This may be done out of spite, or for the purpose of getting the man into a situation where he may need her help or be required to delay a planned departure from the city or country—all for the purpose of "getting him back again." In summary, it is always a good practice for an interrogator to view with suspicion a "tip" or accusation based upon an anonymous report. To be sure, there are occasions when the report is well founded, but in the vast majority of instances, there is some ulterior motive. (A male, of course, is capable of being just as vengeful with respect to a female who has jilted or deserted him, but his vented feelings are usually exhibited in a more blatant manner, such as physical abuse.)

Whenever feasible, personally interview the purported victim, the accuser, or the professed discoverer of the crime before proceeding to interrogate the suspect. A purported crime victim should be asked to relate the details of the occurrence and to give, whenever possible, a detailed description of the offender or of the place where the offense occurred. If the account of the offense is couched in generalities only, it should be viewed with skepticism, because it is characteristic of a false statement to be lacking in the kind of details that are almost always present in a genuine one. For instance, if an employee has falsely reported a robbery in which company money was involved, he or she will ordinarily be very vague as to a description of the robber or as to when, how, or where the incident occurred. A genuine robbery report will ordinarily reveal such details.

At the outset of the interview of a child victim of a sex offense, the interrogator should clearly identify himself and the purpose of the interview. The interviewer should exhibit a calm, patient, and casual manner, and it is usually advantageous to initiate the interview with a general discussion of the child's interests, daily activities, the names of brothers and sisters, etc. Once a rapport has been developed and the interviewer has established some basic understanding of the child's manner of speech and use of words, the child should be encouraged to relate in his or her own words the event in question. It is essential, however, to elicit the information "bit by bit" rather than to seek it in a full recitation. When discussing parts of the body, it may be very helpful to have a doll or a book of pictures available for reference. Extreme caution must be exercised, however: 1) to avoid suggesting what was allegedly done to or with those parts of the body, and 2) to avoid overquestioning a child, especially by several persons on different occasions, because the child may ultimately feel obligated to supply information the questioner seems to want.

Ask a child victim of sex offense to describe the scene of occurrence. For instance, if the crime is alleged to have occurred in the home of a particular individual, the child should be asked to describe the room—its curtains, wall colors, floor rug, bed, and other such objects. If the description is accurate, that fact will serve to corroborate the child's accusation; moreover, when the child's revelation of such details are disclosed to the suspect, it will have a very desirable impact.

Exhibit concern, sympathy, and understanding toward sex crime victims who generally are very reluctant to reveal the details of the offense. Such victims often have difficulty in relating precisely what the offender did and said. The interrogator can ease this burden by suggesting they consider the interrogator very much in the same light as a doctor whom they might consult regarding a sensitive problem. This tends to relieve the victim of much of her embarrassment. Avoid asking questions in a forceful tone of voice. Also, allow the victim to tell her story without interruption, and then delicately ask specific questions concerning aspects of the occurrence that were unclear or incomplete. Care must be taken, however, not to sympathize to the point where the interrogator, in an effort to avoid traumatizing the victim, asks leading questions such as, "I'm sure you went along with him because you were intimidated by this man's size. Is that right?"

In interviewing victims who are ultrasensitive about verbally discussing the event, provide writing materials to enable the victim to record on paper, while being left alone, the details of what the offender did and said. Resorting to a written account of a reported offense or accusation may also be of value in those instances where a doubt prevails as to the validity of the alleged victim's assertions, assuming, of course, that the victim is able to do the necessary writing. She may be requested to write a detailed account of her whereabouts, activities, and observations over a reasonable span of time before and after, as well as during, the alleged event. For example, if a woman claims to have been raped at 10:00 p.m., the interrogator should tell her to write (if she can) everything that happened to her between 8:00 and 10:30 on the night of the rape. This is preferable for several reasons: 1) a person who is falsely accusing someone tends to provide much more detail as to occurrences prior to and following the incident than during the actual incident; conversely, the truthful person usually will focus the written account primarily upon the crime itself; 2) truthful victims will often include emotional comments such as, "Then he struck me in the face and it hurt a lot"; a falsifying person usually is not creative enough to include in the written account the emotional impact of the crime; and 3) an account that provides a perfect sequence in terms of events is more likely to be false than an account that contains some events out of sequence. These principles for evaluating a sex victim's written (or oral) account of events are applicable in the evaluation of accounts related by the purported victims of other types of crime as well.

During an interview with the presumed victim or other reporter of a crime that involves money or property rather than physical offense, a skillful interrogator may ascertain that no crime was in fact committed. For instance, an interview with the person who reports as a theft the disappearance of money, jewelry, or other property may reveal information that will subsequently establish that the missing item was either misplaced or perhaps deliberately disposed of by the owner in order to perpetrate a fraud on an insurance company. An accuser, upon being skillfully interviewed, may admit or otherwise reveal the accusation to be false by reason of revenge, an extortion attempt, or for some other purpose. And there are occasions when the person who professes to have discovered the commission of a crime, or to have found evidence of it, was in fact the offender, and the reported discovery was merely a ploy to divert suspicion from himself.

Summary

When full credibility has been established regarding the victim, the accuser, or the crime discoverer, the facts that are learned may be extremely helpful in determining the procedure to be followed in the interrogation of the suspects themselves.

In certain types of cases where the victim of the occurrence is in a position to influence the disposition to be made of a case solution, as in the case of a theft by an employee, the interrogator should inquire about the victim's attitude with respect to what action, if any, he expects to take toward the perpetrator. The interrogator should be mindful, however, that in some jurisdictions, as discussed in Chapter 8 of this text, it is a criminal offense to condition a restitution or compensation agreement upon a promise not to seek or participate in a criminal prosecution. Legally permissible, however, is the settlement of a civil claim for the loss or injury incurred by the victim.

One basic principle to which there must be full adherence is that the interrogation of suspects should follow, and not precede, an investigation conducted to the full extent permissible by the allowable time and circumstances of the particular case. The authors suggest to interrogators, therefore, the guideline: "Investigate before you interrogate."

SPECIFIC INFORMATION OF VALUE TO INTERROGATORS

There are many kinds of information that an interrogator should have available before beginning the interrogation of a suspect:

Information about the Offense Itself

1. The legal nature of offensive conduct, e.g., forcible or statutory (under-age) rape, robbery, burglary or plain theft, and exact amount and nature of loss
2. Date, time, and place of the occurrence (in accurate detail)
3. Description of the crime area and of the crime scene itself
4. The way in which the crime seems to have been committed and known details of its commission, e.g., implement used, place of entry or exit
5. Possible motives for its commission
6. Incriminating factors regarding a particular suspect

Information about the Suspect or Suspects

1. Personal background information, such as age, education, marital status, financial and social circumstances, and criminal record, if any
2. Present physical and mental condition, as well as medical history, including any addictions to drugs or alcohol
3. Attitude toward investigation, e.g., hostile, cooperative
4. Relationship to victim or crime scene
5. Incriminating facts or possible motives
6. Alibi, or other statements (oral, written, or recorded) that the suspect related to investigators
7. Religious or fraternal affiliations or prejudices
8. Home environment
9. Social attitudes in general
10. Hobbies
11. Sexual interests or deviations *but only if directly relevant to investigation*
12. Abilities or opportunities to commit offense

Information about the Victim or Victims

1. Companies or other institutions:

Attitudes and practices toward employees and public
Financial status (insurance against losses, etc.)
2. Persons:
Nature of injury or harm and details thereof
Age, sex, marital status, and family responsibilities (number of dependents)
Social attitudes regarding race, nationality, religion, etc.
Financial and social circumstances
Physical and mental characteristics
Sexual interest or deviations, *but only if directly relevant to investigation*
Blackmail potentialities

If an interrogator feels that the information received is inadequate for an effective interrogation, he should consider the advisability of postponing the interrogation until the investigation has been resumed in pursuit of further details. In some instances, of course, a delay for that purpose is not feasible, and the interrogator may have to proceed on the basis of the limited information that is available.

The following case situation illustrates the value of the forgoing types of information: The office building of a corporation was partially destroyed by a nighttime fire. An investigation of the scene clearly established that the fire was deliberately set and that it started in the bookkeeping section of the company office, to which the entrance seems to have been effected by means of a door key rather than by force. Not only had the fire started in the bookkeeping area, but also the company's financial records had been burned outside the cabinet in which they were customarily kept. Moreover, the fire occurred the day before a scheduled audit was to have been made by an independent auditing firm. Although these facts clearly indicated that the fire had been deliberately set to conceal an embezzlement, the interrogation of the personnel in the bookkeeping office was delayed until some background information became available. An investigation revealed that a recently employed cashier was considerably in debt, and that his wife spent money excessively. Also, interviews with the cashier's previous employer disclosed that his accounts had been short on several occasions, and that whenever the shortage was called to his attention, he readily offered to make up the deficit out of his own funds. Furthermore, the former employer had experienced a sizable loss, which had never been traced or otherwise explained.

Equipped with this information about the cashier, the interrogator was in a far better position to conduct an effective interrogation than if such facts had been unknown or unavailable. In the latter situation, even if the interrogator had not detected the fact of deception or otherwise had suspected the cashier, there would still have been lacking, to the interrogator's definite disadvantage, the interrogation leads implicit in the information about the possible motive and the losses at the cashier's previous place of employment. Moreover, and perhaps of equal importance, the interrogator who is equipped with such interrogation leads is better able to avoid certain pitfalls that could have a very detrimental effect, particularly with regard to his rapport with the suspect. For instance, in the previous case, if the interrogator had been unaware of the wife's extravagance as a possible reason for the embezzlement, he may well have questioned the cashier on the basis of unfounded references, such as gambling activities or "another woman," both of which may have justifiably angered the suspect because the real reason was his wife's extravagance. On the other hand, using information about the wife's conduct as a contributing factor permitted the interrogator to invoke the very effective technique of placing the moral blame for the offense upon someone else—in this case, the wife. This technique is described later in Chapter 6.

In cases where a suspect has given an alibi, it is imperative that the alibi be checked, if at all possible, before the interrogation begins. Any known defects in it will assist the interrogator very materially. Moreover, an alibi check may actually establish the innocence of the suspect, despite other circumstances that may point to his guilt. In such instances, the interrogator's full attention can be directed toward obtaining helpful leads from the suspect regarding other possibilities, or the interrogation may be abandoned altogether. All too often, time and effort are unnecessarily and unfairly expended in the interrogation of an innocent suspect where an alibi check would have readily established his innocence.

Another example with respect to a valid alibi possibility is the case where police investigators were so thoroughly convinced that a certain prostitute committed a murder that they proceeded to immediately interrogate her in an effort to obtain a confession. Eventually, when the date of the murder was mentioned, she said: "You're wasting your time on me; I was in jail at the time." A check revealed the truthfulness of her alibi. This type of incident occurs all too often.

CONSIDERATION OF CASE SOLUTION POSSIBILITIES

As case information is being given, the interrogator should begin thinking about possible solutions. He should raise many important preliminary questions, such as the possible method used to commit the crime, the probable suspect or suspects, the possibility of a false report of stolen money, and whether inside assistance may have been accorded the person or persons who burglarized a place of business. For instance, if a store manager has reported as a theft the disappearance of money from a safe, the following possibilities could be considered:

1. Was there evidence of a forcible entry into the premises?
2. Had the safe been locked?
3. Who knew or might have known the safe's combination, or had access to it or to supplemental keys to the safe?
4. Is there any reason why the manager or owner himself might have taken the money?
5. Might the owner of the store have had a motivation for a false theft report, such as dwindling income or business losses, that would be alleviated by insurance coverage?
6. Was the store locked for the night?
7. Could some customer or outsider have concealed himself in the store after hours?
8. What is the possibility that an employee set up the burglary and helped thieves steal the money?
9. Is it possible that an insider (employee) stole the money himself?
10. Was the money accidentally left out of the safe?

The following example shows this probing analysis approach: The manager of a large company reported that upon several occasions, money had been stolen, including some of his own, along with a signet ring that he had temporarily placed in a money box. Arrangements were made for polygraph tests to be conducted on a number of employees, all of whom were reported as being truthful with respect to the missing money and ring. Finally, the polygraph examiner suggested that the manager himself submit to an examination. He failed the test and admitted the theft of all that had been reported as stolen by someone else. He had concocted the story about his ring to divert suspicion from himself.

In theft cases such as this one, where the reported loss is covered by insurance, consideration must be given to the possibility of a fraudulent claim. The first investigation or preliminary interrogation procedure should ascertain whether or not a loss or an offense did, in fact, occur. This principle is valid even in reported car theft cases because it is a fact that many such reported losses involve fraudulent claims for insurance, even to the extent of filing claims for nonexistent cars that had been insured on the basis of false credentials.

The following case also illustrates the value of applying this basic principle: A man moved into a suburban home next to an insurance salesman, who became very anxious to supply his new neighbor with all the various kinds of insurance he might need. Finally, the new neighbor agreed to insure a coin collection for $40,000. The agent was so elated over the sale that he arranged for an immediate issuance of the policy. When the insured individual inquired as to when the coin collection would be appraised, the agent replied "eventually," and payment was made of the first annual premium. Eleven months later — without any appraisal having been conducted — the coin collection was reported stolen in the course of a burglary, and only then did the insurance company realize that the collection had not been appraised. The company's adjusters, operating on the assumption that perhaps the collection was overly valued, arranged for the insured person to submit to a polygraph examination. Following the examination, which disclosed deception even as to the existence of a coin collection, the insured confessed that the claim was completely false — that obtaining the policy was done "in jest" due to the insurance salesman's pressuring him for business. Although the two forgoing cases involved polygraph testing, they illustrate the point that such possible solutions should not be overlooked in a strictly interrogation situation.

The following illustration further demonstrates the value of considering case solution possibilities: Several burglars, all brothers, had effected arrangements with certain dishonest businessmen to burglarize the business premises for a sum to be paid off after insurance coverage had been received for the losses. In one instance, a furrier who had encountered a business reversal arranged for the group of brothers to burglarize the store, to get into the storage vault, and to carry off furs insured at a value of $40,000. After the furrier had collected the full coverage, the burglars were paid $30,000, which netted the furrier $10,000 plus a secret return of all the $40,000 worth of furs — to be sold during the next season. This family team was known as "burglars by arrangement."

In the forgoing case, had no consideration been given to the possibility of a fraudulent scheme of this sort, employees of the fur shop would have been under suspicion and probably would have been subjected to investigation and interrogation as to their possible involvement. Therefore, in instances of this type, the owner himself should be considered a possible suspect, and he should be questioned thoroughly before the employees are interrogated.

Employees have been known to take advantage of an actual crime (such as a robbery or burglary) by stealing some of the money or goods presumed to have been stolen by an actual robber or burglar who had taken less than the reported loss, as is demonstrated in the following example: Burglars broke through the skylight of a large supply company and stole $75,000 in merchandise. The first employee on the premises reported the burglary, and after a short, unsuccessful investigation, the company fixed the skylight and replaced the supplies. Soon thereafter, burglars again broke the skylight and stole approximately the same amount in supplies. The discovery of both burglaries was made by the same employee.

While the second burglary was being investigated, a cashier reported $750 missing from her cashbox, which she kept concealed in a file cabinet. This theft clearly indicated the possibility that a company employee had stolen the money, and it aroused suspicion that the person who stole the $750 may have assisted in setting up the burglaries. An interrogation of the discoverer of the burglaries revealed that he had taken the $750, although he had not been involved in either of the burglaries. He explained that, unknown to the cashier, he had observed her placing the cashbox in the cabinet. He thought he could profit by stealing the money from the cashbox without detection and that the company officials would attribute the theft to the second burglary.

In another comparable case: A delivery truck driver, whose route was in a high crime area, expected to be robbed during the pre-Christmas season Anticipating such an occurrence, he placed a major portion of the cash received for his deliveries in a secret hiding place within the truck. Then, when the anticipated robbery did occur, he reported that all of the cash he had collected was taken by the robber. An effective interrogation of him elicited an admission that he himself had converted to his own use that portion which he had successfully concealed within the truck.

Despite the fact that the circumstances surrounding a theft-type crime seem strongly to indicate that a custodian or watchman may have been involved as an accomplice, an interrogator should not foreclose the possibility of that person's noninvolvement. The following case illustrates the advisability of proceeding with that precaution in mind: A big city department store was burglarized late one night, and a large amount of jewelry was stolen. The thieves had broken several jewelry display counters, which obviously would have caused considerable noise. A night watchman, who was supposed to have been in a nearby area at the time, disclaimed hearing any such noise. This rendered him suspect as an accomplice in the theft, and he was subjected to an interrogation based upon that theory. He steadfastly denied any such involvement, but he did admit that every night, including the one when the burglary occurred, he would, at a certain time, leave the store area unattended and go to a nearby diner for coffee and a sandwich. His account for the night in question was ultimately substantiated by the actual burglars after they were apprehended while attempting to sell their loot. They admitted that they had thoroughly cased the store, had learned about the coffee/sandwich routine of the watchman, and had arranged to adjust the lock on the door he used so that it would not lock automatically when the door closed.

In considering possible case solutions, it is important to remember, as previously suggested, that "discoverers" or "reporters" of crimes are sometimes the actual perpetrators. The following case is an example: A college student on leave from school was found shot to death in his bed at home. An older brother reported that he had discovered the dead body. The only person under any suspicion was an elusive petty thief who had stolen a small item from one of the farm motors on the premises and who, on another occasion, had been suspected of attempting to burglarize the farmhouse where the victim lived. The investigation, however, eliminated him as a suspect in the murder.

The victim's older brother, who reported the discovery of the body, soon criticized the police for complacency and negligence in their efforts to solve his brother's murder. He even claimed that the police were "covering up" the murder, and he accused the city officials of sponsoring an inept police department and of ignoring their responsibility. The prosecuting attorney of the county arranged for polygraph tests on various suspects, primarily as a defensive gesture. When they were cleared, the brother of the victim was asked by the examiner to take a test. He failed the test and, when confronted with the results, confessed that he had shot his brother as a result of an intense jealousy of him. He tearfully related how his father had favored his brother over him, had sent the brother to college, and had treated him better in every respect, even to the point of seeking his counsel on many matters; the confessor felt that he had been completely ignored and had been treated as just another farmhand. The castigation of the police for not solving his brother's murder was a final overt effort by the killer to gain his father's favor and recognition.

When taking facts from a person representing himself as the victim or witness, if the interrogator receives the impression that this person actually may be the perpetrator of the offense, it is suggested that the actual interrogation of him be postponed until other available information is accumulated. Inquiry should then be made about the discrepancies in the victim's version of the event, and a seemingly casual effort should be directed toward an explanation. If no explanation is forthcoming, there should be a further delay in questioning until all others in the case have been questioned and eliminated as suspects. An accusatory confrontation at this later time offers a much greater chance for a successful interrogation.

There are various subtle factors that should not be overlooked by the interrogator in terms of possible case solutions. The following case is an example: An employee of Company X was suspected of stealing $3,000 from the company. In examining his employment record, it was learned that he had worked formerly for a public utility company, which he had left to take a lesser paying job with Company X without any potential offsetting opportunities for promotion. It was also ascertained that in changing jobs, he even had forfeited the seniority rights that he had acquired at the public utility company. A question arose, therefore, as to why the suspect should have left his employment with that company. The interrogator called the utility company and learned that the suspect had stolen $3,000, which he had said he needed to pay for an operation to correct his newborn child's clubfoot. The only penalty he had incurred for this was his dismissal as an employee. Thereafter, he had accepted employment at Company X with the lesser benefits.

The suspect was confronted with the utility company dismissal and the clubfoot story. He then confessed that he had stolen the same amount—$3,000—from Company X and for the same reason: a second child born with a clubfoot! Although the odds of two children in the same family being born with a clubfoot are astronomical, this nevertheless proved to be true.

Another case solution factor to be borne in mind is that what may originally seem to be irrelevant information will many times provide a valuable lead. The following is an example: A young man and woman were shot to death while they parked in the "lovers' lane" section of a city park. Persons in the area at the time reported having seen a young man riding a bicycle to and from the "lovers' lane." Also, a young boy had complained to the police that an older boy had knocked him off his bicycle not very far from the park and had taken the bicycle, saying that he wanted to ride it to the park. The police initially ignored this complaint, considering it unfounded. Later, however, the young boy was questioned, and he revealed the identity of the older boy who had taken the bike. When questioned about the theft and the shooting, the older boy confessed that he not only had shot and killed the two lovers in the park but also had robbed two other couples there on a previous occasion after "peeping" at their activities. The point of this case is that if the seemingly irrelevant initial information had not been pursued, the double murder may have remained unsolved.

GENERAL SUGGESTIONS TO INTERROGATORS

It is important for the interrogator to keep in mind some basic principles that often are overlooked:

1. A suspect's alibi should be thoroughly checked out, whenever possible, prior to any interrogation.
2. When a series of money thefts occurs within a single establishment or unit, usually only one person is the thief. The theft of merchandise may be an exception, especially if it is of a large quantity and presumably required two or more persons to remove it.
3. The suspect must have had access to a missing item in order to steal it. He may only have had an excuse for being in the area. It is much easier for a person to steal when he has a definitely legitimate reason for being there.
4. Crimes of homicide and arson are usually committed by a single individual. Gangland killings are an exception and so are killings by terrorists or by religious cults.
5. As previously indicated, in some instances the reporter or discoverer of

a crime should be given prime consideration as a suspect. Also, in some types of offenses, relatives or close friends of a victim should be checked out before proceeding to an investigation of other possibilities.

6. A sexually-motivated arsonist will usually remain at the scene of a set fire or at least be a spectator long enough to achieve sexual gratification from the experience. For example, in one arson case, the policeman at the fire repeatedly had to tell a bystander: "I told you to stand back; If I have to tell you again, I'll arrest you!" This spectator later confessed to having set the fire.

7. Before conducting an interrogation, an effort should be made to learn if the suspect had been interrogated previously by someone else investigating the case, and to ascertain how a custodial suspect had been treated during his period of incarceration. Was the individual actually accused of the crime or of other crimes? Was he physically abused in any way, threatened, or offered any promise of leniency? Did he have a sufficient amount of rest, adequate food or drink, and an opportunity to use toilet facilities? Did the person make any significant admission or confess the crime and then subsequently retract it? Did he retract after having talked to a parent, friend, member of the family, or some other person? If the interrogator can find no evidence of abuse, threats, or promises that might have induced an innocent person to confess, then a prior confession is probably true. In the event that a suspect had been cleared of suspicion by the first interrogator, this information will assist in evaluating the suspect's state of mind, and it will also be helpful in determining whether to proceed with an interrogation immediately or to wait for a more opportune time.

8. Does the suspect have any known physical, mental, or emotional impairments? Has he been taking any medication? This information is important to know in evaluating his reactions during the interrogation. A flaw in a physical, mental, or emotional condition may mislead the interrogator.

9. The interrogator should ascertain the suspect's previous attitude about the anticipated interrogation. As discussed in Chapter 5, innocent suspects are usually very cooperative during an investigation, whereas guilty suspects are usually uncooperative and try to avoid or delay being interrogated.

CHAPTER TWO

Initial Precautionary Measures for the Protection of the Innocent

CAUTION AS TO EYEWITNESS IDENTIFICATIONS AND POSSIBLE MOTIVATIONS FOR FALSE ACCUSATIONS

In eyewitness identification cases, interrogators should be mindful of the fact that there is a very high degree of fallibility regarding such identifications, even in cases involving multiple identifiers. Indeed, of all the factors that account for the convictions of innocent persons, the fallibility of eyewitness identifications ranks at the top, far above any of the others.

One of the finest books on the subject, although written primarily for utilization by lawyers who participate in the trials involving eyewitness testimony, contains some excellent information for interrogators and other investigators.[1] Along with much other valuable information, the author, Patrick M. Wall, listed a number of "danger signals." Of particular importance to criminal interrogators are the following danger signals:

1. The identifying witness *initially* had stated he would be unable to identify the perpetrator.
2. The identifying witness had known the suspect prior to the crime, but had made no accusation against him when first questioned by the police.
3. A serious discrepancy exists between the identifying witness's original description of the offender and the actual appearance of the suspect.

---

[1] WALL, EYE-WITNESS IDENTIFICATION IN CRIMINAL CASES (1966). Also with regard to the fallibility of eyewitness identifications, see LOFTUS, EYE-WITNESS TESTIMONY (1979).

4. Before identifying the present suspect, the witness had identified someone else.
5. Other witnesses to the crime had failed to identify the suspect.
6. Before the crime was committed, the witness had had a very limited opportunity to see the suspect.
7. The identifying witness and the suspect are of different racial groups.
8. During his original observation of the offender, the witness had been unaware that a crime situation was involved.
9. A considerable period of time had elapsed between the time of the witness's view of the offender and his identification of the suspect.
10. The crime had been committed by a number of persons.
11. The witness fails to be "positive" in his identification.

The authors of the present text offer the following suggestions, which may be implicit in or auxiliary to Wall's suggestions:

Consideration should be given to the possibility that the identifying witness may report what he perceives the offender to have looked like rather than what he actually looked like.

The crime victim or witness may be biased not only as to race but also by reason of nationality, religion, organizational or fraternal affiliation, or, in an employer-employee situation, the factors of managerial or union status.

Perception is psychologically affected by general attitudes and environmental factors. A traumatic experience in a prisoner-of-war or concentration camp, or even a prior favorable or unfavorable police experience, may affect the validity of an identification of a criminal suspect.

In cases of sexual abuse, if a child can identify the person suspected of being his or her abuser, and can also relate an account of the event itself, his eyewitness identification is rarely invalid; however, interrogators should be aware of the possibility that the child may have been exploited by an adult seeking an ulterior objective. Classic examples of this are in cases where an influencing adult seeks vengence against the suspect. An innocuous experience of a child could be embellished by such an adult so as to constitute a criminal act. For instance, an innocent touching of a female child by someone toward whom her mother harbors a feeling of vengefulness—and particularly an estranged or divorced husband exercising a visitation privilege with the child—may, with suggestive prompting, evoke a tale of criminal sexual conduct. The authors are aware of a number of such instances that could have resulted in tragic consequences were it not for skillful questioning of the person responsible for the false accusation.

Implausible motivations can be bases for false sex offense charges. In a rare case, for example, a Congressman's daughter accused a man she had formerly dated of trying to rape her. The accused male vehemently denied that any attempted rape had occurred, or that he had ever indulged in sexual intercourse with her. He stated that after having advised the young woman he would discontinue dating her, she had vowed to "get even with him," and, indeed, she had made that effort. One night she concealed herself in his car, and after he had driven away, she announced her presence and got into the front seat. As the driver stopped his car, she threw herself upon him. He stopped and tried forcibly to eject her, which he accomplished only after a considerable struggle. The girl then reported the event to the police as an attempted rape and, indeed, displayed the torn condition of her clothing. The accused was arrested and formally charged. He insisted upon a polygraph test, the results of which supported his truthfulness. Then the girl was tested, with results indicating deception. An ensuing interrogation resulted in her admission that she had been very much in love with the accused man and could not tolerate his rejection of her. She further explained that she herself had torn her clothing in order to lend plausibility to her false accusation.

In sex offense case situations involving adolescent females who accuse their fathers of criminal sexual conduct, consideration should be given to possible motives on the part of the daughter. One actual case of this type involved a false accusation motivated by the father's restriction on his daughter's dating and her breaches of his curfew rules.

In summary, interrogators (as well as investigators) should always exercise caution in evaluating eyewitness identifications, and also the accusations of alleged victims in sex offense cases that are unsubstantiated by evidence beyond the accusations themselves.

CAUTION AS TO CIRCUMSTANTIAL EVIDENCE

There are many instances where the initial discovery or presence of physical evidence at the scene of a crime seem to point convincingly toward some person as the perpetrator of the offense under investigation. This evidence may be in the form of an article of clothing, such as a hat, coat, glove, or handkerchief; or it may be in the form of other personal property, such as a wallet, pen, notebook, glasses, key, or even firearm. Although evidence of that nature will often serve to identify the offender or at least lead to him as a suspect, it may on occasions give rise to a completely false assumption, and an interrogator must always be mindful of that possibility.

An outstanding example of the risk of attaching investigative conclusiveness to the finding of items of the forgoing nature is the following famous case of Suzanne Degnan, which occurred in Chicago in the early part of 1941: Suzanne, age 6, had been kidnapped from the bedroom of her home and her dismembered body was later found in a sewer. In her mouth was a handkerchief that contained the laundry serial number of a soldier stationed in the Chicago area, and the initials monogrammed on the handkerchief were the same as the soldier's! Moreover, the soldier's parents lived near the Degnan home and while on military leave, he had stayed with them shortly before and after the kidnapping. When questioned by the police, he stated that at the time the kidnapping occurred, he had been alone on one of Chicago's elevated trains and had been riding it for several hours—obviously not a convincing alibi. Subsequent developments, however, completely exonerated him and revealed that the actual killer had committed a number of burglaries, many of which had occurred in living quarters of females, and that his entries into the places had been basically sexually motivated. Presumably, it was in the course of a burglary of the soldier's parents' home that the killer had acquired the handkerchief with the earlier suspect's initials on it.

Although circumstantial evidence against the soldier suspect was sufficient to warrant fully the suspicion that it had created, the same cannot be said for the appraisal that police investigators gave to certain circumstantial evidence against another suspect in the same case—a janitor of an apartment building in the basement of which Suzanne Degnan's body had been dismembered. First, the janitor, of course, had had a key to the basement, as well as keys to other adjoining buildings that he serviced. Second, these circumstances recalled to the police a case that had occurred in Chicago some years earlier, a case in which a woman had been murdered by a janitor in the basement of one of his buildings. Those were, however, the only two factors on which the police could base their deduction that the janitor in the Degnan case must be guilty. They were so convinced of the janitor's guilt that a police sergeant working on the case proceeded to attempt to extract a confession by putting the janitor on what was referred to as a "trapeze." The device consisted of an adjustable horizontal bar over which the janitor's arms, handcuffed behind him, were placed at a height that allowed only his toes to lend him any support. Despite this unconscionable treatment, the janitor never confessed. Subsequently, the actual killer, 17-year-old William Heirens, was apprehended and convicted. The janitor filed a civil suit against police officials and others, which was settled for a sizable sum, but he did not live very long thereafter to enjoy it. It is highly probable that the "interrogation" ordeal to which he had been subjected expedited his demise.

This unfortunate event could have been averted if the police had paused long enough to have had tests made in the police department's newly acquired scientific crime detection laboratory to determine whether blood was on the janitor's clothing or in his fingernail scrappings or other parts of his body. The body or clothing of the person who had dismembered the child's body undoubtedly would have borne some trace of the victim's blood. Furthermore, a polygraph examiner had been available to test the janitor suspect. (Many suspects had been tested in the same case, including the previously mentioned soldier suspect.) However, no test was made of the janitor.

CHAPTER THREE

Privacy and the Interrogation Room

PRIVACY

The principal psychological factor contributing to a successful interrogation is privacy—being alone with the person under interrogation. Interrogators seem instinctively to realize this factor in their own private or social affairs, but they generally overlook or ignore its importance in criminal interrogations. In a social situation, an interrogator may carefully avoid asking a personal friend or acquaintance to divulge a secret in the presence of other persons; he instead will seek a time and place when the matter can be discussed in private. Likewise, if an interrogator is troubled by a personal problem, he will usually find it easier to confide in one other person. Even a problem that concerns more than one other person is usually discussed with each of the persons on separate occasions. However, in criminal interrogations, where the same mental processes are in operation, and to an even greater degree by reason of the criminality of the disclosure, interrogators generally seem to lose sight of the fact that a suspect or witness is much more apt to reveal any secrets in the privacy of a room occupied only by himself and the interrogator rather than in the presence of an additional person or persons.

The following three cases illustrate this point. The first case took place in a small Midwestern town. A man was being questioned concerning the killing of his wife, who had been shot on a lonely road not far from a main highway. According to the husband's story, while he and his wife were riding in their automobile, they were held up and robbed. The robber took a ring off the woman's finger and then fired upon her as she called for help. For a number of reasons, the husband's account of the occurrence was viewed with considerable skepticism, and he was suspected of being the actual killer.

For several hours, upon two or three different occasions during the 24 hours following the shooting, the husband was subjected to considerable questioning—but always in the presence of several persons. Later, at the request of the prosecuting attorney, one of the authors of this text interrogated the suspect. A private room was selected for this purpose, and everyone else was excluded.

From the very moment the suspect entered the room, he displayed every indication of guilt; from the outset, it seemed quite evident that here was a person *who wanted to confess*. As the interrogator already knew, the suspect had experienced a very unhappy married life—sexual incompatibility, meddling relatives, etc. Now, he actually wanted to unburden himself of these and other troubles generally. He needed some sympathy; he wanted to be told that the shooting of his wife was something that anyone else might have done during weaker moments under similar circumstances. It was essential, however, that he was allowed the opportunity to be alone with the person who would listen to his troubles and offer him the sympathy his mind craved. Until his discussion with this interrogator, he had not had the opportunity to do so. When the opportunity presented itself, however, he very readily told how he had killed his wife and why, and he revealed the location where he had discarded the weapon and the ring.

This was the easiest sort of case. It should have been unnecessary for the local authorities to seek outside assistance. All that was really needed was a little privacy.

The second case involved an investigation into the rape and murder of a young girl who had been employed as a hostess in a cafeteria. She had disappeared while on her way home from work one night, and her nude body had been found in a ditch by the side of a cemetery road the following morning. She had been last seen in the company of a busboy who worked at the same restaurant in which she had served as hostess. The busboy stated he had merely walked to the streetcar with her and had seen no more of her after that.

In an effort to obtain information concerning the character and habits of the deceased, and the relations between her and the busboy—insofar as such information might furnish some clue to her murderer—the local authorities began questioning other employees of the restaurant. This was undoubtedly a good starting point, but the procedure that followed deserves no recommendation. In the presence of 18 persons gathered in a large office, five waitresses from the restaurant were asked to divulge any confidential information they might have as to the character and habits of the deceased and of the busboy, who upon several occasions had been the escort and companion of two of these girls. In answer to questions concerning the character and habits of the victim, the waitresses invariably replied, "She was a good girl." When questioned about the boy and his behavior when alone with a girl, the answer was: "He is a good boy; on dates, he behaves like a gentleman." What other sort of answers could be expected—even if the victim had been a girl of very loose morals or the boy overly aggressive in his sexual behavior? It so happened, however, that further, more thorough, investigation resulted in a solution of the crime; the busboy was cleared, and the good moral character of the victim was confirmed. But suppose one or more of the five girls had possessed valuable information regarding either the victim or the busboy. Was it not expecting too much of them to provide such sensitive information in the presence of 18 persons, including several local politicians?

In the forgoing case, each one of the girls should have been questioned alone, with no one else present but the interrogator. However, for cases where the girl or woman to be questioned is the suspect, especially if she is a person of an unsavory character with a possible motive for hampering the investigation, it may be advisable to have a female police officer or some other reliable female in a position to hear and see what transpires if a male is to conduct the interrogation. In this way, the interrogator may protect himself from the possibility, although remote, of an accusation that while in the interrogation room, he made a sexual advance toward the suspect. If the female observer must be in the room, that person should be seated in back of and to the side of the suspect and be instructed to remain seated and to refrain from taking any part in the interrogation. In this way, the element of privacy is essentially fulfilled. (The next section discusses this suggested seating arrangement and also recommends the utilization of an observation room so as to avoid the need for an observer in the interrogation room itself.)

In the previously discussed *Degnan* murder case (see Chapter 2), the importance of privacy was impressively revealed by the 17-year-old murderer himself, William Heirens, whose fingerprints were found on a ransom note left in the Degnan home. The handwriting on the note was identified as his. There was also evidence that he had killed two other persons and had committed 29 burglaries. His attorneys, to whom he apparently had admitted his guilt, advised him to confess to the prosecuting attorney, thereby providing him an opportunity to be saved from the electric chair. Arrangements were made between Heirens's counsel and the Cook County State's Attorney for Heirens to make a confession, but at the appointed time and place, Heirens refused to confess. The reason for his last-minute refusal appears in the following headline from the *Chicago Daily News* of August 2, 1946: "Youth Asks Privacy at Conference. Blames Refusal To Talk on Large Crowd at Parley." The newspaper account further stated:

> It was learned that Heirens balked at a conference arranged for last Tuesday because [the state's attorney] had invited almost 30 law enforcement officers and others to be present . . . . It was at the conference between the youth and his lawyers that he told them for the first time that there were "too many" present

on Tuesday. He said he would go through with the confession arrangements to escape the electric chair if it could be done under different conditions. The state's attorney told reporters that he had invited the police officials to the conference because they had all played a leading part in the investigation and he felt they should be "in on the finish."

The *Chicago Times* of August 2, 1946, reported the Heirens confession incident in the following terms:

It was hinted the original confession program was a flop because the youth was frightened by the movie-like setting in [the state's attorney's] office. Presumably he was frightened out of memory, too. To every question about the murders he answered, "I don't remember." His self-consciousness reportedly was deepened by the presence of several members of the police department, especially [the police officer] whose handiness with flowerpots as weapons brought about Heirens' exposé in a burglary attempt.

At the second setting for the taking of Heirens's confession, the number of spectators was reduced by about one-half, but a reading of the confession gives the impression that Heirens, although admitting his guilt, withheld—for understandable reasons—about 50% of the gruesome details and the true explanations for his various crimes, including the sexual motivation for the burglaries in the living quarters of females.

It is indeed a sad commentary upon police interrogation practices when a 17-year-old boy has to impart an elementary lesson to top-ranking law enforcement officials, i.e., that it is psychologically unsound to expect a person to confess a crime in the presence of 30 spectators.

Although case experiences of the type illustrated by the last two examples are not likely to occur at the present time, there continues to be a widespread disregard of the essential condition of privacy by the presence of a second, third, or fourth person during the interrogation of a criminal suspect. In some police departments, it is common practice to interrogate a suspect in an open area in the corner of a crowded police station, with phones ringing, individuals walking in and out, and constant interruptions. Usually two, and sometimes three or more, officers join in the interrogation simultaneously, one attempting to outdo the other or trying to ask the one lucky question that will cause the suspect to confess. Such interrogations seem to emulate television or movie programs that portray actors as police officer interrogators. The scenes are dramatic and very fascinating to the viewers but, in the real world, are counterproductive.

The authors of this volume are fully aware of the practical difficulties that may be encountered in arranging for a private interrogation, even after the interrogator is convinced of its desirability. In a case of any importance, each investigator wants to be in on the interrogation, or at least be present when a suspect confesses or when an informer or a witness divulges valuable information. Each interrogator wants to improve his efficiency rating or otherwise demonstrate his value to the department or office. In addition, the publicity in the community is considered desirable—to say nothing of the satisfaction to the individual's own ego. All this is perfectly understandable and nothing more than normal human behavior, but it is something that must be controlled in the interest of interrogation efficacy.

The person in charge of the investigation, or someone with command rank, should direct that the interrogation be conducted under conditions of privacy. In instances where all investigators are of equal rank, and each one seems to want to participate in the interrogation, they should work out some arrangement among themselves to ensure the element of privacy. It is suggested that the interrogation be conducted by the officer who has demonstrated his skill as an interrogator or, under ideal conditions, by the one who has received special training as a professional interrogator.

Privacy in an interrogation can be maintained without denying to any investigator assigned to the case due credit for his efforts. An understanding may be reached among the various investigators to the effect that if a "break" comes when any of them have absented themselves from the interrogation room for the purpose of ensuring privacy between the interrogator and the suspect or witness, they will all share the credit for whatever results the interrogator himself obtains.

In personnel investigations, a security officer, or other interrogator acting on behalf of the employer may encounter a legal impediment to the achievement of the condition of privacy. The National Labor Relations Act has been interpreted as giving an employee the right to have, at his request, a union representative or fellow union employee present whenever there is to be an interrogation about a matter for which there may be disciplinary action.[1]

---

[1]National Labor Relations Board (N.L.R.B.) v. Weingarten, 420 U.S. 251 (1975). The issue is uncertain as to the right of a nonunion employee to have someone present. The N.L.R.B. ruled that the right existed, and that decision was upheld in DuPont v. N.L.R.B., 724 F. 2d 1061 (3rd Cir. 1983). However, the board subsequently announced that it wanted to reconsider its ruling, whereupon the federal court vacated its decision. 733 F. 2d 296 (1984). Since then, the N.L.R.B. has ruled that the right is confined to union employees. Sears, Roebuck & Co., 274 N.L.R.B. No. 55, 2/22/85, 53 LAW WEEK 2422 (1985).

SUGGESTIONS FOR SETTING UP THE INTERROGATION ROOM

Establish a sense of privacy. The room should be quiet, with none of the usual "police" surroundings and with no distractions within the suspect's view. (If existing facilities permit, a special room or rooms should be set aside for this purpose.) The room should be as free as possible from outside noises and should also be a room into which no one will have occasion to enter or pass through during the interrogation. This will not only instill a sense of privacy, but also the less the surroundings suggest a police detention facility, the less difficult it will be for the suspect or arrestee who is really guilty to implicate himself. The same surroundings will also be reassuring to the innocent suspect. Therefore, there should be no bars on the windows. (There should be an alternative means of protection against any attempts to escape.) In a windowless room that has no air-conditioning system, a mechanical blower or exhaust system may be installed without much difficulty to improve ventilation and to eliminate, or at least to minimize, noises. (The room should have its own thermostatic controls.)

Remove locks and other physical impediments. For nonpolice, private security interrogations, there should be no lock on the door of an interrogation room, nor should there be any other physical impediment to an exit by the suspect if he or she desires to leave the building itself. This will avoid any claims of false "imprisonment." The room should also be devoid of any large objects or drapes that might cause the suspect to believe that a concealed third person can overhear his conversation with the interrogator.

Remove all distractions. Interrogation rooms should be of plain color, should have smooth walls, and should not contain ornaments, pictures, or other objects that would in any way distract the attention of the person being interviewed. Even small, loose objects, such as paper clips or pencils, should be out of the suspect's reach so that he cannot pick up and fumble with anything during the course of the interrogation. Tension-relieving activities of this sort can detract from the effectiveness of the interrogation, especially during the critical phase when a guilty person may be trying desperately to suppress an urge to confess. If pictures or ornaments are used at all, they should be only on the wall behind the suspect. If there is a window in the room, it, too, should be to the rear.

Select proper lighting. Lighting fixtures should be arranged in such a way as to provide good, but not excessive or glaring, illumination of the suspect's face. Certainly, any lighting that interferes with the interrogator's full view of the suspect's facial features and expressions should be avoided. Also, there should not be any glaring light on the interrogator's face. This would not only interfere with the interrogator's observations of the suspect, but also may distort the interrogator's facial indications of understanding, sympathy, etc. Diffused, overhead lighting is more appropriate.

Minimize noise. No telephone should be present in the interrogation room because among other disadvantages, its ringing or use constitutes a serious distraction. Also, any noise emanating from the heat or ventilating system should be minimized to reduce the distraction.

Arrange chairs properly. The chairs for the interrogator and suspect should be about 4 or 5 feet apart, and they should directly face each other, without a desk, table, or any other object between them. The chairs should be of the type normally used as office equipment.

Straightback chairs should be used for the suspect as well as the interrogator. Other types of chairs induce slouching or leaning back, and such positions are psychologically undesirable. A suspect who is too relaxed while being interrogated may not give his full attention to the interrogator, and this will create an unnecessary hurdle. Similarly, this is no occasion for the interrogator to relax. His full attention and alertness are highly essential. Whenever possible, the seating arrangement should be such that both the interrogator and the suspect are on the same eye level. Most certainly, to be scrupulously avoided are chairs with lowered front legs or other deviations that place the suspect in an "inferior" posture or prevent him from making normal adjustments in sitting.

Set up an observation room. If available facilities and resources permit, there should be an observation room adjoining the interrogation room. The authors of this text recommend a smaller adjoining room, in the wall of which there is inserted a "two-way mirror"—a panel of glass chemically treated so as to permit someone from within a relatively dark observation room to see into the lighted interrogation room without being seen. The mirror should be off to one side—away from the suspect (see Figure 3.1) or at least above the eye level if its location has to be in front of the suspect. The interrogation room also should be equipped with a concealed microphone so that the person or persons in the observation room may hear as well as see what occurs in the interrogation room. (State and local laws should be checked first, however, to ascertain whether or not there is any legal prohibition against "electronic eavesdropping.")

An interrogation-observation room arrangement of the suggested type can be of considerable value in several respects:

1. It affords an opportunity for investigating officers to observe and hear the interrogation while the necessary privacy is maintained.
2. The suspect's behavior symptoms (discussed later in this volume) can be evaluated by fellow interrogators who have to prepare themselves for later involvement.
3. In cases where a female is the suspect, a policewoman or other female

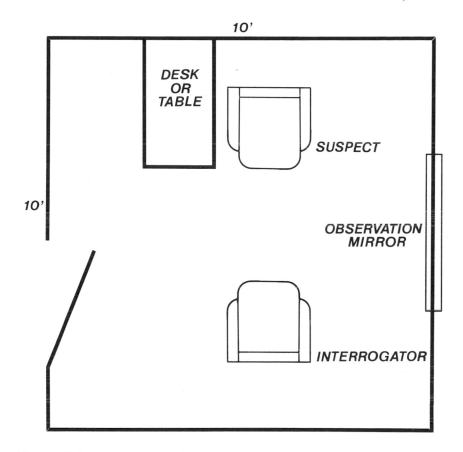

Figure 3.1.

may be stationed in the observation room to witness the proceedings as a safeguard against possible false accusations of misconduct on the part of the interrogator. The presence of any such witness, whether male or female, is also helpful in other types of situations as a safeguard against false accusations of physical abuse, threats, or promises on the part of the interrogator.

4. When a suspect is left alone in the interrogation room, he can be kept under observation as a precaution against any effort to escape or perhaps even the remote possibility of an attempt at suicide. Moreover, the observation room mirror arrangement may protect the interrogator from physical harm by a violence-prone suspect.

Although the probability of the last reason is remote, it is within the realm of possibility, as is evident from the following incident: A young, vicious-looking, multiple-rape suspect who was about to be interrogated requested some food, saying he had not eaten anything since his arrest. Food was brought to him and, also pursuant to his request (and inadvisably, as later events established), a bottle of soda. After being permitted to eat and drink alone, the suspect was observed standing next to the interrogation room door with the bottle in an upraised hand, obviously for the purpose of using it on the interrogator's head when he entered. The observer rushed out of the observation room and warned the interrogator of the impending danger. After a deliberately prolonged entrance delay by the interrogator, the suspect was observed to sit down, whereupon the interrogator entered and quickly, but discreetly, removed the bottle without making any comment about the occurrence. The ensuing interrogation resulted in the admission of a number of rapes in addition to the ones for which the suspect had previously been identified as the perpetrator.

Another possible usage of an interrogation room of the type described is illustrated by the following case: Two warehouse employees were suspected of being accomplices in the theft of tires from the company. During their individual interrogations, guilt was evidenced by their behavior symptoms. However, neither made any incriminating statement. It was decided therefore, to put them together in the interrogation room and to observe what occurred. Immediately, one of them placed a finger over his lips, signifying that silence was to prevail. Following the observation of this gesture, the interrogator removed the signaling suspect from the room and advised him that his incriminating behavior had been observed from the adjacent room through the mirror. He thereupon confessed, and when the other suspect was confronted with this development, he, too, confessed his participation in the theft.

A similar procedure may be followed in other case situations. For instance, in one case in which an interrogator had unsuccessfully interrogated a man suspected of murder, the evidence indicated that his wife, who was in the police station at the time of his interrogation, was aware of his guilt. So a decision was made to ask her to go into the room where her husband was and to wait there for a short while. The purpose was to be able to observe how they reacted to this situation. The interrogator surmised that if, in fact, she believed him to be innocent, she would be very upset and, by her actions and words, would exhibit that concern. On the other hand, if she knew he was guilty, she would probably remain rather passive and would probably indulge in whispering to him or making a gesture to remain silent. What transpired not only verified the interrogator's original belief but also was used advantageously in obtaining the husband's confession of guilt.

As earlier mentioned, in certain case situations, there may be a necessity to have a third person actually present in the interrogation room because of no observation room facility or because of some other factor. In a personnel case investigation, for instance, an employee may exercise his

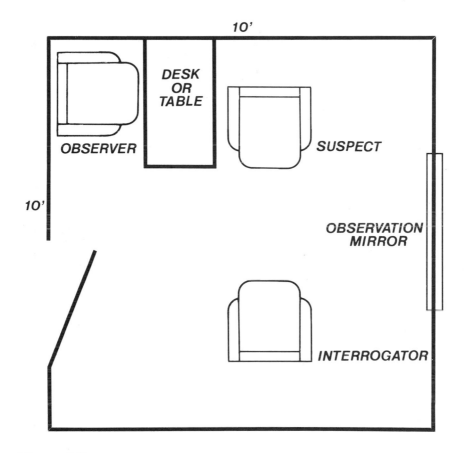

Figure 3.2.

right to have a union representative or some other fellow union employee present. Also in such cases, an employer may want to exercise the precaution of requiring that whenever a female suspect is to be interrogated by a male, another female must be present. Some police departments without an observation room facility follow a similar practice, particularly when the female suspect is of an unsavory character and perhaps prone to falsely accuse a police interrogator of making sexual overtures. Some state statutes specify that a juvenile suspect can only be interrogated in the presence of a parent or guardian. In all such instances, the third party should be seated in back of and to the side of the suspect, as illustrated in Figure 3.2.

Whenever an interpreter is needed to assist in the interrogation, the interpreter should be seated alongside the interrogator, who should be, of course, directly in front of the suspect. Figure 3.3 illustrates this seating arrangement.

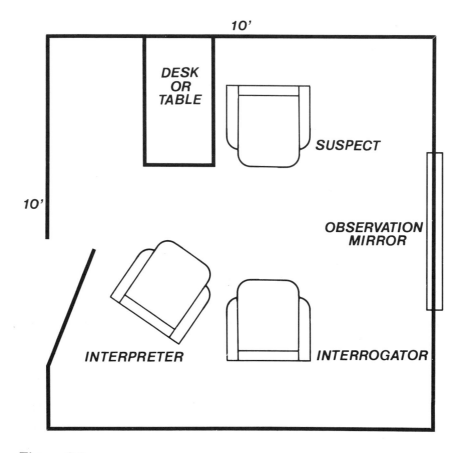

Figure 3.3.

Finally, in view of the forgoing guidelines, it becomes obvious that a suspect's own home or office is an inappropriate setting for an interrogation. It is advisable, therefore, to avoid whenever possible an interrogation in a home or office.

CHAPTER FOUR

Qualifications, Attitude, and General Conduct of the Interrogator

INTERROGATOR QUALIFICATIONS

Ideally, every police department and private security unit should have among their personnel specially trained professional interrogators. The responsibility of interrogating suspects should not automatically go to arresting officers or others who may not possess the required personality traits or may lack the special training needed to conduct effective interrogations. One reason for this is that the same traits that make a police officer or private security officer highly efficient in locating witnesses, procuring evidence, and performing other investigative tasks may prove to be disadvantageous when it comes to interrogating criminal suspects. For instance, impatience to complete an assignment may be a great asset insofar as investigations are concerned, but impatience is a handicap in the interrogation room.

An interrogation specialist should fulfill certain qualifications. First, special personal attributes should be present. For example, the person should be intelligent and should have a good practical understanding of human nature. He should possess suitable personality traits that are evident from a general ability to "get along" well with others, including acquaintances and fellow officers. As already mentioned, patience is another indispensable attribute.

Second, the specialist should have an intense interest in his field. He should study texts or articles regarding the art of criminal interrogation tactics and techniques and should attend one or more seminars conducted by competent, experienced interrogators. These can be of considerable value.

Third, it is essential for the specialist to become aware of the legal rules and regulations that govern interrogation procedures and the taking of confessions from persons upon whom these interrogation tactics and techniques have proved productive. (Such rules and regulations for interrogators are discussed in Chapter 8 of this text.)

Professionalizing the interrogation function within a police department would have three benefits: 1) there would be a considerable increase in the rate of confessions from criminal offenders; 2) the confessions will more likely meet the prescribed legal requirements; and 3) there would be the expeditious and dependable elimination from suspicion of persons innocent of the crimes for which they have been incarcerated or subjected to questioning on a theory of their involvement in the offense. Comparable benefits will accrue to a private security unit staffed by one or more professionally trained interrogators.

ATTITUDE AND GENERAL CONDUCT OF THE INTERROGATOR

It is difficult to formulate or to propose any set rules with regard to the attitude and conduct of an interrogator during the interrogation. Much depends on the circumstances of each particular case. However, in general, the following recommendations should be helpful, particularly with respect to the interrogation of the criminal suspect himself:

Avoid creating the impression of an investigator seeking a confession or conviction. It is far better to fulfill the role of one who is merely seeking the truth.

Keep pencil and paper out of sight during the interrogation. Recording or making notes of the suspect's statements or comments during the course of an interrogation may grimly remind the suspect of the legal significance or implication of an incriminating remark. It is better to avoid note-taking, or at least to postpone it until the latter stages of the interrogation. If the suspect mentions a name or an address that the interrogator wants to be certain to remember, pencil and paper can be used to note that information but then should be removed from the suspect's view.

Dress in civilian clothes rather than in uniform. Otherwise, as in the previous recommendation, the suspect will be reminded constantly of police custody and the possible consequences of an incriminating disclosure. If the uniform cannot be avoided altogether, the coat, star, gun, and holster should be removed for the duration of the interrogation. The interrogator should wear conservative clothes (suit, jacket, or dress) and should avoid colorful ties or other conspicuous clothing accessories. Unless weather conditions demand otherwise, a male interrogator should wear a coat or jacket throughout the interrogation. A short-sleeved interrogator does not command the respect that the situation requires.

Do not use realistic words, such as murder, rape, strangle, stab, or steal, except in certain situations. It is much more desirable, from a psychological standpoint, to employ inferential terminology by talking about the offense as "this thing," "it," or "that." The suspect will know, of course, that the reference is to the offense, but the connotation is less disturbing to him or her than harsh legalistic labels. For similar reasons, a suspect should not be confronted with photographs gruesomely displaying a victim's wounds or injuries.

In order to properly set the stage for the interrogation, someone else should escort the suspect into the interrogation room. That person should also point out the chair in which the suspect is to sit while waiting for the interrogator to arrive. The escort should then say: "Mr., Mrs., or Miss _____[naming the interrogator] will be in to see you in a few minutes." (The escort also may be the one to issue the Miranda warnings of constitutional rights.) Prior identification has two advantages: 1) it eliminates the need for the interrogator to introduce himself to the suspect when the two meet, and 2) its formality tends to heighten the apprehension of a guilty suspect by reason of the apparent exalted status of the interrogator, and whatever confidence the suspect may have had in his ability to evade detection will be somewhat diminished. At the same time, an innocent suspect will be favorably impressed by this professional arrangement and thereby will be relieved of any apprehension over the possibility of being falsely determined to be guilty.

In the early stages of an interrogation, sit about 4 or 5 feet from the suspect. (Later, this distance can be shortened.) Also, as earlier stated, there should be no table, desk, or other piece of furniture between the interrogator and suspect. Sitting or standing a long distance away or the presence of an obstruction of any sort constitutes a serious psychological barrier and also affords a guilty suspect a certain degree of relief and confidence not otherwise attainable.

The suggested close seating arrangement also is reminiscent of such commonplace, yet meaningful, expressions as "getting next" to a person or "buttonholing" a customer, terms that signify that when a person is close to another one physically, he is also closer psychologically. Anything, such as a desk or table, between the interrogator and the suspect defeats this purpose and should be avoided.

To preserve and maintain the advantage of this close seating arrangement, it is very important that the interrogator be free of any offensive breath odor, whether due to food, such as garlic, or to some other factor. As a precaution, it is advisable, whenever possible, to pursue the practice of talking at close range to a fellow interrogator or other colleague just before entering the interrogation room. In this way, the interrogator may be made aware of an offensive breath odor. In the event that any such odor is present, a mouthwash or breath cleanser should be used. An advisable precaution, of course, is to avoid eating food that will cause offensive odors. For example, garlic will cause offensive odors for many hours after its consumption and therefore should be avoided, and this is true, albeit to a lesser extent, in regard to onions.

An understanding should prevail among interrogators, and others working with them, that if an offensive breath or body odor emanates from anyone, that condition will be brought to his attention. The same should be true in regard to any distracting facial appearance or clothing disarray. It is far better for an interrogator to be told of this by a colleague than to have a suspect sustain the annoyance or distraction and thus be deterred from the effectiveness of an interrogation.

Remain seated and refrain from pacing about the room. To give undiverted attention during the interrogation makes it much more difficult for the suspect to evade detection of his deception. Moreover, the actions of jumping up and down and walking around give evidence of the interrogator's impatience, with its consequent encouragement to a lying suspect that if he continues to lie a little while longer, the interrogator will give up. An entirely different impression is created by the interrogator who remains seated throughout the interrogation.

The interrogator also should avoid fumbling with a pencil, pen, or other accessories. This action tends to create the impression that the interrogator lacks confidence or even is seriously uninterested.

Avoid smoking. First, if the suspect is a nonsmoker, smoking by the interrogator may be offensive. Second, if the interrogator is not smoking, the suspect is less likely to attempt to smoke in an effort to relieve emotional tension or to bolster his resistance to an effective interrogation. If a request to smoke is made, the interrogator may suggest, with justification and fairness, that the suspect postpone smoking until he leaves the interrogation room.

To facilitate matters with respect to an avoidance of smoking by a suspect, it will be helpful if there are no ashtrays present; otherwise, they represent a tacit invitation to smoke.

Use language that conforms to that used and understood by the suspect. In dealing with an uneducated or unintelligent person, the interrogator should use simple words and sentences. And where, for instance in a sex crime case, the suspect uses slang or commonplace expressions and gives evidence of being unfamiliar with more acceptable terminology, the interrogator should resort to similar expressions. This can be done in a reserved manner without the loss of the suspect's respect for the position occupied by the interrogator. No attempt should be made, however, to imitate the suspect's style of speech.

When interviewing persons of low socioeconomic status, address them as "Mr.," or "Mrs.," or "Miss" rather than by their first names. Of course, it is usually better to address persons of high socioeconomic or professional status by their first name or by their last name without attaching "Mr.," "Mrs.," or "Miss." However, to avoid seeming impertinent, it may be well in some instances—especially where a suspect is older than the interrogator—to preface addressing the suspect by the first name by asking: "You don't mind if I call you Helen [or John], do you?" Thereafter, if no objection is voiced, the suspect can be referred to by the first name.

For the suspect of a high socioeconomic or professional status, using the first name or last name only (without the accustomed "Mr.", "Mrs.," or "Miss") may defuse his or her usual feeling of superiority and independence. However, the practice of using "Mr.," Mrs.," or "Miss" with someone of low socioeconomic status can be advantageous because it may flatter the person; a feeling of satisfaction and dignity may acrrue from such unaccustomed courtesy. By according the suspect this consideration, the interrogator will enhance the effectiveness of whatever he says or does thereafter.

An exception to this forgoing practice should be made in a case involving the interrogation of a married female criminal suspect who is known to have been indulging in sexual relations with other men. It is better to address her by her first name rather than as "Mrs." In this way, the interrogator minimizes to some extent the guilt feeling or embarrassment that may prevail because of the wife connotation of "Mrs."

If the interrogator believes that a female suspect has loose morals, or is even a prostitute, the chance to interrogate her is not an invitation to treat her rudely; in fact, the interrogator defeats his own purpose when that is done. The following two case situations, which were encountered by one of the authors some years ago, serve well to illustrate this point.

In the first case, a woman of about 60 years of age was suspected of murdering a male boarder in her rooming house. She had called the police to report that the man had died, apparently of natural causes. An autopsy revealed, however, that he had been killed with a small-caliber bullet in his back. Suspicion was directed toward the woman for several reasons, one of which was the fact that she had been the deceased boarder's sleeping companion. Arrangements were made for one of the authors of this text to interrogate her. At the time of the scheduled interrogation, she was accompanied by a police captain of about 20 years' experience as a police officer. He related the case history to the interrogator while the suspect remained seated in another room. Then, when the interrogator was ready to proceed with the interrogation, the captain called out for the suspect to come to the interrogation room. As she approached, he pointed to the room and said, "Get on in there, you old whore; this man wants to talk to you!" She looked at him with considerable scorn as she entered the room. After the captain departed, the interrogator proceeded to address her as "Mrs. _____" and asked her to have a seat. He then inquired if she had been given any food while in police custody and while being questioned earlier by the police. She said "no," and readily accepted the interrogator's invitation to have coffee and a sandwich delivered to her in the interrogation room. Thereafter, the interrogator treated her as a "lady" rather than as a "whore." She soon confessed to the killing of the boarder and supplied information that definitely established her guilt. Moreover, before she was through talking, she confessed to the killing, several years before that, of her husband, who was known to have died under suspicious circumstances.

In the second case, a prostitute was suspected of a robbery that had followed the administration of a drug to the victim, who was seated at the bar of a tavern at the time. After the suspect removed her coat in the interrogation room, the interrogator observed that a broken shoulder strap on her dress had caused one of her breasts to be exposed. Before proceeding with the interrogation, the interrogator procured a towel and placed it over the prostitute's shoulder. After a relatively brief interrogation, during which she was addressed as "Miss" rather than by her first name, she confessed the crime and disclosed the identity of her accomplice. Without doubt, the interrogator's treatment of her as a "lady" facilitated his task, for here was a woman who basically preferred that status to her own calling.

In the interrogation of homosexuals, some police are prone to refer to them as "queers" or "fruits." As a result, resentment develops, and the interrogation is rendered far more difficult. It is much more effective for the interrogator to treat such suspects as though their homosexual conduct is morally acceptable to him. Homosexuals or their companions should never be referred to as "queers," "fruits," or other similar derogatory labels.

Treat the suspect with decency and respect, regardless of the nature of the offense. No matter how revolting or horrible a crime may be (e.g., a sexually-motivated, brutal killing of a small child), the suspect should not be treated or referred to as a despicable, inhumane individual. A sympathetic, understanding attitude and interrogation approach (see Chapter 6) is far more effective. In one of many cases that could be used to illustrate this point, a sex offender, after his confession, said, "I would have told the officers about this earlier if they had only treated me with some decency and respect."

After catching a suspect in a lie, never scold or reprimand him by the use of such expressions as "Why in the hell did you lie to me?" or "You lied to me once and you'll lie to me again." It is much better to conceal any reaction of resentment, or even of surprise. In fact, the more effective handling of the situation is merely to convey the impression that the interrogator knew all along that the suspect was not telling the truth.

Do not handcuff or shackle the suspect during the interrogation. Not only would this show fear of the suspect, but under such circumstances, a confession may be rejected on the ground of coercion.

Do not be armed. The interrogator should face the suspect as "man-to-man" and not as police officer-to-prisoner. Another, although unrelated, reason for not being armed, is the fact that in close quarters, the suspect, if so inclined, might be able to seize unexpectedly the interrogator's weapon for use on the interrogator or others who may seek to prevent his escape.

Also, with respect to weapons, precautionary measures should be taken in certain types of situations to ensure that the suspect himself is not armed. If in police custody, there is little likelihood of his being in possession of a weapon, but consider the following actual case example of this possibility and the advisability for precautionary measures: A probationary city police officer was arrested for taking indecent liberties with small neighborhood children. The police had been investigating the murder of another child from a nearby locale. It was thought possible that the policeman under arrest may have been responsible, and he was asked to submit to a polygraph test. He was accompanied to the site of the testing laboratory by two police officers and a deputy superintendent of police. When the suspect was seated in the interrogation room and the examiner attempted to place the pneumograph tube around the suspect's chest, a gun was discovered hidden under his armpit. By a quick move, the examiner was able to remove the gun from him. The police officers who witnessed the occurrence from an observation room rendered immediate assistance. After the disturbance and a stern reprimand to the officers by the examiner for their not searching the suspect previously, the test was conducted.

What could have happened if that gun had not been accidentally discovered?: The suspect could have: 1) while alone, shot himself; 2) shot the examiner; or 3) used the gun to effect an escape. It was learned later that because the suspect was a fellow police officer, only a casual search of his person had been made before he arrived for the test. The camaraderie of the police in this instance may have caused a serious shooting incident or may have provided the necessary means for the suspect to escape.

Rather than an interrogator being armed, various other precautionary measures may be substituted to ensure that no escape will occur or that no physical harm will be sustained by the interrogator. For instance, where circumstances so warrant, a guard may be placed outside the door of the interrogation room, on the alert for an attempt to escape or for possible acts of violence toward an unarmed interrogator.

In the interrogation of any person, whether a suspect or merely a witness or other prospective informant, try to think in terms of what you yourself would be thinking, doing, or saying if subjected to an interrogation. In other words, the interrogator should "place himself in the other fellow's shoes." Consider the story about a farmer and his lost mule. It seemed that several persons had searched long and laboriously for the mule, but with no success. Finally another searcher, who made the least physical effort of anyone, returned with the missing animal. When questioned about the secret of his success, he replied, "Well, sir, I just thought to myself, 'If I were a mule where would I go?'; that's where I went, and there was the mule."

Recognize that in everyone there is some good, however slight it may be. The interrogator should seek to determine at the outset what desirable traits and qualities may be possessed by the particular suspect. Thereafter, the interrogator can capitalize on those characteristics in the efforts toward a successful interrogation. The following example may seem to be an implausible one, but it actually happened during an ultimately successful interrogation of the perpetrator of a brutal crime. Reference was made to the kind treatment he had rendered his pet cat! The suspect was told that if he himself had been treated similarly by fellow humans, he would not have developed the attitude that led to his present difficulty. This proved to be very helpful in eliciting his confession.

As stated earlier, not everyone in law enforcement or private protective security has the qualifications for conducting effective interrogations. Conversely, many fine interrogators would be ineffective as investigators. There should be no reluctance, therefore, on the part of anyone to make that differentiation, whether he be the administrator who controls the assignments or the person who is to express a preference for the kind of work to be performed. What the authors do urge is that if the assignment or selection is that of an interrogator, it is imperative that he function in the manner described.

CHAPTER FIVE

Tactics and Techniques for Interrogating Suspects Whose Guilt or Innocence Is Considered Doubtful or Uncertain

As a prelude to this chapter, as well as to the one that follows, the authors of this text want to make unmistakably clear the sense in which the words "guilt" and "innocence" are used. Legally speaking, of course, a person is "guilty" only after a determination of that fact has been made by a judge or jury. They start from the premise of a presumption of innocence and that guilt can only be established by proof beyond a reasonable doubt. That obviously is not the prerogative of an interrogator. Consequently, the words guilt and innocence are used here to signify nothing more than the interrogator's *opinion* (and sometimes only a tentative one). It simply means that it is his belief that the suspect either committed the act in question ("guilty"), or that he did not do it ("innocent"). It carries no legal implication whatsoever.

For the initial differentiation between the guilty and the innocent, the present chapter covers three areas: 1) the value of simply observing and evaluating the suspect's verbal and nonverbal behavior symptoms for indications of truthfulness or deception; 2) the behavioral analysis interview, which, in part, is designed to elicit the suspect's behavioral responses; and 3) a discussion of what has been designated as the "baiting question," along with the procedure for dealing with an alibi.

THE VALUE OF DIRECT OBSERVATION AND EVALUATION OF BEHAVIOR SYMPTOMS

There is a kind of confession in your looks, which your modesties have not craft enough to color (Hamlet to Rosencrantz and Guildenstern, in Shakespeare's *Hamlet*, Act 2, Scene 2).

Physicians, psychiatrists, psychologists, and many other professionals have long recognized the value of evaluating a person's behavior in order to arrive at a diagnosis. This attitude has been based upon the principle that there are many levels of communication, and that the true meaning of the spoken word is amplified or modified by many factors, including posture, gestures, facial expressions, and other body activities. In other words, a person can say one thing while his body movements, facial expressions, or tone of voice reveal something entirely different.

Pioneers in the field of criminal interrogation, as it is known today, gave little consideration to behavior symptoms. Overlooking the professional importance and potential value of such individual characteristics, the early interrogators relied almost completely upon the content of what the suspect said. Some had nothing more than a "gut feeling" that the suspect was guilty or innocent. Evidence of behavioral differences between truthful suspects and lying suspects was thought to be of questionable merit and generally were not given conscious consideration. Most certainly, however, some interrogators had developed a skill for assessing behavior, but few disclosed it, or perhaps lacked the ability to articulate or record their observations. Furthermore, it was not unusual for some of them to believe that they were endowed with a "sixth sense" when, in fact, their skill was derived from a special application of their natural five senses, developed through practice, and from a reliance upon a very good memory bank.

Beginning in 1942, one of the authors of this text (Reid) decided to systematically record the behavior symptoms of all suspects who were given polygraph examinations at the Chicago Police Scientific Crime Detection Laboratory. In the research, he compared behavior symptoms and polygraph test results. It was reasoned that since the polygraph records physiological changes during the time questions are asked, and since behavior symptoms are signs accompanying physiological changes, there may be a correlation between polygraph test results and the verbal and nonverbal responses of a suspect. Responses of the subjects were noted during the interview prior to taking the test, while taking the test, and during the interrogation that followed. Observations were also made by someone who looked through a transparent wall mirror at each subject during the entire time he was in the polygraph examination room, either alone or with the examiner. When the polygraph test results were confirmed by evidence of guilt (e.g., a confession or the finding of substantiating facts) or of innocence (e.g., the interrogator's definite diagnosis to that effect or the establishment of another person's guilt), a comparison was made between those results and the observed behavior symptoms of the suspects.

After a compilation of verified cases and a statistical analysis of the behavior symptoms exhibited by polygraph test subjects, it was encouraging to find that the majority of the verified truthful individuals had been tentatively identified as such by the polygraph examiner during the pretest interview, and a considerable number of the verified lying subjects had been tentatively identified as liars, even before the polygraph tests had begun. It was established, however, that truthful suspects were easier to recognize from behavior symptoms alone and that lying suspects were more difficult to identify in this manner.[1]

Evaluation of Verbal and Nonverbal Responses

Verbal responses include both spoken words and gestures that serve as word substitutes, such as a nodding of the head indicative of "yes" or a side-to-side head motion as "no". Also within the category of verbal responses are such vocal characteristics as tone, speed, pitch, and clarity.

The careful listener is aware not only of the significance of a verbal response, but also of the timing, words, and emphasis associated with the response. Fundamental to the psychology of verbal behavior is that the normally socialized individual does not enjoy lying; deception leads to a conflict that results in anxiety and stress. When a suspect offers an evasive answer or an objection in response to a direct question, he does so because of an attempt to avoid the internal anxiety associated with an outright denial.

Nonverbal responses include body movements and position changes, gestures, facial expressions, and eye contact. Nonverbal behavior is internally motivated to reduce anxiety. Whether through distraction (like shifts

---

[1]For a detailed discussion of a similar later study, see Reid and Arther, *Behavior Symptoms of Lie-Detector Subjects*, 44 J. CRIM. L., C. & P.S. 104–108 (1953), and Horvath, *Verbal and Nonverbal Clues to Truth and Deception During Polygraph Examinations*, 1 J. POLICE SCI. & ADM. 138–152 (1973).

Following is a list of additional publications regarding the subject of verbal and nonverbal behavior along with relevant bibliographies: EKMAN AND FRIESEN, UNMASKING THE FACE: A GUIDE TO RECOGNIZING EMOTIONS FROM FACIAL CLUES (1975); Ekman and Friesen, *Detecting Deception From the Body or Face*, 29 J. PERSONALITY & SOC. PSY. 288–298 (1974); Zuckerman, Defrank, Hall, Larrance, and Rosenthal, *Facial and Vocal Cues of Deception and Honesty*, 15 J. EXP. SOC. PSY. 378–396 (1979); Zuckerman, Koestner, and Alton, *Learning to Detect Deception*, 46 J. PERSONALITY & SOC. PSY. 519–528 (1984); De Paulo, Rosenthal, Eisenstat, Rogers & Finkelstein, *Decoding Discrepant Nonverbal Cues*, 36 J. PERSONALITY & SOC. PSY. 313–323 (1978); De Paulo, Zuckerman, and Ronsenthal, *Humans as Lie-Detectors*, 30 J. COMMUNICATION 129–189 (1980); and EKMAN, TELLING LIES (1985).

in body posture, bringing a hand to the face, or crossing the arms) or through displacement behavior (such as picking lint off the clothing; pacing; or repetitious, fast movements), all nonverbal behavior that accompanies a deceptive response emanates from a guilty suspect's efforts to relieve anxiety.

VERBAL RESPONSES

The period of time within which a verbal response is made to a probing question may be the first indication of truth or deception. An immediate response is a sign of truthfulness; a delay in answering indicates the possibility that the answer may be deceptive. This analysis is based upon the theory that a simple, direct, and unambiguous question does not require much deliberation before an answer is given. A delayed response, however, usually reflects an attempt to contrive a false answer. Another significant factor is whether or not the suspect answers the question directly. An answer such as "Who me?" or "I was home all day" or "I don't own a gun" are not responsive answers to the direct question concerning the crime itself. They are evasive answers and typically are deceptive. The same is true of a suspect's attempt to deviate from the subject matter altogether by injecting a comment that is unrelated to the objective of the question.

Also indicative of deception is a suspect's repetition of the interrogator's question or a request that the interrogator repeat it or clarify it. For example, the suspect may say, in regard to an inquiry of his whereabouts on the day prior to the crime, "Do you mean yesterday, sir?," or in an arson case, he may respond to a comparable question by asking "Do you mean did I start the fire?" even though he had just been asked a question only as to his whereabouts at the time of the fire. What this signifies is that the suspect is stalling for time in order to formulate what he thinks will be the most defensible response.

A suspect who hesitates in answering a question by saying "Let me see now," prior to saying "no" is seeking to achieve two objectives: 1) to borrow time to deliberate on how to lie effectively or to remember previous statements, and 2) to camouflage true guilty reactions with the expression of a pretended serious thought.

The truthful suspect does not have to ponder over an answer. He really has only one answer, and it will be substantially the same, regardless of any repetition of the inquiry. Truthful suspects are not required to depend on a good memory, whereas liars are vulnerable and must be particularly careful to avoid making conflicting statements.

The added burden of keeping a story straight sometimes causes a lying suspect to have a mental block that may prevent him from answering at all. An example of this is the case of a state legislator who accused a representative of an architectural firm of offering him a $50,000 bribe to influence a state committee to hire the architectural firm to build a state office building. The legislator agreed to submit to a polygraph test, which he successfully passed. When the person he accused appeared for his test, he was almost unable to talk at all, even to the point of encountering difficulty spelling his own name. This prompted the examiner to take time out to inquire of others as to the suspect's apparent disability to communicate, whereupon it was learned that, despite his present problem, the suspect had been called upon frequently to serve as toastmaster at formal dinners, and that he was an excellent speaker. Following the suspect's ultimate confession, he offered the explanation for his mental block; it was due to the fact that he was so distraught over the accusation that he had become completely disorganized in his attempt to evade the detection of his deception.

A lying suspect sometimes will speak in fragmented or incomplete sentences, such as "It's important that..." "I'll do anything if..." "If you think..." or "I... I hope that you...." He also may feign a memory failure when confronted with a probing question or in responding to a direct accusation of lying. The person will respond with a half-lie, such as "I don't remember," "As far as I know," or "I don't recall;" or, the person may try to bolster his answer with such phrases as "To be perfectly honest with you," or "To be quite frank." The more sophisticated liars may use the same type of evasions, but they usually plan beforehand so that their answers include a protective verbal coating, such as: "At this point in time," "If I recall correctly," "It is my understanding," "If my memory serves me right," or "I may be mistaken, but...." By using these tactics, lying suspects seek to establish an "escape hatch" rather than risk telling an outright lie. On the other hand, some lying suspects may exhibit what seems to be a remarkably good memory, even as to some irrelevant details. The end result, however, will be so patently implausible as to reveal the attempted deception.

Any suspect who is overly polite, even to the point of repeatedly calling the interrogator "sir" may be attempting to flatter the interrogator to gain his confidence. The suspect who, after being accused, says "No offense to you, sir, but I didn't do it," "I know you are just doing your job," or "I understand what you are saying" is evidencing his lying about the matter under investigation. A truthful suspect has no need to make such apologetic statements, or even to explain that he understands the interrogator's accusatory statements. To the contrary, the truthful suspect may very well react aggressively with a direct denial or by using strong language indicating anger over the implied accusation.

A suspect who "swears to God" or offers to "swear on a stack of Bibles," or utters other oaths to support his answers, is, in many instances not telling the truth. Typical examples of expressions used by lying suspects who try to make their statements believable are: "I swear to God, sir;" or "With God as my witness." The suspect may even go so far as to state "On my poor dead mother's grave, sir." On the other hand, truthful suspects are confident of their truthfulness and do not need any such props. The interrogator should bear in mind, however, that within some cultural surroundings, swearing and similar expressions may be rather common-place, and do not necessarily mean that the suspect is lying.

A truthful suspect will give concise answers because he has no fear of being trapped. The person knows that truth is being told and has no reason to qualify or to delay answers. Furthermore, the truthful suspect is not afraid to say that the interrogator is wrong in suspecting him. The truthful suspect is also able, without any difficulty, casually to answer an irrelevant question, such as "By the way, where do your children go to school?" and he is more apt to quickly correct an interrogator who makes a mistake about some irrelevant detail. The liar is far less likely to do so.

As a test to discern whether the suspect's mind is free and clear, the interrogator may deliberately err when referring to such matters as the suspect's home or business address. Usually, the truthful person will correct the interrogator, but the liar, due to his concentrated mental concern with deception, may completely miss the error. The lying suspect may be so disorganized that he will even delay giving his own home or business address.

Truthful suspects will not only respond directly, they also will speak with relative clarity. Liars, however, tend to mumble or to talk so softly that they cannot be heard clearly. Perhaps they hope that if they lie softly, they will be misunderstood; then, if later confronted with the falsity of an answer, they can deny it was said or else allege that they did not under-stand the question. On the other hand, some liars may speak at a rapid pace or may display erratic changes in the tone or pitch of their voices. Similarly, a verbal response coupled with nervous laughter or levity is a common attempt to camouflage deception.

Lying suspects tend to deny guilt with specific language such as, in a fatal shooting, "I didn't do it with that gun." Truthful suspects, however, tend to voice general denials like "I never shot her or anyone else in my life." Truthful suspects are not afraid to use harsh, realistic words, such as "steal," "rape," "kill," "rob," "stab," but the deceptive ones usually avoid such language in order to assuage their guilty feeling. Even when less harsh terms are used, the liar's tone of voice will sound weak, in contrast to the strong utterance of a truthful suspect.

Although verbal responses are not absolute in their indications, the following list represents typical verbal responses, both truthful and un-truthful, to questions that only require a straight, simple, one-word answer—"no":

Truthful Responses

1. A direct, crisp, and almost angry "no"
2. A "no" given in seemingly sincere disbelief of the suspicion or accusation
3. A "no" that seems to imply "Are you crazy?"
4. A "no" given in a challenging manner

Untruthful Responses

1. A delayed answer, followed by an emphatic "no"
2. A delayed statement, such as "Let me see now," accompanied by an appearance of deep thought before answering
3. An apologetic or pleading "no" answer
4. A staring about the surroundings, somewhat hypnotically, before answering "no"

In summary, Table 5.1 differentiates the verbal responses typical of the truthful and of the untruthful suspects.

Table 5.1. Differences between Typical Verbal Responses of Truthful and Untruthful Suspects

Truthful Verbal Responses	*Untruthful Verbal Responses*
Denial in general, sweeping terms	Denial confined to specific aspects of crime
No lack of reluctance to using harsh, realistic words to describe crime	Avoidance of harsh, realistic words when referring to crime
Direct and spontaneous answers	Delayed, evasive or vague answers
Unqualified answers	Qualifications attached to answers
Display of only reasonable memory rather than remarkable one	Unusually poor or else unusually good memory
No introduction of irrelevant matters into conversation	Injection of irrelevant matters into conversation
No requests for repetition of questions that were clear and direct	Requests for repetition of interrogator's questions, even though they were clearly, directly, and audibly stated

Table 5.1 (Continued)

Truthful Verbal Responses	*Untruthful Verbal Responses*
Rationality displayed in answers	Mental blocks or inability to answer rationally
Distinct and clear tone of voice	Mumbling or subdued tone of voice
No need to reinforce denials with oath taking or references	Resorting to swearing or reference to religion as supportive of answers
Appropriate assertiveness and defiance in answering questions	Overpoliteness in answering questions
Apparent seriousness and concern	Laughter or other levity accompanying some answers
Insistence on knowing after interrogation if he or she is still considered suspect	In a hurry to leave interrogation room without inquirying whether he or she is still considered suspect

NONVERBAL RESPONSES

The true meaning of the spoken word may be amplified or modified by any one or more of many nonverbal cues, such as posture, gestures, facial expressions, and other bodily activities; hence, the commonplace expressions "Actions speak louder than words," and "Look me straight in the eye if you're telling the truth." In fact, according to various social studies, as much as 70% of communication between persons occurs at the nonverbal level.

It is one thing for a suspect to answer the question, "Did you shoot James Smith?" with a "no" response while looking the interrogator directly in the eye and leaning forward in an upright posture without any accompanying movements; it is quite another matter for the suspect to say "no" while looking to the floor or crossing legs, or folding arms across his chest. Activities of the latter type are usually symptomatic of untruthfulness, resulting from unknowing attempts by the suspect to release the anxiety and stress of lying.

One of the most important transmitters of nonverbal behavior symptoms is the degree of eye contact maintained by the suspect with the interrogator. Deceptive suspects generally do not look directly at the interrogator; they look down at the floor, over to the side, or up at the ceiling as if to beseech some divine guidance. They feel less anxiety if their eyes are focused somewhere other than on the interrogator; it is easier to lie while looking at the ceiling or floor. Consequently, they either try to avoid eye contact with the interrogator by making compensatory moves or else they overact by staring at the interrogator in a challenging manner.

Truthful suspects, on the other hand, are not defensive in their looks or actions and can easily maintain eye contact with the interrogator. Even though they may be apprehensive, they show no concern about the credibility of their answers. Although attentive, their casual manner is unrestrained. They need no preparation because their answers are truthful:

There are five guidelines to follow when using eye contact to assess whether the suspect is truthful or untruthful:

Generally speaking, a suspect who does not make direct eye contact is probably being untruthful. However, some consideration should be given to the possibility of an eye disability, inferiority complex, or emotional instability, any of which may account for the avoidance of eye contact. Also, some cultural or religious customs consider it disrespectful for a person to look directly at an "authority figure." Background information on the suspect, of course, may alert the interrogator regarding these or similar nondeceptive causes of a lack of eye contact.

Under no circumstances should an interrogator challenge the suspect to look him "straight in the eye." Many lying suspects will accept the challenge and will very promptly do precisely that; they may even continue to stare at the interrogator throughout the interrogation. Thus, the challenge and follow-up stare will destroy the chance for the display of any further meaningful behavior symptoms and may even render futile a continuation of the interrogation.

Instead of staring at the suspect, the interrogator should somewhat casually observe his eyes and other behavior symptoms to avoid making the suspect feel uncomfortable. A casual glance or two at the suspect's eyes, followed by a sharp change in eye contact by the suspect, will be sufficient to determine that he is purposely avoiding a direct look. It provides an effective method for observing eye movement without making the suspect aware that his behavior is being studied; otherwise, the individual may become more guarded in his actions, thus depriving the interrogator of the observation opportunity.

An interrogator should not expect a suspect to constantly look at him; in fact, it is unnatural for either party in a normal conversation to stare at each other with consistency. It is very important, however, for the interrogator to maintain casual eye contact with the suspect, because the lying suspect himself may be watching the interrogator for indications of insecurity or lack of confidence.

A suspect should not be permitted to wear dark glasses during the interrogation unless there is a medical condition requiring their use indoors. A suspect wearing dark glasses should be requested to remove them at the outset, and the interrogator should then set them off to the side, out of reach. Dark glasses during an interrogation will conceal eye contact and thereby permit the suspect to develop a feeling of confidence in the effort to avoid detection. Most certainly, the interrogator should not wear dark glasses because the suspect should be able to observe the appearance of sincerity in the interrogator's eyes as the interrogation proceeds.

An interrogator must, in effect, "bleed" sincerity. The interrogator must seem so sincere that in certain types of case situations, moisture may actually appear in his eyes. To achieve this effect, the interrogator might envision himself as a possible offender, for instance, in a reckless automobile homicide or in the killing of an unfaithful spouse who for years had behaved miserably toward the other. By placing himself "in the shoes of the suspect," an effective interrogator can, without difficulty, actually cry as he sympathizes with the suspects. The confession from a guilty suspect will be greatly expedited by this tactic. However, unless the interrogator actually experiences, or clearly appears to experience, sincerity in what he says, this will be totally ineffective. Suspects will usually be able to recognize insincerity by the "emptiness" of the interrogator's eyes, even though the suspect, of course, will not be consciously analyzing behavior symptoms in the same way the interrogator does.

In summary, the authors submit the following, in loosely phrased terminology: A lying suspect's eyes will appear foggy, puzzled, probing, pleading (as though seeking pity), evasive or shifty, cold, hard, strained, or sneaky. On the other hand, a truthful person's eyes will appear clear, bright, wide awake, warm, direct, easy, soft, and unprobing.

The interrogator should bear in mind, of course, that if the suspect's eyes look tired, this may be attributable to his having worked all night or, if guilty, to having lost much sleep by worrying or by rehearsing his story in order to avoid detection. Ordinarily, however, an innocent person who has worried about being questioned and thereby has lost sleep probably will reveal that fact to the interrogator without being prompted to do so. A liar, on the other hand, is not apt to reveal his apprehension because of a concern about opening up another facet of suspicion to the interrogator's scrutiny.

In a serious case situation, a liar will have incurred such a great strain upon himself that during the interrogation his breathing may become somewhat labored, and the suspect may sigh uncontrollably. Such stress may even cause stomach growls, the result of an upset digestive system or nervousness over fear of detection.

A variety of facial expressions may be caused by a guilty suspect's fear of detection, uncertainty of success at evading detection, or perhaps an awareness that his deception already has been revealed and, therefore, he might just as well confess. The mere fact of variation of expressions may be suggestive of untruthfulness, whereas the lack of such a variation may be suggestive of truthfulness. Of all the facial expressions, one of the most difficult to evaluate is that which reveals anger. (It is the subject of discussion in the following section.)

A suspect's body posture also can be very revealing. An innocent suspect will generally sit upright, but not rigid, directly positioned in front of the interrogator. He may even lean forward toward the interrogator. In general, an innocent suspect will seem relaxed and casual, and any posture changes will seem smooth and natural. On the other hand, the guilty suspect often will slouch or lean back in the chair, or may be unnaturally rigid and stiff, perhaps with legs and feet pulled back under the chair. Usually the guilty suspect will not sit in a direct frontal alignment with the interrogator, but rather at an angle in the chair or off to its side, as though unwilling to face the interrogator. The guilty suspect may sit in a posture with elbows close to his side, or the arms may be folded and locked in front, accompanied perhaps by the crossing of legs at the knees or ankles. A guilty suspect also may exhibit rapid, erratic, and otherwise unnatural posture changes.

In summary, physical activities of the lying suspect may be categorized into the following general types:

1. *Gross body movements* Posture changes; movement of chair back from interrogator; an indication of being about to stand up, or perhaps to even leave room
2. *Grooming gestures and cosmetic adjustments* Rubbing and wringing hands; stroking back of head; touching nose, earlobes, or lips; picking or chewing fingernails; shuffling, tapping, swinging, or arching feet; rearrangement of clothing or of jewelry; dusting, picking lint or pulling threads on clothing; adjusting or cleaning glasses; and straightening or stroking hair
3. *Supportive gestures* Placing hand over mouth or eyes when speaking; crossing arms or legs, hiding hands (by sitting on them) or hiding feet (by pulling them under the chair); holding forehead with hand; or placing hands under or between legs

When a suspect repeatedly engages in any of the forgoing nonverbal reactions in conjunction with verbal responses, that fact is a strong indication the verbal responses may not be truthful ones.

It is exceedingly important—indeed very critical—that a suspect's behavior symptoms are assessed in accordance with the following general guidelines:

1. Look for deviations from the suspect's normal behavior. The normal behavior may be established either from the background investigation or by questioning the suspect about matters unrelated to the offense under investigation. The assessment of the norm should be based on the suspect's style of speech, mannerisms, gestures, and eye contact. Once this norm has been established, subsequent changes that occur when the suspect is questioned about the crime will become significant.
2. Evaluate all behavioral indications on the basis of when they occur (timing) and how often they occur (consistency).
3. To be reliable indicators of truth or deception, behavioral changes should occur immediately in reponse to questions or simultaneously with the suspect's answers. Furthermore, similar behavioral responses should occur on a consistent basis whenever the same subject matter is discussed.

PRECAUTIONS WHEN DIFFERENTIATING BETWEEN BEHAVIOR SYMPTOMS OF TRUTHFUL AND UNTRUTHFUL SUSPECTS

Although behavior symptoms are very helpful in differentiating truth from deception, they are not to be considered determinative of the issue. This is also true with respect to any diagnostic effort respecting human behavior. Moreover, even when behavior symptoms seem to the interrogator to be absolute in their indications, they should be evaluated only as *tentative indicators* of truth or deception. They should be utilized, therefore, only as directives as to how the interrogator should proceed with the actual interrogation. It is also important for the interrogator to realize that *no one behavior symptom should be evaluated apart from the rest; they must be given collective consideration.*

Reticence

Being reticent at the beginning of an interview is a behavior symptom common to both guilty and innocent suspects. A guilty suspect who is afraid to speak because of a fear of being trapped will find it is much easier to defend himself by being as nontalkative as possible. Any comments at all usually will be very brief. Questions may be answered with a succint "No," "I don't know," or "I couldn't say"; and the suspect may attempt to seem casual about it. On the other hand, a truthful suspect may be reticent because of an apprehension over being mistaken as guilty or may fear being unable to articulate his position properly. If the interrogator is patient and understanding, even the most reticent truthful suspect will become less apprehensive and more naturally responsive over time.

Nervousness

It is not uncommon for innocent as well as guilty suspects to exhibit signs of nervousness when questioned by law enforcement investigators or interrogators. Innocent persons may be nervous for several reasons: 1) the possibility of being erroneously considered guilty, 2) a concern as to the treatment they may receive, or 3) a concern that questioners may discover some previous, unrelated crime or act of indiscretion the suspect committed. The third reason would be particularly true in those instances where the previous crime was of a more serious nature than the present one. On the other hand, of course, the nervousness of guilty persons can be fully accountable by a personal awareness of guilt regarding the present crime, the possibility of it being detected, and the prosecution and punishment that may follow. The principal difference between the nervousness of the innocent and that of the guilty is in the degree of nervousness. A guilty person's nervousness will be considerably greater. Also, it is often readily observable from such indicators as excessive perspiration on the forehead or object touched, erratic speech, a peculiar tone in a "laugh" and frequent yawns or deep breaths. In general, the nervousness of the innocent diminishes as the questioning progresses.

Impertinence

Impertinence may be displayed by both truthful and untruthful suspects. This reaction is usually confined to youthful suspects who may resent authority in general, and who may attempt bravado, especially if questioned when their peers are present or know of the interrogation. Consequently, little significance can be placed upon this particular behavior as to whether such persons are lying or telling the truth. As for adults, an act of impertinence by a suspect can be a shield to fend off questions presented by the interrogator. This trait is seldom displayed by a truthful suspect. On the other hand, a lying adult may be impertinent because of the awareness of being caught and the feeling of a need to show defiance and lack of fear.

Anger

A very difficult behavioral reaction to evaluate is anger. For instance, a resentful scowl may result from a guilty suspect's feigned anger, but it may also be the genuine reaction of an innocent person. Although making a differentiation presents a problem for the interrogator, it can usually be resolved by an awareness that a guilty person's "anger" is more easily appeased than the true anger of an innocent person. The innocent person will persist with his angry reaction, whereas a guilty person will usually switch to a new emotional state when he realizes that feigned anger has not deterred the interrogator.

Whenever a suspect is resentful of the fact that he is under suspicion, the interrogator should allow for a vent of that feeling. This will give the impression that the interrogator is really weighing and considering what the suspect is saying. Also, if the interrogator knows or finds out about any hobbies or special interests the suspect has, the latter should be engaged in a conversation about such matters. Without too much delay the interrogator can thereafter bring the suspect back to the realities of the case itself. Meanwhile, the interrogator will have established a better rapport with the suspect. If he is innocent, that fact may be readily ascertainable; if guilty, the suspect is brought much closer to a disclosure of the truth.

Despair and Resignation

If a suspect adopts an attitude of despair and resignation (which is usually more common with the guilty) and says something like, "I don't care whether you believe me or not; I'd just as soon go to jail; there's nothing for me to look forward to anyway," he should be invited to talk about his general troubles and misfortunes. The interrogator should then listen and console the suspect with sympathetic understanding. The interrogator may say, "Joe, I guess life has treated you rather roughly, hasn't it?" Such a question will very likely "open up" the suspect. He will probably begin with a simple "yes" answer, after which the interrogator can delve into the matter with specific questions regarding childhood difficulties, etc. After a relatively brief period of attentive listening, the interrogator can shift the discussion toward the offense itself.

The gravity of the offense under investigation will, of course, have a bearing on the extent and quality of a suspect's behavior symptoms. For instance, a guilty suspect will display greater and more reliable symptoms when questioned about a rape than when questioned about a petty theft or other relatively minor offense.

Generally speaking, a truthful suspect will display an attitude or demeanor that may be described as composed (in control of his actions and speech), cooperative (willing to do anything reasonable to establish his innocence), sincere, concerned, and interested. On the other hand, the guilty suspect may display one or more of the following negative attitudes: unconcerned, uncooperative, insincere, excessively polite, apologetic, or overanxious.

Factors That May Lead To Misinterpretation of Behavior Symptoms

USE OF MEDICATION

The legitimate use of medication for physical or psychological problems can distort an innocent suspect's behavior. For example, a sedative prescribed to reduce nervous tension can cause a person to seem withdrawn and disinterested. Also, intentional abuses of other medication, drugs, or alcohol may cause an innocent suspect to seem confused or disoriented in offering an alibi or some other disclosure, such as the sequence of events. Similar factors might also cause a display of misleading behavior symptoms. For example, withdrawal effects from drug misuse may cause a suspect to seem nervous, fidgety, sweaty, or shaky. The use of some drugs (whether for medical or nonmedical reasons) may cause a "dry mouth," and certain prescribed drugs can cause users to have a "clicky dry mouth." The same drugs may also affect the activity of the Adam's apple, causing it to move up and down. In summary, these reactions should be carefully evaluated in order to avoid misinterpretation of them as indicative of deception.

MENTAL ILLNESS

Interrogators should be highly skeptical of the behavior symptoms of a person with a psychiatric history or psychopathic traits. No matter how clear-cut the symptoms are, extreme caution should be exercised. Such a person who has committed a criminal act may seem to be innocent; on the other hand, an innocent person with a psychological affliction may seem to be guilty. The following case illustrates the risk that may be occasioned by such factors: A young woman reported to the police that she had received several indecent phone calls, and finally an invitation was received to visit the caller in his hotel room. She reported the matter to the police. They advised her to go to the hotel room and that they would follow her and afford her adequate protection. She went to the room, knocked on the door, and was let in by a man. Soon thereafter, the police entered and arrested him. He vehemently denied having made the phone calls and said that he had been under the impression that the woman who had knocked on his door was a prostitute and he had been interested in procuring her services. Being a member of a prestigious businessmen's club and an employee of a reputable oil company, his fellow club members and officials of the company came to his defense, assuring the police he could not possibly be the person who had made the phone calls. When he was subjected to an interrogation, his behavior symptoms were indicative of truth telling, and he persisted in his protestations of innocence. In view of the circumstantial evidence, however, the police investigators were advised to conduct a thorough investigation of his background. It revealed that he had a history of making sexually motivated phone calls of the type in this case, and indeed, he had been in several mental institutions for treatment. None of this, of course, had been known by the individuals who had vouched for his good character. Upon the basis of the disclosures produced by the investigation, the accused was again interrogated. When confronted with his past record, he confessed to making the calls in the present case.

The following case produced the opposite effect: A policewoman was suspected of making obscene calls to a Catholic convent. The basis for the suspicion was a nun's report to the police department that very soon after the policewoman's visit to the convent as the investigator assigned to the case, another call had been received from a woman whose voice sounded like that of the policewoman herself. On the basis of this and other circumstances that did not rule out such a possibility, the policewoman was interrogated. She seemed to be highly nervous and so distraught emotionally that the interrogation had to be suspended temporarily, despite some behavior symptoms of untruthfulness. Shortly thereafter, another call was traced to a different person, who admitted being responsible for all of the calls. The policewoman's past history revealed an "unstable personality," which undoubtedly accounted for the misleading behavior symptoms.

INTELLIGENCE, SOCIAL RESPONSIBILITY, AND MATURITY

The evaluation of behavior symptoms in terms of truth or deception should take into general consideration the suspect's intelligence, sense of social responsibility, and degree of maturity. As a rule, the more intelligent a suspect is, the more reliable behavior symptoms will be. The intelligent individual will usually possess a higher concern over the importance and consequences of the interrogation; his appraisal of right and wrong will be more acute; and, if the person is deceptive during the interrogation, he will experience a greater degree of internal conflict and anxiety. Social responsibilities, such as the person's family, job, and reputation, will affect his degree of emotional involvement in the interrogation process, which may be generally lacking or else prevail to a lesser degree in a person who is without such responsibilities. This will be especially true among suspects who have had a dependency upon alcohol or drugs. Without the usual values, they have very little at stake and will exhibit fewer emotional reactions and behavior symptoms from which the interrogator may assess guilt or innocence. Similar characteristics prevail in youthful suspects or others who lack maturity. Ordinarily, it seems to matter rather little to these suspects whether what they say is truthful or untruthful; they tend to envision themselves as socially unaccountable for their conduct. As a consequence, their behavior symptoms tend to be unreliable.

In summary, although the verbal and nonverbal behavior displayed by a suspect during an interview or interrogation may provide very valuable and accurate indications of possible innocence or guilt, the interrogator should evaluate the behavior according to the guidelines stated earlier in this chapter. Furthermore, the following factors, which may affect the validity of behavior symptoms, should be considered: the gravity of the offense; the mental and physical condition of the suspect; psychological history, level of intelligence, degree of maturity; and the extent or absence of social responsibilities.

EMOTIONAL CONDITION

In addition to precautions regarding the behavior symptoms of suspects, where doubt arises as to the validity of a crime reported by the purported victim, it is imperative to consider that the traumatic experience of the crime itself may produce reactions of nervousness or instability, which might be misinterpreted as indications of falsity. For example, a normally nervous-type victim who has just been robbed at gunpoint may be honestly confused or disoriented by the experience, and consequently may seem to be untruthful about the report of the incident. Or, a wife whose husband has been shot to death in her presence may have been so shocked by what she observed that her version of the incident soon thereafter may seem untruthful, when in fact she truthfully reported what occurred.

Another example of how misleading behavior symptoms may surface is one in which a male friend of a female murder victim was interrogated about her death. He displayed a number of guilty symptoms, according to his initial interrogators. It was reported that he could not look them "straight in the eye," that he sighed a lot, that he had a disheveled appearance, and that he seemed to be going through a great deal of mental anguish. An investigator reported that "He looked guilty as hell!" During a subsequent interrogation, conducted by a professionally competent interrogator, however, it was ascertained that the suspect was emotionally upset because of the young woman's death and that he had been crying uncontrollably over it. He simply had not verbally or demonstrably disclosed to the interrogators the extent of his grief. The investigators mistakenly confused his emotional behavior as indicative of guilt, and therefore, he became the prime suspect. Later developments in the case produced factual evidence that totally exonerated him from any part in the murder.

INITIAL INTERVIEW PROCEDURES

As discussed in detail in Part II of this text, before a *custodial* suspect may be interrogated, even for the limited purpose of making a tentative determination of truthfulness or deception, he must be given the warnings of constitutional rights that were mandated in the United States Supreme Court's 5-to-4 decision in the 1966 case of *Miranda v. Arizona.*[2] Also, after the issuance of the warnings, no interrogation of a person in police custody may be conducted unless he has waived the prescribed rights to remain silent and to the presence of a lawyer. Consequently, the interview procedures discussed in this section may be employed only when: 1) the suspect is not in custody, or 2) the suspect is in custody and has waived both the right to remain silent and the right to a lawyer.[3] All that follows presupposes a fulfillment of either of these two conditions.

The information initially available in the early stage of a criminal investigation is usually insufficient for an interrogator to even tentatively determine whether the suspect is guilty or innocent. In such a case situation, therefore, there are three approaches available to the interrogator: 1) to interview the suspect upon the assumption of guilt, 2) to interview the suspect upon the assumption of innocence, or 3) to assume a neutral position and to refrain from making any statement or implications one way or the other until the suspect has disclosed some information or indications pointing either to guilt or innocence. What are the advantages and disadvantages attending each one of these three possible approaches?

Assumption of Guilt

This approach possesses the desirable element of surprise. As a result, the guilty lack composure and may disclose the truth about certain pertinent information or perhaps even confess guilt. Another advantage of this approach is how the suspect generally reacts when treated as though he were considered guilty. A guilty person usually will display no resentment to such treatment; an innocent suspect usually will express resentment to the extent of being very forceful or perhaps even being highly insulting. A guilty suspect is also more likely to react nonverbally to the suggestion of guilt—fiddling with clothing, crossing and uncrossing legs, squirming in the chair, dusting off clothes or turning the head away as the interrogator talks. As already pointed out, noting these differences in reaction can be very helpful in determining whether or not the subject is guilty.

---

[2]384 U.S. 436 (1966).
[3]The *four* specific warnings that are required, and the sufficiency of *oral* waivers, are discussed subsequently in Chapter 8.

There are, however, two disadvantages to this first approach when there is very little, if any, evidence to support the assumption of guilt. The guilty suspect who does not immediately make some incriminating "slip-up" or confess guilt will be on guard during the remainder of the interview, and if the suspect eventually senses the fact that the approach is nothing more than a bluff, he is that much more fortified, psychologically, to continue with lying and resistance to telling the truth. On the other hand, the suspect who is innocent may become so disturbed and confused that it will be more difficult for the interrogator to ascertain the fact of innocence, or even to obtain possible clues to helpful information that might otherwise have been obtainable.

Assumption of Innocence

This approach possesses two distinct advantages, but these are offset to some extent by an attending disadvantage. The advantages are:

1. The interrogator's statement or implication of a belief in the suspect's innocence will undoubtedly place an innocent party at greater ease and, as a result, the fact of his innocence may become more readily apparent to the interrogator. Moreover, under such circumstances, the interrogator can more successfully elicit whatever pertinent information or clues the innocent suspect may be in a position to divulge.
2. This approach may cause a guilty suspect to lower his guard and to become less cautious or even careless in answering the interrogator. As a result, the individual is more apt to make a remark or contradiction that will not only make evident the fact of his guilt, but which also can be used as a wedge for eliciting a confession.

The disadvantage of this approach is that once an interrogator has committed himself as a believer in the suspect's innocence, he must more or less confine inquiries to those based upon an assumption of innocence, for to do otherwise would tend to destroy the very relationship or rapport that was sought in using this approach. In other words, the interrogator is handicapped to the extent that he cannot freely adjust methods and questioning to meet the suspect's changing attitudes or inconsistencies. This is not an insurmountable difficulty, of course, but it is nevertheless a possible disadvantage that the interrogator should consider before embarking upon this particular course.

Assumption of a Neutral Position

This approach obviously possesses neither the advantages nor the disadvantages of the other two. For this very reason, therefore, it may be considered the best approach to use in the average case where the interrogator's case information and observations have given no encouraging indication that the suspect might be particularly vulnerable to either one of the other two approaches.

When the suspect is *not in custody* (and therefore no *Miranda* warnings are required) and has not been questioned by other investigators, it is well for the interrogator to ask a question such as: "Do you know why we have asked you to come here?" or "Do you know why I have come here to talk to you?" A guilty person who is asked a "know why" question is immediately placed in a vulnerable, defensive position. If the suspect professes ignorance when the circumstances clearly indicate his awareness of the purpose of the interview, that fact alone becomes considerably important to the interrogator for its diagnostic value as well as for its effect upon the suspect's resistance when it is later referred to as an indication of guilt. On the other hand, the suspect who admits knowing why he is being questioned may be asked: "Well, what do you know about it [the offense]?" By being impelled to offer an explanation, a guilty person may at the very outset of the interview make some significant remark or exhibit certain symptoms of guilt that otherwise might not have been so readily provoked.

If the suspect is innocent or ignorant of the particular offense under investigation, but guilty of another offense or in possession of pertinent information concerning such other offense, the "know why" question may result in a lead to the solution of the other offense. For instance, a reply of "Yes, you think I had something to do with that break-in last week" (referring to an unsuspected offense), would obviously prompt the interrogator to make further inquiries about it. Information gained in this unexpected manner has led to the solution of cases that otherwise might have escaped the interrogator's attention.

It is very important for the interrogator to realize that the use of the "know why" and "what do you know" questions must be confined to noncustodial suspects. For those in custody, the *Miranda* warnings and waivers are required, and, obviously, there can be no waiver without the suspect being aware of the matter about which he or she has consented to be questioned.

Subsequent to the above-described initial procedures, the interrogator should embark upon a *behavioral analysis interview*, which consists of asking: 1) standard investigative questions, such as the suspect's relationship with the victim, his whereabouts prior to and at the time of the crime, as well as thereafter, the nature of their last visit and other relevant matters; and 2) selected questions designed to evoke *verbal* and *nonverbal* responses that will be helpful in making a tentative determination as to whether the suspect is lying or telling the truth.

THE BEHAVIORAL ANALYSIS INTERVIEW

Although standard investigative questions are for the primary purpose of obtaining information rather than to evoke responses for behavior analysis, the responses should nevertheless be given analytical consideration. In other words, the interrogator should look for clues of truth or deception from the very outset of the interview. This should be done in accordance with the guidelines presented in the first section of this chapter regarding the need for acute observations. The core of behavior analysis, however, is the asking of noninvestigative questions that are specifically designed to evoke behavioral responses. The following hypothetical case illustrates the process of behavior analysis. (The same process is appropriate, of course, for all other types of cases, including those involving a private security officer's interview of an employee suspected of a theft from his employer. See Chapter 7.)

Assume that Mary Jones was found stabbed to death in her apartment at 9:00, the morning of December 7, 1984. All the circumstances clearly indicate it occurred about midnight, and there was no evidence of a forcible entry. Subsequent investigation disclosed that on a number of recent occasions, Mary and a male friend of hers, Jim Smith, were overheard having loud arguments, primarily about Mary's relationship with several of her male co-workers. There seems to be good reason, therefore, to interview Jim, but clearly there is no basis for an arrest.

At the outset of the interview, the interrogator should spend a few minutes asking the suspect a series of innocuous questions, such as his complete name, age, address, current place of employment, and other general background questions. The purpose of this is twofold: 1) to acclimate the suspect to the environment and, at the same time, 2) to afford the interrogator an opportunity to evaluate the suspect's normal verbal and nonverbal behavior patterns.

Following such initial questions, the interrogator should ask a "know why" question: "Do you know why you are here?" or "Do you know why we're here?" Since Jim knew Mary and very probably had read or had heard about her death, a naive or evasive reply to the "know why" question would be viewed with suspicion. For instance, if Jim states that he had no idea of the purpose of the interview, or if he makes a vague comment such as "I suppose you want to talk about what happened to Mary," that should be viewed in a different light than if he very bluntly states "You are trying to find out who killed Mary." The latter response is more characteristic of that of an innocent person.

Following the "know why" question, it is generally appropriate to say: "Jim, we have interviewed many people regarding Mary's death and the pieces are falling together quickly. Jim, if you had anything to do with this, you should tell me." This seemingly casual statement will afford him an opportunity to readily admit his involvement if that be the case. In the absence of the unlikely occurrence of a sudden admission of guilt, the interrogator's statement will nevertheless serve the purpose of inducing a display of behavioral responses suggestive of either guilt or innocence.

If Jim was involved in Mary's death, he may respond verbally to the interrogator's statement by stating "You mean, did I do this? No." Coupled with the verbal response, there will probably be a nonverbal response, such as shifting in his chair, avoiding eye contact, or crossing arms or legs. On the other hand, if Jim is innocent, he very likely will immediately say something such as "I had nothing to do with it! I loved that girl. I never hurt her and never would have." As these words are being spoken, he probably would be leaning forward and looking the interrogator straight in the eye, using appropriate hand gestures to emphasize his point.

The next step for the interrogator would be to ask a few general questions regarding Jim's knowledge about the event, the victim, and possible suspects. If Jim is innocent, he is thereby given an opportunity to divulge possibly helpful information that might not have been disclosed if his discussion had been confined to answering specific questions. On the other hand, if guilty, he is placed in a vulnerable defensive position. He may make a remark that would be indicative of guilt or would lead to a specific line of questioning.

The following series of questions should be asked for the purpose of evoking behavioral responses indicative of either guilt or innocence:

Jim, why do you think someone would do this to Mary?   The purpose of this question is to ascertain the suspect's perception of the motive for the crime. If Jim is guilty, he will be faced with a dilemma when asked the question because, in essence, he is being asked to reveal why he killed Mary. In an effort to conceal any indication of his involvement, he may hesitate or else repeat the question as a stalling tactic in order to construct what he believes to be an acceptable answer. On some occasions, a guilty suspect may even reveal his true motive by offering an explanation such as, "Maybe there was an argument, or maybe someone was drinking or on drugs." If the guilty suspect does not offer such an excuse, he usually will respond with "I never thought about it." When a person's spouse, family member, or close friend is killed, it is only natural to think about a possible motive or cause for the incident. In conjunction with this type of verbal response, the guilty suspect may engage in a variety of nonverbal gestures suggestive of his discomfort and concern over the question.

If Jim is innocent, when asked why someone would kill Mary, he might say, without hesitation, that the killer must be insane or "I don't know why anyone would do this. Mary didn't have an enemy in the whole world." In making those comments, he would maintain direct eye contact and would probably lean forward in his chair.

Jim, of the people that you and Mary knew, whom do you feel would be above suspicion regarding Mary's death? In other words, who among them would never do anything like this?   This question is an implied invitation to the suspect to assist in the investigation. If Jim is being truthful, he will readily name specific individuals whom he feels would be above reproach or for whom he would vouch as not being involved in Mary's death. He will not be afraid to eliminate certain persons from suspicion. If, on the other hand, Jim is guilty, his response might be noncommittal. Guilty suspects usually do not want to eliminate any one individual from suspicion because that would tend to narrow the search down to them. They might respond, therefore, by saying, "I don't know, it's hard to say what people might do." Meanwhile, they may shift around in the chair or engage in some other type of movement.

If a suspect responds to this question by naming himself as above suspicion, no absolute inference should be drawn, but it must be noted that this type of response is more typical of the deceptive suspect than of the innocent.

Jim, who do you think might have done something like this to Mary?   Whereas the previous question called for the elimination of suspects, this one seeks information of an affirmative nature. By asking Jim to reveal his suspicions as to the guilty person, the interrogator may thereby evoke a very significant and reliable indication of guilt or innocence. This is particularly true of cases where any one of several persons, all acquainted with each other, may have committed the offense.

A guilty suspect usually will not reveal a suspicion about anyone else, no matter how much effort is made to have him to do so. In other words, when asked "From among the people you and Mary knew, which one of them do you think might have done this?" Jim probably would say, "I don't know," or "I haven't the faintest idea." No matter what the interrogator says thereafter, he probably will remain adamant in his denial of harboring any suspicion. On the other hand, if Jim is innocent, he may, after some persuasion, tell of his suspicion, even though it has a very flimsy basis or is perhaps based upon nothing more than a dislike or prejudice toward another individual. When first asked the question regarding his suspicion, he may respond, in a rather unsure manner, "I don't know. I can't believe anyone I know could do something like this." The interrogator should then say:

> Jim, I'm not talking about actual knowledge or proof. Here's what I mean. There is no question that someone you know may be involved in this. That being so, which one, from among all the people you and Mary ever knew, do you think could or might have done such a thing? Now, let me assure you that I will not reveal to him that you told me anything. My primary purpose in asking the question is to give you an opportunity to relieve yourself of any thoughts along that line, so that your holding back won't make it look like you're the one who's involved in this. If you had no part in it I want to know that, without having any doubt about it. So let me now ask you, Jim, who do you think might have done this?

If Jim is innocent, such persuasion will probably cause him to disclose a suspicion about someone else. However, if Jim is guilty and previously had failed to mention any suspicion, he probably will maintain that attitude, regardless of the interrogator's persuasion efforts.

Jim, what do you think should happen to the person who did this to Mary?   In responding to this question, if Jim is innocent, he probably will indicate some significant punishment, such as going to the penitentiary, or receiving the death penalty. In contrast, if he is guilty, he will try not to answer the question. He likely will say "It's not up to me," or "I'm not a judge," or he may indicate that the offender should be asked the reason for committing the crime. The underlying explanation for this evasion is that were he to suggest a penalty, he would in effect be prescribing his own punishment. In the event a guilty suspect does indicate severe punishment, any accompanying nonverbal behaviors will likely belie the sincerity of the answer.

Jim, did you ever think about hurting Mary, even though you didn't go through with it?   If Jim acknowledges that he had thought about hurting Mary, this is suggestive of possible guilt, even if in his acknowledgment, he very likely would have added to his "yes" answer, "but not seriously." If, however, Jim is innocent, his response probably would be a simple "no," even though, in fact, such an idea may have occurred to him but may have been dismissed without consideration.

In utilizing this technique, if the interrogator does not receive an acknowledgment that the suspect had been thinking about committing the offense or one similar to it, the interrogator should then say to the suspect: "The reason I'm asking you if you ever thought about doing this is because if you ever did, then that may account for the fact that your looks and appearance might create the impression that you're not telling the truth." A guilty person is apt to try to explain away this impression by admitting that he had thought about committing the act in question or one similar to it. An innocent person will usually persist in denying any such thoughts.

Once a suspect admits having thought about the offense or a similar one, the interrogator should ask about the kind and frequency of such thoughts. If the thoughts went as far as plans or preparation, and especially an actual attempt, then the interrogator should become even more secure in the belief of the suspect's guilt.

In some case situations, such as the investigation of a sexually-motivated murder, a suspect may be asked, "Have you ever dreamed about doing something like this?" A question of this nature was asked by one of the authors of this text during the interview of a person suspected of a sexually-motivated murder, in which the offender had sexually assaulted and decapitated the victim and then had performed a sex act upon the dead body. He admitted that he had dreamed about "placing naked women into a knife machine." Thereupon, the interrogator asked him to give the full details of the dream, which he did. During a subsequent interrogation, the suspect admitted his guilt. His confession was fully substantiated by the finding of the girl's wristwatch at the place where the suspect stated he had thrown it, and by additional evidence of guilt.

Although this sexually-motivated case is unique, perhaps further case experiences of a similar nature may establish a dream-act relationship comparable to that already frequently observed between thinking about a criminal act and its actual commission.

Jim, would you be willing to take a polygraph test to verify that what you have told me is the truth?   If Jim is guilty, he is likely to refuse to be examined, or he may offer some excuse for not wanting to be tested at that time. Guilty suspects sometimes object to taking the test on the basis of no confidence in them—that they are not infallible, and that the refusal of courts to admit test results in evidence is proof of lack of accuracy. Whenever the suspect indicates that he feels this way, the interrogator should say: "Some courts do allow the tests, and certainly it is allowed for investigation purposes." On the other hand, if Jim is being truthful, he probably will accept the opportunity to take such a test. This customary difference in reactions to the suggestion of a polygraph test provides a very helpful indication as to whether the interrogator has before him a guilty or an innocent person. Caution must be exercised, however, to avoid attaching too much significance to a person's reluctance (or perhaps even an outright refusal) to be examined. The unfavorable publicity that has been given in recent years to polygraph testing may be believed by innocent persons. Nevertheless, the suggestion of a polygraph examination, even when an examination is unavailable, is often very helpful in evoking behavior symptoms for analysis by the interrogator as to probable guilt or innocence.

In all instances where suggestions are made about a polygraph examination, the interrogator should carefully avoid creating the impression that the suspect is required to take the test. Indeed, it is essential that the proposal be presented in such a way that the suspect will know that it is only an invitation or an opportunity to establish truthfulness.

Upon a suspect's expressed willingness to take a polygraph test, it may be advisable to ultimately arrange for one whenever the interrogator may be uncertain as to guilt or innocence, or in the event he feels that the suspect is attempting a bluff. However, there should be no interruption of the interview at this time. Arrangements for the test should await the conclusion of the interview.

Jim, how do you think that you would do on a polygraph test regarding the death of Mary?   This question may be asked of the suspect who has already indicated his willingness to take a polygraph test. However, if Jim has refused to be tested, the question should be altered as follows: "Let's assume you would be willing to take a test, how do you think you'd come out?" If Jim is guilty, he probably will respond by expressing doubt about the accuracy of polygraph tests. He may say "I hope I'd do all right," "I don't know, because I'm nervous," or "I never did well on tests in school." He may even say that he might fail the test, adding that he had a friend who failed a test although that friend was telling the truth. If Jim is being truthful, he probably will indicate a very positive attitude toward the test outcome by saying: "I'm sure I'll do fine" or "I'll do 100% because I am telling the truth." His statement will be supported by a sincere facial expression, direct eye contact, and a demeanor that expresses a confidence in the outcome.

Jim, did you discuss Mary's death with your family [or close friends]? Experience has indicated that if Jim is guilty, he may say "no" to this question. Not only will he want to conceal the fact that an event occurred for which he anticipated to be questioned, but he probably also wanted to avoid actually being asked by a family member or friend any probing questions bearing on his possible involvement. He may account for his failure to disclose the event to family and friends on the grounds that he did not want to cause them any worry or concern. If Jim is innocent, however, he probably has discussed the matter with a family member or friend and will acknowledge that fact to the interrogator. He also may relate the reactions of those persons.

Jim, if we can establish who the person is who did this to Mary, do you think that person should be given a second chance? This is a question similar in principle to the punishment question. A truthful person rarely is in favor of giving the offender a second chance; the guilty suspect, on the other hand, will often indicate some type of leniency or be noncommittal about it. If truthful, Jim might say something to the effect of "Hell no! Whoever did this should get as much of a chance as he gave Mary!" If Jim is guilty, however, he may respond by saying, "That's hard to say . . . ." Again, consideration must be given to the nonverbal behavior symptoms that accompany the verbal response to determine the credibility of the spoken answer.

In addition to the behavior-provoking questions already described, each interview should include a baiting question, as well as an assessment of the suspect's alibi. These two points will be separately addressed.

THE USE OF BAITING QUESTIONS

An interrogator may use "baiting questions" during the behavioral analysis interview. Such a question is nonaccusatory in nature but at the same time presents to the suspect a plausible probability of the existence of some evidence implicating him in the crime. Its intended purpose is to induce a deceptive suspect to change, or at least to consider changing, an earlier denial of guilt. The following example illustrates its application.

In the Mary Jones murder case, presented in the previous section of this chapter, assume that Jim, the suspect, had stated that he was home at the time of the crime. The interrogator may ask: "Jim, is there any reason you can think of why one of Mary's neighbors would say that your car was seen parked in front of her home that night?" Without waiting for an answer, the interrogator should state: "Now, I'm not accusing you of anything; maybe you just stopped by to see if Mary was home." If Jim is innocent and was not there at that time, he will emphatically deny his car was near Mary's home. On the other hand, if Jim is guilty, he must pause to evaluate the possibility that someone did see his car at the scene. He must decide whether to lie about it or to take his chance on an acknowledgment of that fact and consider what explanation he should offer. In any event, there will be a delay in his response. Most often, the forthcoming answer would be a denial, but it will be accompanied by the significant nonverbal behavior described in the preceding section of this chapter. However, on some occasions, a guilty suspect in Jim's position will change his denial and say "I'm sorry, I forgot; I now remember that I did stop by there momentarily but left when I did not see any light in Mary's apartment."

A baiting question may be used in almost any type of case situation. When using it, however, the interrogator must avoid any positive, challenging statement, such as "You were seen coming out the back door," because the suspect may have exited through a side door. Similarly, a statement that the suspect's fingerprints were found on a bedroom dresser will evoke a truthful denial from a suspect who knows full well that he was not anywhere near the dresser. The interrogator who issues such unfounded statements is getting out on the proverbial limb, to be easily sawed off by the suspect's awareness of the statement's falsity. Moreover, once the interrogator is caught in a lie, further effectiveness is lost. There is no risk, however in asking a nonspecific, nonchallenging question, such as: "*Is there any reason why* some neighbor should say your car was parked in front of Mary's residence?"

Baiting questions should only be used *after* the suspect has made an appropriate denial; otherwise, they serve no useful purpose. For instance, in the case of Mary Jones, if the interrogator had presented the baiting question before Jim denied being near Mary's house the night of the crime, a subsequent acknowledgment that he was there would not have had the same significance as when he changed his story from a prior denial.

When a baiting question is used, the interrogator must present it as a plausible, sincere inquiry. It also must be accompanied by what the suspect may perceive to be a nonincriminating excuse for explaining away the incriminating effect of the bait evidence itself. The following examples are illustrative:

Joe, fingerprints have been lifted from the safe by the police crime lab technicians. Is there any reason why, when they are compared with yours, the report would show that yours are the same as the ones on the safe? Perhaps you accidentally put your hands on the safe on some prior occasion, without having anything to do with the missing money?

Now, Harry, you told me you had been drinking the night this happened. Is it possible that you could have done this and simply don't remember because of the alcohol?

As you may now know, Frank, the store had concealed security cameras in that area. Is there any reason why, when the films are developed, they will show you being there? Not that you took the money, you understand; maybe you just happened to be walking over there to get something?

A baiting question can deal with either real or nonexistent evidence. It may refer to such items as footprints, tire tracks, personal belongings left at the crime scene, or dirt on the suspect's shoes of the same kind as that at the scene.

Use of Baiting Questions To Evoke the Truth

As is discussed later in this chapter, a guilty person who is presented with a baiting question will usually hesitate before rejecting the bait, try to offer a possible explanation, or ask for some further information about the matter mentioned by the interrogator. An innocent person will usually reply with some such statement as: "No, because I didn't do it" or "No, because I wasn't there." Although this reply is not proof of guilt or innocence, the nature of a suspect's response or reaction may be very helpful, along with other factors, in determining guilt or innocence.

Another form of a baiting question carries the strong implication that the answer is already known, when in fact it is unknown. Its purpose is to dissuade the suspect from responding falsely and to encourage him to reveal the truth. For example, when the interrogator has reason to believe that the suspect possesses or knows the whereabouts of an instrument or article that might have had some connection with the crime, instead of merely asking, "Do you have such-and-such?" or "Do you know where such-and-such is?" it is much better to assume in the question that the suspect does have it or else knows where it is. The effectiveness of this approach is well illustrated by the following case.

During the course of an interview with a rape-murder suspect, and based upon information developed by the investigators, the interrogator received the impression that, regardless of guilt or innocence, the suspect was a sex deviate (in a very substantial sense). The interrogator's previous experience in the interrogation of sex deviates of various sorts brought to mind the possibility that the suspect may have been keeping a diary of his sex affairs and practices. Since such a document might be of some value in an interrogation, the interrogator was interested in finding out if one existed. Toward this end, he asked the question: "Where is your diary?" The suspect paused momentarily and then replied, "It's home—hidden underneath my desk." His permission was obtained to pick up the diary. Officers dispatched to his home discovered an extraordinary and almost unbelievable diary, replete with entries about numerous sexual experiences. Some of the entries referred to "struggles" with girls he had picked up in his car, usually at places where they had been awaiting public transportation under inclement weather conditions. Other entries pertained to "struggles" with a few willing girlfriends, who had feigned resistance to accommodate his particular desire in that respect. Other recorded experiences concerned sexual conduct in the privacy of his home, whereby he would reach a climax by the mere reading of his recorded sex acts.

When confronted with diary entries of the "struggles" with the girls he had picked up, the suspect readily admitted that they had been actual rapes. Although the diary contained no mention of the latest rape-murder, the interrogator became thoroughly convinced that the suspect was in fact responsible for it. He was reminded of his previous offenses, particularly one in which the modus operandi was quite similar in many respects to the principal offense. He was also told that, morally speaking, his latest offense was "no worse" than his previous nonfatal rapes. This and other techniques resulted in a confession to the rape-murder.

There is every reason to believe that in the forgoing case, if the issue of the diary had been brought up in any way other than by the question "Where is your diary?" the suspect probably would not have divulged its existence or whereabouts, and the interrogator would have been deprived of a very valuable means of eliciting the rape-murder confession. Had the interrogator merely asked, "Do you have a diary?" the suspect probably would have inferred that its existence was not already known and therefore would have denied having one. With the question phrased in such a way as to imply a certainty of its existence, however, it became difficult for the suspect to make a denial, because, for all he knew, the interrogator or other investigators might have already been aware of its existence or actually have had it in their possession.

Another possible application of this baiting question technique is in cases where the interrogator seeks to establish the identity of an accomplice or of another person who is in some way connected with the offense under investigation. Rather than confine the inquiry to "Who is the person?" it is often much more effective to supplement the inquiry with, or perhaps use as a substitute, certain "piecemeal" questions, such as "What part of the city does he live in?" or "What's his first name?" In this way, the questions seem rather innocuous and render much less difficult the suspect's divulgence of the requested information about the individual's complete identity.

The baiting question is also appropriate in a situation where a relevant issue in a case is whether or not the suspect knew "John Jones." Rather than asking: "Do you know John Jones?" there is greater potential to the question "How long have you known John Jones?" The former question carries no indication of possible awareness that the suspect knew Jones; consequently, a denial may be made rather comfortably. With the question presented in the latter form, however, a suspect who is motivated to lie about knowing Jones is placed in a dilemma; he becomes concerned over the possibility that the interrogator has evidence of the fact of acquaintance with Jones and is thus more likely to acknowledge it. Similarly, in a case where the suspect's presence in the company of John Jones at a particular time would be of incriminating significance, but the interrogator does not know that the suspect was in fact there, it is advisable to ask, "How long were you with John Jones that night?" This kind of question is more apt to produce a truthful answer, such as "Only for a few minutes," than if the question were phrased: "Were you with John Jones that night?" The latter question may draw a simple "no" answer.

An adjunct to the baiting question, and at times a very effective one, is the prefacing of a question with the statement: "Think carefully before you answer the next question." This admonition is apt to provoke a truthful reply from a guilty suspect because of the concern that the truth is already known. It can be rendered even more effective if the interrogator has some written papers in his hand or starts looking through some papers on a nearby table at the time the admonition is given.

Whenever the desired acknowledgment does not result from the use of the "think carefully" warning, it is sometimes effective for the interrogator to express skepticism about the reply by asking, "Are you sure about that?" In this way, an opportunity is afforded a lying suspect to reconsider the possible risk entailed by not telling the truth about a fact that seems to be already known to the interrogator.

Use of Baiting Questions To Reveal a Lie

The previous baiting questions involved situations in which the interrogator was seeking to elicit a truth-revealing response. A similar tactic may be used to more or less invite a suspect to lie in response to a relevant question, if inclined to do so. This may occur in a case where the interrogator knows what a truthful answer should be to a certain question, but he asks it in a manner that implies a lack of knowledge. Assume, for instance, that in a robbery case, the investigation disclosed that shortly after the robbery, the suspect made a substantial payment on his car, paid off a large debt, or deposited money in a bank under a fictitious name. Instead of calling the occurrence to the suspect's attention and asking for his explanation, the interrogator should casually inquire somewhat as follows: "Except for your salary (or other usual income) have you come into possession of any other money recently?" If he readily admits he has, and offers a satisfactory explanation of it, such a disclosure may serve to exonerate him from further suspicion. On the other hand, however, a lie to the question will be a strong indication of possible guilt and, at the same time, it will be of very valuable assistance to the interrogator who is trying to obtain a confession.

The following case illustrates this use of the baiting question: A male was suspected of having set fire to his store about 10:00 one night. The investigation revealed that about 9:45, he was seen leaving his house through the back door and walking down an alley in the direction of the rear exit of his store. In this case situation, nothing is apt to be gained by confronting him with this information, because, if he is guilty, he would immediately offer a false explanation for his actions. He may even say, for example, that he had gone to the store to get something he had forgotten to bring home at the time he had locked the store at 6:00. It is far better to give him an opportunity to lie about his actions. For instance, the interrogator may ask him to state what time he arrived home after having closed the store and to tell what he did thereafter (e.g., ate dinner, watched television) up to the time he was notified of the fire. Only after the suspect has committed himself to having remained in his home all evening should he be confronted with the evidence of the walk down the alley at 9:45. Once caught in such a lie, a suspect will have considerable difficulty avoiding a confession of guilt.

Another form of baiting a suspect consists of deliberately using an incomplete question such as "Then what she said is. . . .?" leaving it up to the suspect to fill in the remainder. Some well-known television investigative reporters have used this incomplete questioning technique to good advantage.

ALIBI—TRUE OR FALSE?

Unquestionably, the best way to check an alibi is by actual investigative methods. In other words, if a suspect states that he was at a certain place during the time the offense was being committed elsewhere, the best way to determine whether or not this is the truth is for an investigator to check with the place named by the suspect to obtain information or evidence that will either substantiate or disprove the suspect's alibi. There are, however, occasions when this procedure is not feasible or even possible and, therefore, reliance must sometimes be placed on interrogation methods alone.

Whenever an alibi is couched in general terms, such as "I was out riding in my car that evening," it is advisable for the interrogator to have the suspect relate all of his activities during the period covered by the alibi, to name the places visited, to state the route traveled, and also to give the approximate time for each activity or when each place was visited or each route traveled. In other words, suppose the crime was committed at 8:00 p.m., and the suspect states he was riding in his car from 7:00 to 9:00 p.m. He should then be asked to trace the route he took, name the places he visited, and give the time at which he arrived or left. In this manner, he may be placed in a position of being unable to account for the full period from 7:00 to 9:00, or else may find it necessary to offer fictitious details which could easily be detected and proven as false.

Another method for testing an alibi that is given in general terms is to ask the suspect if he had observed a certain occurrence that supposedly happened at the place and time mentioned. The suspect, assuming that the interrogator is referring to an actual occurrence, may acknowledge having observed it, thereby exposing deceit and probable guilt. Assume, for example, that in the Mary Jones murder case, instead of Jim saying he was home at the time of Mary's death he states that he had been out riding in his car. After the disclosure of the details, the interrogator should leave the interrogation room for a few minutes, explaining to Jim that he is going to check out a few things. Upon his return, he should describe a fictitious occurrence on the route that Jim said he had traveled. The description of the occurrence may be something along the following lines: "From what you told me, Jim, you drove on Highway 66 past Central City at about midnight. I understand that this was the time a semitruck had overturned, and traffic was delayed for about an hour. How long were you stuck there? How did you manage things?" If Jim is lying, he is thereby presented with a dilemma. He does not know, of course, whether the accident had actually occurred. He must pause, therefore, before he either acknowledges or disclaims knowledge of the occurence. He may then respond in one of three ways: 1) admit that he did not see the accident, implying, therefore, that the interrogator must have erroneous information, 2) state that he forgot to mention earlier that he had turned off Highway 66 before reaching Central City, or 3) that he only had to wait a short time before the traffic cleared. The second or third selections are, of course, strong indications of guilt. However, even if Jim is smart enough to sense a trap, his delay in making one of the three selections may, in itself, indicate guilt. If, however, Jim is innocent, there will be no delay in saying that he saw no evidence of an accident on Highway 66 at the time he was near Central City.

One favored tactic for evaluating an alibi is to ask the suspect for a detailed account of his activities before and after, as well as during the crime period. Lawyers occasionally use a similar technique in the cross-examination of a witness whose testimony they seek to discredit by showing that although the witness's memory of activities prior to and since the event in question is very bad (or perhaps is very good), his memory of occurrences at the time when the offense was committed is, by comparison, unreasonably good (or unreasonably bad) and is, therefore, an apparent indication of untruthful testimony. Criminal interrogators also may obtain indications of a suspect's guilt or innocence by using this technique. (The investigator should be mindful, however, of the possibility that some special event—a birthday, a parent's death, etc.—may explain a suspect's accurate recall of the date of some other event, or of his activities on or about that time.)

With respect to a suspect's activities prior to the crime, it may not be necessary, in the average case, to go back much further than a few hours or a few days prior to the offense, but there are occasions when it is helpful to obtain information about the suspect's activities over a longer period of time. In any event, the interrogator should gradually lead the suspect up to the day and time of the offense and then let him continue beyond that point, covering whatever subsequent period is deemed desirable.

Recollection of considerable detail as to activities before and after the offense, in contrast to absence of a similar quality of recollection for the period of the offense itself, may very well signify an effort to deceive. Also of significance is any contrast between a recollection of considerable detail at the time of the offense and the lack of it with regard to previous and subsequent events. A third situation might arise, to the ultimate advantage of the interrogator. A suspect, while falsifying a detailed alibi, may realize the need for a comparable recollection of previous and subsequent activities and may proceed to manufacture a set of details that may be easily recognized as false and may be proved to be such by known facts either already in the possession of the interrogator or discovered by subsequent investigation.

Some interrogators follow the practice of having a suspect's detailed alibi statement reduced to writing and signed by him. Then, if the interrogator's subsequent efforts are unproductive of any specific indication of guilt or innocence, another statement regarding the alibi is obtained. This second statement is compared with the first one. If both statements generally agree in their various details, that fact is considered indicative of truth telling because few liars are able to remember all of the details of a previous lie. On the other hand, if inconsistencies are present, that fact can be used to good advantage in the course of the interrogation.

Contrary to the generally prevailing notion, when two or more persons relate a bona fide alibi for themselves or give a truthful version of an occurrence, there will be some variations regarding the details because two persons ordinarily do not observe an occurrence with equal accuracy, nor can they recall or describe the incident in identical fashion. Therefore, an interrogator should view with suspicion an alibi, account, or occurrence given by two persons with a full coincidence of all details. The following case is an example: A husband and wife, who were suspects in a murder case committed several weeks prior to their interrogation, related as an alibi their presence together at a dinner in a neighborhood restaurant. They each told in detail the time of arrival, the means used to get there, and what they had ordered for dinner that night. Their stories were the same with respect to all of the details, but they were also too good to be true. It subsequently developed that the suspects were guilty of the murder, and that they had decided upon the restaurant alibi for the following reason: They were frequent diners at this particular restaurant and were familiar with the menu served there on the various nights of the week. They realized that the restaurant manager, waitresses, and others probably would not remember whether or not they were there on the particular night in question, and therefore probably would be unable to discredit the alibi.

Another illustration of the same psychological principle is a case involving the disappearance of a large sum of money from an armored money truck, to which four men had been assigned as guards. An investigation revealed that there had been no forced entry into the truck, and this fact cast suspicion on the four guards. At the outset of the investigation, each one admitted that in violation of company orders, they had left the truck unguarded for a period of time while all had gone to a restaurant together for lunch. The statements that were taken from the guards varied considerably with respect to some of the details about the events and activities during this lunch period, and that fact had convinced the investigators that the guards were lying. However, when one of the authors of this text was engaged to interrogate the guards, he viewed the minor discrepancies in their statements as evidence suggestive of truthfulness rather than deception. Thereafter, a recently discharged guard was interrogated, and he confessed that while still in the employ of the company, he had managed to have a duplicate key made for the truck door and had awaited an appropriate time for using it to steal some money. He was, of course, familiar with the guards' habit of occasionally leaving the truck unguarded during the time they were eating together, and this afforded him the timely opportunity to take the money. Following his confession, he led the interrogator and other investigators to the place where he had concealed the money, and the entire sum was recovered intact.

CHAPTER SIX

Tactics and Techniques for the Interrogation of Suspects Whose Guilt Seems Definite or Reasonably Certain — The Nine Steps to Effectiveness

The authors again wish to make clear that the word "guilt" as used in this text only signifies the interrogator's opinion. In no way does it connote legal guilt based upon proof beyond a reasonable doubt. Accordingly, it is in that context this chapter presents the tactics and techniques for the interrogation of suspects whose guilt, in the *opinion* of the interrogator, seems definite or reasonably certain. Among them are *the nine steps* to effectiveness.

GENERAL CLASSIFICATION OF OFFENDERS

The selection of interrogation procedures depends to a considerable extent upon the personal characteristics of the suspect himself, the type of offense, the probable motivation for its commission, and the suspect's initial behavioral responses. On the basis of these considerations, criminal offenders are subject to a rather broad, yet flexible, classification into either *emotional offenders* or *nonemotional offenders*.

Emotional offender refers to an offender who ordinarily experiences a considerable feeling of remorse, mental anguish, or compunction as a result of his offense. This individual has a strong sense of moral guilt—in other words, a "troubled conscience." Emotional offenders can be identified behaviorally during an interrogation in that they tend to be emotionally moved by the interrogator's words and actions. As the interrogation progresses, the emotional offender may develop watery eyes and body posture will become less rigid and more open, without crossed arms and legs. The subject's eye contact with the interrogator will become less frequent, eventually culminating in a vacant stare at the floor. Because of the "troubled conscience" feeling, the most effective interrogation tactics and techniques to use on such a suspect are those based primarily upon a *sympathetic approach* — expressions of understanding and compassion with regard to the commission of the offense as well as the suspect's present difficulty.

Nonemotional offender refers to a person who ordinarily does not experience a troubled conscience. He may react emotionally, but usually to a lesser degree than that experienced by emotional offenders. During interrogation, the nonemotional offender may offer token, unchallenging denials of guilt that are stopped easily. The suspect is quite content to allow the interrogator to talk, but the words fall on seemingly deaf ears as the suspect maintains a defensive, closed posture, including crossed arms, erect head, and a cold, hard stare. A remarkable characteristic of the nonemotional offender is a resistance to becoming emotionally involved in the interrogation.

The most effective tactic and techniques to use on the nonemotional offender are those based primarily upon a *factual analysis approach*. This approach means appealing to the suspect's common sense and reasoning rather than to his emotions; it is designed to convince him that his guilt already is established or that it soon will be established and, consequently, there is nothing else to do but to admit it.

As a general rule, the majority of all offenders, emotional and nonemotional, possess emotional traits to some degree. For this reason, the sympathetic and factual analysis approaches often should be intermingled. Greater emphasis will be placed, however, upon one or the other, depending on the type of offender.

As a result of many years' experience, primarily on the part of the staff of John E. Reid and Associates under the guidance of the late John E. Reid, (one of the co-authors of the present text), the interrogation process has been formulated into nine structural components — *the nine steps* of criminal interrogation. These nine steps are presented in the context of the interrogation of suspects *whose guilt seems definite or reasonably certain.* It must be remembered that none of the steps is apt to make an innocent person confess and that all of the steps are legally as well as morally justifiable. For those persons who have qualms or reservations about utilizing some of the steps, this chapter subsequently presents various justification factors.

In utilizing *the nine steps* approach to an effective interrogation, the interrogator should keep in mind two points:

1. The numerical sequence does not signify that every interrogation will encompass all nine steps, or that those that are used must conform to a specific sequence.
2. As each step is used, the interrogator should be on the alert to evaluate whatever behavioral responses the suspect may be displaying, the responses themselves may be suggestive of the next appropriate step.

BRIEF ANALYSIS OF THE NINE STEPS

Step 1 involves a direct, positively presented confrontation of the suspect with a statement that he is considered to be the person who committed the offense. At this stage, the interrogator should pause to evaluate the suspect's response. Before proceeding to the next step, the interrogator should repeat the accusation. The tone and nature of this repetition will depend upon whether the suspect seemed passive or voiced a positive denial after first being accused. If passive, the second accusation should be expressed with the same or even greater degree of conviction. Care must be taken, however, to enunciate very clearly the second accusation so as to obviate the possibility of any misunderstanding. If the suspect's reaction to the second confrontation is as passive as the one to the initial confrontation, that fact in itself is an indication of deception. On the other hand, if the suspect is quite direct and forceful in denying the first accusation, the second accusation may be reduced in tone and nature and the interrogator should proceed to *Step 2*, even though *Step 1* created a lessening of confidence in his initial assumption of the suspect's guilt.

In **Step 2** the interrogator expresses a supposition about the reason for the crime's commission, whereby the suspect should be offered a possible moral excuse for having committed the offense. To accomplish this, the interrogator should attempt to affix moral blame for the offense upon some other person (e.g., an accomplice), the victim, or some particular circumstance (e.g., an urgent need by the suspect of money in order for the suspect to support himself or family). If a suspect seems to listen attentively to the suggested "theme," or seems to be deliberating about it, even for a short period of time, that reaction is strongly suggestive of guilt. On the other hand, if the suspect expresses resentment over the mere submission of such a suggestion, this reaction may be indicative of innocence.

Up to this point, a guilty person, as well as an innocent one, will have denied guilt. The interrogator should then embark upon **Step 3**, which consists of suggested procedures for handling the initial denials of guilt. Basically, this step involves cutting off the suspect's repetition or elaboration of the denial and returning to the moral excuse theme that comprises *Step 2*. An innocent person will not allow such denials to be cut off; furthermore, he will attempt more or less to "take over" the situation rather than to submit passively to continued interrogation. On the other hand, a guilty person usually will cease to voice a denial, or else the denial will be weak, and he will submit to the interrogator's return to a theme.

Step 4 involves the task of overcoming the suspect's comments about the moral excuse element presented in *Step 2*. These comments will consist of what may be viewed as "objections" from the suspect, presented in the form of explanations as to *why the suspect did not* or *could not* commit the crime. These responses are normally offered by the guilty suspect, particularly when they come after the denial phase of the interrogation. They are significant in that they constitute evasions of a bold denial by the substitution of the less courageous statement as to *why* the suspect did not or could not commit the offense under investigation. Such an objection causes less internal anxiety than the utterance of an outright denial.

Step 5 consists of the procurement and retention of the suspect's full attention, without which the interrogation may amount to no more than an exercise in futility. During *Step 5*, the interrogator will clearly display a sincerity in what he says. Helpful in achieving this is an increase in the closeness of the previously described seating arrangement between interrogator and suspect. The same is true of the physical gestures the interrogator can employ, such as a pat on the shoulder or, in the case of a female, a gentle holding of the suspect's hand.

Step 6 involves the handling of the suspect's passive mood. This step should occur when the suspect becomes quiet, displays a tendency to listen, or tries to avoid looking directly at the interrogator. Physical signs of "giving up" may begin to appear. At this point, there should be a reinforcement of eye contact between the suspect and the interrogator. Tears that may appear in the suspect's eyes at this time usually are indicative of deception and also of a "giving up" attitude.

Step 7 is the utilization of an alternative question—a suggestion of a choice to be made by the suspect between an "acceptable" and an "unacceptable" aspect of the crime. This choice will be in the form of a question, such as: "Was this the first time, or has it happened many times before?" Whichever alternative is chosen by the suspect, the net effect of an expressed choice will be the functional equivalent of an incriminating admission.

Following the selection of an alternative, **Step 8** involves having the suspect orally relate the various details about the offense that will serve ultimately to establish legal guilt. These details can include where the fatal weapon was discarded or where the stolen money was hidden and the motive for the crime's commission.

Finally, **Step 9** relates to the confession itself. This step involves the recommended procedure for converting an oral confession into a written one and is presented later in this text.

Figure 4 illustrates the nine steps. Again, the authors wish to make clear that many cases do not require the utilization of all nine steps. Frequently, just a few of them will suffice to permit a resolution of the issue.

PRELIMINARY PREPARATIONS FOR APPLYING THE NINE STEPS

Before proceeding to apply any of *the nine steps*, the *Miranda* warnings must be given to a custodial suspect and a waiver must be obtained. Unless the interrogator knows that this has already been done by the person who presented the suspect for interrogation, or by someone else in authority prior to the interrogation, the interrogator should give the warnings and obtain the waiver. It is preferable, however, that the interrogator be spared this responsibility so that he may immediately proceed with the behavioral analysis interview and the interrogation without the diversion occasioned by the warning procedure. (The form and nature of the required warnings and of the waiver are fully described in Chapter 8 of this text.)

Two points are worth repeating here:

1. The words "guilty," "innocent," "definite," and "reasonably certain," with respect to the issue of guilt or innocence, represent nothing more than labels for interrogation purposes. A final determination of a suspect's status is the province of the judge or jury at a criminal trial.
2. Before the interrogator begins, he should have knowledge of all available, relevant investigative information concerning the crime, witnesses, and discoverer of the crime or accuser, and also regarding the persons under suspicion, including, of course, the one who is about to be interrogated. In the majority of cases, a nonaccusatory interview of the suspect should precede any interrogation.

Before the interrogator embarks upon the actual interrogation, even in those instances where he has previously interviewed the suspect, it is advisable to allow the suspect to sit in the interrogation room alone for about 5 minutes. A guilty suspect will rapidly try to review everything that is going to be said, and this preparation will cause him to become insecure. Additional doubts and concerns will arise in the suspect's mind and thereby further disorganize efforts at deception. Some guilty suspects will be so deep in thought and so concerned with their plight that when the interrogator enters the room, they will become startled and immediately indicate by their eyes and general appearance that they expect their deception to be revealed. On the other hand, an innocent suspect, even though somewhat apprehensive, will usually turn easily toward the in-

THE NINE STEPS TO EFFECTIVE INTERROGATION

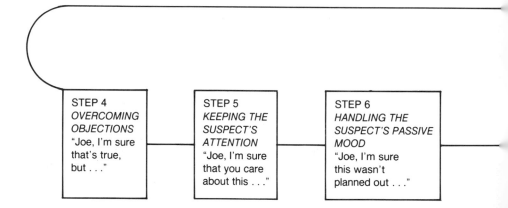

Figure 6.1.

terrogator when he enters; although understandably interested, there will be an "at ease" look in the suspect's eyes and the appearance will be a favorable one.

Before entering the interrogation room, the interrogator should prepare and have on hand an evidence case folder, or else a simulation of one. Then, at the outset of the interrogation, and also at appropriate times

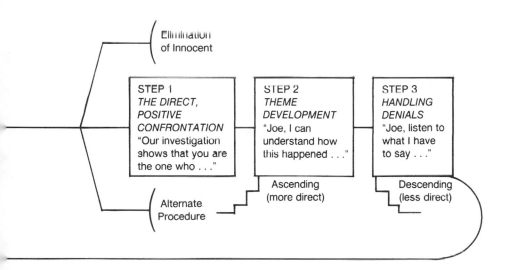

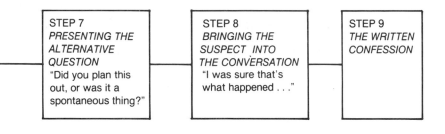

during the various steps that follow the initial confrontation, the interrogator should look into the file as though reviewing its contents. The purpose of doing so is to lead the suspect to believe that it contains information and material of incriminating significance, even though, in fact, the file contains very little. The mere sight of the file will have a desirable effect on both guilty and innocent suspects because of the impression of preparedness on the part of the interrogator.

After the suspect has been waiting about 5 minutes, the interrogator's entrance into the interrogation room should be very deliberate and should be accompanied by an air of confidence. The success or failure of an interrogation depends to a large extent upon the interrogator's initial approach and the first impression that is created. If the suspect is not seated, the interrogator should direct him to do so. On the other hand, if the suspect is seated and starts to rise, there should be a direction to remain seated.

The interrogator should be polite, of course, but at the same time should maintain a degree of professionalism as he enters the room. It is well to emulate somewhat the conduct and behavior of a busy medical specialist who calls upon a hospitalized patient to whom the specialist has been previously identified and who knows of the impending arrival. Although the specialist will extend a brief greeting, usually no handshaking or other social gestures occur. The physician proceeds with his professional duties, such as examining the patient's chart and then interviewing and examining him. It is a strictly professional event.

Likewise, in an interrogation situation, the interrogator should not volunteer any handshaking; if, however, the suspect extends his hand to the interrogator, the response should be a very casual handshake. Although the interrogator should already have been identified, if this has not occurred, or if the suspect inquires about the interrogator's name, only the last name should be mentioned. If the interrogator, for instance, identifies himself as "Jack Wilson," this may encourage the suspect to refer to him as "Jack," thereby establishing a familiarity that will serve as a psychological handicap to the interrogator. The suspect should call him by the more formal "Mr. Wilson" or, at the least, "Wilson."

STEP 1: DIRECT, POSITIVE CONFRONTATION

In those instances where the interrogator has had no prior contact with the suspect, the interrogator, while still standing in front of the seated suspect and using the case folder as a prop, should state clearly and briefly something along the following lines: "You're Joe Burns? I'm in here to talk to you about the break-in at Jason's Jewelry Store last week." As that comment is being made, the interrogator should finger through the case folder to create the impression that it contains material of an incriminating nature about the suspect.

Although the interrogator in this instance has already been insulated from having his own first name used, he has gained a psychological advantage by addressing the suspect by *his* first name. This is particularly so when the suspect is a person with a professional title, or someone of social, political, or business prominence. Such suspects are thereby stripped of the psychological advantage they may assume they have by virtue of their position. It is a very disarming tactic. There are exceptions, however. Whenever there is a significant disparity between an interrogator's young age and the older age of a suspect, it may be inappropriate to call the suspect by his first name. Then, too, as discussed earlier, a psychological gain may accrue to the interrogator by addressing a person of low socioeconomic status by his or her *last* name (prefaced in appropriate instances by Mr., Mrs., or Miss).

The direct, positive confrontation in the aforementioned hypothetical burglary case should be "Joe, the results of our investigation clearly indicate that you broke into Jason's Jewelry Store last week." This direct, positive statement should be emphatically expressed in a slow, deliberate, and confident manner. The words "broke into" have an unmistakable meaning and, at the same time, avoid the legalistic word "burglary." (As earlier stated, there is a psychological disadvantage in using words or expressions that conjure up in the suspect's mind the legal consequences of a confession of guilt.)

Note that in the example given of a direct confrontation, the interrogator referred to "our" investigation. This carries the implication that several investigators have reached that conclusion, and not just the interrogator. The statement, therefore, is more impressive than if the interrogator merely had said: "It looks like you broke into . . ." or "I am confident you broke into . . . ."

Even in case situations where the initial interview with a suspect was conducted by the same person who is to conduct an interrogation, the interrogator should proceed with a direct, positive accusation. Immediately thereafter, the interrogator, while continuing to stand in front of the seated suspect, should pause to ascertain the reactions. The pause should only last 5 or 10 seconds, even though it may seem to be longer to the suspect. Meanwhile, the interrogator can appear busy, thumbing through the evidence folder, while observing the suspect without looking directly at him.

In the event that the confrontation in *Step 1* seems too strong and, therefore, inappropriate for use by private security personnel (because of cautionary company policy, the security officer's personal relationship with the suspected employee, or some other reason), the confrontation statement can be rephrased in the following ways: 1) "Joe, the results of our investigation indicate that you have not told the whole truth about the [missing money, etc.]," or 2) "Joe, as you know, I have been interviewing several people here concerning [the missing money, etc.], and right now, you are the only one I cannot eliminate from suspicion."

This same modification of the confrontation statement may also be advisable in police interrogations if the interrogator develops any reservations as to the actual guilt of the suspect. This is apt to occur in case situations where circumstantial or direct evidence has indicated guilt, but the behavior symptoms displayed during the initial interview were consistent with possible innocence.

If, after the first accusation, the suspect responds by asking the interrogator "What do you mean?" or "What did you say?" he is probably stalling for time or trying to reorganize his thoughts that were disrupted by the surprise accusation. (This inference, of course, is valid only if the accusation was unmistakably clear.) On the other hand, an innocent person will usually have no reason to ask a question as to what the interrogator said or meant, and may immediately express resentment over being accused.

During the behavioral pause, a guilty suspect probably will look at the floor or to the side as much as possible in order to avoid eye-to-eye contact. This will afford him the time to develop a verbal response, which, in many instances, may not in fact represent an answer at all. The suspect may at this stage also exhibit physical signs of guilt—shifting posture, crossing legs, brushing clothing as if to remove dust, slouching in the chair, or moving back in the chair in order to get as far away as possible from the interrogator. To the contrary, the innocent suspect may move forward in the chair, displaying none of the aforementioned gestures. The innocent suspect's face may become flushed, the eyes may concentrate on the interrogator, and he may also respond verbally in a very angry, blunt manner. No attempt will be made to conceal resentment over the accusation. Some innocent suspects, however, will seem completely surprised and taken aback by the accusation, or else will exhibit a moment or two of disbelief. Then, a sincere, spontaneous, and even vehement denial may follow, accompanied by eye-to-eye contact. The innocent person may look truly offended and may attempt to stop the false accusation. On the other hand, a guilty person will usually be passive; he may respond with a rather pleading look and answer in the form of a soft denial or a rather vague inquiry to the interrogator.

A guilty suspect may attempt to evade detection by employing dramatic physical gestures—moving the head back and forth and running fingers through hair in an effort to create the impression of complete desperation. By this means, the suspect can also avoid looking the interrogator straight in the eye. He may speak loudly upon the assumption that this will intimidate the interrogator into terminating the interrogation. These pretenses should not be permitted to mislead the interrogator.

After the behavioral pause following the initial confrontation statement, the interrogator should be seated in front of the suspect and repeat the statement, coupled with the transitional comment, "Joe, as I said, our investigation indicates that you are involved [in this break-in], and I'd like to spend a few minutes with you so we can get this thing straightened out, OK?" If the suspect tries to interject a denial, it is important to say: "Just a minute, Joe, let me explain a few things to you first." Then the interrogator should begin to develop his theme. (This development is further explained in *Step 2*).

One of the interrogator's goals at this point is to keep the suspect from denying involvement in the crime. Without a doubt, of course, the easiest confessions to obtain are from suspects who fail to make a denial after the positive confrontation. In cases where the suspect's guilt seems so certain that the interrogator does not need the positive confrontation behavioral pause to evaluate truthfulness, it is recommended that he only make the initial confrontation statement and then follow it with a question. In the forgoing case, for example, the confrontation may be: "Joe, the results of our investigation clearly indicate that you broke into Jason's Jewelry Store last week. I'm going to sit down with you for a few minutes so we can get this thing straightened out, OK?". Almost all deceptive suspects will retort with something other than a denial when the confrontation is followed up by such a question. Some guilty suspects will simply nod their head in acknowledgment, while others may be evasive with "I don't know what you're talking about." Regardless of the suspect's response to this initial confrontation, when the interrogator is certain of the suspect's guilt, the second statement asserting guilt should not be made in such a way as to afford the suspect an opportunity to utter a denial. After the interrogator sits in front of the suspect, he should then proceed with the theme development (*Step 2*).

On occasion, the interrogator will encounter a suspect who, after the initial confrontation statement, does not exhibit behavior that is clearly indicative of either guilt or innocence. The interrogator should nevertheless make a second confrontation statement and should do so just as firmly as would be done with a suspect whose behavior symptoms were indicative of guilt. Only by doing that can a differentiation be made between the guilty and the innocent. Some persons are so constituted that, even though innocent, they will not make their objections or indicate their resentment until they are fully convinced that the interrogator means what has been said by way of an accusation. Then, too, some guilty suspects will not exhibit symptoms of guilt until after the second confrontation statement is made. Whenever indefinite behavior symptoms persist even after the second confrontation, it is recommended that the interrogator proceed as though the symptoms had indicated guilt.

In instances where the responses to a second accusation are indicative of probable innocence, the interrogator should nevertheless attempt to develop a theme (as described in *Step 2*) in an effort to establish some rapport with the suspect. In the event the suspect becomes adamant in the denial and does not allow the interrogator to develop a theme, it may be necessary for the interrogator to "back down." The procedure for doing this is described in *Step 3* on the handling of denials.

There are two auxiliary aspects of *Step 1*. One deals with the misleading behavior symptoms that may follow the accusatory confrontation; the other pertains to the legal and moral justification for its utilization as an interrogation technique.

Misleading Behavior Symptoms following Accusatory Confrontations

As cautioned in Chapter 5, the interrogator, when assessing guilt or innocence, must always be mindful of the risk involved in a reliance solely upon the initial behavior symptoms. Even though a guilty suspect will usually react to the accusatory confrontation in a passive, evasive, and insincere manner, or an innocent suspect usually will react in a sincere, aggressive, and perhaps even hostile manner, there are exceptions, as the following cases illustrate. Cases 1 and 2 concern innocent suspects; cases 3 and 4 concern guilty suspects.

CASE   1

In this case, investigative information was strongly suggestive of the suspect's guilt. A female employee, suspected of stealing $2,000 from a bank, seemed very distraught. Her eyes were evasive, and she was somewhat disorganized in her speech. The total appearance was one of guilt. When confronted, she began to cry. However, during her crying, she blew her nose, looked the interrogator straight in the eye, and sternly said: "But I didn't steal the money!" Each time she made this denial, she became more intense, but she continued to look dejected. However, because she was so direct, and because of her greater intensity in saying "I did not steal the money!" the interrogator said: "Something is on your mind!—What is it?" She answered, "I can't tell you, I can't! I can't!" After some persuasion, she disclosed she was pregnant by her boyfriend, who also worked at the bank, and he had agreed to marry her, but his mother, who was not informed of the pregnancy, wanted a large church wedding in several months. The suspect's shame of being pregnant, coupled with the boyfriend's mother insisting on a large wedding at a later date, seemed to be the reason why the girl seemed worn down and dejected, and why her concern about the entire matter portrayed the appearance of guilt.

After postponing any further interrogation, the suspect and her boyfriend disclosed the pregnancy to the mother, and the matter was satisfactorily resolved. A subsequent interview brought forth symptoms of innocence and, indeed, further investigation revealed the identity of the actual embezzler.

CASE   2

In the following case, the suspect's postaccusatory confrontation behavior symptoms were also misleading. An official of a company was suspected of embezzling $150,000. His behavior symptoms were strongly suggestive of guilt, but the reason for this, as was subsequently ascertained, was the fact that he had been convicted of a theft 20 years previously and had served time in a penitentiary. After his release, he had been employed by the company and had become so successful that he had advanced to a managerial position. The president of the company, the only person who knew about the previous conviction, had interceded successfully on his behalf to obtain a pardon. This fact had not been disclosed to anyone else until the interrogator, concerned over the suspect's possible guilt as to the $150,000 embezzlement, was confidentially informed by the company president of the suspect's previous record. After this disclosure, and after the suspect was told about it, his whole behavior changed noticeably. He was at ease, his eyes became clear, and he was immediately reported as innocent, an opinion later verified by another employee's confession.

CASE   3

Three hundred and fifty thousand dollars in cash was reported stolen in a burglary from a wealthy lawyer's home. Polygraph tests were given to each of the household employees. An ex-police officer, who was employed as a chauffeur, failed the test. Confronted with the results, he vehemently denied being implicated, and buttressed his loud outbursts of indignation with various portrayals of innocence. The interrogator refused to retract the accusation. Although the outbursts were consistent and loud, they did not seem to be sincere indications of innocence; moreover, the suspect was embellishing his denials by dramatic gestures. The interrogator continued the interrogation on the assumption of guilt. The suspect finally confessed and hastened to add that, because of a spending spree with friends of his, only $69,000 could be returned. Fortunately, some of the remainder of the full amount was recoverable from assets purchased with the stolen money.

CASE   4

A comparatively small sum of $180 was missing from an automatic teller machine at a bank. A 7-year employee failed a polygraph test and was then confronted regarding the missing $180. His response, loud and clear, was "I did not take that money!" The examiner then sat down in front of the suspect and again advised him that the polygraph test showed he had not been truthful about the $180. The suspect slammed his hand down and again said with anger, "I did not take that $180!" The suspect looked the examiner in the eye while making this additional denial and then looked around the room in disgust as if to say, "I can't believe this!" The examiner then began to offer some justification for the theft, but he was stopped by the suspect's loud response: "You're ruining my life and career. I did not take that money!" The examiner, ignoring this statement, said: "I'm sure if you were dishonest you would have been doing things like this from the first day you started, but you're not basically dishonest. You're like me or anyone else who gets into a jam and without thinking does a crazy thing, and I'm sure you're sorry for it now." At this point, the suspect, almost in tears, got up suddenly from his chair and walked toward the door of the room. The examiner continued to talk to the empty chair as if the suspect had not left and said, "Joe, if you needed the $180 for some legitimate expense, I can understand your doing this!" The suspect, still standing and staring at the door, buried his head in his arms against the wall and shouted, "I did not take the money." Then he punched his fist against the wall, actually causing slight damage to it. Immediately thereafter, he dropped to his knees and said "I'm sorry!" The examiner responded excitedly: "Look what you've done to the wall. Now sit down and let's get this matter straightened out." The suspect again stated he was "sorry" and meekly sat down. Once more, he denied, but very meekly, that he had stolen the $180. With tears in his eyes, he admitted that a few months previously, he had stolen $500 from the automatic teller machine, but he continued to deny that he had taken the $180. The examiner, persuaded by the recorded polygraph responses indicative of lying about the latter sum, coupled with the contradictory indications between the wall slamming and the utterance of "I'm sorry," continued with his accusation regarding the $180, but to no avail. However, subsequent developments in the case clearly established that the suspect had, indeed, stolen the $180, in addition to other money beyond the admitted $500. In this case, the suspect had been so committed to his original denial regarding the $180 that he could not reverse himself. Such a reaction is not uncommon in cases where the interrogator permits the suspect to become repetitive with the denial.

Many offenders will admit guilt to a very serious offense, while at the same time refusing to do so regarding a lesser related one that was part of the same series of events. An example of this is the case of a rapist or murderer who will admit his guilt to such a serious offense but will still steadfastly deny stealing a gold crucifix or other religious object from the victim's body or room. In his mind, the incidental offense is more revolting and harder to admit than the main one.

Justification for Accusatory Confrontation

As illustrated, there are occasions when the person on whom an accusatory confrontation has been used is then considered by the interrogator to be innocent of the offense under investigation, even though circumstances were very indicative of his guilt. The accusatory technique nevertheless can be justified, not only on broadly based considerations but even regarding the particular individual suspect. First and foremost, as to an innocent suspect, recognition must be given to the fact that were it not for the interrogation that ultimately terminated in a conclusion of innocence, the person may well have always remained under a cloud of suspicion. Moreover, in a personnel security situation, that suspect may actually have been fired as an employee—if not at that particular time, then at a later date. As between the latter possibilities and the hurt feelings from being wrongly accused (in a strictly private setting), the authors submit that the interrogation experience is the less onerous one.

Once again, the accusations comprising *Step 1* are confined to those interrogations where the suspect's guilt seems to the interrogator to be definite or reasonably certain. They are also utilized under conditions of absolute privacy, which should minimize the suspect's discomfort. The privacy factor, incidentally, is also one that is protective to the interrogator personally because it provides immunity from a subsequent civil suit for slander or defamation of character. That claim can only arise, of course, when a false accusation is made in the presence of some third party.[1]

There are many situations where public welfare requires relinquishment of some personal comfort or even a sacrifice of a measure of protection from governmental intrusion. Examples of this are found in instances where the police are legally permitted to stop and even to frisk a person whom they reasonably suspect of having committed, or being about to commit, a criminal offense. The fact that subsequent developments definitely show that the stop-and-frisk was conducted on an innocent person does not have the retroactive effect of rendering the police action illegal. The same is true where the police, acting on reasonable grounds (probable cause), make an actual arrest, including the taking of a person to a detention facility until released by court order. Subsequent proof of

---

[1]With respect to third parties, however, there is what the law terms a "qualified privilege" that protects the speaker when the third party (or parties) is someone who is an official

innocence does not subject the police to any liability; the only requirement that must be fulfilled is that they acted upon reasonable grounds.

Not only are reasonably based police procedures sanctioned in the public interest, even at the risk of discomfort and embarrassment to potentially innocent persons, but comparable legal sanction also prevails regarding security officers functioning in the private sector. Consider, for instance, the statutory and case law that permits a merchant or a security officer to temporarily detain a person reasonably suspected of shoplifting for the purpose of determining whether the merchandise is in his lawful possession. Where there are reasonable grounds (probable cause) to believe that a person has actually committed the theft by shoplifting, many state statutes specifically authorize an actual arrest by the merchant or security officer. That also is the common law in many states where there is no statute.

An often overlooked factor with respect to the interrogation of suspects is that many criminal offenses can only be solved by the interrogation process, regardless of the availability of sophisticated, scientific investigative aids or highly skilled police or private security investigators. Stripped of the opportunity to interrogate suspects, the investigative process would be emasculated in numerous types of situations. Consider, for instance, a brutal nighttime rape of a woman who had been dragged into an alley. If she is unable to adequately describe her assailant except in a very general way (white or black, tall or short, wearing a coat or coatless, blue or white shirt, etc.), there would be no way to lawfully establish the guilt of a suspected assailant who is apprehended in the vicinity of the rape except by the process of interrogation. The fact that the suspect matched the general description, or that his clothing contained blood, even of the same type as the victim's, or that strands of hair pulled from the head of the assailant were similar to samples taken from the suspect may not establish proof of guilt beyond a reasonable doubt. A confession usually is indispensable in cases of this type. Similarly, a monetary theft on the part of one of a number of employees would often remain unsolved were it not for the opportunity to conduct interrogations of a suspect or suspects.

Public welfare, in both police case situations and in private security investigations, renders vitally necessary the legal approval of interrogation efforts, subject always to the constraint of reasonableness under the particular circumstances. The public can ill afford deprivation of interrogation opportunities from either the police or the operators of business

---

participant in the investigation (e.g., a fellow police or security officer), or else someone who has a financial interest in the subject matter of the investigation (e.g., a merchant or one of his associates or other representative). Such a third person's overhearing an interrogator's accusatory statements is not viewed as a "publication" for purposes of a suit for slander or other defamation. The references in support of this legal principle are presented in Chapter 8 of this volume.

enterprises. Providing immunity for criminal conduct is intolerable within both public and private sectors.

An additional factor for consideration with respect to the utilization of the accusatory technique, and particularly on persons who are later established to be innocent, is that in a properly conducted interrogation, an interrogator will not extend an accusation beyond the point where mental distress becomes a reasonable probability. There should be no prohibition, however, upon the utilization of the accusatory confrontation that is designed and applied only for the purpose of persuading the guilty to confess, while at the same time avoiding the risk of procuring a confession from the innocent.[2]

STEP 2: THEME DEVELOPMENT

Emotional Offenders

Immediately after the direct, positive confrontation described in *Step 1*, the interrogator should begin the development of a "theme." This involves, in large measure, presenting a "moral excuse" for the suspect's commission of the offense or minimizing the moral implications of the conduct. The selected theme may be based upon a simple, common sense analysis of the suspect's unusual circumstantial proximity to the situation that triggered the criminal conduct. Some themes may offer a "crutch" for the suspect as he moves toward a confession; other themes will foreclose any supportable alternative to a disclosure of truth. Because emotional offenders often experience shame and guilt, themes centered around excusing their criminal behavior are effective because such themes permit the suspect to accept physical responsibility for committing the crime while relieving his emotional guilt.

APPROACHES TO BE AVOIDED

During the presentation of any theme based upon the morality factor, caution must be taken to avoid any indication that the minimization of moral blame will relieve the suspect of *criminal responsibility*. (Later, this text discusses how to handle a situation where the suspect asks the interrogator: "What will happen to me if I tell you I did this?")

---

[2]Chapter 8 of this volume discusses in detail the legal distinction between mental distress induced intentionally and the relatively minor stress that may result from a legitimate, well-intentioned interrogation during the course of an investigation of a criminal offense.

It is important to avoid spending excessive time in presenting a theme, particularly in instances where the suspect gives any indication of being on the verge of confessing. When that occurs, the interrogator should immediately invoke *Step 7*, presenting an alternative question. On the other hand, if the suspect seems resolute in the denial, a considerable amount of time may be required to develop an appropriate theme.

A mistake that criminal interrogators frequently make is revealing to the suspect at the outset of the interrogation all that is known about the case and suspect. Seldom is anything gained by this approach, and frequently much is lost. It may be helpful, however, to point out to the suspect a single piece of evidence bearing on his guilt. For instance, in a hit-and-run automobile case, let the suspect know (if it is a fact) that a dent has been observed on the left front fender of his car and that human hair and blood have been found around the dent. In a theft case, perhaps the suspect can and should be told (if it is a fact) that the interrogator knows that a substantial loan was paid off by the suspect soon after the theft. In other words, the suspect should be told just enough to satisfy him that there is good reason for being questioned and that the investigators are not merely on a "fishing expedition."

Once the suspect's attention is called to a particular piece of incriminating evidence, the interrogator must be on guard to cut off immediately any explanation the suspect may start to offer at that time. This can be done by saying, "Wait a minute, Joe; wait until I'm through and then I'll hear what you have to say." In this way, the interrogator not only retains control of the situation but also disallows the suspect a chance to explain incriminating evidence. Such a chance would bolster the suspect's confidence and put the interrogator on the defensive, which should never be permitted. The psychological consideration involved here is very important: The impression created at this early stage of the interrogation may set the pattern for all that follows. This consideration is discussed in detail in *Step 3* on handling denials.

Another form of theme development that must be avoided is "high-pressure salesmanship," whereby the interrogator goes into a rapid-fire monologue, indulging in accusations and perhaps telling the suspect all the interrogator knows about the case and about the circumstances pointing toward the suspect's guilt. In such instances, very little of what the interrogator says will have any impact.

Basic to any theme application is confidence on the part of the interrogator and, more important, a conveyance of sincerity in whatever is said. With respect to the interrogator's self-confidence, the fact that a suspect has a criminal record, or even an extensive one, should not be assumed to present an insurmountable barrier to securing a confession. Persons of that type may still be vulnerable to the tactics and techniques described in this text. In any event, if an interrogator becomes concerned over the fact that the suspect has a criminal record and is probably too "wised up" to confess, the interrogator will have encountered defeat before even starting.

Also with regard to interrogator self-confidence, a person with a background as a law enforcement officer is not any more difficult to interrogate than anyone else; in fact, such a person is frequently more vulnerable to interrogation techniques than persons without a similar background. Perhaps the reason for this is the suspect's acute awareness of the significance that will be attached to even minor contradictions or slip-ups in a false story; he also knows from his own professional experiences that a guilty person may exhibit symptoms of deception by his behavior and general conduct. The suspect may even know of the particular interrogator's skill in obtaining confessions. In short, a suspect with a background in the field of law enforcement may have less confidence as a liar than the ordinary criminal suspect.

An interrogator should never adopt or drift into an indifferent, passive, or lethargic attitude. If those are the interrogator's usual personality characteristics, he probably should not be in the interrogation field at all. However, if such an attitude is the result of only a temporary "letdown" mood, it is advisable to have someone else serve as interrogator until the attitude changes.

The most effective attitude is generally one that reveals a calm confidence, wherein there is a constrained display of a vital, intense interest in the interrogation mission, but one that, at the same time, implies an understanding, considerate, and sympathetic feeling toward the suspect. In conveying a sympathetic, understanding attitude, an interrogator must not indulge in fast or glib talk. Except when actually feigning impatience or displeasure, the interrogator should talk slowly—even to the point of occasionally hesitating, or even seemingly stuttering, in his attempt to formulate a theme.

If the interrogator senses that the first theme selected has not hit a responsive chord, he should either modify it or shift to another theme. In doing so, the interrogator should not indicate disappointment for having presented the first theme. He should just quickly embark upon another one, all the while maintaining, or even accentuating, eye contact with the suspect and displaying confidence in the achievement of his ultimate objective.

THE TRANSITIONAL THEME

Sometimes, the interrogator may feel awkward in beginning a theme that immediately follows a positive confrontation. Consequently, the interrogator, as well as the suspect, requires a transition into the theme. The core of the transitional theme should address the reason why it is important to tell the truth. Also, the transitional theme may be most effective if it does not directly address the suspect, but rather introduces a "third" person into the interrogation environment. This third person could be the interrogator, as he relates a personal story; another suspect in a similar case, real or fictitious; or an institution, such as a fraternal order or church. The transitional theme thereby provides groundwork for the actual presentation of the main theme itself, because now a third person or institution becomes the subject of discussion, and the suspect does not feel an impulse to deny the crime.

The following example illustrates a transitional theme:

> Joe, the reason I want to talk with you today is that you remind me of a fellow we had in here a couple of weeks ago. He was young and ambitious and a real go-getter. By working his way up the ladder at a bank, he went from clerk to teller, and finally he was promoted to auditor within a period of 8 or 10 months. Everything seemed to be going well for him. He had a loving wife, two lovely children, and they were in the process of moving to a newer home in a nice subdivision. One day, while he was balancing the books, he noticed a teller had failed to record a $6,000 deposit. This was the amount the fellow I'm talking about needed to complete a down payment on his home. On the spur of the moment, a decision was made to take the money. I don't think I have to tell you what happened next. The bank noticed the shortage after the customer called. This young auditor came under suspicion, and I remember him sitting right where you are, telling me how sorry he was for taking the money. The reason you remind me of him is that, as with him, you have a lot going for you. You are intelligent, ambitious, and basically very honest. I think what happened to you is that on the spur of the moment you decided to do this to help pay bills for food or maybe clothes for your family . . . .

Once such a transitional theme has been presented, the interrogator can easily direct his comments specifically to the crime the suspect committed.

SPECIFIC THEMES THAT CAN BE USED

The themes for *Step 2* that are presented in this chapter do not constitute the entire interrogation process; they represent only the basic psychological elements of it. Moreover, as a theme is presented, the suspect may not remain quiet and just listen; instead, he may interrupt with a denial or an objection. When this occurs, responses must be handled in the particular manner described in either of the two subsequent interrogation steps (*Steps 3* and *4*). Following successful application of these steps, there may be a return to one or more of the earlier themes of *Step 2*, or the interrogator may have to shift to an alternative procedure. In other words, the themes only represent a general step among the various other specific steps that follow. In order to explain the themes presented in this chapter, each one must be illustrated by some examples that disclose the very interrogation tactics and techniques that are required to render the themes effective. The examples themselves may seem to consume only a few minutes each; however, a considerably longer period of time may be required in order to adequately develop and elaborate upon the basic idea.

Throughout the theme presentation process, the interrogator should not lose sight of the fact that the moral or psychological excuses offered to the suspect do not even have to approximate the true motivation underlying the offense. All that is required is the creation of a perception on the part of the suspect that he is a less reprehensible person, morally speaking, than the bare facts of the case would indicate. The objective of *Step 2*, therefore, is primarily to establish the psychological foundation to achieve an implicit, if not explicit, early, general admission of guilt. (In *Steps 8* and *9*, the interrogator will seek to ascertain from the suspect the actual motivation and the complete circumstances of the offense itself.)

THEME 1: SYMPATHIZE WITH SUSPECT BY SAYING ANYONE ELSE UNDER SIMILAR CONDITIONS OR CIRCUMSTANCES MIGHT HAVE DONE SAME THING

A criminal offender, and particularly one of the emotional type, derives considerable mental relief and comfort from an interrogator's assurance that anyone else under similar conditions or circumstances might have done the same thing. The suspect is thereby able, at least in part, to justify or excuse in his own mind the offensive act or behavior. Yet, the person still realizes that a wrong or mistake has injured or damaged another person or the public in general. Self-condonation, therefore, does not completely satisfy the offender's desire for relief from a troubled conscience. As a matter of fact, the comfort derived from the interrogator's assurances that another person might have committed a similar offense merely offers an added incentive to obtain the greater degree of relief and comfort that would be provided by a confession. While the suspect is in such a frame of mind, the solicitations of a sympathetic interrogator will cast a shadow over the suspect's previous concern about the legal consequences of an exposure of guilt.

The following case illustrates how this technique may be used very effectively: A hit-and-run driver was made to believe that anyone else under similar conditions of panic might also have fled from the scene. He was, therefore, afforded an opportunity to "square himself" with his own conscience. Meanwhile, his realization that he was less savage-like in his behavior than he first assumed himself to be rendered his task of confessing a much easier one than would otherwise have been the case. He was thus permitted to "save face."

The following line of conversation has been found to be effective in the interrogation of an offender such as a hit-and-run driver:

I'm sure in my own mind that a man like you wouldn't deliberately do a thing like this. I think I know what happened; your car hit something. You were not sure what it was, but you had some doubts; so you got excited and drove away. Now you realize you did wrong. You are no different than anyone else and, under the same circumstances, I probably would have done what you yourself did. Now the shock is over and you, as a good citizen, should tell the truth as to what happened. You certainly did not do this deliberately!

In hit-and-run cases, it is helpful for the interrogator to bear in mind the various factors that may account for a person's behavior. The published literature on hit-and-run automobile cases lists a number of reasons why a person may have fled from the scene of an accident, including: 1) panic or psychological numbness from shock, 2) having been under the influence of alcohol, 3) having driven without a license, 4) having feared financial loss or public shame, 5) having had a passenger in the car whose presence would have caused the driver or passenger considerable embarrassment, 6) having had stolen goods or other evidence of a crime in the car, or 7) having feared exposure for some other criminal offense. Suggesting to the suspect any appropriate one of these reasons, and equating the possibility that anyone under similar circumstances, including the interrogator, probably would have done the same thing, will contribute greatly to the success of the interrogation.

In sex offense cases, it is particularly helpful to indicate to the suspect that the interrogator has indulged, or has been tempted to indulge, in the same kind of conduct as involved in the case under investigation. One of many actual cases encountered by the authors of this text concerned a young man, about 17 years of age, who was suspected of rape. The suspect was told that because of the circumstances of the case, he could hardly avoid doing what he did and that, moreover, the interrogator himself, as a young man in high school, "roughed it up" with a girl in an attempt to have intercourse with her. Soon thereafter, the suspect confessed. His father, upon learning of his son being in police custody, arrived at the police station protesting his son's arrest. He was told his son had committed a rape and had admitted to it. The father vehemently protested that his son could not have done such a thing. When the interrogator learned of the protest, he advised the arresting officers to have the father meet his son face to face and learn the truth directly from the confessor himself. When the two met, the father said "Son, did you do this?" The son replied: "Yes, Dad; I just couldn't help what I did. Even Mr. _____ [naming the interrogator] did something like this when he was in high school." Fortunately, the suspect pleaded guilty and, in view of extenuating circumstances, was granted probation, which spared the interrogator the experience of testifying what he had told the suspect. (To be sure, the interrogator would have admitted the fact at trial and, as is seen in Part II of this text, such a statement, although false, would have been ruled legally permissible.)

Once again, interrogators are cautioned that in utilizing the presently discussed theme, they should not make a promise of immunity from prosecution or a diminution of punishment as an inducement for a confession. There is, of course, no legal objection to extending sympathy, as described here, in an effort to elicit the truth.

THEME 2: REDUCE SUSPECT'S FEELING OF GUILT BY MINIMIZING MORAL SERIOUSNESS OF OFFENSE

Although this theme is of value in many types of cases, it is particularly effective in sex crimes. In such cases, it is desirable for the interrogator to pursue a practice of having a male suspect believe that his particular sexual irregularity is not an unusual one, but rather one that occurs quite frequently, even among so-called "normal" and respectable persons. In this connection, it has been found effective to comment as follows:

> We humans are accustomed to thinking of ourselves as far removed from animals, but we're only kidding ourselves. In matters of sex, we're very close to most animals, so don't think you're the only human being—or that you're one of very few—who ever did anything like this. There are plenty others, and these things happen every day and to many persons, and they will continue to happen for many, many years to come.

In sex crimes, it is also very helpful for the interrogator to state that he has heard many persons tell about sexual activities far worse than any the suspect himself may relate. This will serve to encourage the suspect to admit a particularly "shameful" kind of sexual act. His embarrassment will be minimized.

Whenever referring to the particular sexual act about which the suspect is being questioned, the interrogator should not use vulgar terms unless, of course, the suspect is incapable of understanding more acceptable terminology. If, in connection with the offense under investigation, homosexuality on the part of the person being questioned becomes an issue, it should never be discussed or referred to as "abnormal" behavior. To the contrary, the interrogator should convey the impression (irrespective of his own values) that homosexuality of a consensual nature is within the bounds of normality.

The following case involving a suspect who killed his wife illustrates the application of minimizing guilt feelings. Investigation of the case had revealed that the deceased wife had treated her husband very miserably over the years. The interrogator proceeded to say:

Joe, as recently as just last week, my wife made me so angry with her nagging that I felt I couldn't stand it anymore, but just as she was at her worst, there was a ringing of the doorbell by friends from out of town. Was I glad they came! Otherwise, I don't know what I would have done. You were not so lucky as I was on that occasion. Was it something like that, Joe? Or did you find out she was running around with some other man? It must have been something of this sort that touched you off; or maybe it was a combination of several things like that. You've never been in trouble before, so it must have been something like what I've just mentioned—something that got you on the spur of the moment and you couldn't stop yourself. Anyway, she's gone, so we must depend upon you to find out the reason for what happened. You're the only one who can tell us.

Not only is it effective to compare the suspect's conduct with that of "lots of other people," including the interrogator, but when circumstances permit, it is also helpful to compare the suspect's present offense with prior similar (or lesser) offenses committed by the suspect. This too, serves to minimize the moral seriousness of the present offense. The application of this theme in the interrogation of a rapist-murderer was instrumental in eliciting his confession of the killing of his latest rape victim. In this case, the interrogator told the suspect that his rape-murder was no worse than the many other nonfatal rapes he had committed (and to which he had confessed during an earlier period of his interrogation). He was told that in the one case, where death had resulted, he merely "got a tough break"—as was true to a considerable extent because, from all indications, he apparently only had wanted to subdue his victim's resistance rather than to kill her. (He had choked the victim in a fit of passion, which was his usual practice with others, but in this particular instance, the girl failed to recover consciousness soon enough. As a result, he had assumed she was dead and had disposed of her body by throwing it from his car. Her life might have been spared if he had only given her sufficient time to recover from the effects of his earlier violence.) During an interview with one of the authors of this text a few days before the suspect's execution, the rapist-killer stated that at the time of his interrogation, just prior to his confession, he had been comforted by the interrogator's remarks regarding the "no worse" aspect of his present offense in comparison with his previous ones.

As earlier stated, the interrogator must avoid any expressed or intentionally implied statement to the effect that because of the minimized seriousness of the offense, the suspect is to receive a lighter punishment. Nevertheless, there is no legal objection to minimizing in the suspect's mind the *moral* seriousness of the offense.

Although the theme under discussion is particularly suitable for emotional offenders, it also is effective on suspects who classify as nonemotional. For instance, in a case of employee theft, a suspect's attention may be called to published reports on the high incidence of larceny and embezzlement among employees, etc. A published article by one of the authors[3] might be used for this purpose; the article contains the statement that "about 85 out of every 100 persons will 'steal' if a favorable opportunity to do is presented to them."

In 1983, the National Institute of Justice (the research branch of the Department of Justice) published a report that is also of value to interrogators in employee theft cases. It is entitled "Theft by Employees in Work Organizations" (published by the U.S. Government Printing Office), and is based upon research involving 9,175 employees of 47 businesses, including 16 retail establishments, 21 hospitals, and 10 electronic firms. Following is a summary of the findings:

One-third of the employees reported theft from their employers within the prior 12-month period.

Two-thirds of the employees reported counterproductive behavior, such as long lunches and breaks, slow or sloppy workmanship, sick-leave abuse, and the use of alcohol or drugs while at work.

The highest levels of theft were reported by unmarried male employees between the ages of 16 and the mid-20s.

Property theft and counterproductive behavior were more likely among employees expressing dissatisfaction with their employment, and particularly with their immediate supervisors.

The single factor most predictive of theft was the employee's perception of being caught; in other words, the greater the perceived risk, the fewer incidences of theft.

Lower levels of employee theft were experienced by organizations with clearly defined policies on theft, an inventory control system with theft reduction as a major priority, and a policy of evaluation of prior job histories during preemployment screening procedures.

---

[3]Inbau, *The Social and Ethical Requirements of Criminal Investigation and Prosecution*, 3 CR. L. QUAR. (Canada) 329, pp. 347–348 (1960). The article is a reproduction of a lecture by the author at "The First Canadian Conference on Criminal Law" in Toronto, Ontario, September 23, 1960.

*THEME 3: SUGGEST A LESS REVOLTING AND MORE MORALLY AC-
CEPTABLE MOTIVATION OR REASON FOR THE OFFENSE THAN
THAT WHICH IS KNOWN OR PRESUMED*

A good example of the utilization of this theme are cases of sex-motivated arsonists, especially where deaths result from the fire. Upon reflection, an arsonist may find his conduct highly reprehensible, and his conscience can become greatly troubled. The interrogator may diminish that feeling by starting off with a suggestion of an accidental setting, something far easier to admit than the deliberate act for sexual gratification. Once again, the objective is to have the suspect place himself at the scene of the crime.

The same theme can be effectively applied in the interrogation of a person suspected of setting a fire for the financial gain of procuring reimbursement from an insurance company. Committing such an act is, of course, a criminal offense, and obviously the suspect would encounter great difficulty in admitting the true facts, despite physical and other circumstantial evidence against him. The person must be eased into an admission, and this can be accomplished by the interrogator's suggestion of the possibility that the suspect started the fire *accidentally*. The objective at this point is to have the suspect place himself at the scene of the fire. Once this occurs, the interrogator can confront the suspect with evidence that indicates a deliberate setting, along with the reason for committing the act, such as business losses and the financial pressure of creditors.

Another good illustration of this theme's application is the case of a male, sex-motivated killer. The sexual feature of the killing is now not only extremely troublesome to him, but he also may realize that it will be viewed by others as more revolting than killings for most other reasons. Therefore, when he reaches the confession stage—when he feels a compulsion to admit the offense—it will be much easier for him to start by attributing the victim's death to an accident or to some other such factor. Therefore, in order to secure the initial statement to that effect, the interrogator should suggest possible moral excuses. The important thing is to have the suspect place himself at the scene or to connect himself with the event in some other way. Thereafter, it will be relatively easy to obtain a full, truthful disclosure of the actual reason or motivation. Here is the specific language the interrogator may use: "Joe, what happened? Did this girl go along with you at first, and then she had a change of mind, and all of a sudden she let out a scream? You then had no alternative but to stop her yelling, and that's all you were trying to do. Is that the reason, Joe? That's how it happened?"

Intoxication is a guilt-diminishing factor, which can be used for suspects who are interrogated regarding the crimes that are, to say the least, embarrassing to the suspect. For example, consider the case of a respected citizen who has been accused by a neighborhood child of taking indecent liberties with her. The suggestion that alcohol was responsible for his objectionable conduct permits the suspect an opportunity to "save face" by blaming alcohol for his conduct. Although intoxication usually is not a legal defense, except in certain specific intent types of crime (e.g., theft), the interrogator can submit it as a reasonable explanation and as a "face saver" for an otherwise respectable citizen. This approach affords the suspect some comfort with regard to the reaction of relatives, friends, and other persons when they hear about his admission, particularly when a child victim is involved.[4] Once the act itself is admitted to the interrogator, the task of obtaining a truthful account will be greatly facilitated.

A suspect's use of drugs may be approached in the same way as alcohol consumption. It, too, will serve to render a crime less reprehensible in the offender's mind. Moreover, drug addiction can also be presented as the actual motivation for a crime such as robbery or burglary—the impelling need for money to support the drug habit.[5] In other words, the suspect had to rob, burglarize, or commit some other money-objective crime in order to physically survive. The interrogator may also point out that when an addict is without drugs, his perceptions and judgments are clouded, causing him to do things that otherwise would not have been done. Furthermore, the person may be told that he is not someone who would seek to commit crimes just for the sake of committing them or who would earn a living that way; what happened was the result of the mistake of becoming dependent on drugs, for which taking another person's money was the only available means to obtain them. By accepting this excuse, the suspect becomes more amenable to a confession.

In a robbery-killing case, the interrogator should suggest that the suspect had not intended, or had not planned, the killing, and that the only motive was to get some needed money; nevertheless, the shooting was necessary in self-defense after the person being robbed had pulled a gun or knife. This self-defense excuse can also be used in other types of killings or near-killings for the purpose of obtaining an initial admission of guilt. For instance, where the known or presumed motive for a shooting was revenge, the interrogator may say to the suspect:

---

[4]In suggesting that intoxication may have been a factor underlying a suspect's criminal offense, a reference could be made to a 1979 study by the United States Department of Justice, which showed that nearly one-third of state prison inmates drank very heavily just before committing the crimes that led to their imprisonment. The study is entitled *Prisoners and Alcohol* (U.S. Dept. of Justice, Bureau of Justice Statistics, published Jan. 1983).

[5]A study conducted by the U.S. Department of Justice, published in October, 1983, contains statistics that reveal a high correlation between criminal offenses and the use of drugs by the offenders at the time of their crimes. See particularly p. 39 of the *Report to the Nation on Crime and Justice: The Data*, Document # U.S.J. - 87068.

Joe, you probably didn't go out looking for this fellow with the purpose of doing this. My guess is, however, that you expected something from him and that's why you carried a gun—for your own protection. You knew him for what he was—no good. Then when you met him, he probably started using foul, abusive language, and he gave some indication that he was about to pull a gun on you. Then you had to act to save your own life. That's about it, isn't it, Joe?

When the suspect admits the shooting, the interrogator can then proceed to point out that the circumstantial evidence (location of the wound, position of the body, etc.) negates the self-defense explanation. Thereafter, with relative ease, the interrogator will be able to secure the true explanation. Even if the interrogator fails to do so, the inconsistency between the suspect's original denial of the shooting and his present admission of at least doing the shooting will serve to preclude a self-defensive "out" at the time of trial.

In the interrogation of a suspected embezzler, the suggestion may be offered that there was only the intent to "borrow" the money rather than to steal it and that had it not been for the untimely discovery of the shortage, he would have replaced the money somehow. Another approach with an embezzler is to suggest that the money was taken for the benefit of a spouse, child, or other person. This is particularly effective when the interrogator knows that another person had been in need of financial aid and had actually received aid from some source. For instance, in one case, a suspected bank teller was known to be financing his son's attendance at a theological seminary, which the teller could not have afforded on his bank salary. The interrogator suggested that the teller's desire to assist his son was the motive for the embezzlement, although the interrogator knew that the embezzled funds far exceeded the money needed for the son. The suggested motive, however, served the purpose of securing the initial admission, after which the suspect eventually disclosed the real reason for the theft—his gambling activities.

Occasionally, the reason for an embezzlement is actually the suggested one—a sick child or pregnant wife and the subsequent need to pay doctor and hospital bills. In some such instances, the authors of this text have recommended to the employing company that it continue such confessed embezzlers in its employment. Apart from the humanitarian considerations involved, a persuasive argument in support of this practice is the fact that there is no assurance that a replacement of the confessed embezzler would be any better security risk. On the other hand, if the motive for embezzlement was to cover up or recoup gambling losses, the embezzler should be dismissed. He is a poor security risk. Moreover, for the person's own future welfare, it is probably better that he not continue in a tempting situation where there is ready access to cash belonging to a bank or other employer.

A female thief or embezzler is particularly vulnerable to the suggestion that her stealing was for the benefit of someone else—a child, her husband, her boyfriend, etc. In fact, that is very often the reason why a female steals. Her thievery ordinarily is less selfishly motivated than a man's.

In a theft case, the suggestion may be offered that the suspect took the missing item (purse, money, etc.) by mistake and then later was afraid to return it because he thought the owner might not believe that it really had been taken by mistake. Also, in a theft case where the interrogator knows or has good reason to believe that gambling losses or the suspect's propensity to gamble constitutes the probable reason for his thievery, it is advisable to talk to the suspect somewhat as follows:

> Joe, we are all human beings and we all have our faults and weaknesses. There's the good and the bad in all of us. Some people go nuts over women; others over alcohol; others over gambling. In your case, it's gambling and, except for the fact that it got too strong a grip on you, you're no different from a lot of other people. Ninety-nine out of a hundred people gamble at one time or another, and a good percentage of us are chronic gamblers—we can't keep away from it. But one thing about gambling; it's a cleaner weakness than some of the others—like an irresistible urge to rape, or to drink excessively, or to use dope. So let's get this thing straightened out, Joe.[6]

When an interrogator uses the technique of suggesting a less revolting and more morally acceptable motivation or reason than the one that is known or presumed, it is legally important, of course, for the interrogator to attempt to learn the true explanation for the offender's conduct, even though what has already been disclosed reveals, in itself, a criminal offense of some degree. In any event, following whatever the suspect finally states, the interrogator should proceed to obtain a disclosure of all the details that are procurable.

The primary importance of securing a true explanation for the offense lies in the fact that in many cases, the real reason or motivation may be subject to corroboration by subsequent investigation, whereas an untruthful one is obviously not subject to supporting proof. There will be occasions, of course, when a suspect will adhere to the face-saving explanation suggested by the interrogator. This risk, however, is not serious, particularly in view of the fact that many persons will resort to this face-saving

---

[6]With respect to compulsive gamblers, the National Council on Compulsive Gambling, based in New York City, has reported that 61 percent of the adult American population participate in some form of gambling; that 15.5 million gamble illegally; and that approximately 1.1 million are compulsive gamblers. Compulsive gambling is described by the Council as a "progressive behavior disorder in which an individual has a psychologically uncontrollable preoccupation and urge to gamble," and that "The cardinal features are emotional dependence on gambling, loss of control and interference with normal function."

device without the benefit of any suggestion from the interrogator himself. Moreover, as stated earlier, it is also a fact that most confessors to crimes of a serious nature will lie about some aspect of the occurrence, even though they may have disclosed the full truth regarding the main event. They will lie about some detail of the crime for which they have a greater feeling of shame than that which they experience with respect to the main event. For instance, a sex-motivated murderer may make a complete and truthful disclosure of the killing, but at the same time, he may lie about the nature of his actual sexual act. A burglar-murderer may freely reveal all the details of killing but, as earlier illustrated, may lie about taking a gold crucifix from the victim's home.

The forgoing are psychological realities and it is advisable for judges, prosecutors, defense counsel, and criminal interrogators to be aware of them in evaluating the trustworthiness of confessions that are obviously lacking in completely accurate disclosures of the details of the admitted offense.

THEME 4: SYMPATHIZE WITH SUSPECT BY CONDEMNING OTHERS

This theme is three-pronged: 1) condemn the victim, 2) condemn the accomplice, or 3) condemn anyone else upon whom some degree of moral responsibility might conceivably be placed for the commission of the crime under investigation. The psychological basis for these approaches can be appreciated quite readily by anyone who has committed noncriminal wrongdoings and has had to "own up" to them. There is a natural inclination to preface an admission with a condemnation of the victimized person or thing, or with a statement purporting to place part or even all of the moral blame upon someone else. The same mental forces are in operation in matters involving criminal offenses—and to an even greater degree because of their more serious nature.

In view of the fact that self-condonation of this type so frequently accompanies a confession of guilt—with the offender seeking by this means to more or less justify or excuse the offense in his own mind—it seems only reasonable to presume that an interrogator's condemnation of the offender's victim, accomplice, or others would prove to be effective in provoking or expediting a confession. Moreover, actual experience has demonstrated this to be so.

The following description of several case situations illustrates the manner in which this technique can be applied.

Condemning the Victim

The propensity of a wrongdoer to put all or part of the moral blame for his conduct upon the victim will be readily apparent by a reflection upon the childhood experiences of most individuals. The following event, which assumes the participation of two young boys, one of whom is the male reader of this text himself, is illustrative:

One Sunday morning you see little Johnny, your next door neighbor, standing on the sidewalk all ready for Sunday school or church. Just because of your own disagreeable mood, and for no other recognizable reason, you push Johnny down. The fall tears a hole in the knee of his trousers. He runs crying to his mother, and then your mother has you before her for an explanation of the event and a possible reprimand or punishment. What was your initial reaction? To deny it all; to deny you pushed Johnny. But that cannot be done under present circumstances because his mother, or perhaps your own mother, saw you push Johnny, and she only inquires of you, "Why did you do it?"

If you conducted yourself according to the usual pattern, you probably responded somewhat as follows: "Mother, he pushed me first," or "He called me a bad name" (or better yet, "Mother, he called you a bad name!"). That's why I pushed him." All this was untrue, of course, but you defended your actions in this manner. You condemned the victim, and in doing so you reacted in a perfectly normal way. Even adults resort to an equivalent kind of blame-escaping tactics.

What does the normality and prevalence of this victim-blaming characteristic in wrongdoers suggest for criminal interrogation purposes? It suggests that the interrogator use it in the interrogation of criminal suspects—in other words, during the course of an interrogation, the interrogator should develop the theme that the primary blame, or at least some of the blame, for what the suspect did rests upon the victim.

Consider, for instance, the case of a man suspected of killing his wife. The investigation reveals that the wife had treated the suspect very miserably over the years. Under such circumstances, it is recommended that the interrogator should let the suspect know that the interrogator is aware of what the suspect had been up against. The interrogator should condemn the wife for her conduct, making the point that by her own conduct, she herself had brought on the incident of the killing.

In the type of case just described, much can be gained by the interrogator's adoption of an emotional ("choked up") feeling about it all as he relates what is known about the victim's conduct toward his spouse. This demonstrable attitude of sympathy and understanding may be rather easily assumed by placing one's self "in the other fellow's shoes" and pondering this question: "What might I have done under similar circumstances?"

Some outstanding examples of the effectiveness of this technique are to be found in sex crimes where the victims are children. In such cases, when a male adult offender confesses, he frequently places the blame upon his victim, even though the victim may be a very young child. The presence of this trait in itself should suggest the technique to be used in the interrogation of offenders of this type—the condemnation of the victim; the placing of the blame upon the victim, even though a child, for doing something that triggered the suspect's emotional outburst. This suggested technique may be viewed with skepticism by some persons who either cannot conceive of themselves as committing such an offense or who, even if they could get past that first hurdle, would never blame a child. However, the persons who commit offenses of this type are basically moral cowards; for them, it is not difficult to affix blame upon the child.

In one case that involved the interrogation of a 50-year-old man accused of having taken indecent liberties with a 10-year-old girl, the suspect was told:

> This girl is well advanced for her age. She probably learned a lot about sex from the boys in the neighborhood and from the movies and TV; and knowing what she did about it, she may have deliberately tried to excite you to see what you would do.

The offender then confessed, but, true to the characteristics of his group, he proceeded to place the blame on the child. Even if this had been so, he would, of course, have been just as guilty in the eyes of the law.[7]

Whenever a sex offense involving a very young female has resulted in some actual physical harm to her, it is advisable for the interrogator to supplement the placing of blame on the child with a statement that the suspect must have been only trying to please her—just trying to make her happy—and that any harm to her was purely accidental.

The interrogation technique of condemning the victim can also be used advantageously in other types of sex crimes—for example, a forcible rape—by suggesting to the suspect that the victim was to blame for dressing or behaving in such a way as to have unduly excited a man's passion. The discussion might go somewhat as follows:

> Joe, no woman should be on the street alone at night looking as sexy as she did. Even here today, she's got on a low-cut dress that makes visible damn near all of her breasts. That's wrong! It's too much of a temptation for any normal man. If she hadn't gone around dressed like that you wouldn't be in this room now.

---

[7]Child sexual abuse is medically known as pedophilia, the abnormal sexual desire or erotic craving of an adult toward children. A detailed discussion of the characteristics of such offenders and their victims appears in two publications of the International Association of Chiefs of Police: *Child Sexual Abuse* (Training Key # 323) and *Sexual Exploitation of Children—Chickenhawks* (Training Key # 311). The subject is also discussed in the January, 1984 issue of the FBI Law Enforcement Bulletin.

Two other IACP Training Keys of value to criminal interrogators are *Interviewing the Child Sex Victim* (Training Key # 224) and *Interviewing the Rape Victim* (Training Key # 210).

If the forcible rape occurred in the suspect's car or in his or the victim's residence, she can be blamed for behaving in such a way as to arouse the suspect sexually to a point where he just had to have an outlet for his feelings. For instance:

Joe, this girl was having a lot of fun for herself by letting you kiss her and feel her breast. For her, that would have been sufficient. But men aren't built the same way. There's a limit to the teasing and excitement they can take; then something's got to give. A female ought to realize this, and if she's not willing to go all the way, she ought to stop way short of what this gal did to you

Where circumstances permit, the suggestion might be offered that the rape victim had acted like she might have been a prostitute and that the suspect had assumed she was a willing partner. In fact, the interrogator may even say that the police knew she had engaged in acts of prostitution on other occasions; the question may then be asked, "Did she try to get some money out of you—perhaps more than you actually had, but once you were that close to her you couldn't help but complete what she started?" Any such condemnation will make it easier for the suspect to admit the act of intercourse, or at least his presence in the company of the victim.

The degrading of the character of the victim can also be used in cases such as one in which the suspect is being interrogated regarding the killing of a fellow criminal or even a police officer. The victim can be pictured as "no good," and as one who had always been involved in crooked deals and shakedowns.

In assault cases, the victim may be referred to as someone who had always "pushed other people around," and that perhaps he finally got what was coming to him. Furthermore, the victim may be blamed for having initiated an argument, or perhaps for even having threatened physical harm.

The main objective of the interrogator in many instances is to have the suspect place himself at the crime scene or in some sort of contact with the victim. Once that is accomplished, the interrogator will later be able to have the suspect relate the true facts of what occurred. For instance, in an assault case, once the suspect admits having been involved in the incident, the exercise of a little patience will ultimately result in a disclosure of a guilty person's full responsibility for the occurrence.

In a robbery case, the victim may be blamed for having previously cheated the suspect or perhaps for stealing some property from him, and it may be brought out that the suspect's intent had been merely to settle the account.

In theft cases involving employees, particularly first offenders and those whose motives arose from an actual need for money rather than from some other circumstances, the employer should be condemned for having paid inadequate and insufficient salaries, or for some unethical or careless practice that may have created a temptation to steal. For example, in interrogating a bank teller, the suspect might be asked, "How much money do you make, Joe?" after which the interrogator could mention a purposely overstated amount. Then when the suspect states the actual salary figure, the interrogator may say:

Ye gods, man, how in the world can anybody with a family the size of yours get along on that kind of money in this day and age? Look at the temptations you face every day! You handle thousands upon thousands of dollars for a salary like that?! And you're not only supposed to live on it, but be a first-rate dresser as well. That's something common laborers don't have to do. They can go around in old, dirty clothes, and they make twice as much money a day as you do. I know how financially pressed you were. You were so hemmed in you could see no way out except to do what you did. Anyone else confronted with a similar situation probably would have done the same thing, Joe. Your company is at fault. You work hard but can't get by on your small salary; so you arranged for a loan and of course you had a hard time paying it back and you missed some payments. Then you probably tried to get another loan some place else to pay off the previous one. So you're forced to do something like this to pay your bills and now you're being questioned about it. I can tell you this—if you received a decent salary in the first place, you wouldn't be here and I wouldn't be questioning you. Joe, I'm sure that's the answer. Now tell me, was it because you couldn't get along on your salary, Joe, or was it because you were looking after some woman on the side? I'm sure you couldn't get by on your salary alone. I'm also sure that if you received an adequate salary in the first place, you wouldn't have had to get a loan and you wouldn't be here now. [The preceding three sentences actually represent the "alternative question" technique discussed in *Step 7*.]

In certain case situations, an employer may be blamed for some perceived unfair treatment of the suspect, such as a demotion, a promotion with additional responsibilities but without commensurate pay, or the denial of a promised raise in salary.

Following is an example of how the technique of condemning the employer for his carelessness may be used with employees such as household maids. Assume that the missing item under investigation is a fur coat.

Helen, your employer had several fur coats and I'll bet she threw them down all around the house or else treated them like they were cheap pieces of cloth. Many times you probably had to pick them up and put them away yourself. You probably got the idea she didn't much care for the coats and wouldn't even miss one if it did disappear. That's probably what gave you the idea. Then after you did this, maybe you got to thinking about what you had done and would like to have brought it back but couldn't.

The following case illustrates a variation of this concept of blaming the victim: A man was found decapitated in his bed at home. He had been a very unruly alcoholic for several years, living with his wife and 15-year-old son. The wife became the chief suspect, and the interrogator attempted to blame her husband for having mistreated her and their son, for having spent all of their money on alcohol, and for having made their lives miserable. The wife remained impassive and unconcerned. As a last resort, the interrogator told the suspect, "Okay, if you say you did not do it, then it must have been your son." As the interrogator made a move toward the door, the suspect said, "Leave my son alone. He had nothing to do with it. I did it myself." Thereafter, the suspect gave a detailed account of the murder.

CONDEMNING THE ACCOMPLICE

For much the same reason that a youngster with a baseball bat in hand alleges to an irate homeowner near the playing field that "we" (he and his teammates) broke the window rather than stating "I" did it (meaning the boy who struck the ball its damaging blow), the criminal offender is naturally inclined to have someone else share the blame or even be blamed altogether for the commission of the crime in question. Any line of interrogation, therefore, that tends to lift from him some of the burden of guilt for the criminal act will make the suspect that much less reluctant to confess.

It has always been a temptation, or even an instinctive reaction, for children to blame their playmates, in full or in part, for the mischief they themselves did, either alone or with their help. For instance, recall such an occurrence as this one: A youngster and his friends were at a loss as to what to do some summer afternoon. The youngster gazed at a neighbor's tomato patch and got the idea that it would be fun for everyone to engage in a "tomato war"—plucking the ripe tomatoes and throwing them at each other. This they did, all as a result of the one youngster's own bright idea, but when his father began to question him about the event after receiving the neighbor's complaint, what did the boy say? Did he own up to the deed and accept responsibility for leading his playmates into the tomato patch? He did not! First, he tried to lie about it all, to deny any participation whatsoever in the act of destruction. But someone saw him throwing the tomatoes, and this his father knew. So what next? He instinctively tried to put the blame on "the other fellows": "Dad, I didn't pull any tomatoes off the bushes. The only ones I threw were the ones that had been thrown at me." Adults often seek the same way out when confronted with an accusation of wrongdoing that involved the participation of other persons. Therefore, interrogating a suspect in a case involving another participant or participants, it is advisable to suggest that the primary blame, or at least some of the blame, belongs to the other fellow.

The manner in which the technique of condemning the accomplice may be utilized is aptly illustrated in the following description of an interrogation of a property owner accused of arson: The suspect had invested heavily in a real estate project which, as it neared completion, seemed doomed as a financial failure. In charge of the property in question was a handyman whose mental capacity was somewhat deficient. After a fire of suspicious origin, in which a large and heavily insured building was destroyed, the handyman, upon being questioned by investigators, confessed that he had set fire to the place at the request of the owner. On the basis of this confession, together with the evidence that the fire was of incendiary origin, the owner was arrested. At first he denied his guilt, and he continued to do so even when confronted with the testimony of his employee. Then, an interrogator proceeded to apply the above-suggested technique of condemning the accomplice. The interrogator's expressions in this respect were somewhat as follows:

> We all know—and you know—that there's considerable truth to what your employee says about the fire. We also know that a man of your type may not have done such a thing had it not been suggested or hinted at by someone else. It looks to me as if this fellow you have working for you may be the one who conceived the idea. He knew you were having a tough time financially, and he probably wanted to be sure his pay would go on, or perhaps he was looking for even more than that. For all I know, he might have done this just for the purpose of getting you in trouble. Maybe he wanted to get even with you for something he thought you had done to him. That I don't know, and we won't know the true explanation unless you tell us. We know this much: The place was set afire; your employee did it; he says you told him to do it. We also know you haven't told the whole truth.

The suspect admitted that he had known that the property was to be set afire and had approved of the burning. At first he insisted, as the interrogator had indicated as a possibility, that it was the employee's idea, but this version, of course, was false. Nevertheless, for a few minutes the interrogator permitted the suspect to bask in the sunshine of this partial and reflected guilt and to derive therefrom the attending mental comfort and relief. However, soon thereafter, the interrogator began to point out the lack of logic and reasonableness in the suspect's fixation of primary blame upon his employee. The suspect was told that he still did not look as relieved as a man should look after telling the truth. Then the interrogator proceeded to explain sympathetically that by coming out first with only part of the truth, he had done what all human beings would do under similar circumstances. Finally, as a climax to such comments, the interrogator urged him to tell the whole truth. The suspect then admitted that the idea of burning the building was his own. For the purpose of inducing him to begin his confession, however, it was necessary and effective for the interrogator to start off by first blaming the accomplice.

Another example of the "condemning the accomplice" technique is the following case of a robbery-murder, in which the police were convinced of the guilt of a 72-year-old man and a 30-year-old accomplice. The younger man, during his interrogation, was told: "That guy's always getting younger people into trouble. He's been in trouble all his life, but he's never been in jail himself, although he's certainly been responsible for some younger fellows going there. It's time he got what was coming to him; he's long overdue."

Another example of the "condemning the accomplice" technique is the case of the robbery-murder of an old recluse that had remained unsolved for 20 years, even though the police were convinced that a certain known hardened criminal was responsible along with two unidentified young men. The police finally learned the identity of one of the two young men. When he was arrested, it was noticed that his hair was partially grey, and he seemed very nervous and apprehensive. The interrogator was informed that for many years, the older, experienced criminal had lured young men into his robbery gang and had trained them to commit robberies such as the one in which the old recluse was shot to death. In the interrogation of the suspect, the interrogator first commented about the suspect's prematurely grey hair and said:

> I'll bet ever since that day 20 years ago, that old man stands as a ghost at the end of your bed, which prevents you from sleeping and scares you to death so that you don't even want to go to bed. You're feeling miserable, Jim, because you are living with that man's death on your conscience. If it wasn't for that old reprobate who got you into this, your hair wouldn't be grey at your age and you would not be feeling as you do all the time. Your life has been ruined by that old S.O.B. He got lots of young guys like you into trouble. Everyone out there knows that, but you got the unlucky break of being with him when he shot that fellow. Jim, you won't get any rest until you get that off your conscience by telling the truth about it.

After the interrogator had commented several times about the color of the suspect's hair and why he was prematurely grey, and after he had berated the old reprobate partner for getting the younger suspect into this trouble, the suspect confessed and substantiated that the older man had led him and another young man to the cabin of the recluse, where, without warning, the older man had shot the recluse because he had not moved fast enough in giving up his money; then, they set fire to the cabin in an attempt to cover up the murder.

Another case in point is one that also indicates how to select the first of two joint offenders for interrogation. A man was being robbed in a wooded area and, as he resisted, the bigger and more forceful of two robbers grabbed an ax and split the victim's head wide open. A witness reported that the other robber, the smaller of the two, had searched the victim thoroughly and had stolen his watch, wallet, and ring. It was quite evident that the more forceful robber seemed too stern to be the first one to be interrogated because when any preliminary questions were put to him, he answered with a grunt or else merely exhibited an angry look. It was then decided to interrogate the smaller robber who had stolen the valuables after the victim had been hit on the head and left to bleed to death.

The interrogator confronted the suspect with the fact that basically he was only a thief but had been made into a killer because of his partner's conduct. The interrogator stated that practically everyone in the world steals, but very few persons are murderers. "Your partner is a murderer," stated the interrogator, "whereas you only wanted to take something. It is important, however, for you to get the truth in as to what you did and show that you yourself did not kill this man." The interrogator concentrated on this theme of having the suspect reveal exactly what he himself had done. The suspect then told how he had stolen the man's watch, wallet, and ring after the victim was on the ground. Following this, the suspect told what he had done with the watch, wallet, and ring. He was then asked about the ax-slaying by his partner. The interrogator was convinced that the ax-wielding robber probably would not give a detailed confession, but, after indicating his disgust with his babbling partner, he did, reluctantly, acknowledge his guilt by simply confirming the smaller man's formal confession.

In applying this technique of condemning the accomplice, the interrogator must proceed cautiously and must refrain from making any comments to the effect that the blame cast on an accomplice thereby relieves the suspect of legal responsibility for his part in the commission of the offense. By suggesting the application of this technique, the authors merely recommend a moral condemnation in the form of expressions of sympathy for the suspect's "unfortunate" experience in having been influenced by a "criminally minded associate."

CONDEMNING ANYONE ELSE UPON WHOM SOME DEGREE OF MORAL RESPONSIBILITY MIGHT CONCEIVABLY BE PLACED

In addition to victims and accomplices, there are others who may be condemned to good advantage. Sometimes, the interrogator may find it effective to cast blame on government and society for permitting the existence of social and economic conditions that are conducive to the commission of crimes such as that for which the offender is accused. On other occasions, even the offender's parents may be alleged worthy of blame for the offender's conduct. Numerous other possible recipients of the interrogator's condemnation might also be mentioned, but the following case descriptions will suffice to illustrate the application and effectiveness of this technique.

In the interrogation of an accused wife-killer (the one referred to in the previous discussion of privacy), the interrogator proceeded to condemn the wife's relatives, who were known to have meddled in the offender's marital affairs. They were blamed for having deliberately set about to render the suspect's married life unhappy. At one point, the interrogator remarked that probably the relatives themselves deserved to be shot. During the discussion, the interrogator did not spare the wife, of course, nor wives in general. The suspect's wife was alleged to be a provocative, unreasonable, and unbearable creature, and was portrayed as a woman who would either drive a man insane or else to the commission of an act such as the present one in which she herself was the victim. In this respect, however, the interrogator stated that the suspect's wife was just like most other women. He was also told that many married men avoid similar difficulties by becoming drunkards, cheats, and deserters, but unfortunately the suspect tried to do what was right by "sticking it out," and it got the better of him in the end. All of this, of course, rendered the offense less reprehensible in the suspect's own mind, thereby overcoming his desire to avoid an exposure of guilt.

In an arson case, an ambitious young man, who had worked hard to accumulate a sizable amount of money, was anxious to become successful in merchandising a new product. Some promoters led him to believe it was a "sure thing," and he was so convinced by them that he purchased a substantial amount of it, rented a store, and invested in a sizable unused warehouse upon a long-term lease. Within a short time, the merchandise proved worthless. The young man attempted to cancel his lease, but the landlord refused. A friend of the young man suggested he soak the premises with gasoline and set fire to them so as to terminate the lease. He followed this advice, but when he set the warehouse afire, an explosion blew him out a first-floor window. By quickly removing his clothing he survived with a few bodily wounds. He left town until his wounds had healed. Upon his return, he was interrogated about the occurrence. The interrogator proceeded to place the blame on the landlord for not releasing him from the lease, whereas the suspect was lauded for his ambition and his honest desire to become successful. He was told there was still a possibility for him to ultimately get a new start, and that he should be grateful for still being alive and in good health. The suspect then disclosed the facts about setting the fire. He also stated that his anger toward the landlord was a factor in his use of an excessive amount of gasoline, which, of course, resulted in his being blown out the window.

During the interrogation of a married rape suspect, sometimes blame may be cast effectively upon the suspect's wife for having not provided him with the necessary sexual gratification. The discussion may proceed upon the following lines.

If your wife had taken care of you sexually, as she should have done, you wouldn't be here now. You're a healthy male; you needed, and were entitled to, sexual intercourse. And when a fellow like you doesn't get it at home, he seeks it elsewhere. Moreover, since you're not able to search for and date a female as a single man is free to do, a fellow like you has to take what he finds; and sometimes, because of his terrific, pent-up urge, he has to go about it in a rather hurried-up fashion, as you did here. That's the reason, isn't it, Joe?

When the offense is theft or embezzlement, a spendthrift wife or the financial burden of a child may be blamed for the suspect's thievery. He may be told:

Your wife [or daughter, or son, if such is the case] had been pressuring you for more money than you were earning. You cared enough for her so that you wanted her to have all she asked for—even though you didn't have it to give, Joe. What you did here was for her, not for your own selfish interests. She shouldn't have asked for all she got from you. Now she will probably understand, and she should stick by you in your present difficulty. It's time now, Joe, for you to tell the truth.

A person who has taken indecent sexual liberties with a young girl may be told that her parents are to blame for letting her roam around by herself as they did. In instances where the suspect had lured the child into his car or elsewhere by offering candy, or something else in the way of a gift, the parents may be blamed for not providing such things themselves. Along with the blame-fixing upon the parents, the child herself may be blamed, as was suggested in the discussion of the earlier technique of condemning the victim. A moral coward of this type finds it very comforting to have his conduct understood on the basis of one or more of these considerations.

A burglar or robber may be told that if there were no "fences" who bought and sold such stolen goods, the thief probably would not have done what he did. The interrogator may talk to the suspect somewhat as follows, particularly where the principal objective is to build up a case against the "fence" himself:

Men like you wouldn't do the things you do if there were no fences. Fellows like that are making monkeys out of people like you. You go out and risk your neck doing the job and taking all the chances of getting shot and killed. Then you bring what you took to one of these jerks and he gives you about 10 percent of its value, after which he unloads it at a 90 percent profit, minus, of course, what he has to give to the police as a payoff. He makes a big haul. You take the chances; he makes the money. If there were no such people like that, men like you probably wouldn't get into this kind of trouble, because if you couldn't get rid of the stuff, there would be no use taking it. Did any of these fences ever help you or any other men like you when you got in trouble? Hell, no! When a fellow like you gets put away, the fence gets himself someone else to do business with, and when that one gets sent away, he finds another replacement. Everyone knows this, but when a fence is questioned, he grins and says, "You don't have anything on me; I didn't do anything." We want to get at these fellows. If we can shut them off, you and a lot of others wouldn't be getting in trouble. They've been making suckers out of you guys long enough. It's time they be put out of business. They've been riding in Cadillacs long enough. What's this guy's name, Joe?

Blame may be cast on high-interest moneylenders (the so called "loan sharks") for pressuring a suspect for the payment of his loan at a time when he was unable to pay; in other words, his creditors "forced" him to steal. In such instances, the suspect may be told:

Joe, I know that it's hard today to get by without going into debt. I'm in debt myself, but fortunately I'm not over my head and my creditors are not loan sharks. You, however, have those fellows breathing down your neck, and they don't give a damn about men like you. All they're interested in is the big interest rates they get. And they suck people like you into believing that they are giving you a pretty good, easy-to-handle deal when they make a loan to you. I can't understand why they are allowed to get by with that kind of operation. They know damn well at the time a loan is made that you can't possibly keep up with it. It's hard enough just to make the high interest payments, to say nothing of the loan itself. You end up working for the loan sharks, and finally when they have you backed to the wall, you find that the only way out is to do something just like you did the other day. Joe, I'm sure that's how you were forced to do this; you got in over your head and didn't know what to do, so you did this.

In an arson case, blame may be placed upon the insurance company for permitting the accused and others to take out excessive insurance and to insure property far in excess of its actual value. The point to be made by the interrogator is that by this excessive insurance practice, the insurance company presented too much of a temptation to set property afire for the insurance money, particularly in those cases where the owner was hard-pressed financially.

When a person has committed an embezzlement or other theft because of the apparent or surmised necessity of replenishing losses sustained as a result of his own gambling activities, it is advisable for the interrogator to blame the police, prosecuting attorney, or community as a whole for permitting gambling opportunities to exist. For instance, a suspect may be told:

Joe, I know you've been doing a bit of gambling, and you got into the habit through little or no fault of your own. Too much temptation was put in front of you. The police and politicians are the ones to blame for permitting illegal gambling to exist. Now a complete blessing is even being placed on gambling by state lotteries and the like. The authorities are to blame; they should know that this only increases the temptation to take money from employers and others. If you have a tendency to gamble, and all of us do, and if you do gamble, you are forced to make up for your losses because gambling is a losing game. If it were stopped, you wouldn't be here now. We ought to put the blame where it really belongs!

A suspected embezzler can be told, to good advantage, that everyone is living in times when money is treated rather casually, particularly by the national government. Therefore, the old-time regard for the money or possessions belonging to others is lost. As an illustration, a suspect may be told that since the government squeezes citizens with burdensome taxes to obtain money to waste on foreign countries, it is no wonder that individuals like him lose their own sense of values with respect to the money and property of other persons.

When a suspect's home or neighborhood environment seems to be a factor accounting for his criminal conduct (as is so often the case), the interrogator should point out that fact.[8] The application of this technique is illustrated later in this chapter when theme development of youthful (juvenile) suspects is discussed.

In a burglary or robbery case, a theme may be developed on the basis that the suspect's life circumstances (e.g., unemployment for many months with a family to support) are to blame for driving the person to do what he did out of frustration and desperation.

THEME 5: APPEAL TO SUSPECT'S PRIDE BY WELL-SELECTED FLATTERY

It is a basic human trait to seek and enjoy the approval of other persons. Whether in professional activities or in ordinary, everyday living, most individuals receive a satisfying amount of approving remarks or compliments. However, those who engage in criminal activities, particularly those who operate alone, may seldom receive approving remarks and compliments; moreover, the need for such attention and status is just as great or even greater than it is with everyone else. In the course of the interrogation of a criminal suspect, therefore, the establishment of effective rapport between interrogator and suspect may be aided very considerably through praise and flattery.

---

[8]For statistics regarding the high correlation between criminal offenders and the environmental factors such as "turbulent home life, lack of family ties, and poor education," see p. 37 of *Report to the Nation on Crime and Justice: The Data*, published by the U.S. Department of Justice Bureau of Justice Statistics in October, 1983.

Consider the case of a juvenile or even an adult who is being interrogated as the suspected driver of a "getaway car" used in the robbery-murder of a gas-station attendant. Assume that a police patrol car had given chase but was outdistanced by the fleeing vehicle because the officers could not run the risk of injuring innocent pedestrians or motorists. The driver of the fleeing vehicle, of course, had no such consideration, and his reckless driving made the escape possible. In such cases, there is much to be gained by speaking to the subsequently apprehended suspect somewhat as follows: "Joe, the officers who were chasing that car tell me that in all their years on the force, they have never seen a car maneuvered like that one was. It really took the corners on two wheels."

Why is flattery of this type helpful? Perhaps the explanation rests upon the following considerations, and again, for purposes of illustration, the case of the driver of the "getaway car" is used. The driver may have developed into a criminal offender by reason of parental neglect or other such circumstances. At home, he had been accorded no attention, love, affection, or status. In school, the only way he could attract attention or acquire any status was by being unruly and mischievous. To further distinguish himself, he may have resorted to destructive acts, such as breaking windows, stealing store merchandise; then automobile tires, automobiles, etc. A natural development beyond that was robbery—and murder. Here, then, may be a person starved for attention, recognition, and status. Such suspects are, in many instances, particularly vulnerable to an interrogator's compliments and flattery. This does not mean, of course, that ordinarily a confession is immediately forthcoming because of flattering remarks; however, along with all else the interrogator says and does, it can be very helpful in obtaining a confession of guilt, and even though one is not obtained soon, or perhaps not at all, if the suspect gives clear indications of lying, the interrogator nevertheless will have achieved a considerable measure of success because other investigative efforts can be concentrated on that particular suspect.

In one case involving a robbery suspect, the suspect was told, with good effect:

I've been in investigative work a long time and I've talked to a lot of people who have done things like what you did, but I've never seen or talked to anyone who had as much guts as you do. I don't know how you could be as calm as you were under those circumstances. Moreover, this was the best planned job I've ever come across for a guy working alone. It's amazing how you found out where those materials [the stolen articles] were kept. And then when you got into action, you made John Dillinger look like a piker. [The reference here is to a notorious gunman in the early 1930s, but there are other, more current names the interrogator may select.] He had all kinds of help from others, but you worked alone. Joe, how did you feel before you pulled off that job? I guess your nerves of steel didn't have any room for nervousness.

In one case involving a rapist who was in military service and had aspired to an advanced military career, the interrogator flattered him regarding his desire for public service and suggested that his interest in a military career was good evidence of his basically honorable character. The interrogator then urged that the suspect should be honorable as regards the case under investigation and should tell the truth. A confession followed shortly thereafter.

In another case involving a jail chaplain accused of taking indecent liberties with a child, the interrogator commented upon the chaplain's "dedication to God" and all the sacrifices he had made as "a man of God." It was then suggested that basically, he had the same human frailties as everyone else and that on this unusual occasion, he just could not sufficiently suppress his feelings. He was then advised to go into the chapel of the jail where the interrogation was being conducted and there, while alone "with God," to write out an account of what had happened. Within an hour, he presented the interrogator with a fully detailed confession. (A result of this type is exceedingly rare, regardless of whether or not the suspect is a clergyman. It does illustrate, nevertheless, the potential of flattery, as well as of one of the previously discussed themes.)

Flattery is especially effective when it is in reference to a person's youthful appearance, attire, family background, good reputation, unselfishness, etc. Also, the uneducated and underprivileged are more vulnerable to flattery than the educated person or the person in favorable financial or social circumstances. With the latter types, flattery should be used sparingly and very discreetly.

Occasionally, a suspect may attempt to utilize flattery on the interrogator in order to make a favorable impression. He may address the interrogator by a title obviously beyond that which the interrogator actually possesses —"Captain" instead of "Sergeant" or "Doctor" instead of "Mr." In such instances, the suspect should be corrected. Suspects should never be allowed to think that they can reverse their role with that of interrogators. Therefore, in a title promotion situation, the interrogator should inject the appropriate correction—"I'm Sergeant"[or Mr.] _____ without making any further comments. The suspect who has consciously indulged in the flattery will get the point.

THEME 6: POINT OUT POSSIBILITY OF EXAGGERATION ON PART OF ACCUSER OR VICTIM, OR EXAGGERATE NATURE AND SERIOUSNESS OF EVENT ITSELF

In some instances in which an offender is accused by the victim, or by a witness to the crime, the interrogator should tell the suspect that even though there must be a basis for the accusation, there is the ever-present possibility of exaggeration, and that the truth can only be determined by first obtaining the suspect's own version of the occurrence. For example, in a rape accusation case in which the suspect denies not only the rape but even the act of intercourse itself, it is effective to talk to the suspect in the following terms:

> We know the girl is telling the truth about your having sexual intercourse with her. We also know that you're not telling the whole truth, even though she may be lying about force being used. Suppose she had intercourse with you voluntarily, and then after it was all over, she became fearful of a possible pregnancy or of a venereal disease, or of her indiscretion being otherwise discovered by her parents [or husband], or else her hair or clothing was ruffled up and, when questioned about that, her only out seemed to be the rape story. If this is what happened, we have no way of finding out—unless we hear your own explanation. Now I'm not saying that this is what occurred. I'm merely looking at this from all possible angles; in any event, we're interested in knowing the truth. If the truth is what she states, we want to know it; on the other hand, if it's anything less, we're just as anxious to find that out. My advice to you, therefore, is to tell the truth. [All this may be preceded or supplemented, of course, by a condemnation of the victim, as discussed in Theme 4.]

After an offender has succumbed to this technique, he may try to cling to the partial admission as a representation of the whole truth, but once it is acknowledged that he previously had lied to the interrogator, it becomes very difficult for the suspect to continue his resistance. The person then can be told that if the present admission represented the complete truth, he would not have delayed so long in stating it, and that the person still does not have the relieved look of one who has told the truth.

Pointing out the possibility of exaggeration on the part of accuser is not only helpful in obtaining confessions from the guilty, but it may also serve the purpose of exonerating the innocent. A good illustration of the point is a case in which the 35-year-old daughter of a police lieutenant accused a taxicab driver of rape. The interrogator was satisfied that the accused was telling the truth when he denied the rape, but he surmised that the cab driver was lying when he denied having the accuser as a passenger. The interrogator then talked to him as follows:

> Joe, you're not telling the whole truth. We also know that this woman is at least telling part of the truth. It may well be that she's grossly exaggerating what happened. But she was in your cab, and she probably had intercourse with you voluntarily. Then when she left, she may have feared a pregnancy, or a venereal disease, or she may have had some other reason for coming up with this rape story. But unless you tell us the truth as you know it, we'll just have to take what she says at its face value. My advice to you, Joe, is to tell the truth.

To this, the suspect responded: "All right. Now that you put it up to me that way, I'll tell you what actually happened." He then related that the woman had hailed his cab from in front of a tavern; that she had been intoxicated;

that as he approached the address she had given him, she directed him to go into an alley in back of her family home and told him to stop at a particular place and to turn the lights out; and that she invited him to have sexual intercourse with her, which he did.

Following this disclosure, the interrogator confronted the woman with the driver's statement, whereupon she admitted that he had told the truth. She explained her false accusation by saying that after the affair, she had feared pregnancy and also had been concerned over the possibility that a member of her family had seen her get out of the cab in the alley, and that her ruffled clothing would provoke suspicion. Furthermore, she had not thought the cab driver would be located because she had only hailed a passing cab and was not in one sent to the pickup location by the cab company, which probably would have had a record of the driver who was sent out on the call. Once she started with her lie, however, it had been difficult for her to retract her accusation. In this case, therefore, had it not been for the utilization of the exaggeration technique, the accused may have been prosecuted for a crime he had not committed.

Following are a number of cases when the theme of exaggeration on the part of interrogator may be useful: In the interrogation of a person suspected of the offense of having sexual intercourse with a female under the prescribed age of consent (i.e., "statutory rape"), the interrogator may state that the girl has said she had been forced to submit. The offender will usually react immediately by making a denial of force, thereby admitting by implication the intercourse itself.

Where the case involves a theft of money or property by means of larceny, embezzlement, or burglary, the interrogator should refer to the reported loss in terms of just about double or triple the actual amount involved. For instance, where the amount is reported to be $500, the interrogator may talk in terms of $1,000 or $1,500. He may also say that at the time the money was taken, other items of value were also carried away (e.g., a diamond ring or negotiable bond), according to the statement of the victim of the loss. The interrogator should then suggest that the actual amount of the loss may be much less than reported, that perhaps nothing but money was taken, or that the person or company reporting the loss may be trying to cheat the insurance company covering the risk by adding to the loss actually sustained. As an alternative, the interrogator may suggest that perhaps the person who reported the loss—for example, a company manager—may have stolen some money or property himself and is now trying to cover his own thievery by adding that amount to the actual loss in question. The suggestion that the manager or other boss may be dishonest will frequently strike a responsive chord because of the employee's dislike of him for one reason or another. In some instances, of course, the suggestion that a manager or other boss may be covering up his own thievery by exaggerating the loss is well founded in fact!

For an idea of the specific conversation that may develop between the interrogator and an embezzler during the application of this exaggeration technique, consider the following case situation: A company sustained a considerable loss of merchandise over a period of several months. An audit and inventory disclosed the amount to be about $20,000. The manager of the company warehouse was strongly suspected. He had been observed in the warehouse on a Sunday night in the company of two other men, but the warehouse was closed for business, and there was no reason in the interest of the company for the presence of anyone there at that time. Furthermore, auditors ascertained that carbon copies of a number of invoices were missing; the safekeeping of such carbon copies had been the manager's responsibility.

When the manager was interrogated, on the well-founded assumption that he was responsible for all or part of the loss, the interrogator began by saying:

> Joe, there's a big shortage of merchandise here at the company, and it looks like you're in the middle of it. You were seen at the warehouse with two other men on Sunday night, February 16th and the auditors found that a lot of carbon copies of your invoices were missing. I know you're a fair man and you will want to make up for what you did [and here the interrogator should pause briefly, then follow with the question:] Did you steal $40,000 worth of merchandise? [The harsh word "steal" is here used deliberately.]

"Hell, no!" was Joe's reply, and the conversation thereafter was along the following lines:

Interrogator:	Was it about $30,000?
Joe:	Hell, no!
Interrogator:	Was it about $20,000?
Joe	[speaking less firmly now]: No.
Interrogator:	Was it as little as $15,000?
Joe:	Not even that much.
Interrogator:	Well, how much was it, Joe? Be fair and honest about it. Was it $14,000?
Joe:	It's not even $10,000 worth. [By this statement, Joe has, in effect, admitted the theft.]
Interrogator:	Joe, it's certainly more than $10,000 worth!

At this stage of the interrogation, and without pursuing the amount issue, the interrogator asked Joe to relate the details of the thefts—the ways and means employed, the specific items taken, and the disposition made of them or their present location. Then Joe was confronted with the actual audit of the loss—$20,000. The point was also made that because all the merchandise had disappeared in the same manner, Joe must be responsible for the entire loss. He soon thereafter admitted a total theft of $20,000. He also revealed that he had set up a store of his own as an outlet for the stolen merchandise!

Where the exact amount of a loss is not presently known, the figure-lowering procedure may furnish a clue as to the amount known to the suspect. For instance, acting on the assumption that the theft loss of merchandise in a particular case is a five-digit figure below $30,000, the interrogator may receive a very firm response, such as "Hell, no," when that particular figure is mentioned. The interrogator should then lower the amount by about one-third by asking if it could be $20,000. The response to this may still be "No," but it will be stated less firmly than when the larger amount was mentioned. Then, when the figure is further lowered by $5,000 to the amount of $15,000, the suspect may say, with an air of uncertainty: "It couldn't be that much." At this point, the interrogator should begin to reduce the figure in $1,000 steps. If the answer to questions about $14,000, $13,000, $12,000, and $11,000 is "No," the interrogator should then say in a somewhat irritated tone of voice: "Could it be as little as $10,000?" The answer, stated rather squeamishly and hesitatingly, may be, "It's not even that much." This will indicate that the amount stolen was approximately $10,000. In this type of case situation, the interrogator should be mindful of the fact that a person who steals over a period of time and disposes of the "loot" immediately may not actually know how much has been stolen; the suspect may really believe that the value was only $10,000, whereas it could have been twice that much.

In cases where the figure-lowering "peak of tension" technique is used, the interrogator should carefully observe the suspect's physical activities—squirming about in the chair, the dusting of trousers, the crossing and uncrossing of legs, the picking of fingernails, and the fumbling with a ring or other object. Activities of this sort, along with the suspect's verbal responses, will furnish some indication of a forthcoming incriminating admission.

Also to be considered is the revealing difference between the response of an innocent person and that of the thief when an inflated amount as to how much he may have stolen appears in the question. A response such as: "Hell, no; they don't have that much around the whole place" is not the response of an innocent person; the innocent one will almost always respond by saying, in a resentful way: "I didn't steal anything!"

Relative to the interrogator's task when using this technique are several important factors. First, the person who becomes involved in a series of losses is usually one who is well liked by fellow employees and who has been in a position to give them or let them take company property, or to permit them to violate company rules. For that "benevolence," of course, there is a strong ulterior motive—to seek immunity from other employees against the probability of their reporting his own irregular activities, such as violating various company rules or even his own thievery. The person may say to a new employee, as he hands over some item of merchandise, tool, etc., "Here, take this home with you." If the new employee says, "But that would be stealing," or words to that effect, the response is apt to be: "This company's rich. And you're a damn fool if you don't take something; all the rest of the employees do." On rare occasions, of course, such efforts may backfire; the induced employee may become conscience-stricken and confess to the employer his own wrongdoing and at the same time reveal what he knows about the other employees, too.

Second, in the interrogation of an employee suspected of being the principal thief, the interrogator should seek acknowledgment that he knew of minor thievery of other employees. That acknowledgment is very helpful in obtaining the suspect's own confession to a larger amount of thievery.

Third, when an investigation of a series of losses involving a substantial sum of money or merchandise is being conducted, it is advisable to first interrogate the newly employed personnel, telling them that: "Someone is a big thief around here and it's got to be stopped." New employees confess their own wrongdoings more readily than the confirmed thief, and they are less reluctant to reveal what they know about those who are responsible for the much larger thefts.

The interrogator, however, must be careful in evaluating a readily forthcoming minor admission from a newly employed person because he too, may have already stolen a considerable amount and may assume that by making minor admissions or by identifying an even bigger thief, suspicion will be diverted from his own substantial thefts. Therefore, when an admission is made rather quickly, without much prodding, the interrogator must be concerned as to the extent of truthfulness. A good interrogator will take into account the haste with which a suspect makes an admission as well as how he looks while making that admission. An admission reluctantly given is more reliable than a volunteered admission; the latter may be an attempt to cover up a much larger theft.

The exaggeration theme also may be utilized by exaggerating the intent of the suspect with respect to the offense. For instance, a suspected burglar may be told that a rapist has been terrorizing residents in their homes in the same neighborhood, and that the interrogator is concerned over the possibility that the burglary suspect may be a rapist as well as a housebreaker. Another example of exaggeration of intent is to suggest that the burglary suspect may have been the person who attempted to set fire to one of the burglarized houses. In general, the psychological principle to employ is to minimize in the suspect's mind the act he committed when compared with more offensive behavior possibilities. Stated another way, the idea to be conveyed is that the suspect is not so bad a person after all.

THEME 7: POINT OUT TO SUSPECT GRAVE CONSEQUENCES AND FUTILITY OF CONTINUATION OF CRIMINAL BEHAVIOR

During the course of their criminal careers, many offenders experience a fleeting desire or intention to reform. This is particularly true with youthful offenders, or with adults who are first offenders or in the early stages of their careers of crime. Such a mood at times is manifested during an offender's period of failure, that is, when he is accused or under arrest and thus brought face to face with the stark realities on the debit side of such activities. During this time, the suspect can become quite vulnerable to comments regarding the future consequences and futility of a continuation of the criminal behavior, especially when the offense is not of the most serious sort and when the offender is not too well seasoned by a long series of offenses and police experiences. Under these circumstances, the individual might be convinced (momentarily, anyway) that for his own sake, it is a good thing to have been caught "early in the game" because this experience may serve to avoid much more trouble later. In a larceny case, for instance, the interrogator might say:

> You know what will happen to you if you keep this up, don't you? This time you've taken a relatively small amount of money; next time it will be more, and then you'll do it more often. You'll finally decide it's easier and more exciting to get what you're looking for at the point of a gun. Then someday you'll get excited and pull the trigger when the muzzle's resting against somebody's belly. You'll run away and try to hide out from the police. You'll get caught. There'll be a trial, and when it's all over, despite the efforts of your parents and relatives, who in the meantime have probably spent their last dime trying to save your neck, you'll probably have to spend the rest of your life in the penitentiary. Now's the time to put the brakes on—before it's too late. And remember this too, Joe: Do you know what's the average amount of money that's taken in robberies? About $18. So for a lousy $18, a guy puts his life on the line. It's downright crazy, Joe. There are better ways to live.

It is advisable, whenever possible, to point out the relative insignificance of the offense in terms of how much worse it could have been. In a burglary case, for instance, the interrogator might say to the suspect:

> Joe, all that happened the other night was the taking of money. But if you keep this up, some night you'll crawl in a window thinking that no one is home, but someone is home, and he comes at you with a gun or a knife. To save your own life, you grab the gun or the knife and you have to use it on him; or, if you don't kill someone yourself, eventually someone may kill or cripple you for life. One of your intended victims, or perhaps a policeman, may do this to you. Let me give you an actual example of this. [Here the interrogator may use a similar case within his own experience.] When I was a kid, there were two young fellows in my neighborhood who were always doing flashy things. They were well dressed

and dated the best-looking girls around. Yet neither one of them worked, and their families had no money to support their style of living. Well, the mystery was solved one night when a tavern owner who had been robbed twice decided to be prepared for the next attempt. When the two young men I told you about entered the tavern, the owner, who suspected what they were up to, ducked behind a partition where he had a pistol, and as the two fellows drew their guns and forced the cashier to hand over money, he shot and killed both of them. Had they been caught when they were new at the stealing game, their young lives would have been saved. Joe, you may not fully realize it now, but getting caught early like this may prevent something like that from happening to you. Put the brakes on now before it's too late.

Youthful offenders or adults who are not confirmed criminals, or who have not committed serious crimes, may be told:

Everyone makes mistakes, and we can all profit by such mistakes. A person with any brains at all can look upon them as lessons regarding his future conduct. And, after all, that's really what the judicial system is all about—to teach a fellow a lesson, in the hopes that he'll straighten himself out. Joe, if you don't own up to your present mistake and you think you've gotten away with something, you're bound to get yourself in worse trouble later on, and maybe then you won't have a chance to straighten yourself out. The police may do it for you when they catch you in a burglary or robbery; you may end up straightened out on a marble slab in the morgue. What a heartbreak that would be for your mother to go to the morgue and identify your body with a tag on your big toe and nothing else but the bullet in your head.

Interrogations that are handled in the manner of the above examples tend to make an offender feel that he is indeed rather fortunate in having escaped more serious difficulty. Once in that frame of mind, the suspect may become less reluctant to confess a crime.

The basic validity and effectiveness of the present technique may be explained by the fact that many offenders do have some awareness of the ultimate consequences of their continued criminal behavior. Moreover, when an offender vows that he will go straight, he usually means it at that time. Perhaps that is the reason for the appealing effect of pointing out the grave consequences and futility of continuing with a criminal career.

Nonemotional Offenders

As previously stated, the nonemotional offender attempts to avoid becoming emotionally involved in the interrogation; in effect, he insulates himself from the interrogator's words and actions. This form of defensiveness often renders the previously discussed sympathetic themes ineffective.

Psychologically, the nonemotional offender perceives the interrogation as a contest of endurance, pitting his own willpower against the interrogator's persistence. To this type of offender, the consequences of lost pride or embarrassment weigh somewhat as heavily as would any consideration about losing a job or going to prison. Regardless of the interrogator's sincerity or credibility, the nonemotional offender tends to be suspicious of anyone offering assistance or seeking his trust. For these reasons, the use of sympathy, exaggerations of the crime, or condemning other persons for the crime are themes that by themselves are unlikely to elicit a confession.

THEME 1: SEEK ADMISSION OF LYING ABOUT SOME INCIDENTAL ASPECT OF THE OCCURRENCE

A suspect who has been caught in a lie about some incidental aspect of the occurrence under investigation loses a great deal of ground; thereafter, as the suspect tries to convince the interrogator that he is telling the truth, he can always be reminded that he was not telling the truth just a short while ago. Under no circumstances, however, should the suspect be told "You lied to me once, and you'll lie to me again." The reminder of lying should be expressed in polite fashion, not in the form of a reprimand. To state it otherwise may result in a defiant attitude.

A simple example of this theme is a case that involved a male suspect who, having been accused of indecent liberties with a child, denied to the investigators that he had even seen the child. In such instances, the interrogator should try to get the suspect to admit having seen, and having talked to, the child. The interrogator may say:

> Joe, there's no question but that you were in this kid's presence and that you talked to her, and there's nothing wrong with that! There's also nothing wrong with giving her candy, or even patting her on the head. Joe, what did she say to you?

If Joe is guilty, he may think he can avoid any further suspicion by acknowledging the conversation with the child. Thereafter the interrogator can proceed to utilize other appropriate techniques, such as blaming the child. (Here, of course, is a reversion to earlier discussed techniques.)

In the application of this technique, the interrogator should bear in mind that there are times and circumstances when a person may lie about some incidental aspect of the offense without being guilty of its commission. Here is an actual case illustration: An investigation of the murder of a married woman disclosed that the suspect, who was also married, had been having an affair with her. When questioned by investigators about his whereabouts at the time of the murder, the suspect gave an alibi, which was quickly established to be a falsehood. This so convinced the investigators that he was the murderer that one of them subjected him to physical abuse in an effort to obtain a confession. He did not confess. Subsequently, however, a professionally skilled and ethical interrogator, seeking to ascertain the reason for the false alibi, was able to elicit from the suspect the fact that at the time of the murder, he had been in bed with another married woman. This was the reason for his having lied when he gave his previous alibi; in other words, he lied in order to avoid exposure of his latest indiscretion. The second alibi proved to be a truthful one!

Whenever a suspect seems to be telling the truth regarding an event under investigation but is reluctant to tell where he was at the time of its occurrence, the interrogator may say:

> Joe, if what you were doing at the time has nothing to do with this case, I give you my word I'll treat whatever you tell me as confidential. I'm not interested in your personal affairs. So tell me where you were at the time. [Whatever an innocent person says in response should, of course, be kept confidential!]

The following case illustrates that a person may be telling the truth about a principal offense but lying about some particular aspect of it. As earlier described with respect to the "preliminary preparations" of an interrogator, the case involved a delivery truck driver who reported to the police that he had been robbed of his employer's money collections. Because of the driver's general behavior and certain other factors, the police suspected him of making a false report and of having taken the money himself. He finally admitted that although a robbery had actually occurred, only a small amount of money had been taken because he had previously hidden most of the collected money in the truck as a precaution against just such an eventuality; however, after the robbery, he had decided to steal the remaining funds himself.

Another practical consideration that must be kept in mind regarding this theme is that in the investigation of a particularly large embezzlement, an employee suspect who will admit taking a much smaller sum or sums of money is rarely the one who is guilty of taking the principal sum under investigation. The guilty party, however, will seldom admit any smaller thefts or even any kind of wrongdoing; the person knows he is guilty of taking the large sum and assumes that any minor admission will create a presumption of guilt regarding the principal sum. An exception to this general rule occurs, of course, in cases involving a series of losses, such as stock shrinkage of merchandise over a period of time, or a series of relatively small money shortages; in these types of cases, the minor admissions of any employee are of considerable significance regarding his possible responsibility for all, or a large part of, the accumulated losses.

THEME 2:   HAVE SUSPECT PLACE HIMSELF AT SCENE OF CRIME OR IN CONTACT WITH VICTIM OR OCCURRENCE

The value of this theme—having the suspect place himself at the scene of the crime or in contact with the victim, even though he denies doing the act itself—is referred to earlier in the discussion of certain other themes; however, since the theme is, in itself, a major one, it is treated as such under the present heading.

The technique's basic validity is illustrated in the questioning of a child regarding mischievous conduct, or even the taking of something which did not belong to him. If the child admits having been present when the act occurred or having seen the missing object earlier, acceptance of full responsibility is not remote. For instance, if a boy is thought to have taken some money or some object from his parents' bedroom, he may first be asked, "Johnny, did you see a dollar bill on the dresser in my room a while ago?" An admission that he had seen the money, or that he had merely been in the room from which it was taken, warrants his being questioned further. His admission of presence and seeing the money will constitute a substantial step toward a disclosure of the truth.

In an actual criminal case situation, the technique can be utilized in the following fashion. Assume that money has been taken from a company safe, to which only a few employees had had access during the day on which it was kept open. The interrogator may say to the actual suspect: "Joe, I understand that the company safe is left open all day. That's right, isn't it? [Assume "yes" is the answer.] You saw it open last Friday. Right? [Assume again that the answer is "yes".] Joe how many times did you go into the office that day? These questions will then be followed by others of a more specific nature. Depending upon the employee's verbal and nonverbal responses, the interrogator may be in a position to proceed on the basis that the suspect had taken the money. The interrogator then may utilize other appropriate themes for such cases.

The placing of the suspect at the scene should be done early during the interrogation and before the suspect fully realizes the implication of his presence there. Even if a lying suspect denies being present at the scene, the resulting uneasiness will very probably reveal indications of deception.

When a suspect denies any contact with the victim on the day of the crime, an interrogator may successfully use the following ploy:

Joe, there isn't any doubt but that you were with [naming the victim] last Tuesday over at the [scene of the crime]. We have witnesses, but Joe, maybe they are mistaken as to just exactly when they saw you there. If, in fact, you were there several hours earlier or after this thing happened, it's important to tell me that. That might explain why the witnesses say they saw you when this occurred.

THEME 3: POINT OUT FUTILITY OF RESISTANCE TO TELLING TRUTH

With all offenders, in particular the nonemotional type, the interrogator must convince the suspect that not only has guilt been detected, but also that it can be established by the evidence currently available or that will be developed before the investigation is completed. In other words, an effort should be made to have the suspect realize that it is futile to continue resisting telling the truth. To accomplish this, it may be necessary to reveal to the suspect several of the various pieces of incriminating information or evidence already in the interrogator's possession, and then to ask the suspect, "Joe, if you yourself had that information, or evidence against some other person, you'd believe he was the one who did it, wouldn't you?" Without waiting for a response, the interrogator should continue: "Whether or not you acknowledge your involvement is almost meaningless; the evidence will speak for itself! My only reason for spending this time with you is to give you the opportunity to explain any mitigating circumstances that you think might make a difference. For example, if this was your partner's idea...." The interrogator may then suggest various "acceptable reasons" which may have led to the suspect's commission of the act.

If the offense under investigation was committed by two or more persons, and the suspect under interrogation presumes or knows that he is the only one in custody or the first to be questioned, it can be very helpful to talk to him along the following lines:

> You know as well as I do, Joe, that in all cases like this where two or more persons are involved, sooner or later somebody talks, and in your case it should be you. So let's get going before some other guy leaves you holding the bag. Don't let him get his oars in first and splash all the blame on you. What you say *now*, before that happens, we can believe. But later on, no one is likely to believe what you say, even though at that time you may be telling the absolute truth.

The impact of this type of theme is that, based upon the available evidence, the only logical conclusion that anybody could come to is that the suspect is guilty, and that this may be his only opportunity to present a plausible explanation for this act.

By thus stirring up the already existing concern that eventually an accomplice may talk, the interrogator can achieve either of two objectives. The initial and immediate one is to evoke the truth now; the other is to lay the groundwork for the next theme of "playing one against the other" at a later time, when the accomplice or accomplices are being interrogated.

THEME 4: WHEN CO-OFFENDERS ARE BEING INTERROGATED AND PREVIOUSLY DESCRIBED THEMES HAVE BEEN INEFFECTIVE, "PLAY ONE AGAINST THE OTHER"

When two or more persons have collaborated in the commission of a criminal offense and are later apprehended for questioning, there is usually a constant fear on the part of each participant that one of them will "talk." Individually, each of them may feel confident of his own ability to evade detection and to avoid confessing, but not one of them seems to experience a comparable degree of confidence with regard to the co-offender's ability or even willingness to do so. Uppermost in their minds is the possibility that one of them will confess in an effort to obtain special consideration.

This fear and mutual distrust among co-offenders can be made the basis for the very effective interrogation technique of "playing one against the other." Since this theme involves largely a bluff on the part of the interrogator, however, it should be reserved as a last resort, to be used only after other possible themes have failed to produce the desired result.

There are, in general, two principal methods that may be used in playing one offender against another. The interrogator may merely intimate to one offender that the other has confessed, or else the interrogator may actually tell the offender so. In either event, there are two basic rules to follow, although they are, of course, subject to exceptions: 1) keep the suspects separated from sight and sound of each other (except in regard to the one variation subsequently discussed); and 2) use, as the one to be led to believe the other has confessed, the less criminally hardened, or the follower rather than the leader of the two or more offenders, or the one who acted out the lesser role in the crime—in short, use the one who is likely to be more vulnerable to the ploy. At times, however, the reverse procedure is warranted; perhaps the leader may be the more vulnerable one because of concern that if he does not talk first, he may be left "holding the bag" after the weaker one confesses first. The choice to be made is a judgmental call that the interrogator must make on the basis of the particular case circumstances.

If the co-offenders seem to be very naïve—for example, young first offenders unfamiliar with the possibility of interrogation trickery—a simple form of intimation may consist of the practice of taking one suspect into the interrogation room soon after the interrogation of the first one and then telling him.

> This other fellow is trying to straighten himself out; how about you? Or do you want to let this thing stand as it is? I'm not going to tell you what I now know about your part in this job. I don't want to put the words in your mouth and then

have you nod your head in agreement. I want to see if you have in you what it takes to tell the truth. I want to hear your story—straight from your own lips.

Many are the occasions when the admonition has triggered a confession.

The intimation tactic may be dramatized to add to its effectiveness. Following is an example of this, as it was used by one of the authors of this text on a number of occasions over a period of years. (In relating this example, and the others that follow, it is assumed that the Miranda warnings will be, or already have been, appropriately administered to custodial suspects. When, the suspects are not in custody, there need be no such warnings; moreover, in noncustody cases, the time available for the dramatization is not restricted by the legislative requirement that persons actually under arrest must be taken before a judicial magistrate "without unnecessary delay." Also, although a duplication or approximation of the physical surroundings or circumstances described may not be available to most interrogators, what is related illustrates the potential of dramatized intimation. Complexity is not a prerequisite. It may be achieved in a rather simple setting.)

An investigation of a burglary clearly indicated that it was committed jointly by A and B, and both of them were to be interrogated by the same interrogator. Furthermore, the investigators unsuccessfully questioned both of them, reporting that neither one was likely to confess, particularly A, who was presumably the leader of the two. Both A and B sat in a spacious waiting room with a secretary who was busily typing. The secretary had been coached for her subsequent role.

A was taken to the interrogation room, which was adjoined to the waiting room by a door. After meeting with no success in interrogating A, except for a reinforced belief that A was guilty, the interrogator returned him to the waiting room and then escorted B into the interrogation room. His interrogation was also nonproductive, except for a reinforcement of the belief that he, too, was guilty. The interrogator left B in the interrogation room and returned to the waiting room alone. There, he instructed the secretary: "Please come in the back with your pencil and notebook" (or he signaled her to that effect). This instruction was given within view of A, but in such a natural manner that it did not seem to be an act performed for his benefit. The secretary then proceeded to sharpen her pencils, turned back some pages of her stenographic notebook—all within the observation of A—and then departed in the direction of the interrogation room. After absenting herself for the period of time that would ordinarily be required for the actual taking of a confession, she returned to the waiting room and began typing what seemed to be shorthand notes taken during the period of her absence. She used legal-size paper and also provided for carbon copies; again, within view of A. After several minutes, she paused and inquired of an officer seated near A, "How does this man [referring to A] spell his last name?" (If the name is a simple one, then the inquiry should be directed to his address, etc.) After receiving the information, she continued with her typing. When finished, she took the paper and carbons from the typewriter and, after sorting out the carbon sheets, departed with the typewritten material in the direction of the interrogation room. Thereafter, she returned to her desk without the papers and assumed her usual secretarial duties.

After the lapse of 15 or 20 minutes, the interrogator entered the waiting room and escorted A back into the interrogation room (now vacated by B, who had been taken to another room). After A was seated, the interrogator said: "Well, what have you got to say for yourself?" At this point, A confessed, being under the impression that his co-offender had done so already. Even if A had not immediately confessed, the interrogator was not foreclosed from resuming his interrogation of him and, if A had inquired about what B had said, he should have been told, "Never mind what he said, you tell me what happened; I want it from your own lips."

Whenever several persons are suspected of committing a series of offenses, such as a number of robberies, and one of them confesses to one or two of the offenses, the confession may be effectively used in obtaining confessions from others regarding the entire series, even when the initial confessor has been involved in no more than the one or two to which he has confessed. This may be done in the following manner:

Equipped with the first confession (in writing, time permitting), the interrogator then selects for interrogation one of the suspects who was named by the first one as an accomplice. While holding the written confession (or notes of an oral one), the second suspect is told that what is being held is the statement of one of the other fellows. Joe is then asked: "What do you have to say for yourself?" If Joe makes a vague denial or evinces a quizzical look, the interrogator should say: "I'll give you a start, and you tell the rest." At this point, only scant information should be revealed—just enough to satisfy the suspect that this is no bluff. Very likely, an admission will be forthcoming about the one offense, following which the interrogator should say, "Now, what about the others you were in on?" Another one or more, beyond the one or two contained in the initial confession, probably will be revealed. Upon sensing that the present suspect has probably told all he did or knows about, the interrogator should briefly write out the confession and have him sign it. This will then be available for use with the remaining suspect or suspects in the same way the first confession was used.

In one of the many cases where the forgoing technique was used, one of the authors of this text cleared up a series of a considerable number of offenses committed by a group of five young men. The offenses consisted of burglaries, robberies, and even rapes committed upon some of the robbery victims.

Another kind of intimation that may be employed is illustrated by a case in which a father and son are involved in the commission of a crime, and they have consistently maintained that they were innocent, even when questioned separately. In such a case situation, the interrogator may say to the father, "OK, if you are both telling the truth, as you say you are, here's a piece of paper and a pencil. Write a note to your son; tell him that you have told the truth and that he, too, should tell the truth. You don't have to say anything else." As this is said, the actions and facial expressions of the suspect should be carefully observed. If he delays in responding, or if he equivocates in his answer, this will be further assurance of deception because if he and his son are telling the truth, there should be no reluctance or unwillingness to write out such a message. The dilemma that is thereby presented to the suspect may result in his writing and signing of the messsage to his son. Then, when the message is presented to the son, his actions, facial expressions, and verbal responses will be of helpful significance. If he is innocent, he will respond, unruffled and with confidence, by saying something to the effect of: "I am telling the truth, and so is my father; I don't know what you're trying to do. Why don't you bring him in here?" On the other hand, if the two are guilty, a confession from the son is apt to be forthcoming. If the son is guilty and confesses, his subsequent written confession can then be shown to the father, or the interrogator may have the son orally relate to the father what he has already stated in his signed confession.

The following case is an excellent illustration of the advisability of having some sound basis for any statement offered to one offender by way of proof that the co-offender has confessed; otherwise, the interrogator may get himself out on the proverbial limb and have it sawed off. Several years ago, one of the authors interrogated two boys (brothers) who were suspected of committing a series of burglaries. Each one persisted in his denial of participating in any of the offenses, including the particular offense that brought about their arrest and that was the chief object of the present interrogation. Finally, the younger of the two boys made an admission concerning one burglary. He stated that he had assisted the other offender, his older brother, in throwing into a river some of the loot from a burglary. Equipped with this bit of information, the interrogator resumed his interrogation of the other suspect, this time with a view to making him believe that his younger brother had made a complete confession of all the burglaries. The suspect was told, "Well, your kid brother has told us everything; now let's see if you can straighten yourself out." Since the suspect seemed unimpressed with what the interrogator had said, he was then told, "Just to show you I'm not kidding, how about that job when you and your younger brother unloaded the brass metal in the river when things got too hot for you?" Thereupon, the suspect smiled and said, "You're bluffing; my brother didn't say that because it isn't true." Feeling quite confident that the younger boy had told the truth about the brass disposal job, the interrogator decided to have him repeat the statement in the presence of the older boy. This was done, and the two then began to argue over who was telling the truth. However, soon thereafter, the younger boy stated that he was mistaken about this particular job—adding that in regards to this one particular offense, he had his brother confused with another boy, whom he named and identified as his confederate in the theft of the brass. Nevertheless, he did implicate his brother in several other burglaries. When confronted with such admissions, the older boy also acknowledged his guilt.

In this case, the boy to whom the interrogator had transmitted the incorrect information had every reason in the world to believe it was a bluff. Quite naturally, he was not influenced by such a statement, and the same would be true in any case in which an interrogator was inaccurate in his guess as to some detail submitted as proof of the fact that a co-offender had already confessed.

Whenever the more direct bluff is attempted—that is, whenever the suspect is actually told that his co-offender has confessed—the interrogator must be careful not to make any statement purporting to come from the co-offender, which the person to whom it is related will recognize as an inaccuracy and, therefore, as a wild guess and a falsehood on the part of the interrogator. Once the interrogator makes such a mistake, the entire bluff is exposed, and then it becomes useless to continue with the act of playing one against the other. Moreover, the interrogator is then exposed as a trickster, and thereafter, there is very little that can be done to regain the suspect's confidence. Therefore, unless the interrogator is quite certain of the accuracy of any detail of the offense that he intends to offer to one suspect as representing a statement made by his co-offender, it is better to confine statements to generalities only.

An exception to the forgoing precautionary measure is to be made in a case where one of the offenders is definitely known to have played a secondary role in the commission of the offense. In such a case, the one may be told that the other offender has put the blame on him for the planning of the offense, or for the actual shooting, etc. At the same time, the interrogator may add, "I don't think this is so, but that's what he says. If it's not the truth, then you let us have the truth." In this way, the interrogator can avoid any danger to his bluff because he concedes the possibility of the statement being a falsehood.

In addition to its application to the "playing one against the other" technique, there is a basic utility in emphasizing to an offender that he performed the less offensive role in the commission of the crime, as illustrated in the previous discussion of condemning the accomplice.

THEMES FOR YOUTHFUL (JUVENILE) OFFENDERS

In the interrogation of youthful (juvenile) suspects, the principles and many of the case examples that have been discussed with respect to adult suspects are just as applicable to the young ones. There are, however, several additional theme developments and guidelines particularly applicable to them.

To prepare for the interrogation of a youthful suspect, the interrogator should attempt to learn from the case investigators whatever information is available regarding the suspect's background, such as parental relationship and general attitude as observed by the investigators. Often, a youthful offender has been deprived of proper parental guidance, love, or affection. The interrogator's awareness of such facts can be of considerable assistance in the interrogation.

As earlier suggested in this text, caution must be exercised in evaluating a youthful person's behavioral responses. Due to immaturity and the corresponding lack of values and sense of responsibility, the behavior symptoms displayed by a youthful suspect may be unreliable. Nevertheless, they are deserving of cautious consideration.

One theme that the interrogator may utilize is that all young persons have a tremendous amount of restless energy, but they experience considerable boredom; consequently, consideration must be given to their propensity for making mistakes and doing things that are morally or legally wrong. This factor is one of the very reasons why the judicial system separates adult offenders from juvenile offenders. Automobile insurance companies reflect this differentiation by the much higher liability rates charged for youthful drivers. A 26-year-old man, for instance is viewed to have learned to control his conduct beyond that which prevailed when he was 17; therefore, he presents a much safer risk.

Another theme may be based upon the many temptations to which the youth of today are exposed because of the easy availability of alcohol and drugs, and also upon the fact that in many instances, youthful persons are in homes where both parents are working and, therefore, their supervision and guidance may be practically nonexistent. Such conditions and circumstances place youths in a much more vulnerable position for wrongdoing than most of their counterparts in former times.

Consistent with the earlier discussion of placing blame on someone other than the suspect when interrogating a youthful person (provided the parent is not present, of course), the interrogator may place the blame for the suspect's conduct on his family life and ensuing difficulties. The application of this technique may be illustrated by the following statements, made to a young robbery-murder suspect who had actually encountered many of the experiences to which the interrogator referred:

Joe, you started out about the same way as a lot of kids, and I myself had a similar problem when I was a kid. You had a mother and father, and then things changed when your father died when you were 10. Your mother had other children, too, with very little to live on. You had to scratch around as best you could. Whatever you got by way of money or things to eat you had to share or give to your mother and brothers. A child is a child, and soon you probably had to take things from other people; otherwise, you got nothing. That became a habit when you were a kid and it looked easy, and then this thing happened [referring to the offense under investigation]. This would not have happened to you if your father had lived and been able to care for you, to provide for you, your mother, and your brothers the necessities of life. If he had lived, you probably wouldn't be in this room today. Society should be blamed for not having found some way to help your poor mother when your father died so that it would have been unnecessary for you to develop the habits you did.

In a case where one or both parents were alcoholics or for some other reason neglected the suspect as a child, the interrogator may say:

I can pretty well understand what would have happened to me if that condition existed in my home. No one to cook meals or perhaps even care if I lived or died. No wonder you finally got into something like this. You were worse off than an orphan. There are good homes of one sort or another for orphans, but you couldn't have gotten into one because you were supposed to already have a home and a father and a mother. Actually you didn't, and that's why you have this problem now.

The neighborhood in which the suspect lived as a child may be blamed for not providing suitable alternatives to mischievous conduct. In other words, there were no activities such as baseball or basketball, and not even any park facilities, and this contributed to the vulnerability to peer pressure from other kids involved in unlawful conduct who wanted the suspect to join them in those activities. He was left with no other choice.

Along with the presentation of any of these themes, the youthful suspect should be told that despite background experiences, he must embark upon restraints and corrective action before more serious consequences develop. This entails the utilization of the previously described tactic of pointing out (as in *Step 2*), the grave consequences and futility of a continuation of relatively minor criminal behavior.

A fairly characteristic trait of youthful offenders is their tendency to present an alter-ego defense by claiming to have knowledge of the person who committed the offense. When pressed for a description of that person, the guilty suspect's usual reaction makes apparent the fact that the so-called offender is none other than the suspect himself. The interrogator should view any such claim with considerable caution.

A few states provide by statute that a youthful (juvenile) suspect cannot be interrogated unless one parent or guardian is present. (The law pertaining to this subject is discussed in Chapter 8 of this text.) Under this requirement, the interrogator should spend some time with the parent before questioning a son or daughter. During this session, the interrogator should take a very positive approach and impress upon the parent that the only interest in talking to the youth is to ascertain the truth. The interrogator should emphasize that he is just as much interested in establishing innocence as responsibility. The interrogator should also advise the parent that there is a basis for wanting to conduct the interrogation, and one or more reasons may be mentioned without revealing all that is known.

In dealing with a parent who has an overprotective attitude toward his or her child, an interrogator should emphasize three primary points: 1) no one blames the parents or views them as negligent in the upbringing of their child, 2) all children at one time or another have done things that disappoint their parents, and 3) everyone (the interrogator as well as the parent) has done things as a youth that should not have been done. Once the interrogator has effectively gained the cooperation and support of the parent for the task of ascertaining the truth from the child, any subsequent interview or interrogation, particularly if the parent is going to be in the room, should be that much easier.

A parent who is present during the interrogation should be advised to refrain from talking, confining his or her function to that of an observer. The parent should be asked to sit in the chair set aside for an observer as diagrammed in Chapter 3. The interrogator should then proceed with the interrogation as though he were alone with the suspect, utilizing not only the themes specifically applicable to juveniles but any that are deemed appropriate from among the ones earlier discussed for the interrogation of adults.

The following case illustration may help to further clarify the utilization of some of the themes for the youthful offender: Someone had set fire to a bundle of paper products in a company warehouse in the early afternoon of a normal workday. The perpetrator had disarmed the ceiling firefighting system so that the fire spread before several employees were able to stop it with fire extinguishers. Subsequent investigation focused on a 17-year-old employee, whose father was an executive with the company. The father had been portrayed as a hard-driving business executive, and the son was said to have had a very unsatisfactory relationship with his father. The interrogator based his primary interrogation theme upon the cold relationship that had evolved between a rebellious teenager and his goal-oriented parent. Specifically, it was the interrogator's intention to focus upon the excessive amount of time and effort the suspect's father invested in his career at the sacrifice of the personal development of his 17-year-old son. The language the interrogator employed was somewhat as follows:

Jimmy, there is a fence which divides the hardened criminals, who have no respect for the lives and property of others, and a misunderstood kid who becomes involved in an act of vandalism that gets a little out of hand. Right now you stand on top of that fence teetering toward one side or the other, and it is your choice as to which side of the fence you will finally fall on. The fact you now have an opportunity to explain your reason for doing this [starting the fire] and state what was actually in your head at the time this happened will determine where you land.

It is not uncommon for teenagers to experience feelings of uncertainty and rebelliousness that put them at odds with their parents. Just as often, a parent who is achievement-oriented may lose touch with the uncertainties experienced by an adolescent. Sometimes, in an all-out effort to provide for the material needs of their children, a parent, by concentrating almost exclusively on a career, might unwittingly neglect the emotional needs of a son or daughter. Under those circumstances, it is easy to understand how a child may feel neglected by a parent and do something drastic to try and gain that parent's attention. After a period of time in which an adolescent is subjected to this type of pressure, he might react in a manner such as this, like you did, Jimmy.

It's human to make errors in judgment, and you made a mistake when you decided that by getting involved in this thing, you could make your father stand up and take notice of you. But the critical question is whether you did this out of malice to try and kill someone or whether, in fact, you did it out of an impulse of desperation in trying to gain the respect of your father.

It may be a difficult thing to admit to your parents that you did something wrong, but you should look ahead to those times in the future when you will ask your father to rely upon your word against those who might make false accusations against you. How are you to be believed then if you don't resolve this cloud of suspicion over your head now? Furthermore, consider that time in the future when you will be the father of a teenager who might get into trouble. Wouldn't you expect your son or daughter to level with you? If not, how could you expect to rely on them in the future? You should not be hypocritical; instead, you should set an example of the same standard of honesty that you will expect your own children to maintain.

The difference between a hypocrite and an essentially honest person is that the latter has guts enough to stand up for the truth when he gets caught. Although everyone has something in the "closet" of his life, only a strong person is able to tell the truth about it.

A person's family relationship is the most important thing to preserve and your relationship with your parents is clearly at issue here. The fact that people sometimes hurt those they love the most has been proven in this instance. While your father was preoccupied with his business, you were hurt by his subsequent lack of attention. And while you truly loved him, you saw no way of commanding the desired attention other than by subconsciously hurting your father. Don't allow this incident to permanently break your family relationship by continuing to live a lie.

At this point, the suspect began crying and, as he raised his head up to look at the interrogator, the alternative was presented: "Did you do this thing out of *malice* to try to kill someone, or did you do it out of *love* for your parents to try and gain their respect?" The suspect answered: "Love."

Before discussing the remaining steps, the authors reiterate the statement made earlier that an interrogator need not utilize the steps in the exact order in which they appear in this text. In fact, it would be impossible to do so in any given case situation, since various developments in the early stages of an interrogation may require a shifting in the sequence of the remaining recommended steps. Moreover, there may be times when two or more steps will have to be intermingled so that they may seem to represent only a single step; consequently, the themes comprising *Step 2* will have to be reused from time to time during the course of an interrogation. In other words, it is impossible in a text of this nature to comparmentalize or categorize the various tactics and techniques as though each one was self-supportive and exclusive of the others. They are all interrelated. Unavoidably, however, they must be discussed individually; otherwise, any discussion of them would be rambling and confusing. It is, therefore, essential for the interrogator to exercise his own ingenuity when embarking upon an interrogation. This text must be used only as a set of principles rather than as a set of fixed, inflexible rules.

STEP 3: HANDLING DENIALS

Confessions usually are not easily obtained. Indeed, it is a rare occurrence when a guilty person, after being presented with a direct confrontation of guilt, says: "OK, you've got me; I did it." Almost always, the suspect, whether innocent or guilty, will initially make a denial. It may be "No, I didn't do it" or a similar expression, or perhaps a meaningful gesture to that same effect. A denial is basically a response that an allegation is false. It is an indicated refusal to believe, recognize, or acknowledge the validity of a claim. This denial phase of an interrogation is one of the most critical stages for the interrogator. Unless it is handled with expertise, the interrogator's subsequent efforts may be exercises in futility.

The following childhood experience illustrates the importance of skillful handling of a suspect's denial. Two children are involved in a dispute over the breaking of a toy, such as a water gun. They confront each other: "You broke my gun!" "No, I didn't!" "Yes, you did!" "No, I didn't." And on it goes — "yes," "no," "yes," "no." Theoretically, the last speaker wins, but in actuality, there is no winner in that kind of combat of words. The same is often true in a criminal case setting—a meaningless exchange of words.

In another type of childhood experience, a child's intuitive denial of wrongdoing results in no small measure from the impact of parental admonitions such as, "You know what will happen if you do that again!" Similarly, in the adult world, there is a considerable amount of social conditioning toward denials of wrongdoing. There is in fact a certain amount of conditioning even toward the refusal to answer questions at all—for example, the awareness of the constitutional privilege against self-incrimination, and the judicially imposed requirement that before persons in police custody can be interrogated, they must be advised that they have the right to remain silent and that anything they say may be used against them. Then, too, adults learn from their own experiences, or from the experiences of others, that denials in many case situations do result in a successful avoidance of unfavorable consequences that might otherwise accrue from an admission of guilt.

For the forgoing reasons, as well as others, no interrogator should be disturbed over a criminal suspect's denial of an accusation, even when the circumstances of the offense clearly seem to warrant an admission of some sort. He should recognize the normalcy of denials.

From the initial accusatory confrontation (*Step 1*), and throughout the development of the theme (*Step 2*), the interrogator should have conveyed to the suspect the attitude and position that the investigation into the case has clearly indicated his guilt, and, consequently the only reasons for the interrogator to be talking to him at all are to determine the circumstances of the crime and to obtain an explanation for its commission.

Step 3 specifically concerns the affirmative reactions and the behavior the interrogator should display as the suspect attempts to deny involvement in the offense under investigation. It has a twofold purpose: 1) to assist in the ascertainment of the suspect's guilt or innocence, and 2) to aid in the procurement of a confession from the suspect who is, in fact, guilty.

The first denial of guilt usually occurs immediately after the direct positive confrontation, when the interrogator accuses the suspect of having committed the offense under investigation. The suspect will have been told, in no uncertain terms, something like this: "The results of our investigation clearly indicate that you are the person who broke into Jason's Jewelry Store." The interrogator should then allow for a 5-or 10-second pause, during which he should listen to and carefully observe the manner in which the suspect makes a denial. This will give the interrogator a fairly clear indication of the suspect's probable guilt or innocence.

The suspect's initial denial should be allowed without making any attempt to stop him from completing it. From this point on, however, the interrogator must seek to prevent the suspect from indulging in further denials. The manner in which the suspect reacts to the cutting off of additional attempted denials will be of great assistance in distinguishing the innocent from the guilty, and at the same time further aid in moving the guilty suspect toward the confession stage. As to the latter, the principal interrogational gain of stopping denials is that it deprives the guilty suspect of the psychological fortification that would be derived from repetitious disclaimers of guilt, because the more often a guilty suspect repeats a lie, the harder becomes the task of the interrogator to persuade the suspect to tell the truth. Not only would there be the basic reluctance to admit guilt but also the reluctance to acknowledge that he previously had lied to the interrogator. For these reasons, every discreet effort should be made to prevent the utterances of denials subsequent to the first one. The innocent, truthful suspect will not be adversely affected by this tactic, whereas it will very materially assist in the procurement of a confession from the guilty suspect.

An innocent suspect, as a rule, will respond to the interrogator's first accusation (*Step 1*) with a spontaneous, direct, and forceful denial of guilt. He will likely express or otherwise indicate anger and hostility over the accusation and may even insult the interrogator because of it. While making the initial denial, the innocent suspect will look the interrogator "straight in the eye" and may very well lean forward in the chair in a very rigid or even aggressive posture. The verbal content of the innocent suspect's denial may be something like: "You're wrong. You've got to be crazy if you think I did something like that!"

A guilty suspect will usually offer a very different type of initial denial than that which emanates from the innocent, and the verbal content may assume a variety of forms. There may be an evasive implied denial, such as "Why do you think I did that?" or else a qualified denial like "Honestly, I didn't do it" or "On my mother's grave, I'd swear I didn't do it." Perhaps it may be an excuse-offering denial such as, "I didn't even know this happened." There might also be a denial couched in the form of a delaying tactic, such as: "What did you say?" or "Who me?"

Some denials of guilty suspects may contain simulated expressions of surprise; for example, "What? I can't believe this is happening to me!" Another variation is a rehearsed anticipated denial: "I knew this would happen to me," or "That's what I thought you'd say." Regardless of the type of denial, however, the tone of the guilty suspect's voice will ring hollow and evince insincerity.

In conjunction with the verbal denial, a guilty suspect will usually engage in such nonverbal actions as avoiding eye contact with the interrogator, moving back in the chair or moving the chair itself back, or shifting posture, including crossing and uncrossing arms and legs. Although there are occasions when a guilty suspect may simply remain quiet without saying anything after the accusation, considerations of self-preservation will usually impel some sort of verbal retort.

Following the interrogator's first confrontation statement and the behavioral pause, during which the interrogator listens to and observes the anticipated denial from the suspect, the interrogator should repeat the accusatory statement (*Step 1*) and immediately attempt to begin the development of the interrogation theme that is considered appropriate (*Step 2*).

During the development of a theme, most suspects, innocent as well as guilty, will attempt to interject statements of denial. It is imperative, therefore, that as the interrogator develops a theme, he should be watchful for indications that the suspect is going to attempt to make a denial statement of one sort or another beyond the initial denial. In other words, the interrogator should be able to evaluate the suspect's actions so as to anticipate when the suspect is preparing to offer a second denial. The reason for this preparedness is to be able to stop the suspect, whenever possible, from even voicing the words, "I didn't do it" or an equivalent statement.

Innocent suspects disclose very little warning during the theme development stage that they are about to verbally deny involvement in the crime. They may give some general nonverbal signs that they are about to speak, such as shaking the head or leaning forward while making some hand gesture or arm movement, but they will usually give no verbal clues that a denial is forthcoming. Instead, they simply voice the statement, "I didn't do it," without any prefatory remark. On the other hand, a guilty suspect will usually preface the denial with a "permission" phrase, so as not to upset or insult the interrogator. Typically, it takes the form of a remark such as, "But sir"; "Please sir"; "Can I just say one thing?" "Let me say"; "If I can explain"; "If you will just listen"; or "I understand what you are saying, but. . . ."

Following the permission phrase, a guilty suspect will be impelled to add: "I didn't do it"; however, the interrogator should seek to prevent this from occurring. It is incumbent upon the interrogator, therefore, to recognize the significance of the permission phrase and then, upon hearing it, he should interject a comment that will get the suspect's attention and stop the completion of the denial statement. The type of comment should first include an accentuated reference to the suspect's first name (e.g., "Joe!"), to be followed by: "Before you say anything else, let me explain how important this is" or "Joe! Listen, I want you to understand this." To further forestall a denial, the interrogator should signal disinterest by turning his head to one side and holding up a hand to make a well-recognized "stop" gesture, or by accompanying the head turning with a light touch to the suspect's arm. Moreover, in order to assert control over the situation, the interrogator may want to change the tone of voice by either speaking louder or, in some instances, by speaking softly; or the rate of speech may be changed to underscore the significance of the statement.

The statement, "Joe, before you say anything else, let me explain how important this is," will usually stop a guilty suspect from completing a denial statement. Following this remark of "importance," and the subsequent silence of the suspect, the interrogator should immediately return to the development of his theme. As the interrogator proceeds with theme development, sooner or later the suspect will attempt to reenter the conversation with a denial. Once again, as the guilty suspect attempts to introduce a denial with a permission phrase (e.g., "But sir"), the interrogator should immediately interject a statement advising the suspect to "just listen" because of the importance of what the interrogator is saying. The dialogue presented in Table 6.1 illustrates this process:

Table 6.1. Elements of Dialogue in Step 3

Interrogator: Joe, the results of our investigation clearly indicate that you are the person who broke into Jason's Jewelry Store last week.	**Positive Confrontation Statement**
Joe [After pause.]: You think . . . I could do something like that?	**Suspect's Initial Denial during Behavioral Pause**
Interrogator: Joe, there isn't any doubt about it. What I would like to do now is to sit down with you to see if we can't get this thing straightened out.	**Restatement of Accusation**
You see, Joe, in situations like this, the most important thing for us is to understand the circumstances that led into this kind of thing. Now, I know how tough things have been for you since you got laid off last year. The way the . . .	**Theme Development**
Joe: But, sir . . .	**Permission Phrase for Denial**
Interrogator [interrupting Joe]: Joe, just listen to me for a minute. I want you to know how important this is. Joe, the way today's economy is destroying so many lives with inflated prices and unemployment, we	**Stopping Denial**

Table 6.1. Continued

see people like you making mistakes like this all the time. You, see, Joe, I know you would have never done something like this had you not felt that there was no alternative. Your family . . .	**Returning to Theme and Stopping Further Denials**
Joe [interrupting the interrogator]: Please, sir, can't I just say one thing?	**Permission Phrase for Denial**
Interrogator: Joe, let me finish this because I know the pressure you must have been under to pay your family food bills, the rent, and to buy clothes for your kids. (These suggested reasons may be unfounded, of course; the suspect may have committed the offense in order to pay a gambling debt of for some other less redeeming reason that the ones mentioned by the interrogator.)	**Stopping Further Denials and Returning to Theme**
Joe [interrupting the interrogator]: Listen, sir . . .	**Permission Phrase for Denial**
Interrogator [interrupting Joe]: I will, Joe, just as soon as I finish, because this is so important for you to understand	**Stopping Further Denials and Returning to Theme**

[Continuation of dialogue]

The type of exchange presented in Table 1 may take place several times during the early stage of the interrogation. Usually, a guilty suspect can be stopped from voicing denials by the interrogator's response, which may be physical gestures, such as the "stop" hand gesture, the mention of the suspect's first name, or a reference to the importance of what the interrogator is saying. However, there may be occasions where those tactics will not stop the suspect from denying the crime. In such instances, the interrogator may have to escalate his response statement to include comments that imply more incriminating evidence coming, such as, "Joe, I haven't finished! Let me tell you the whole story [or, exactly what we have against you] before you say anything else!"

A guilty person is always interested in hearing the whole story or in finding out exactly what may be known about him so that an assessment may be made of the situation. As a result, most guilty suspects become quiet when told, in essence, that more incriminating information is coming.

In some instances, it may become necessary for the interrogator to feign annoyance as a tactic to stop a guilty suspect from repeating denial. For example, when the interrogator's theme is interrupted with permission phrases such as, "But, just let me say one thing," the interrogator, in a tone of apparent annoyance, should say, "Joe! quit interrupting me! I'll hear from you when I'm finished, so just sit quiet and listen until I'm through." Following this, the interrogator may add: "Joe, I'm sorry I got upset like that, but I just want to be sure that you're listening to me because I know what you've gone through. You see..." (Here, the interrogator should return to the theme).

As a general rule, this latter tactic will either terminate a guilty suspect's denial attempts or at least cause him to do so less frequently as the interrogation continues. The interrogator will have thereby thwarted the suspect in relying upon the protest, "I didn't do it." A guilty suspect soon realizes that the attempt to deny committing the crime has been fruitless and has not discouraged or stopped the interrogator in pursuit of the truth. As a result, the guilty suspect will usually develop a change in tactic in an effort to achieve some control over the conversation. At this point, the interrogator should move on to *Step 4:* Overcoming Objections. However, before discussing this phase, it is necessary to review the behavior of the innocent suspect during the initial denial phase of the interrogation.

As stated earlier, an innocent suspect will generally make a very direct, sincere, and spontaneous denial after the interrogator's first positive confrontation. Nevertheless, in order to minimize the risk of an erroneous diagnosis, the interrogator should continue a short while the assumption that the suspect may be guilty. Again, the focus here is on suspects against whom there is reasonable evidence or certainty of guilt. In other words, before the interrogator ever accuses a person of committing a crime, there should at least be reasonable basis for believing that the person actually committed it. Furthermore, *none of what is recommended will induce an innocent person to confess*! (This point is embellished in the earlier discussion of *Step 1*).

Even though a suspect may respond to the first accusation in a manner consistent with that of an innocent person, the interrogator should proceed with the theme development based upon a tentative assumption of deception. An innocent suspect usually will not let the interrogator continue for long before forcefully interjecting a denial into the conversation. Unlike guilty suspects, the innocent ones, as previously mentioned, will not "preface" their denials with permission phrases; rather, they will unequivocably state something to the effect of, "You're wrong; I didn't do it!" Nevertheless, the interrogator should attempt to stop denials in much the same way as was done with the denials of person displaying symptoms of guilt.

In the majority of instances, innocent suspects will not allow the interrogator to stop their denials; in fact, the intensity and frequency of denials from the innocent will increase as the interrogation continues. An innocent suspect will become angry and unyielding and often will attempt to take control of the interrogation by not allowing the interrogator to talk until the suspect has made very clear the point that he did not commit the crime under investigation.

There are exceptions to the general "innocent" pattern of resistance when dealing with suspects from certain cultural backgrounds. Some innocent individuals, because of ethnic or environmental characteristics, harbor such a respect for authority that it is difficult for them to indulge in forceful or disrespectful denials, and they may meekly allow the interrogator to stop their attempts at denial. They may seem to listen to the interrogator and may even nod their heads in apparent agreement as the interrogator develops the theme. Only when finally asked an incriminating question will they deny any involvement in the crime, or will they finally express frustration with a statement such as, "What kind of conversation is this—it's all one way!" At this point, such an individual will seem genuinely offended and very sincere in his denials, but this attitude will be slow in development.

Innocent suspects often emphasize their denials by distinctly enunciating their words, and their eyes may convey an injured or angry look similar to that of a person who has been deeply offended. Furthermore, they will rarely move past this state of denials during an interrogation; they will remain adamant in their position and refuse to allow the interrogator to continue with an unchallenged development of the interrogation theme.

At this point during the interrogation, when the interrogator is unable to stop the suspect from making denials, and the interrogator may still be somewhat uncertain as to the suspect's guilt or innocence, a considerable advantage may be gained in a theft case by asking the suspect if he is willing to make restitution. Except for a most unusual case situation, no innocent person will agree to pay the victim the amount of the loss, or even any part of it. A guilty person who is able or who has the ultimate potential to make any kind of restitution may be quite willing to do so. Therefore, the interrogator should ask the suspect the following question respecting a willingness to make restitution: "Joe, this fellow [or the company] is entitled to the return of that money. How about seeing that he gets it back?" An innocent person might respond, "I know he is, but I didn't steal it!" On the other hand, the guilty person may hesitate and ponder over an answer before saying "no," but he will seem uncertain, as though evaluating the benefits of such an act; or he or she may immediately say, "All right, I'll see that he is reimbursed, even though I didn't take it."[9]

In instances where an ordinary thief or an embezzler agrees to make restitution for the loss of the missing sum (e.g., $300), the interrogator should then say, for the purpose of more complete self-satisfaction regarding a conclusion of guilt: "Now, what about paying back the other loss, the $200 one? (Here the interrogator refers to a fictitious loss, which should always be of a lesser sum or value than the actual loss.) In such a situation, the suspect will probably respond by saying, "No, I will not!" Then, when the interrogator says, "Why not?" the typical reply is, "Because I didn't take it!" Such a response will confirm the reasonable inference warranted by the suspect's initial willingness to make restitution for the actual loss; consequently, the interrogator should continue with the attempt to develop an appropriate theme for the eventual admission of guilt.

An innocent person will remain steadfast in denying guilt, regardless of the attitude or statements of the interrogator. A guilty person, however, may try to placate the interrogator by expressing a willingness to admit the offense while at the same time denying that he committed it. For instance, the suspect may say "All right, I'll tell you what you want, but I didn't do it." An interrogator, therefore, may be materially assisted by an awareness that a statement of this type is characteristic of the guilty suspect. The psychological factors that prevail are comparable to those involved when a suspect in a theft case expresses a willingness to make restitution to the victim.

When the interrogator senses that the suspect may be innocent, he should begin to diminish the tone and nature of the accusatory statements. Rather than concentrate on the fact that the suspect committed the act in

---

[9]Whenever the matter of restitution is discussed, the interrogator, and particularly one who is acting on behalf of an employer or other private person who has been the victim of a financial loss, must carefully avoid making any statement to the effect that if restitution (of any amount) is made, there will be no report or formal complaint of the matter to law enforcement authorities. To do so would be in violation of the statutory law of some jurisdictions. For instance, in Illinois, Section 32-1 of its Criminal Code (Ch. 38, Ill. Rev. Stats.), contains the following provisions regarding "Compounding a Crime": "A person compounds a crime when he receives or offers to another any consideration for a promise not to prosecute or aid in the prosecution of an offender." It is punishable by a $500 fine.

Note should be made of the fact, however, that there is no prohibition upon the settlement of a *civil* claim upon the basis of a restitution of part or all of the stolen money or property.

There is also a somewhat comparable federal offense known as "Misprision of Felony." The statute provides that "whoever, having knowledge of the actual commission of a felony (under federal law) conceals it and does not as soon as possible make (it known to a federal judge or other authority) shall be fined not more than $500 or imprisoned for not more than three years or both." The statute has been interpreted by the courts to require not only knowledge of a crime but also an affirmative act of concealment. 18 U.S.C. § 4.

question, the interrogator should soften the accusation to the point of indicating that the suspect may not have actually committed the act but was only involved in it in some way, or perhaps merely has some knowledge about it, or else harbors a suspicion as to the perpetrator. This process of "stepping down" the intensity of the accusation is a very deliberate one; the interrogator should continue with the evaluation of the suspect's verbal and nonverbal behaviors. Moreover, he should look for indications of something the suspect may have done of a less relevant nature that evoked the suspicion about his commission of the principal act. For example, in a $5,000 embezzlement case, the interrogator should explore the possibility that the suspect stole a smaller amount of money, unrelated to the larger amount and that this could account for the behavior symptoms displayed during the initial phases of the interview regarding the $5,000.

The interrogator may find it advisable to expand the interrogation into such areas as the possibility that the suspect gave a false alibi for some personal reason unrelated to the crime under investigation. Perhaps the alibi that was offered, which proved to be false, may be accountable to an impelling need to prevent the disclosure of an indiscretion, such as having been in the company of an individual other than the suspect's spouse at the time of the commission of the crime in question. The possibility of the suspect's commission of some other crime similar to, but unrelated to, the one under investigation might also be explored.

Whenever the verbal and nonverbal behavior exhibited by the suspect during an interrogation seems sincere and indicates that the suspect was not involved in the offense under investigation, no statement should be made immediately that he is clear of any subsequent investigation. The suspect should merely be told that as a result of cooperating with the interrogator, other leads will be pursued in an attempt to substantiate the suspect's claim of innocence. Similarly, if the interrogator is convinced of a suspect's guilt, but is unable to move him past the denial phase of the interrogation, the suspect should be advised that the investigation will continue in an effort to establish the suspect's true status.

On some occasions, it may be appropriate at this stage of the interrogation to provide the suspect with a means of demonstrating "innocence" by offering him an opportunity to take a polygraph test. The interrogator may say: "I can arrange right now for a test to be given to you." The suspect's reaction to this may be very helpful. If he agrees and seems willing to take the test as soon as possible, this usually is an indication of possible innocence. On some occasions, however, a guilty person may agree to a test because he thinks the proposal is a bluff. In either event, an effort should be made, if possible, to obtain a polygraph examination. However, if a test is to be conducted, there should be a reasonable time delay between the interrogation experience and the test.

A guilty person to whom a proposal has been made for a polygraph test will usually seek to avoid or at least delay submission to the test by offering such comments as: "I'm not taking a lie detector test; they say the lie detector makes mistakes" or "Hold on—I've got to talk to my lawyer first." Responses of this nature are usually strong indications that the suspect is guilty. However, a refusal may be made by an innocent person who is aware of the importance of examiner competence and will therefore insist upon first knowing something about the examiner.

Following a suspect's refusal to take a polygraph test, the interrogator can (at least for its effect upon the suspect) point out the incriminating significance of a refusal. This, as well as the mere suggestion of a polygraph, or a "truth serum" test, will frequently result in confessions from the guilty.

When a suspect maintains innocence, and the interrogator is unable, or prefers not to, arrange for a polygraph test, the suspect should be advised that arrangements may be made for a subsequent interview in the very near future.

An innocent suspect is usually in no hurry to leave the interrogation room; in fact, there is a reluctance to leave, primarily because the suspect wants to be sure that the interrogator believes he is innocent. On the other hand, a guilty suspect will be very anxious to make an exit and will not relish the possibility of a return engagement.

Upon arriving home and relating the interrogation experience to a spouse or other family members or friend, a suspect may be urged to prove his truthfulness and to offer to take a polygraph test. If the suggestion is met with evasion by the suspect, the spouse or other person may become suspicious and then insist that the suspect make a clean breast of the situation with the promise that he will receive that person's support. Such developments have occurred with some frequency. Moreover, a troubled conscience, or an augmented concern over forthcoming proof of guilt, may prompt a guilty suspect to return to the interrogator without encouragement from anyone, and then to proceed to confess.

When the various techniques of sympathy and understanding have proved to be ineffective in stopping the denials of a suspect whose guilt is definite or reasonably certain, the interrogator may consider using a so-called "friendly-unfriendly" act. This act may involve two interrogators or else one interrogator working alone.

The following procedure applies when two interrogators are involved: Interrogator A, after having employed a sympathetic, understanding approach throughout his interrogation, expresses regret over the suspect's continued lying. A then leaves the room. Interrogator B enters and proceeds to make uncomplimentary statements to the suspect, by pointing out his objectionable characteristics or behavior. (Or, B may enter while A is still in the room, and B can start his efforts by admonishing A for wasting his time on such an undesirable person; whereupon *A* will leave the room with pretended hurt feelings over the suspect's refusal to tell him the truth.)

After Interrogator *B* (the unfriendly one) has been in the interrogation room for a short while, Interrogator *A* (the friendly one) reenters and scolds *B* for his unfriendly conduct. *A* asks *B* to leave, and *B* goes out of the door with a pretended feeling of disgust toward both the suspect and *A*. *A* then resumes his friendly, sympathetic approach.

This technique has been effectively applied by using a detective as the friendly interrogator and a police captain as the unfriendly one. As the captain leaves the room after playing his unfriendly role, the detective may say:

> Joe, I'm glad you didn't tell him a damn thing. He treats everybody that way—persons like you, as well as men like me within his own department. I'd like to show him up by having you tell me the truth. It's time he learns a lesson or two about decent human behavior.

The psychological reason for the effectiveness of the friendly-unfriendly act is the fact that the contrast between the two methods used serves to accentuate the friendly, sympathetic attitude and thereby renders that approach more effective. Interrogators must bear in mind, of course, that in the employment of the friendly-unfriendly act, the second (unfriendly) interrogator should resort only to verbal condemnation of the suspect; under no circumstances should physical abuse or threats of abuse or other mistreatment ever be employed.

Although the friendly-unfriendly act is usually performed by two persons, one interrogator can play both roles. In fact, the authors are of the opinion that this is the more effective way to apply the technique. When a single interrogator acts out both parts, he feigns impatience and unfriendliness by getting up from his chair and addressing the suspect somewhat as follows: "Joe, I thought that there was something basically decent and honorable in you but apparently there isn't. The hell with it. If that's the way you want to leave it, I don't give a damn. The interrogator sits down on the chair again and after a brief pause, with no conversation at all, may say, "Joe, you'd tax the patience of a saint the way you've been acting. But I guess there is something worthwhile in you anyway." Or, the interrogator may even apologize for his loss of patience by saying, "I'm sorry. That's the first time I've lost my head like that." The interrogator then starts all over with the reapplication of the sympathetic approach that formed the basis for his efforts prior to the above-described outburst of impatience. Now by reason of the contrast with which he has been presented, the suspect finds the interrogator's sympathetic, understanding attitude to be much more appealing. This places him in a much more vulnerable position for a disclosure of the truth.

The friendly-unfriendly act is particularly appropriate in the interrogation of a suspect who is politely apathetic—the person who just nods his head, as though in agreement with the interrogator, but says nothing in response except a denial of guilt. With a suspect of this type, a change in the interrogator's attitude from friendly to unfriendly and back to friendly again will at times produce a change of attitude. The suspect may then become more responsive to the interrogator's efforts at truth disclosure.

STEP 4: OVERCOMING OBJECTIONS

The guilty suspect who realizes the futility of merely uttering a plain denial usually resorts to a change in tactic in order to achieve some control over the conversation. This change will ordinarily take the form of a reason as to why the accusation is wrong. It will fall far short, however, of presenting evidence of innocence, but the guilty suspect assumes that it may be sufficient to satisfy the interrogator. Statements of this type may be termed "objections." For instance, in an armed robbery case situation, the objection may be: "I couldn't have done that; I don't own a gun!" The suspect thereby tries to lend support to the denial. The presumed logic behind the objection is: "I don't own a gun so I couldn't have committed the armed robbery."

Whenever the suspect resorts to voicing an objection, the interrogator's efforts up to this point clearly have had a desirable impact. Moreover, the suspect's move from a denial to an objection is a good indication of a concealment of truth. An innocent suspect, on the other hand, will usually remain steadfast with the denial alone and will feel no need to embellish it at all. He considers "I didn't do it" to be entirely adequate.

The manner in which the interrogator may overcome a suspect's objection is a rather recent development in the art of criminal interrogation. Previously, interrogators were inclined to view objections in the same way as denials, and they dealt with them in the same manner. They would attempt to stop the suspect from voicing any objections. Now, however, there is the awareness among effective interrogators that when a suspect resorts to the tactic of offering objections, this signifies a different frame of mind than when he simply denies commission of the crime; consequently, instead of stopping the suspect, the interrogator should permit an indulgence in the voicing of an objection. The reason for this is that it will provide the interrogator with helpful information for the development of interrogation themes. Instead of discouraging objections, the interrogator should let the suspect voice an objection and then seek to overcome it.

Before proceeding with a presentation of the detailed procedures for overcoming a suspect's objections, it is helpful to consider the terms used by an effective automobile salesperson in overcoming a prospective purchaser's reluctance to commit himself to a sale. Some salespersons actually refer to the tactic as "overcoming objections."

A person enters a sales display room and starts to look at a particular car. If, when a salesperson says "I see you're interested in the 280Z," the response is "I'm just looking," a sale is unlikely to result; the conversation stalls at this point of a denial. The same will be true even after the following limited conversation occurs between the salesperson and the potential customer:

Salesperson: You know, this is the last week we are giving $500 rebates on that model; it's a real buy.
Customer: I'm just looking.
Salesperson: What kind of package would you like me to put together on this baby so you could drive it home today?
Customer: I'm just looking.

Suppose, however, that the potential buyer begins to offer reasons (objections) for not buying. The dialogue might continue as follows:

Customer: Even with a rebate, I could not afford it.
Salesperson: I know what you mean, but you see, after this week is over, not only is the rebate off, but we will have a 10 percent increase across the board. You'll never see a price like this again. Come on over here and I'll show you how we can work something out.
Customer: But even if I could afford it, I'd be interested in some different options than this one has.
Salesperson: No problem, we have over 50 cars on the lot. Let's see what kind of package we can put together so you can drive one of these home today.
Customer: Well, we can talk about it, but I'm not saying I'll buy it. I'd have to talk to my wife first.
Salesperson: Fine. I'm sure she'll love it. How about calling her and have her come over?

Obviously, considerable progress was made toward a sale. By using comparable tactics, an interrogator may overcome the objections that are offered by a guilty suspect in response to the accusation by the interrogator. The interrogator, too, is on the way to making a sale—selling the suspect on the idea to tell the truth.

Suspects will often inject an "introductory phrase" as a prelude to voicing their objections. These may take form of such expressions as "I couldn't have done it," "I wouldn't do a thing like that," "That's impossible," "That's ridiculous," or "How could I ever do something like that?"

Upon hearing such introductory phrases, the interrogator should seek an elaboration by asking the suspect such questions as: "Why couldn't you have done this?" or "Why would it be ridiculous?" The importance of doing this is similar to the reason the automobile salesperson allowed the prospective customer to express his objections to committing himself to the purchase of a car; the interrogator may thereby ascertain the specific nature of the objection.

The majority of objection statements that suspects offer can be categorized into the following general groups:

1. *Emotional Objections*
   "I'd be too scared (nervous) to do something like that." "I loved her." "I like my job."
2. *Factual Objections*
   "I don't even own a gun." "I wasn't even there that day." "I don't even know him." "It's impossible because the security is too good." "I wouldn't even know how to do something like that." "I don't need money, I have $5,000 in my account." "I don't even have the combination to the safe."
3. *Moral Objections*
   "I'm a good Catholic [Protestant; Jew] and that kind of thing is against our religion." "I wasn't brought up that way." "A person who would do something like this is really sick."

Statements of this type are feeble explanations, even in those instances where they may be partially true. In any event, the interrogator should not argue with the suspect over the statement, nor should there be any indication of surprise or irritation. The interrogator should act as though the statement was expected. Such a reaction will have a discouraging effect upon the suspect, who will perceive that he made the wrong statement, or at least an ineffective one.

Following is an illustration (again using the armed robbery suspect situation) of the inappropriateness and ineffectiveness of an *argument* by the interrogator with the suspect over his statement in objection to the accusation:

Interrogator:	You said it's ridiculous. Why, Joe?
Suspect:	Because I don't own a gun.
Interrogator:	Sure you do, and you used it that night!
Suspect:	Hey, I just said I don't own a gun; I've never bought or owned one. You think I own a gun? Prove it!
Interrogator:	Look, fellow, you used your damn gun that night. Quit being a wise guy!
Suspect:	I don't have a gun, damn it!

This type of exchange allows the suspect to gain control of the interrogation. It puts the interrogator on the defensive and causes a great deal of unnecessary hostility and frustration for the interrogator to overcome.

In contrast to the forgoing expressions of the interrogator, the appropriate response would have been a statement of agreement or understanding, such as: "I hope that's true," "I'm glad you mentioned that," "I was hoping you'd say that," "I certainly understand what you're saying," or "I know that may be true." Immediately following a response of this type, the interrogator should attempt to reverse the significance of the suspect's objection and return to the interrogation theme without delay. Table 1 shows an example of the dialogue that should occur between the interrogator and the suspect in a case situation involving the armed robbery of a liquor store.

Table 6.2. Elements of Dialogue in Step 4

Interrogator: Joe, I don't think this was your idea or something you planned well in advance. I think that you and some of your buddies went into that liquor store, saw that there weren't any customers around and one of your buddies told you to go up there and get the money and you just didn't know how to stop it. Then this whole thing happened with the gun and everything else.	**Theme Development**
Suspect: But that's ridiculous.	**Follow-Through**
Interrogator: Why is it ridiculous, Joe?	
Suspect: Because I don't even own a gun.	**Objection**
Interrogator: I'm glad you mentioned that, Joe, because it tells me that it wasn't your idea to do this; that one of your buddies talked you into this, handed you the gun, and then the whole thing happened. You see, Joe, if you did own a gun and carried it in that night, ready to use it, to kill	**Overcoming Objection by Agreement and Understanding, and by Pointing Out Negative Aspects of Situation if Objection was Untruthful**

Table 6.2. Continued

somebody if they got in your way,
that's one thing. But if the other guy
stuck it in your hand, to use just
to scare everybody, that's
something else again . . .

[Continuation of dialogue]   Continuation of **Theme**
                                    Development

Another explanation of *Step 4* is the following case situation where a suspect's objection comes after the interrogator has presented the essence of his selected interrogation theme. Assume that the case under investigation involves a series of neighborhood burglaries. Although no sex offenses were connected with any of them, the suspect under interrogation is told that some of them occurred and that the description of the assailant, as given by two young female victims, fitted the suspect. At this point, the suspect says: "But I could never do something like that. I'd be too scared just by being in the home." The interrogator then expresses his agreement and begins to discuss the negative aspects of the fictitious situation as though it were a true one:

> "I believe that's true, Joe, because if you wouldn't be scared that tells me you're capable of anything, even those rapes. But the fact that you were scared tells me that you're not the kind of guy who would be climbing in windows to attack girls, but you just went in there to pick up a few things for some money because you were desperate. I know how tough it can be these days . . . [The interrogator continues with his theme].

On occasion, the interrogator may be confronted with an objection that is very difficult to deal with or to transpose into material for development of the theme. For example, in a child molesting case, it would be inappropriate for the interrogator to accept, or to agree with, a suspect's objection such as, "I'd never do something like that because whoever did that is a pervert." The interrogator's response should be one of a general nature, perhaps describable as an "absolute declaration," such as: "Exactly, Joe, don't you see, that's why we should get this thing cleared up." In effect, this declaration is merely a vehicle by which the interrogator sidesteps the objection. It actually does not mean anything to the suspect, but it creates the impression that the interrogator is encouraged by the suspect's statement, and this is the opposite effect from that which the suspect anticipated when he offered the objection. The guilty suspect is usually not perceptive enough to question the interrogator's statement at this point. The interrogator can then resume the interrogation theme.

A second method of sidestepping difficult objections is to use a response such as: "That's possible I suppose, Joe, but let me tell you this . . . ." or "That may be true, Joe, but the important thing is this . . . ." An example of sidestepping and then properly overcoming a difficult objection is illustrated in the following sequence during an interrogation in a child molesting case:

Interrogator: Many times I've seen people, including myself, do things under the influence of alcohol that we would never do on our own.

Suspect: But I'd never do anything like that because whoever did that is a pervert.

Interrogator: Exactly, Joe. Don't you see? That's why we should get this thing cleared up, because I don't want anyone to think that about you. I know that you would never do something like this when you're sober. The people who might do that when sober have a real problem. But all of us do things when we're drinking that are totally out of character, like this thing you did. This isn't like you normally; I know that. This thing happened because you weren't yourself . . . .

When multiple objections are offered during the course of an interrogation, the suspect is probably guilty. As previously mentioned, innocent suspects usually remain steadfast with their denial statements. If an innocent person is going to offer an objection, it usually occurs very early in the interrogation, not after numerous attempts to deny the crime.

At this stage of the interrogation, when a guilty suspect's objections have been properly handled and even used against him or her, the suspect may become very uncertain about the situation and may become withdrawn. This development requires the utilization of *Step 5*.

STEP 5: PROCUREMENT AND RETENTION OF SUSPECT'S ATTENTION

Review of Previous Steps

At the outset of the interrogation, the suspect is accused of committing the offense under investigation, as described in *Step 1*. Following this first confrontation statement, the interrogator begins to develop the selected theme or themes from among those discussed in *Step 2*. During the theme development, the suspect, whether innocent or guilty, usually attempts to simply deny any involvement in the crime. *Step 3* outlines tactics to stop such denials. At this stage of the interrogation, the innocent suspect usually remains adamant with the denial or becomes very insistent with respect to his innocence; the guilty suspect tends to reveal a weakness in his position and, in an attempt to gain control over the conversation, begins to offer objections pointing toward noninvolvement in the crime. In *Step 4*, the task of the interrogator is to overcome these objections. Thereafter, the guilty suspect often begins to shunt aside the interrogator's comments. There will also be some indications of apprehensiveness. The suspect now begins to feel moments of indecision, and will struggle to avoid the consequences he knows or presumes will follow as a result of the criminal act and his aroused impulse to confess. Psychologically, this constitutes the suspect's withdrawal from the interrogation environment. The suspect becomes pensive, talks much less, and gives the impression of not even listening to what the interrogator is saying. The suspect may turn his head aside; fiddle with a tie clasp, coin, or other object; pick fingernails or indulge in some other distractive action, such as dusting off clothes with his hand; exhibit a wry smile; or display a "faraway" look while pondering the question: "Shall I tell the truth or keep on lying?"

When the suspect is in this frame of mind, if the interrogator remains silent or leaves the suspect alone in the interrogation room, or accedes to the request for a cigarette, the suspect may quickly regain his composure, and all of the interrogator's prior efforts will be lost. It is extremely important, therefore, that this critical stage of the interrogation be recognized immediately, for it suggests that the time is now for the interrogator to move closer to the suspect so as to procure and retain the suspect's attention.

Essential Elements

PHYSICAL GESTURES

During the period of a guilty suspect's indecision over whether to tell the truth or lie, the interrogator should move his chair physically closer to the suspect than the 4 or 5 feet that prevailed at the outset. This will decrease the suspect's confidence while simultaneously increasing anxiety. Moreover, as stated in Chapter 3, it is a recognized fact that the closer a person is to someone physically, the closer he becomes to that person psychologically. Additionally, there will be occasions, particularly in the interrogation of the emotional offender, as previously stated, when it becomes very effective to gently pat the male suspect's arm or shoulder or to gently hold a female's hand in order to retain his or her attention. That physical gesture will also serve to convey to the emotional offender, as well as to some of the nonemotional ones, that the interrogator understands or sympathizes with the suspect's predicament. It can convey that impression far better than words themselves. However, if the suspect withdraws, even casually, from any such tactile contact, the interrogator should make no further attempt. Nevertheless, he should maintain the physical proximity already achieved.

Considerable discretion must be exercised when using the suggested gestures. The pat on the shoulder should be reserved for males who are: 1) younger or of approximately the same age as the interrogator, or 2) of the first offender type. It should not be employed on a career criminal or on a "cocky" type of person. Only rarely should it be used on older persons because, to them, the pretentiousness of the gesture may be too obvious. Female offenders may prefer to have their hand held.

Before an interrogator contemplates either moving closer to a suspect or touching him or her, the situation must be carefully evaluated. Any premature action may destroy the atmosphere created to this point. In general, the suggested actions should take place only when the suspect is not looking directly at the interrogator, when he seems to be listening, and when the suspect is past the stage of making denials and offering objections.

CHAIR PROXIMITY

The interrogator's physical action of moving closer to the suspect should be a gradual, unobtrusive process, and should seem to be the natural result of the interrogator's interest and sympathy. It would be inappropriate and unnecessarily distractive for the interrogator all of a sudden to pick up his chair and to place it directly in front of the suspect, as though for a "nose-to-nose" confrontation. As recommended in Chapter 3, the original position of the interrogator's and suspect's chair at the outset is to directly face each other about 4 or 5 feet apart.

The interrogator should first move his body to the front edge of the chair and should lean forward. This posture change immediately reduces the distance between the interrogator and suspect. From that point on, movements by the interrogator should consist of pulling his chair forward in small increments until he is close enough to reach out easily and to touch the suspect, if and when appropriate.

As the forward movements are made, the interrogator should not focus attention on them by pausing in his conversation. The interrogator should continue to talk and to maintain eye contact with the suspect, without looking down at the chair as it is moved. A guilty suspect will usually be aware of an increased feeling of uneasiness as the interrogator moves closer but often will not consciously recognize that the cause for it is the physical proximity of the interrogator. The suspect simply senses or perceives that lying is becoming more uncomfortable.

As the interrogator moves closer to the suspect, he should watch and evaluate the suspect's response. If the suspect just sits there without any physical reaction, the interrogator is making a great deal of progress. However, if the suspect physically moves his chair back or readjusts his position to the rear of it, perhaps the interrogator is progressing too quickly; the interrogator should then slow down the movements. Also, because the purpose of moving the interrogator's chair closer to the suspect is to keep his attention, if the attention is maintained while the interrogator is at the original distance from the suspect, it may not be necessary to move closer. Where an arm, shoulder, or hand touching is contemplated, the chair moving will be required, of course.

EYE CONTACT

It is important for the interrogator to maintain steady eye contact with the suspect by such actions as mention of the suspect's first name, tone of voice, and, where appropriate, touching of the suspect. Constant eye contact may be broken momentarily by the suspect as he looks down or away from the interrogator, but this may not mean loss of attention; in fact, the suspect may at that time be weighing what has been said.

MAINTAINING ONE THEME

During this stage of the interrogation, the interrogator should not switch themes. Once attention has been secured, the interrogator should continue using the essential elements of the selected theme, although he may begin working toward the alternative question.

STEP 6: HANDLING SUSPECT'S PASSIVE MOOD

At the conclusion of *Step 5*, the interrogator should have achieved a desirable rapport with the suspect. As a consequence, the suspect, if guilty, will have become very reticent. He becomes more willing to listen, attributable in part to an increasing awareness that the deception does not possess its anticipated effectiveness. The suspect may begin to assume a defeatist posture—slumped head and shoulders, limp legs, and glassy eyes. In general, the guilty suspect will seem downcast and depressed. At this stage, the interrogator should begin to concentrate on the central core of the selected theme while preparing the groundwork for the possible alternatives that are described in *Step 7.*

Whereas earlier the interrogator merely suggested the possible reasons why the suspect committed the offense and coupled them with embellished statements designed to offer psychological escapes, the interrogator should now start to distill those reasons from the general framework of the theme and concentrate his verbal statements on the specific basic one implicit in the theme. The following example of this procedure is useful because of its factual simplicity, although the same principle may be utilized in more serious cases, such as a robbery-murder: A suspect is being interrogated about a theft of money from his employer. The interrogator may have developed a theme along the following lines:

> Joe, I know how tough it is in today's economy to make ends meet. Every paycheck you get has to stretch further and further to cover the costs of the basic things we all need: food, home, car, and other necessities. But what has happened over the last few years is that as prices have gone up, more money is needed just to buy the same things we bought earlier. And it seems like employers, the people we work for, forget this. Instead of getting the pay raises we need just to keep up with things, we are stuck with the same pay month after month. Pretty soon an honest person like you finds himself in a position where his pay just doesn't cover the necessities, and he begins to wonder how he'll ever make ends meet. Then one day, when someone leaves work in a hurry and money is accidentally left out, you begin to give in to the temptation that you've been able to fight off up until that time. The pressure becomes unbearable, and in one split second, you give in and make a mistake in judgment and do something like this. We all face these pressures and have to scramble these days to make ends meet.

The interrogator should continue with the development of this specific theme as long as the suspect maintains interest, even though he may have committed the theft in order to purchase alcohol or drugs, or to gamble, or to provide entertainment for himself that he could not afford with his legitimate income. Throughout it all, the interrogator must, of course, fend off the suspect's denials and objections in the manner previously described.

As the suspect drifts into a passive mood, the interrogator should move closer to the suspect (if this has not occurred thus far) to recapture attention to the theme. Then, when the suspect begins to display the indications of being about to give up, the interrogator must focus more intently on his statements about the possible central reason for the theft, as in the following example:

Joe, I'm sure you were just over your head in bills at home, and this money appeared to solve your problem; it seemed to be the only way out, or maybe someone in the family was sick and needed an operation or some medical attention that you couldn't take care of, but yet you couldn't ignore it. And so this money was there and this seemed to be the solution to an impossible situation.

The various reasons that the interrogator offers for the motive of the theft are designed to prepare the suspect for the alternative question, which is discussed in *Step 7*. As each reason is presented, the interrogator must closely observe the suspect's behavior for signs of acceptance or rejection, to determine whether or not the offered reason presents an acceptable possibility for the commission of the act.

At this time, it is very important for the interrogator to continue displaying understanding and sympathy in urging the suspect to tell the truth. As the interrogator repeats and reiterates reasons for the commission of the offense, it may be appropriate to interject statements that if the suspect were his own brother (or father, sister, etc.), the interrogator would still advise telling the truth. The interrogator may also urge the suspect to tell the truth for the sake of his own conscience, mental relief, or moral well-being, as well as "for the sake of everybody concerned."

In urging or advising an offender to tell the truth, the interrogator must avoid expressions that are objectionable on the grounds that they constitute illegal promises or threats. However, by speaking in generalities, such as "for the sake of your conscience" or "for the sake of everybody concerned," the interrogator can remain within permissible bounds.

The following line of discussion has been used to good advantage on many occasions (particularly in sex or embezzlement cases): The suspect is advised that by telling the truth, he can perform somewhat of a mental operation on himself—an operation equally as important and necessary as the removal or destruction of injurious tissue in a cancer patient. In this respect, it may be helpful to draw a circle on a piece of paper, mark off a small area on the rim of it, and tell the suspect that, in effect, the marked-off portion represents a piece of infected tissue on his mind or soul that if untreated or not removed, will continue to spread and produce other and more serious offenses than the present one. The suspect should then be told that there is only one way that the necessary mental operation may be performed, and only he can do it—and that is by telling the truth.

"For the sake of everybody concerned" is an expression that lends itself to many interpretations conducive to truth telling, for example, the suffering of the victim or of his dependents or the harm caused to other persons adversely affected by the offender's conduct. It is advisable, therefore, to briefly mention these consequences for the purpose of placing the suspect in a more regretful mood.

The expression, "It's the only decent and honorable thing to do," constitutes somewhat of a challenge for the offender to display some evidence of decency and honor. This is particularly applicable in sex crimes where, in the absence of a plea of guilty, it would become necessary for the victim to undergo the ordeal of publicly relating the details of the offense committed against the victim; in such instances, it is occasionally helpful to ask a male suspect how he would like to have his own sister or mother appear in court as his victim may have to do. In playing upon this potential weakness, if the suspect happens to mention that he is a religious person, discuss with him the tenets of his particular creed. Mention to him the fact that his religion becomes meaningless until he tells the truth with regard to the offense in question. Likewise, if he belongs to a fraternal order, appeal to him in its name. It is also quite helpful if the interrogator can state that he or his parents or close friends belong to the same church or fraternity and that, therefore, he, the interrogator, knows and appreciates what the suspect's moral obligations are in the present situation.

In a sex murder case, in which the interrogator knows that the suspect has an invalid mother, the appeal to his "decency" can be as follows: "Joe, a mother—and particularly one like yours—is the most understanding person in the world. Her real concern is about the reason for your doing this. That's what we all want to know—the reason. And your mother, in particular, is entitled to know." In one such case, the suspect eventually responded by saying, "I'll tell you the whole story if I can first talk to my mother." The interrogator agreed and said he would send a car for the mother, but within a few minutes after making the request to see his mother, the suspect made a full confession.

During this stage of the interrogation, a suspect may begin to cry. The interrogator should not leave the room and give the suspect a chance to "cry it out"; the suspect who is given that opportunity may fortify himself and return to the denial stage. When a suspect begins to cry, the interrogator should commiserate with the suspect and offer encouragement by attempting to relieve his embarrassment. Crying is an emotional outlet that releases tension. It is also a very good indication that the suspect has given up and is ready to confess. The suspect's emotional outburst is evidence of remorse and often is perceived by the suspect as exposing his inner feelings of guilt. A positive attitude on the part of the interrogator will cause the suspect to feel that a confession is expected at that time.

Sometimes female suspects cry as a ploy, or as a final, yet insincere effort to gain sympathy.

When a male suspect cries, which is usually tantamount to an admission, it is suggested that the interrogator proceed as follows:

You know, Joe, the problem today is that men are too ashamed to cry and everything is bottled up inside. They are afraid to let it out. That's why men have so many more heart attacks than women. It is good to cry, Joe, because it shows me that you are sorry for what you did.

If the suspect seems willing at this time, the interrogator can seek an admission by getting the suspect to say that he is sorry, but if there is any doubt about that readiness status, it is best to wait until later, when the alternatives of *Step 7* are offered.

The majority of suspects do not cry at this stage. They do, however, indicate defeat by a blank stare and complete silence. They are no longer resistant to the interrogator's appeal for the truth. This blank stare and complete silence is an indication that the suspect is ready for the alternatives in *Step 7*.

STEP 7 : PRESENTING AN ALTERNATIVE QUESTION

In the context of interrogation techniques, an alternative question is one that presents to the suspect a choice between two explanations for possible commission of the crime. It is a face-saving device that renders easier the burden of the suspect's start toward telling the truth. It may be phrased in such terms as: "Did you plan this, or did it just happen on the spur of the moment?" or "Was this your own idea, or did someone talk you into it?"

To this point, the interrogator will have focused on such techniques as minimizing the moral seriousness of the crime or on offering psychological excuses or justifications for the suspect's criminal behavior. The alternative question technique climaxes those basic concepts by presenting to the suspect a choice between an inexcusable or repulsive motivation for committing the crime and one that is attributable to error or the frailty of human nature. For example, in an armed robbery case in which the victim was shot, the alternative question may be: "Joe, did you shoot him on purpose, or did the gun go off accidentally?" Intentional shooting obviously presents an indefensible choice, whereas an accidental shooting constitutes an acceptable alternative. Even though the selected option is the shooting by accident, the answer nevertheless will be an admission of the shooting, and from then on, the ascertainment of the full facts will be greatly enhanced.

In using the alternative question, the interrogator must bear in mind the need to phrase it in terms of an assumption of guilt; for instance, "Joe, is this the first time you did something like this, or has it happened many times before?" In other words, the question must not be phrased in such a manner as to permit the suspect to make an easy denial, as would occur if he is merely asked "Did you do it, or didn't you?"

An alternative question must be based on the assumption that the suspect actually committed that act, irrespective of whether it connotes legal guilt or not, such as an admission to a killing in self-defense. Following an admission, the interrogator can proceed to determine the true details regarding the commission of the crime.

An interrogator should always be mindful of the fact that when a criminal offender is asked to confess a crime, a great deal is being expected of him. First of all, it is not easy for anyone to "own up" to wrongdoing of any kind. Furthermore, in a criminal case, the suspect may be well aware of the specific serious consequences of telling the truth— the penitentiary or even the electric chair. Therefore, the task of confessing should be made as easy as possible for the suspect. Toward that end, the interrogator should avoid a general admission of guilt questions, such as: "You did kill him, didn't you?" "You did rape her, didn't you?" "You did hit him with your car, didn't you," or "Tell us all about it, Joe." Any such questions will recall to the suspect's mind a revolting picture of the crime itself—the scream of the victim, the blood spurting from a wound, or the pedestrian's body being thrown over the hood of an automobile or dragged along the street. No person should be expected to blurt out a full confession of guilt; the interrogator must ease the ordeal. As the great Austrian criminal investigator, Hans Gross, stated in his 1907 book, *Criminal Investigation* (at p. 120):

> It is merciless, or rather psychologically wrong, to expect anyone boldly and directly to confess his crime. . . . We must smooth the way, render the task easy.

When the interrogator presents the alternative question to the suspect, it is not enough simply to ask the question and then to wait for the suspect to answer. The interrogator must encourage the suspect to select one of two options. This is accomplished through the use of a "supporting statement."

A supporting statement is one in which the interrogator reinforces his belief that the correct choice is the one that seems to be morally excusable or at least one that represents a less socially revolting reason for committing the act. Generally speaking, the supporting statement emphasizes the negative aspects of the undesirable alternative choice, followed by pointing out the positive aspects of the desirable choice and thereby encouraging the suspect to choose that one. The following example illustrates this process. (The questions are usually asked one right after the other; they are here separated only for the purpose of identifying their individual nature and purpose.):

Alternative Question: Joe, was this money used to take care of some bills at home, or was it used to gamble?

Negative Option: You don't seem to be the kind of person who would do something like this in order to use it for gambling. If you were that kind of person, I wouldn't want to waste my time with you, but I don't think you're like that.

Positive Option: I'm sure this money was for your family, for some bills at home. It was for your family's sake, wasn't it, Joe?

The last statement may be made even though the interrogator knows that the money was used for some other purpose.

In a case where the victim was shot by an armed robber, and the suggested alternative question is: "Joe, did you purposely do this, or did it just go off accidentally?" the supporting statement would be: "I'm sure you didn't plan on doing this, did you Joe? I think that the gun just went off accidentally. All you wanted was a few bucks; you didn't want to hurt him, Joe, did you?"

A supporting statement closes with a question that calls for a one-word answer or a nod of the head in acceptance of the less offensive of the two options. In appropriate instances, the supporting statement should be coupled with a gesture of understanding and sympathy, such as a pat on the shoulder. This indication of sincerity, coupled with the timing of the supporting statement, is the key to success in this particular procedure.

In presenting the supporting statement containing an undesirable alternative choice, the interrogator's facial expression should display disgust and rejection; when describing the desirable alternative choice, the interrogator should display a gratifying demeanor.

The alternative question usually focuses on the reason *why* the suspect committed the act, but it does not necessarily have to be thus limited in scope. The alternative question may focus on some detail of the offense, preferably something preceding or following the occurrence itself. A "detail" question is based on the *where, when,* or *how* of an act or event pertinent to the crime under investigation, but yet is removed in point of time or place from the main occurrence itself. In an armed robbery case, for instance, the question may be: "Did you bring the gun yourself, or did one of your buddies give it to you?" In a rape case, where the suspect has denied ever seeing the victim, an appropriate question would be: "Were you with her for a long time before this happened or for just a few minutes?" In an arson case, the question may be: "Did you use a match or a lighter?"

Depending upon the nature of the crime and the suspect's demeanor during the interrogation, occasionally it becomes advisable to use a one-sided alternative question, for example, "You are sorry about this, aren't you, Joe?" The negative possibility—the absence of any feeling of remorse—is not stated, but the implication of its presence is readily apparent to the suspect.

Even though the alternative question may be directed toward some detail of the crime, or may be of a one-sided nature, generally speaking, the most effective format of the alternative is when it deals with the reason for the commission of the act. Its effectiveness is founded upon the basic principle that even in ordinary, everyday, noncriminal experiences, it is much easier to admit a mistake or any kind of wrongdoing if, at the time of the admission, a person is permitted to explain *why* it was done. Similarly, in a criminal case situation it is much easier for a criminal offender to confess a crime if given an opportunity to couple his admission with an explanation or excuse for the conduct. The alternative question and subsequent supporting statement offers the suspect that opportunity.

Alternative questions, when asked at the proper psychological moment, have a number of advantages that make them much more effective than inquiries or solicitations calling for an outright or general admission of guilt. First, by delving into details of where, when, how, or of the reason for the offense, the interrogator effectively displays a greater certainty of the suspect's guilt; otherwise there would be no interest in details. This, in itself, has a tendency to weaken the suspect's resistance to telling the truth. Second, there is the very desirable element of surprise in a question of this type. It catches the suspect off guard at a very crucial time, and it stimulates to greater activity the already aroused impulse to confess. Third, a question with respect to the reason for the crime, when asked of a suspect who feels impelled to confess but who is thwarted by the task of bursting forth with the complete admission all at once, offers an opportunity to preface or combine an admission of guilt with whatever excuses or explanations the person cares to make in an effort to ease his conscience, as well as to have the interrogator believe that the crime is less odious or less reprehensible than is actually the case. Fourth, an inquiry into a detail of the offense implies a rather sympathetic attitude on the part of the interrogator. It gives the impression that the interrogator is not particularly interested in a confession but rather in ascertaining and understanding the reasons for the offender's behavior, or in being informed of the circumstances or conditions that contributed to the consummation of the act.

Occasionally, in the application of the alternative question procedure, the interrogator will encounter a suspect who may grasp any one of the suggested explanations or excuses (e.g., an accidental act) and persist thereafter in relying upon it for a legal defense, even though it may not represent the truth. Once the suspect has admitted the act itself, however, the interrogator can almost always follow through successfully and obtain the accurate version by pointing out the flaws in the explanation or excuse given. (The procedures for doing this are described in *Step 8*.)

Nevertheless, despite such eventualities, the tactical advantages to be gained from any admission that contradicts the suspect's previous denials will sufficiently compensate for the risk of having an occasional suspect refuse to retrench from his adoption of the explanation or excuse offered by the interrogator.

In selecting the alternative question, primary consideration should be given to the theme that the interrogator has been using. The alternative should be a natural extension of the theme. It puts into focus, in one question, the central core of the theme that was emphasized by the interrogator, especially in Step 6. For example, while questioning a suspected embezzler, the interrogator may have used the theme that the suspect had originally intended to merely borrow the money for a short period. The alternative question may then be: "Joe, did you plan to keep that money all along, or did you only borrow it with the plan of paying it back?" Following this would be a supporting statement such as: "Joe, I'm sure you intended on paying that money back. If you didn't, you don't deserve the chance to get this thing straightened out. You did plan on paying it back, didn't you, Joe?"

In phrasing the alternative question, the interrogator should avoid any emotionally charged words that would recreate a revolting recollection of the event. For example, in a rape case, there would be an avoidance of expressions like: "Is this the first time you raped a girl, or have you raped a lot of girls before?" Instead, the question should be phrased: "Is this the first time something like this has happened, or has it happened a lot of times before?" The suspect will know, of course, what the interrogator means when reference is made to the event as "this."

The decision regarding when to ask the alternative question can be critical to the success of the interrogation. If it is presented while the suspect is still denying involvement in the commission of the crime (*Step 3*), or when he is still offering objections (*Step 4*), the presentation of the alternative question will usually lead to an argument from the suspect in which he maintains his innocence. Therefore, the proper time to present the alternative question is when the suspect has stopped making denials and objections and seems to be quietly listening to the interrogator. This stage is usually reached at the conclusion of *Step 6*. Occasionally, however, after a direct confrontation has occurred, the interrogator may quickly realize that the suspect has become quiet and that his nonverbal behavior indicates proneness for an admission. At that point, the interrogator should introduce a theme (*Step 2*), but soon thereafter invoke the alternative question without applying *Steps 3, 4, 5,* or *6*. To ramble on and delay the alternative question may cause the suspect to change his frame of mind and to act negatively with denials.

When the alternative question is first presented, the suspect may not make any comment, in which event the question should be repeated in basically the same form, unless the suspect's behavioral responses are suggestive of a total rejection. If that occurs, the question should be rephrased in such a way as to be more acceptable so as to avoid losing the suspect's attention.

Step 7 is frequently the real key to a successful interrogation. Unfortunately, many interrogators simply do not know what to do at that stage in order to trigger a confession. Use of the alternative question along with its supportive statement would probably produce a favorable result.

The following case example clearly illustrates the potential of the alternative question; note the focus on a detail of the crime: Jack was suspected of stabbing to death his estranged wife, along with their three children. The interrogator used the theme that every man's patience has a breaking point, and that the suspect probably went over to the wife's apartment with the best of intentions, but the more he attempted to be reasonable, the less reasonable she became. The interrogator then said:

> Jack, you're an honest guy and I am sure you wanted to be fair to your wife. You went over to her apartment with the intention of talking to her about the marriage separation and money settlement like normal human beings, but she probably started an argument with you, and she got so mad and unreasonable that she even backed you up to the kitchen table. Now, if you were backed up to the kitchen table, and she was raising complete hell with you, and your hand accidentally rested on a knife, and you used it without thinking, I can understand that, and I can easily see how this could happen. That's one thing, but if you took the time to look into the drawer to find one and then you used it, that's different; if that's what happened, I don't want to talk to you further. However, if it was on the table and not in the drawer, and in backing up while she was sticking her finger in your face and screaming at you, and your hand then landed on it and you used it on her without thinking, I can well understand how this happened. Now, Jack, was it on the table or in a drawer? I'm sure it was on the table and not in the drawer. It was on the table, Jack, wasn't it? I'm sure you didn't have to look through the drawer to find it! Jack, was it on the table or in the drawer? This is a most important point, Jack. Was it on the table or in the drawer?

After proposing alternatives—"on the table" or "in the drawer"—a number of times, and indicating the importance of his decision, the suspect finally mumbled the word "table." This was the first admission and the start of his confession. (Later the suspect revealed that he had actually reached in the drawer for it.)

An important point is that the interrogator in the case made no mention of the death of the children. Psychological justification was only assessed toward the wife. Obviously, the children were absolutely blameless for the tragic event. To include them in any questioning would have had an adverse effect on the interrogation.

STEP 8: HAVING SUSPECT ORALLY RELATE VARIOUS DETAILS OF OFFENSE

When the suspect accepts one of the choices presented in the alternative question, he has, in effect, made the first admission of guilt. The objective of *Step 8*, then, is to develop this admission (which only tends to establish the suspect's guilt) into a legally acceptable and substantiated confession that discloses the circumstances and details of the act.

As stated in the discussion of the *Step 7*, the alternative question and its supportive statement should be phrased so that the suspect only needs a nod of the head or a one-word response to indicate acceptance of one or the other of the alternative choices. At the precise moment when the suspect accepts an alternative, it is critical that the interrogator immediately proceed to have the suspect further commit himself to a discussion of the details of the crime. If the interrogator gives the impression of being uncertain or hesitates after the suspect accepts one of the alternative choices, the suspect will thereby be presented with an opportunity to retract his statement. The interrogator should encourage the suspect to continue beyond the acceptance of an alternative by making a reinforcement statement, such as: "Good, that's what I thought all along."

If a suspect accepts an alternative that the interrogator does not believe to be the truth, it is inadvisable to challenge him at that particular time. A correction of the alternative choice should be sought, however, after the suspect has given a general description of the criminal act. (The manner of doing this is described later in this chapter.)

As the interrogator makes a statement of reinforcement, he should seem elated and should, while still looking directly at the suspect, ask a question calling for some additional detail regarding the suspect's act, such as: "Then what happened, Bob?" The interrogator may have to repeat this question a few times or even change the question slightly to: "What happened next, Bob?" The interrogator should then proceed with questioning the suspect in an attempt to develop a general description of the criminal act. The questions presented to the suspect during this initial phase of the confession should be brief, clear, and designed so that they can be answered in only a few words. Furthermore, the questions should not contain any harsh or emotionally charged terminology. An example of this is the case discussed in *Step 7* in which the husband, Jack, was suspected of having stabbed to death his wife and three children. When Jack mumbled the word "table" in response to the alternative question, "Was the knife on the table or in the drawer?" the interrogator followed with a statement of reinforcement: "Good Jack, that's what I thought all along. Then what happened, Jack?" The following dialogue ensued:

Jack [after a pause]:	I did it to her.
Interrogator:	You mean you used the knife?
Jack:	Yeah.
Interrogator:	How many times did you use the knife, Jack?
Jack:	A couple of times.
Interrogator:	Did you use it in the front or in the back?
Jack:	Front.
Interrogator:	Did you stick her in the back at all, Jack?
Jack:	No. [The interrogator knew from the facts in the case that she was only stabbed in the front, but several times. The details of the number of times she was stabbed should be left to a later time when it will be much easier for the suspect to tell the number of times he estimates that she was stabbed. Also, the interrogator should bear in mind that in his frenzy, the husband may not know the exact number of times he stabbed his wife.]
Interrogator:	Then what happened?
Jack:	The kids were crying.
Interrogator:	And what did you do?
Jack:	I put them in the tub.
Interrogator:	You mean the bathtub?
Jack:	Yeah.
Interrogator:	What did you do then?
Jack:	I used it on them.
Interrogator:	You mean you used the knife on them, Jack?
Jack:	Yeah.
Interrogator:	What did you do then?
Jack:	I thought about using it on myself, but I didn't have the guts, so I left.
Interrogator:	What did you do with the knife, Jack?
Jack:	I left it in the bathroom.
Interrogator:	Where in the bathroom?
Jack:	With them in the bathtub.

At this point, the interrogator has the suspect, Jack, totally committed to the murders. The interrogator should then pursue in detail the circumstances of the act, as well as what the suspect did before and after he committed the crime. The interrogator would now use, for the first time, fully descriptive, incriminating words, such as stab (or in other cases, shoot, steal, rob, burglarize, etc.), so that when these words are used in the formal written confession, the suspect will be accustomed to them. It is also at this point that the suspect (in this case, Jack) should be asked more details about the manner and the number of times he stabbed his wife.

The interrogator should attempt to develop information that can be corroborated by further investigation, and he should seek from the suspect full details of the crime and also about his subsequent activities. What should be sought particularly are facts that would only be known by the guilty person (e.g., information regarding the location of the murder weapon or the stolen goods, the means of entry into the building, the type of accelerant used to start the fire, and the type of clothing on the victim).

During an oral confession, the interrogator should refrain from taking any written notes. To do so may discourage the suspect from continuing with his confession.

After a suspect has related his general confession, the interrogator may return to the incorrect alternative that the suspect may have selected earlier, provided that it pertains to an essential legal aspect of the case. At this point, it is relatively easy to obtain a correction from the suspect because of his present penitent frame of mind, whereas previously it would have been inadvisable to do so. He now will usually answer any question as truthfully as he can. In other words, after a suspect begins to confess, he will continue to do so unless the interrogator becomes abrasive or offends the suspect by an impertinent attitude.

Consider once again the homicide case illustration in which Jack killed his wife and three children. Jack accepted the alternative choice that the knife was on the table. If the interrogator believes that the knife was actually in the drawer, and that the suspect carefully looked for and chose the knife he was going to use, then it becomes important to correct his original alternative choice so as to establish his actual purpose and intent. The suspect should be confronted with the interrogator's belief that the knife was in the drawer. He may do this by utilizing a second alternative in which the location of the knife in the drawer becomes the more acceptable choice. For instance:

> Jack, you said earlier that the knife was on the table and not in the drawer. Now, Jack, it is important to get to the whole truth. We know the knife was not on the table. My concern is whether it was just in the drawer, or if you brought it there with you, knowing all along that you were going to use it. Now Jack, was the knife in the drawer or did you bring it with you? It was in the drawer, wasn't it?

If the interrogator is accurate in his belief that the knife was in the drawer and not on the table, then, when first confronted with this statement, the suspect will seem uncomfortable, perhaps look down to the floor and change his posture or move around in the chair. This deceptive nonverbal behavior would be a clear signal for the interrogator to seek an admission that the knife was in the drawer and not out on the table.

To further illustrate this procedure for rectifying the suspect's acceptance of an incorrect alternative choice, consider the case of a man who is accused of taking indecent sexual liberties with a child by placing his finger into her vagina. As discussed in *Step 2* (Theme Development), the interrogator may develop the theme that the victim's parents were at fault for not expressing any love, affection, or concern for the child. As the interrogator approaches the alternative question stage of the confession, he may say:

> Art, did you only rub her down there or did you put your finger into her. I'm sure you only rubbed her a little bit down there and then stopped immediately. I know who's to blame. It's her mother for letting that girl run around like that. Art, tell me, did you put your finger in all the way or did you only rub her a little bit down there. Did you put your finger into her or only rub her a little bit? You just rubbed her didn't you, Art?

After the suspect nods his head signifying yes, the interrogator compliments the suspect for telling the truth and then proceeds to obtain the details of the act. Later, a correction can be obtained for an untruthful choice by the interrogator saying:

> Art, I know you're trying to tell the whole truth, and that's very important. But I'm sure that you did put your finger into her. Art, when you put your finger inside of her, were you trying to hurt her or did you just want to see how she would react? I know you weren't trying to hurt her. Did you put it in all the way or just a little bit? Art, I want the truth. How far did you put your finger into her, all the way or just a little bit?

The suspect may respond by saying, "a little bit." Thereafter, the interrogator should ask: "Up to the first joint or to the second one?" He should then have the suspect so indicate by pointing to the appropriate joint on his own finger. If the suspect in this child molesting case had told the truth originally about just rubbing the victim, he would not have allowed the interrogator to proceed with his questioning without making a strong denial of anything other than "rubbing."

During an oral confession, it is important that the interrogator be the only one in the room with the suspect. The presence of any other persons may discourage suspects from giving any details about their actions. Later, however, when the interrogator is satisfied that adequate details surrounding the commission of the crime have been obtained, he may decide that it would be appropriate to get another person to witness the oral confession. In such cases, the suspect should be told that the interrogator is going to step out of the room for a minute, but will return shortly. The interrogator should then locate someone to witness the suspect's general acknowledgment of guilt. This should be done without delay; otherwise, the suspect will have time to reconsider what was said and may decide to retract his confession.

The purpose of having the suspect's oral confession witnessed is two-fold: 1) after he has told two persons, instead of just one, that he did commit the crime, he has so fully committed himself that he will be less likely to refuse to give and sign a written statement, 2) in the event the suspect does refuse to give or sign a formal statement, there will be two persons available, the interrogator and the witness, to testify at trial to the fact that the suspect did confess orally. This will be more effective than the testimony of the interrogator alone.

Before the interrogator reenters the interrogation room with the witness, the witness should be told what the suspect's admissions were and what the witness should do after the interrogator and the witness enter the room together. The witness should also be told not to say anything at the outset; that the interrogator will initially do all the talking. Furthermore, the witness ought to be instructed to stand to the side, near the seated suspect, to look directly at the interrogator rather than at the suspect, and that the interrogator will relate to the witness the fundamental points of the suspect's confession.

When the suspect's oral confession is witnessed, he should *not* be asked to repeat the details; to do so would create an added burden for the suspect, who may then reassess his situation and retract the confession. Therefore, upon entering the room with the witness, the interrogator should say, "This is Officer Smith. He has been working with me on this case." Following this brief introduction, the interrogator should then repeat to the witness (Officer Smith) the essential elements of the suspect's confession. To illustrate this approach, in the previously described wife-killing case, the interrogator would state: "Jack said that he stabbed his wife last week, that the whole thing happened on the spur of the moment and without any previous planning; in fact, he said he went to her apartment to get some information for his lawyer about the divorce and that she started an argument with him. He also told me that he stabbed the children but only because they were crying and he didn't know what to do. He also said he intended to stab himself, but didn't do it and then left." Following this statement by the interrogator, the witness, pursuant to an earlier instruction to him, would ask a few confirmatory questions. The ensuing dialogue would be as follows:

Witness: Now, Jack, is what Mr. _____ [interrogator's name] just told me the complete truth?

Jack: Yes it is.

Witness: Jack, did you plan doing this before you went to the apartment?

Jack: No sir, it just happened. I can't even believe it happened.

Witness: Was anybody with you when you stabbed your wife and kids?

Jack: No, I was alone.

The purpose of having the witness ask a few questions is to have the suspect actually verbalize to the witness what had already been told to the interrogator. This will be more effective than a mere acknowledgment of the truth of what the interrogator told the witness.

In some cases, the witness may function as a supplementary interrogator to elicit, with more extensive questioning, details not disclosed to the principal interrogator. For instance, in an employee theft case the witness may ask questions about additional company thefts to the one or ones already admitted.

After the suspect has fully committed himself, the witness should leave the room and the interrogator then should proceed to obtain a full written confession. The essential elements necessary in a written confession and the appropriate procedural considerations are discussed in *Step 9.*

After having first heard the suspect's oral confession, if the interrogator senses that the suspect may change his mind if left alone while the interrogator went for the witness, a short, handwritten, and signed confession should be obtained from him before leaving the room for any period of time.

STEP 9: CONVERTING AN ORAL CONFESSION INTO A WRITTEN CONFESSION

Most confessed criminal offenders will subsequently deny their guilt and allege that they either did not confess or else were forced or induced to do so by physical abuse, threats, or promises of leniency. Occasionally, the defendant in a criminal case will even go so far as to say that he was compelled to sign a written confession without reading it or having had it read to him, or that he was forced to place his signature on a blank sheet of paper and all that appears above it was inserted later.

In a community or jurisdiction where the police enjoy the respect and confidence of the public, false claims of that nature are rather easily overcome; the prosecution may even secure a conviction on the basis of an oral, unwritten, or unrecorded confession with very little corroborating evidence. In most cases, however, the problem is much more difficult, and a written or recorded confession is considered far preferable to an oral one. When the confession is in writing, the controversy between the prosecution and the defense becomes more than merely a matter of whether or not the court or jury is to believe the oral testimony of the police or the accused; the written statement also lends considerable support to the prosecution's contention that the accused did, in fact, confess.

Although a confession may be sound-recorded or even videotaped, the preference among law enforcement officials including prosecutors, is for a written one. Among the various practical disadvantages attending the use of a sound-recorded or videotaped confession is the fact that a law enforcement agency that uses this means of preserving a confession may find it necessary to do so in all cases, despite the fact that in some cases, it is not feasible for one reason or another, to make a recording. A failure to follow the practice in a particular case will afford defense counsel an opportunity to effectively contend that the reason no recording was made is because the investigators employed interrogation methods that they did not want to have revealed by a sound-recorded or videotaped one. Moreover, when a law enforcement agency uses electronic equipment to record confessions, the argument may be advanced that all of the interrogation itself should have been recorded. This is obviously impractical, particularly within a large metropolitan police agency. Another point to consider is the fact that even a sound or videotaped recording of a confession is not immune from attack upon its validity. It does not constitute the kind of unassailable evidence that is sometimes attributed to it.

An excellent analysis of the issue of the utilization of tape-recordings, audio or visual, is presented in a 1982–83 report of a special study prepared for members of the Australasian Forces, entitled "Scientific and Technical Aids to Police Interview-Interrogation." The report was prepared by Detective Sergeant Luppo Prins of the Tasmanian Police, who extensively explored the practices for recording interrogations and confessions in the United States and England.

In his review of some police departments that have tape-recorded interviews and interrogations, the author reported the following observations:

1. Frequently both police officers present are engaged in the actual questioning. The tape does not indicate who is speaking and, therefore, transcribers who are unfamiliar with the voices would not be able to identify the speaker.
2. There tends to be consistent overspeaking. Both the interviewer and interviewee speak at once and, as a result, neither can be understood.
3. Both interviewer and interviewee sound very staid—almost mechanical—obviously extremely conscious of the tape recorder.
4. Background noises such as coughing, papers rustling, and chairs being moved, often interfere with audibility.
5. Foreign-speaking persons or those with broad accents are extremely difficult to understand on tape. Speech rapidity, slurring, etc. are also apparent. Some poorly educated suspects are almost incoherent.
6. Descriptions by head, eye, or hand movement are unable to be conveyed on tape to a listener. They require verbal clarification.
7. Evidence that would be ruled inadmissible, e.g., prejudicial to accused, is often on tape, thus creating problems of tape-editing for court purposes.

8. Much irrelevant material on tape can prolong interview and court proceedings.
9. Several tapes had malfunctioned and part of the interview was lost, thus destroying the credibility of the whole interview.

The report concluded:

"Significantly, since the tape-recording experiment commenced, the number of persons interviewed at the station has decreased; the number of persons making confessions during interrogation has decreased, and the number charged has decreased. As a result, the crime clean-up rate has also decreased. Increases have been shown of the following: 1) refusal of suspects to speak at all, 2) refusal to admit other offenses, and 3) refusal to nominate co-offenders."

It is essential that an oral confession be reduced to writing and be signed as soon as possible. The next morning, or even a few hours after the oral confession, may be too late, because the confessor may have reflected upon the legal consequences of his confession and retract it. No time should be lost, therefore, in preparing for and obtaining a written, signed confession. If time and circumstances do not afford the opportunity for a stenographic transcription, or even for writing out a detailed confession, the interrogator should write or type a brief statement of what the suspect orally related—even if only two or three sentences long—and present it to the confessor for signature. Once an offender has committed himself in writing, regardless of its brevity, there is a reduced probability that he will refuse later on to make and sign a more detailed version of the crime.

Many good cases have been lost because an interrogator assumed that the next morning, or a few hours later, would be time enough to have a confession written and signed, only to find that, in the meantime, the offender had changed his mind about admitting guilt. It is a safe practice, therefore, to lose no more time than is absolutely necessary in obtaining some kind of signed statement. It may even be in the form of a suggested note or letter addressed to a relative, friend, or employer, explaining why the writer committed the offense. Such a document will serve as security against a change of mind or a denial during the period before the taking of a formal, detailed statement.

In addition to the avoidance of a time delay with respect to a written admission, it is also advisable to obtain the statement, or even the complete written confession itself, in the same room where the interrogation was conducted. A change to another place, or even to another room close by, may have the psychological effect of a retraction of the oral confession.

Warning of Constitutional Rights

Even though the warnings required by *Miranda v. Arizona* to be given custodial suspects have been issued before the interrogation began, it is advisable, nevertheless, to repeat the warnings at the beginning of the written confession, making reference, of course, to the fact that the suspect had received them earlier. One reason for this reference is to establish further evidence that the warnings had been given at the required time, prior to any interrogation, rather than only at the time of the taking of the formal confession. Then, too, because a suspect has a right at any time to revoke his waiver of rights, the incorporation of the warnings in the confession itself will thereby preserve evidence of the fact that the waiver was a continuing one up to the time of the signing of the confession. Moreover, at this stage, because the suspect has already confessed orally, the incorporation of the warnings into the written confession is not likely to deter him from signing the document with the warnings in it. The psychological factors are now different, obviously, from those prevailing at the time when an interrogator seeks a waiver of *Miranda* rights before an interrogation has even begun.

Printed forms are usually available for the typing or handwriting of a confession for submission to the confessor for his or her signature. It should start with a statement such as the following one:

Having been told, before being questioned about the following offense, of my right to remain silent, that anything I say could be used against me, and that I had a right to a lawyer, without cost if I could not afford one, I nevertheless was willing to talk and I also am now willing to give this written statements:

In the event the confessor informs the interrogator that he does not wish to make or to sign the statement, or that a lawyer is wanted, the interrogator must cease any further questioning or recording. Nevertheless, the oral confession is still usable as evidence. A United States Supreme Court decision to that effect is discussed in Chapter 8 of this text.

If the oral confession has been made to the police by a person not in custody when the interrogation began, and to whom, therefore, the warnings did not have to be issued initially, it is advisable, as a precautionary measure, that they be given now at the start of the written confession in the way and manner just described, including the statement of waiver.

A private security officer does not have to issue the warnings to any suspect, even one under arrest, unless the security officer is empowered with full police authority or is acting in conjunction with the police. (The legal authority in support of that proposition is presented Chapter 8 of this text.)

The Preparation and Form of the Written Confession

A written confession may be prepared in the form of questions (by the interrogator) and answers (by the confessor), or in the form of a narration by the confessor. Such confessions may be written out by hand, typed by the interrogator, or taken down by a stenographer and transcribed into typewritten form.

Most prosecutors prefer the question-and-answer format of confession; others prefer the narrative form. Perhaps the best procedure is to effect a compromise whereby the preliminary and concluding aspects of the offense are elicited by means of specific questions from the interrogator, but the details of the actual occurrence are given by the confessor in narrative form. For instance, the suspect may be asked specific questions as to his name, whether or not he is known by any alias, his address, age, place of employment, whether (in some types of situations) he understands and reads the English language, the time he arrived at the scene of the crime, and the names of persons who were with him up to that time; then, after the interrogator's questions have brought the suspect right up to the time and place of the crime, he may be asked, "What happened then?" Thereafter, as long as the suspect confines himself to an orderly recitation of the occurrence, he should be permitted to continue to narrate what happened. If he hesitates or seems to be relating events out of sequence, the interrogator can interpose a specific question in order to have the subject continue in an orderly fashion. At the same time, however, some irrelevant talking should be permitted, because its very irrelevancy may be considered as evidence of the voluntariness of the confession.

After the main occurrence has been covered in the confession, the interrogator may return to the use of specific questions, such as "Where did you go then?" "What time did you get there?" etc. Specific questions may also be used, of course, to bring out previously revealed facts that were omitted from the suspect's narrative portion of the statement.

In addition to the previously mentioned advantages, a question-and-answer format of confession also lends itself more readily to the deletion of certain parts, if the trial court should consider any deletion necessary before the confession is read to the jury. All of the interrogator's questions should be short, very simply worded, and "to the point"; the use of lengthy, complicated questions and the kind of answers that are likely to follow will render the document much less impressive.

Under no circumstances should a confessor be put under oath by a notary public, justice of the peace, or by anyone else before the taking of a confession. Such a practice has been viewed by some courts as a coercive influence that will nullify the legal validity of the confession.

A preference generally prevails for having a stenographer record the confession in shorthand or stenotype for later transcription into a typewritten document that will be read to, or by, the confessor, and then signed by him. Moreover, some interrogators, including the authors, prefer that the stenographer be a woman rather than a man, and that she also sign the confession as a witness. Women stenographers can be excellent safeguards against fake claims of brutality or other improper conduct on the part of the interrogator. A jury is not apt to believe that she would be a participant or observer in any such impropriety. In fact, a male defense counsel is sometimes completely dissuaded from making such a claim once he knows that the stenographer is a woman. In other words, a confession that is taken down and transcribed by a woman can be a much more unassailable piece of evidence than one taken by a male stenographer or typist. In a sex offense case situation, if the confessor seems too embarrassed to talk in the presence of a female stenographer he should be told that she has heard hundreds of statements equal to or far worse than anything he may say.

The stenographer who has a confession assignment should be briefed about the case and be given the suspect's name and other such information before entering the interrogation room. She should also be instructed to sit off to the side of the suspect rather than in front of him and refrain from talking to the interrogator or asking any questions other than perhaps to have the interrogator or suspect speak louder or more slowly, or to repeat something that was not sufficiently audible for recording purposes.

For the psychological effect on the jury when the written confession is read, it is advisable to ask the confessor, very early in the confession, a question that will call for an acknowledgment that he committed the crime. This can be done after initial questions about name, address, age, etc. (For example, "As regards the fire in the store at First and Main Streets, do you know how it started?" Answer: "I started it.") Then, after that acknowledgment, the interrogator can continue with further preliminary questions as he leads up to the main event and asks the suspect to narrate the details of what occurred.

Early acknowledgment of guilt in a confession will serve to arouse immediate interest in the document by the jury as it is read. It makes clear to the jury at the very outset that what is being read is a confession of guilt, and jury members will then follow more closely the details that are subsequently disclosed. An additional advantage of early acknowledgment of guilt is the effect it has on the confessor personally. The suspect who has thus committed himself is far less likely to balk at continuing with the details.

The details of a confession should not only contain the details of the offense itself, such as the date, time, place, motive, and manner of its commission, but also such things as the places where the confessor had been before and after the crime, and the names of individuals he saw and talked to before and after the event. In some instances, the confessor should also be asked to describe the clothing he wore at the time because this may be an important factor with respect to the courtroom identification testimony by the victim or witnesses.

During the taking of a confession, no one should be in the interrogation room other than the confessor, interrogator, and stenographer. In addition to the previously discussed psychological reasons for such privacy, there is a persuasive legal factor. In some jurisdictions, each person present during the interrogation or the taking of a confession will have to be produced as a witness at the trial whenever the defendant contends that improper methods were used to obtain his confession. This obviously imposes a burden upon the prosecution that can and should be avoided.

Even in those instances where the interrogator himself writes or types the confession, there is no need to have a third person present to actually witness its preparation or signing. The confessor's subsequent acknowledgment to a witness or witnesses that the written confession and signature are his will be sufficient.

The person who types the confession should avoid placing a signature line at the end of it for two reasons: 1) the line connotes too much legalism and may discourage the confessor from affixing his signature to the document; 2) in the event that a confessor refuses to sign the confession, the document will look far better without the unused signature line on it. An unsigned confession has been held to be usable as evidence, as long as the interrogator can testify that it accurately represents what the defendant said. Moreover, a preceding oral confession will still be usable, even if a typed one is rejected.

Readable and Understandable Language

Throughout the taking of the confession, the interrogator must always be on guard to see that its contents will be readily understood and easily followed by a reader or subsequent listener who has no other independent knowledge as to what occurred. All too often, the interrogator neglects to realize that although what is going into the confession is perfectly clear to him, its contents may be vague and indefinite to others, including the judge or jury who will hear the case. For instance, when a person has orally confessed to a rape, the interrogator who takes the written confession knows full well what the confessor means when he admits he did "it", but "it" may be rather meaningless to someone else. Also, when a confessor says he set fire to "the place," and that it was on "that night," the person who does not have the benefit of other independent knowledge about "the place" or "that night" is at a loss to comprehend the confession. Moreover, when a confession is that vague and indefinite, a trial judge may refuse to let it be used at all.

The way to clarify indefinite words or phrases is to interrupt the confessor and ask a question that will explain away the uncertainty. For instance, in a rape case, if the confessor speaks in terms of "it," he may be asked, "What do you mean 'it'?" or "By 'it,' you mean sexual intercourse [or the suspect's equivalent terminology]?" In an arson case, the suspect may be asked, "What do you mean by 'place?' ", or "By 'the place' you mean the house at the corner of First and Main Streets in this city?" or "What do you mean by 'that night?'", or "By 'that night,' you mean the night of July 10th of this year?" Furthermore, the language of the statement should clearly identify the legal nature of the act. For example, in a theft case, the word "steal," rather than "take," should be used.

Avoidance of Leading Questions

In a confession in which the interrogator does most of the talking, and which consists primarily of "yes" or "no" answers, it is not nearly so convincing and effective as one in which the interrogator plays the minor part and the confessor the leading role of both informer and confessor. It is highly important, therefore, that the interrogator let the confessor supply the details of the occurrence and, to this end, the interrogator should avoid or at least minimize the use of leading questions.

To illustrate the point, suppose a person is in the process of confessing a murder in which it is a known fact that the gun involved in the crime was thrown away under a certain house. The confessor has been giving various details of the crime and the interrogator is about to inquire regarding the disposal of the gun. At this stage, some interrogators may say, "Then you threw the gun under the house, didn't you?"—a question calling merely for a "yes" answer. Far more convincing to a court or jury is to have the gun details appear in answer to a nonleading question, such as: "Then what did you do with the gun?"—a question calling for detailed information from the confessor himself.

In addition to the forgoing advantages attending nonleading questions, there is another factor to be considered. An interrogator may encounter a situation—although its occurrence will be exceedingly rare—where subsequent to the confession, he may become skeptical as to its validity, particularly when there is some suspicion that the confessor is a pathological liar and may be absolutely innocent of the crime to which the confession was made. In such instances, the interrogator will find considerable comfort in being able to evaluate the confession in the light of certain known facts, and this can ordinarily be done, unless during the interrogation those facts were disclosed to the suspect in the form of leading questions. In other words, in the above-stated hypothetical case situation regarding the gun under the house, the interrogator who asked the suspect what he had done with the gun, and who was told, "I threw it under the house" (where the gun was actually found), is in a far more desirable position than the now skeptical interrogator who tells the suspect, "Then you threw the gun under the house, didn't you?" and merely receives a "yes" answer.

Another case illustration of the advisability of not disclosing all of the details of a crime to the suspect is one in which an elderly woman was brutally assaulted sexually and killed while in the kitchen of her home. The suspect who confessed to the offense did so rather quickly and in such a manner that the interrogator wondered whether the confession was genuine. Fortunately, no one had told the suspect the details of the offense, such as the exact nature of the victim's injuries and the place where certain objects had been thrown; nor had anyone described the kitchen itself to the suspect. An accurate revelation by him of these various details, including an accurate description of the kitchen, quickly allayed the interrogator's concern as to the validity of the confession. Had the suspect been told all this before his confession, the case would have given the interrogator considerable concern.

Confessor's Own Language

In the preparation of the written confession, no attempt should be made to improve the language used by the confessor himself. The language used represents that person's confession and should be in the confessor's original words; otherwise, a judge or jury may be reluctant to believe it emanated from a defendant whose education may have ended at the third grade but whose confession contained the language of a college graduate. Also, in a sex offense case, the confessor's own terminology should go into the written confession without any attempt being made by the interrogator to "clean it up." For instance, the words "sexual intercourse," "vagina," or "anal penetration" should not be substituted for the crude language used by the confessor. Along the same line, if the suspect is to write out a confession, the interrogator should not assist in the spelling of any of the words even if asked to do so. The suspect should be told to do the best he can with the spelling.

Personal History Questions

At the trial, the offender may allege that the confession represents only what he had been told to say—that the interrogator "put the words into my mouth." An excellent precautionary measure to effectively meet such a defense is the practice of incorporating in the confession a number of more or less irrelevant questions calling for answers known only to the offender. For instance, the suspect may be asked the name of the grade school he attended, or the place or hospital in which he was born, or for other similar information. Care must be exercised, however, to avoid questions that call for answers about which the confessor may not be sure (e.g., the name of his grade school principal).

When accurate personal information is included in a confession, the prosecutor may point to it as evidence that the accused actually gave the information contained in the confession and was not merely accommodating the interrogator by repeating what he was told to say.

On occasion the confession should reflect the fact that the suspect had the opportunity to satisfy such physical needs as being able to use the washroom facilities or having something to eat or drink, particularly if the circumstances surrounding the interrogation involved several hours. It also may be important in some situations to clarify with the suspect whether or not any drugs or alcohol had been consumed within the previous 12 hours. This may become relevant in those cases where the defendant later claims to have been under the influence of drugs or alcohol at the time of his alleged confession.

Intentional Errors for Correction by the Confessor

For many of the same reasons that personal history data are incorporated into the confession, it is a good practice to purposely arrange for the inclusion, on each page of the confession, one or two errors, such as an incorrect name of a person or street, which will be subject to later correction by the confessor when the document is read by or to him. Any such corrections, of course, should be in the confessor's own handwriting, accompanied by his initials or signature in the margin alongside the corrections. When confronted at the trial with a confession bearing corrections of this nature, the confessor will encounter considerable difficulty in denying reading the document before signing it.

Reading and Signing the Confession

It is advisable for the interrogator to read aloud a carbon or photocopy of the confession as the confessor follows the original one word for word. When the previously described intentional errors are reached, the suspect will usually call them to the interrogator's attention; to play it safe, however, the interrogator should keep the errors in mind and raise a question about them in the event the suspect neglects to do so.

In addition to placing of initials or signature alongside corrections, the suspect should be requested to place an "OK," followed by his initials or signature, at the bottom of each page after the contents have been read by or to him. Then, at the end of the confession, it is well to have the offender write out, in his own hand, some such statement as the following: "I have read this statement of mine and it is the truth. I made it of my own free will, without any threats or promises having been made to me be anyone." After this should appear the signature.

When the time comes for the signing of a confession, the interrogator should never say, "Sign here." It is much better, psychologically, to say, "Put your name here," or "Write your name here" while pointing out the place for the signature. The word "sign" connotes too much legalism.

A suspect who balks at signing the confession may be told that the already disclosed information is something that only the offender could know, that he has already acknowledged the content of the statement to be true, and that both the interrogator and stenographer can testify that the statement was made. The suspect also may be told that his signature would demonstrate sincerity and would also demonstrate that the suspect cooperated in the investigation.

In the event that the confessor is illiterate, there is very little purpose to be served by having him sign, or even place his mark (an X) on a typewritten confession. Nevertheless, an unsigned typewritten copy may be helpful at the trial. The interrogator would be permitted to testify not only that the copy accurately represents what the accused said, but also that after it was read to him he acknowledged it to be true. In such instances, it is advisable for the prosecutor to offer as a witness the stenographer who recorded the confession and who could testify directly from the shorthand notes.

Another possibility in cases involving illiterate confessors is to make a sound recording of their confessions, even though, as previously stated, written confessions are generally preferable.

Witnesses

In most instances where the offender does not object to the oral confession being reduced to writing, he will readily sing it in the presence of one or more witnesses in addition to the interrogator. As already stated, however, it is better to maintain the element of privacy throughout the signing of the confession. Moreover, there are some occasions when a hesitating and wavering confessor may balk at the signing if other persons, and particularly uniformed police officers, enter the room for the obvious purpose of witnessing the signature.

A written confession actually need not be signed by any witnesses. All that is required is to have some one person authenticate it—someone who can testify that he saw the defendant sign it and acknowledge its truthfulness. Indispensable, of course, will be the testimony of the interrogator that the accused voluntarily made the confession and that the written document was read by or to him before it was signed.

With respect to all of these various considerations regarding written confessions, the fact should be borne in mind that an oral confession is as admissible in evidence as a written one, the only difference being the greater weight and credibility usually given to the written, signed confession.

Only One Written Confession

An interrogator should always seek to take as full and complete a confession as may be necessary for use as evidence at the trial. This does not necessarily mean that it must be lengthy; as a matter of fact, the ordinary crime can be—and should be—adequately related within a relatively few pages if the interrogator is aware of the essential requirements of a confession. A relatively short, although complete, written confession is a much more persuasive document than one that is cluttered with unnecessary verbiage and a lot of irrelevant facts.

If the interrogator's written confession is inadequate, the prosecuting attorney may have to take a second one. This duplication may add to the prosecutor's trial court difficulties, because defense counsel may demand an inspection of the first one, and an attempt will be made to capitalize on whatever differences, even very minor ones, that may be present between the two. In fact, unfavorable inferences may be drawn by the jury itself, without any aid from defense counsel.

Whenever an interrogator is unskilled in the taking of an adequate written confession, or lacks the time or facilities to do so, a suitable alternative is to merely write out, and have the suspect sign, a very brief statement acknowledging the commission of the offense, or else have the suspect write it himself, and then leave to the prosecuting attorney the preparation of one that will incorporate the full details.

On those occasions when a written confession is later considered inadequate, such as those lacking in some essential details, the interrogator should prepare an entirely new confession rather than one that merely supplements the first confession. This will serve to minimize the controversies and legal difficulties that would otherwise be presented by each document's dependence upon the other for completeness.

In the evaluation of a written confession, either by the interrogator or by a prosecuting attorney, consideration should be given to the fact that it is a rather common occurrence for the confessor to a major crime to lie about some incidental aspect(s) of the offense. For instance, a murderer may deny that he indulged in a certain sex activity prior to the killing of a female victim, when the circumstantial evidence clearly established that sexual conduct preceded the killing. The reason for this is that in the suspect's own mind, the killing is not nearly so revolting as the forcible sexual act itself. Therefore, a discrepancy of this kind between the confessor's statement and circumstantial evidence of this type should not be considered as discrediting an acknowledgment of guilt.

In an effort to minimize the possibility or the extent of a confessor's lying about some incidental aspect of the occurrence, the interrogator should follow a practice of having the confessor relate all the details of the crime before any effort is made to reduce the confession to writing (*Step*

8); if there seems to be any false statement or any withholding of pertinent information, then is the time to try to obtain the complete truth rather than during the taking of the written confession.

In instances where the written confession is to be taken by someone other than the interrogator who obtained the oral confession, or where the taking of a second confession is considered necessary because of some shortcoming or defect in the original one, the second interrogator (e.g., a prosecuting attorney) should first familiarize himself very thoroughly with the case and also with whatever is known about the suspect. Following this, he should, as a rule, talk to the suspect alone and listen to the confession before any attempt is made to reduce it to writing. In this way, the interrogator will become acquainted with the suspect and therefore be better prepared to question him at the time when the confession is to be reduced to writing.

Although the authors have referred to the procedure whereby prosecutors exercise the responsibility of taking a second or final statement of the confession, prosecutors must be mindful of the problem they may encounter if circumstances later require their own testimonies as witnesses to authenticate the confession. This is particularly so with regard to those instances where, in a small community, there may be only one prosecutor. The courts view with considerable disfavor the appearance of a prosecutor as a witness in the very case he is prosecuting.

Confining Confession to One Crime

When a person confesses two or more crimes, separate confessions should be taken of each one, unless the crimes are so closely related in point of time, place, or other circumstance that the account of one crime cannot be related without referring to the others. For instance, if a suspect confesses several robberies or several burglaries, or a robbery and a burglary, a separate confession should, as a rule, be taken of each offense. The exceptions occur when several persons are robbed at the same time, or when the occupant of a burglarized home is also robbed by the burglar, or when a kidnapped person is also murdered. In such instances, the crimes are so closely related that it is practically impossible to describe one offense without referring to the other offense or offenses. The situation is different, of course, as regards the robbery of John Jones on Monday night and a robbery of Frank Smith on Wednesday night. Either of such offenses can be described without a reference to the other one. Moreover, the courts hold that it is improper, because of the inherent prejudicial effect, to offer evidence to a jury about a crime other than the one for which the defendant is on trial. There are certain exceptions where, at trial, evidence of another crime or crimes may be presented to establish motive, lack of accident, etc., but those situations are of no practical concern to the person taking a confession. Consequently, each offense should be treated separately when taking written or recorded confessions.

For similar reasons, a confession should never contain any reference to the fact that a suspect had previously been arrested or convicted. Any such statement would have to be deleted from the confession before it could be accepted in evidence at the trial.

Physical Evidence, Photographs, and Sketches

When a crime weapon is referred to in a confession, and the weapon has been recovered and is available (either at the time of, or subsequent to, the written confession) a separate, supplemental statement may be obtained about the weapon itself. It should be shown to the suspect, who should be asked if it is the weapon he used. Following an affirmative answer, the suspect should be asked to put an identifying mark on it — his initials, for instance. Then a written statement should be prepared in which the suspect merely states and signs something to this effect: "This 38-caliber (Colt) revolver [or knife] with my initials (J.B.) on the handle is the gun I used in the robbery and shooting [or in the stabbing] of John Jones last Monday, March 1, 1985, at First and Main Streets in this city of Hamlet." Such a statement may be put on a card and actually tied to the weapon itself.

A separate statement of this type may be more effective than a similar statement incorporated in the confession itself because the latter would break the continuity of the account of what occurred. Then, too, if the weapon is a bloody knife or other such instrument, and it is shown to the suspect during the taking of the written confession, it may cause him to balk at continuing with the confession. Moreover, in the reading of a confession to the jury, the pause for the weapon identification may interfere with an otherwise orderly recitation of the facts of the occurrence.

Photographs of the crime scene may also serve as the basis for a supplemental statement. For instance, if a photograph shows the location of the place where an arson fire started, and it also shows the container in which the flammable fluid was transported, the suspect may be asked to point them out on the photograph and to place a number alongside each one. Then, on the back of the photograph or on a separate sheet of paper that can be attached to the photograph, the confessor should be asked to write out: "On this photograph of the interior of the house at First and Main Street, A is where I started the fire; B is the can in which I carried the gasoline." Such a statement should then be signed, of course.

If no photographs are available, there may be occasions when it will be advisable to have the confessor make a sketch of the crime scene and include in it the location of certain objects or the place where something of significance occurred. Accompanying the sketch should be a signed statement such as has been suggested for use with a photograph.

The value of having a suspect make a sketch of the crime scene is well illustrated by the following case: An elderly recluse was murdered and his cabin was burned in an effort to conceal the murder. Six years later, one of the authors interrogated a suspect and obtained a confession from him. He was then asked to make a sketch of the cabin—locating the bed, the stove, and other such objects. His sketch located these various objects just as they appeared in a photograph that investigators had made immediately after the crime. It proved to be of considerable value as further evidence of the confessor's guilt.

Safeguarding the Effectiveness of the Confession

PRESERVATION OF STENOGRAPHIC NOTES

Although a confession written and signed as previously outlined will be difficult to attack in court, there may be occasions when it will become necessary to refute certain objections to it by calling as a witness the steneographer who prepared the typewritten copy from her shorthand notes. The only way this can be done, of course, is to have the stenographer read to the court and jury the original shorthand notes. It is advisable, therefore, that these notes be preserved until the case has been finalized in court.

NOTES REGARDING CONDITIONS AND CIRCUMSTANCES UNDER WHICH THE ORAL AND WRITTEN CONFESSIONS WERE OBTAINED

At the time of trial, usually several months after the confession, an interrogator may be cross-examined at considerable length regarding the conditions and circumstances under which the confession was obtained. To meet such a contingency, he should never rely solely upon memory. It is desirable, therefore, to keep notes regarding such matters as the issuance of the Miranda warnings, the time when the interrogation was begun and ended, the time when the confession was signed, the names of the persons who witnessed the confession, and also information as to the general condition of the interrogation room, particularly with reference to its lighting arrangements and approximate temperature.

PHOTOGRAPH AND MEDICAL EXAMINATION OF CONFESSOR

In communities where defense counsel indulge in a rather routine practice of attempting to show that the police interrogators employ "third degree" methods to obtain confessions, much can be gained, if time and circumstances permit, by photographing the confessor after the confession. The photographs should include not only a front view but also both side views of him. However, the photographs should not be taken of the suspect in a posed position; it is much better to take them while he is talking to someone and perhaps also while smoking.

Moreover, whenever such defense tactics are anticipated in important cases, it may be well to have a physician examine the confessor so as to be able to establish at his trial the lack of bruises or other alleged evidence of the "third degree."

CONFESSION NOT END OF INVESTIGATION

Many investigators have the impression that once a confession has been obtained, the investigation is ended, but seldom, if ever, is this true.

A confession unsubstantiated by other evidence is far less effective at the trial than one that has been investigated and subjected to verification or supporting evidence. For instance, assume that a confessed murderer has revealed when and where he purchased the knife used in the killing; he also identified a gas station where he had obtained a washroom key so he could wash his bloody hands; and he told of a chance meeting he had had with an acquaintance as he left the gas station. There should then be an immediate investigation regarding the purchase of the knife. If the seller remembers the transaction, he should be asked to give a signed statement about it. This will serve to ensure his cooperation at the time of the trial; furthermore, it will minimize the risk of his possible appearance as a witness for the defense to deny any such transaction. For similar reasons, interviews should be conducted with, and written statements obtained from, the gas station attendant who gave the suspect the key and who may have observed blood on the suspect's hands. Perhaps the suspect may have even made a significant comment about the blood. Then, too, the suspect's acquaintance should be interviewed and a written statement sought from him also.

A confession thus supported and substantiated will be far more valuable than the bare document itself. Moreover, there will be many occasions when a thorough postconfession investigation will produce enough incriminating evidence to render unnecessary the use of the confession itself.

In the case where a postconfession investigation has resulted in the discovery and procurement of overwhelming physical and circumstantial evidence of guilt, it is well for the prosecuting attorney of the jurisdiction to anticipate a possible plea of insanity. It is advisable, therefore, for him to arrange for the immediate taking of signed statements from the offender's relatives and friends, in which they express themselves as to his mental condition (e.g., whether he was normal, whether he had ever sustained a head injury). At this stage of the case, the truth will be more prevalent than at the time of trial.

Another matter that deserves a prosecutor's serious consideration is the advisability of trying the case without even using the confession. Many prosecutors are of the view that if there is sufficient other evidence of guilt, procured either before or after the confession, it is better to rely upon such evidence and not to use the confession as part of the prosecution's case in chief. The confession will be available, of course, for rebuttal purposes or for the impeachment of the confessor if he takes the stand and testifies.

The principal reason for the forgoing practice of omitting the confession from the prosecution's proof of guilt is the fact that an attack on the confession and on the interrogator who obtained it—however unfounded the attack may be—might divert the jury's attention from the significance and weight of all the physical or circumstantial evidence presented by the prosecution. Each case, of course, will present its own separate problem, and, consequently, a prosecutor should not follow any set rule about the use or nonuse of a confession as evidence.

Postconfession Interviews

After a person confesses a crime, he usually is very willing, perhaps even anxious, to talk further with the interrogator—to talk about his troubles generally. The confessor is also usually willing to discuss the reasons why he confessed, even to the extent of answering the interrogator's specific questions as to the impact of particular techniques that the interrogator employed to obtain the confession. Here, then, is an excellent opportunity for an interrogator to improve his knowledge and skill. The authors suggest, therefore, that whenever time and circumstances permit, the interrogator should conduct a postconfession interview. It will be a highly rewarding exprerience in several respects.

First, what the interrogator learns from one confessed offender can be employed to good advantage in the interrogation of others, particularly those who have committed similar offenses. Second, and of even greater importance, such postconfession interviews will permit the interrogator to obtain an insight into human nature that cannot possibly be obtained in any other way or from any other source. Moreover, the greater the insight, the more understanding and sympathetic he will become regarding all criminal behavior and all criminal offenders. Eventually, the interrogator will develop an attitude that will prevent him from ever "hating" anyone— regardless of the kind of crime committed. This attitude is a prime requisite for effective interrogation. Criminal offenders will intuitively recognize whether or not an interrogator has such an attitude, and they will find it easier to talk and to confess to an understanding, sympathetic interrogator than to one who lacks these qualities.

A person who aspires to become a skillful interrogator need not be concerned over the possibility that the development of an understanding, sympathetic attitude will make a "softy" of him and thereby ultimately destroy the very skill that must be achieved. That will not happen—at least not as a consequence of an understanding, sympathetic attitude. Not one of the effective interrrogators known by the authors has ever sustained a diminution of effectiveness by reason of the development of such attitude. To the contrary, it has always produced a higher degree of interrogation skill than that previously possessed.

The authors have conducted postconfession interviews on numerous occasions over the years. In fact, postconfession interviews are the source of much of the information upon which many of the forgoing techniques are based. The authors even followed the practice to the extent that on one occasion, while obtaining case materials for the original (1942) predecessor of the present text, a rapist-murderer was interviewed in his death cell a few days before his execution—for the sole purpose of ascertaining why he confessed. In that death cell, one of the authors obtained the most valuable lesson in criminal interrogation he had ever received from any single source. His "instructor" was well qualified. He had committed a series of rapes that had culminated in the murder of his victim. The night he confessed, there was no opportunity for a postconfession interview, but the opportunity eventually presented itself after the offender's trial at which he unsuccessfully pleaded insanity and after which became reconciled to the fate that awaited him. He not only talked freely, but also frankly specified and discussed the various interrogation techniques that were most effective in persuading him to confess. He also supplied the interviewer with information that permitted the formulation of a new technique, which has been used effectively ever since in other similar cases.

The postconfession interview may be conducted during the time when the stenographer is typing up the confession. In addition to the factor of time conservation, it is well to keep the confessor occupied during this period as a safeguard against a change of attitude and a possible retraction of the oral confession or a refusal to sign the typewritten one.

A postinterrogation interview should consist of asking such questions as the following:

1. What did you think about most during the interview?
2. Did you attempt to say or do anything to throw the interviewer off the track?
3. What was the most difficult obstacle for you to overcome in telling the truth?

4. Could the interviewer have said or done anything differently that would have made it easier for you to tell the truth?
5. Was anything said or done during the interview that prompted you to hold back the truth for a while?
6. What was the most significant thing the interviewer did or said that led you to tell the truth?
7. Are there any other comments or observations you would like to make about your interview today?

CHAPTER SEVEN

General Recommendations and Suggestions to Interrogators

THE EXERCISE OF PATIENCE AND PERSISTENCE

It is merciless, or rather psychologically wrong, to expect anyone boldly and directly to confess his crime.... We must smooth the way, render the task easy. (Hans Gross, *Criminal Investigation*, 1907., p. 120)

An interrogator should never lose sight of the fact that when a criminal offender is asked to confess a crime, a great deal is being requested. A confession may mean the loss of liberty or even life. Moreover, it is ordinarily difficult for anyone to admit even a simple mistake that involves no possible penal consequences, or perhaps not even any social stigma. There is no reason, therefore, why a criminal offender should be expected to confess without hesitation and reluctance, particularly when the case is one in which there is little or no provable evidence of guilt at the time of the interrogation. It is necessary, therefore, that the interrogator possess the quality of patience. The lack of it, or a driving urge to "get the job done quickly," may be an asset insofar as certain other types of police work are concerned (e.g., field investigations), but such characteristics in an interrogator are definitely undesirable.

Once a suspect senses the fact that the interrogator is impatient, he is thereby encouraged to persist in deception. The suspect develops the attitude that by holding out, the interrogator will soon give up. Then, too, the emotional factor of impatience will interfere with the interrogator's exercise of sound judgment and reasoning that the task at hand demands. Moreover, impatience may lead to anger and the interrogator will then become personally involved in what should be strictly a professional undertaking. That anger may produce threats or the use of physical force, endangering the welfare and security of the innocent or else eliciting from the guilty a confession that is legally valueless as evidence.

Not only must the interrogator have patience, but it must also be displayed. It is well, therefore, to get the idea across, in most case situations, that the interrogator has "all the time in the world." He may even express those exact words. (In some cases of a minor nature, however, the opposite impression should be given—that the case is not deserving of a lot of time and effort and that the interrogator has more important tasks to perform.)

Another prime requisite for a successful interrogation, in addition to patience, is persistence. In this respect, the following rule of thumb is a helpful one for an interrogator to follow: *Never conclude an interrogation at the time when you feel discouraged and ready to give up, but continue for a little while longer—if only for 10 or 15 minutes.* The authors have observed many instances in which the offender confessed, or later said he had decided to confess, just at the very time when the interrogator was ready to abandon, or did abandon, his efforts. The reason for this occurrence is the fact that, ordinarily, the time when the interrogator becomes discouraged coincides with the time when the suspect fully realizes the futility of continued lying.

During the above-suggested "overtime" periods, the interrogator should devote attention to the main aspects of the case. Aimless, irrelevant talking at this point will prove fruitless.

When the interrogator feels that he has expended all possible techniques, it is helpful, in many instances, to leave the subject alone in the interrogation room for awhile, but only after saying to him before departing: "Think it over, Joe; I'll be back in a few minutes." Upon returning to the interrogation room, the interrogator should be seated, and then resume the interrogation by first saying something like: "Well, Joe, what about it?" During the period when the suspect is left alone, he will probably do a lot of thinking and may conclude that the time is at hand for telling the truth.

With respect to persistence, it is well for the interrogator to bear in mind that on many occasions, the suspect who seems tough and not likely to confess is actually more vulnerable to an effective interrogation than some suspects who give the impression of being rather easy.

In considering the suggestion of persistence, it is important for interrogators to be mindful of the fact that they are not privileged to conduct unreasonably long interrogations. An unduly prolonged one may render a confession unusable as evidence.

MAKE NO PROMISES WHEN ASKED "WHAT WILL HAPPEN TO ME IF I TELL THE TRUTH?"

Whenever a suspect under interrogation makes an inquiry such as, "What will happen to me if I tell you the truth?" or "Do you think I'll go to jail if I confess?" under no circumstances should the interrogator point out any of the possible consequences of a confession, nor should he hold out any inducement whatsoever. Any such reply would nullify the legal validity of the confession that may follow, and rightly so, because a promise of leniency or immunity may induce an innocent person to confess. Moreover, the interrogator should realize that whenever a suspect raises a question of that sort, he is, in effect, beginning a confession. For these two reasons, therefore, the interrogator's reply should be somewhat as follows: "Joe, I can't tell you what will happen. I'm in no position to say. I don't have the authority, and it wouldn't be fair if I made any commitment to you. Joe, my advice to you is to tell the truth—and to tell it now. Then if you think you have a break coming, talk it over with the district attorney or the judge." Immediately thereafter, the interrogator should ask a detail question, such as where, how, when, or why the subject did the act in question.

By responding to the suspect's "What will happen to me" question in the above-suggested way, the interrogator displays an attitude of fair play, which is quite impressive. Moreover, if the offender later retracts the confession on the grounds that it was obtained as a result of promises and inducements, the interrogator can in all sincerity relate the forgoing comments to good advantage. The issue as to what promises are and are not legally permissible is discussed in Chapter 8 of this text.

VIEW WITH SKEPTICISM THE "CONSCIENCE-STRICKEN" CONFESSION

Criminal offenders whose guilt is unknown to the police will rarely surrender themselves and confess their guilt. The instinct for self-preservation stands in the way. Consequently, an interrogator should view with considerable skepticism any "conscience-stricken" confession. Such a confession is very likely to be false. It may be the product of a mentally ill person, or it may stem from an otherwise normal person's effort to incur a temporary police detention in order to gain some other deliberately conceived objective. Among the latter possibilities are instances where an individual may merely be seeking free transportation back to the state or community where the crime was committed. In other instances, the purpose may be that of being incarcerated, either for a brief or even a relatively long period, in order to evade police consideration of him as a suspect for a much more serious crime. Then, too, there are times when the only motive of a conscience-stricken confession is the publicity the confessor seeks to achieve.

A genuine conscience-stricken confessor will give the appearance of a person who has been broken in health and spirit as a result of a troubled conscience. On the other hand, with the exception of the mentally ill person, the false confessor is apt to be rather lighthearted in appearance and conduct. He recognizes that if and when the prosecution stage is reached, the confession will be retracted, and convincing evidence submitted to establish the falsity of the confession.

One method for checking the authenticity of a conscience-stricken confession, or one that seems to be the result of mental illness, is to refer to some fictitious aspects of the crime and test whether the suspect will accept them as actual facts relating to the occurrence. This tactic presupposes, of course, that all the true facts of the case have not already been disclosed to the subject. As earlier stated, such disclosures should be withheld for this very reason, as well as for other considerations.

WHEN A SUSPECT HAS MADE REPEATED DENIALS OF GUILT TO PREVIOUS INTERROGATORS, FIRST QUESTION HIM, WHENEVER CIRCUMSTANCES PERMIT, ABOUT SOME OTHER, UNRELATED OFFENSE OF A SIMILAR NATURE AND FOR WHICH HE IS ALSO CONSIDERED TO BE GUILTY

As already suggested, an interrogator should make every possible effort to keep the suspect from uttering repeated denials of guilt, because such denials make it all the more difficult for the suspect to tell the truth later. In other words, the suspect will find it hard to then tell the interrogator, in effect, "I've been lying to you, and to the other investigators, but now I'll tell the truth." With this consideration in mind, an interrogator, when called upon to interrogate someone who has repeatedly denied guilt to other investigators should, whenever circumstances permit, first try to obtain an admission regarding another similar, although unrelated offense for which he is also guilty, and regarding which he is presently under suspicion. For instance, if a person has committed a theft, such as stealing a purse in a school, office, or hospital, and repeated denials of guilt have been made, it is far easier to tell about other purse stealings than to admit the one regarding which repeated denials had been made. For this reason, the interrogator should first concentrate efforts on an admission about some other similar, unrelated offense that was committed either in the same or in some other school, office, or hospital. Then, after obtaining an admission for such other offense or offenses, the interrogator can proceed with an interrogation about the main offense in question.

The forgoing procedure is particularly helpful with female suspects. A woman can be much more reluctant than a man to confess a crime about which she has previously made repeated denials of guilt.

AN UNINTELLIGENT, UNEDUCATED CRIMINAL SUSPECT WITH A LOW CULTURAL BACKGROUND SHOULD BE INTERROGATED ON A PSYCHOLOGICAL LEVEL COMPARABLE TO THAT USUALLY EMPLOYED IN THE QUESTIONING OF A CHILD IN RESPECT TO AN ACT OF WRONGDOING

An unintelligent, uneducated offender with a low cultural background presents a different interrogation problem from that encountered with other types of suspects. In some essential respects, this type of offender must be dealt with on a psychological level comparable to that usually invoked during the questioning of a child who has committed a wrongful act.

A guilty suspect of this general type is ordinarily able to indulge in some very effective acting. He has the capacity with such acting to deceive an inexperienced interrogator into believing that the truth is being told. Another common characteristic is that this type of offender ordinarily does not exhibit the observable symptoms of deception that are so helpful to the interrogator with respect to other types of suspects. Moreover, the unintelligent, uneducated offender from a low cultural environment is usually able to sit and listen very calmly to what the interrogator says and may even nod his head as though in agreement—but then the comment will be made, with perhaps a smile, "I don't know anything about this thing."

It is necessary with this type of person to speak in very simple terms. Care must be exercised as to tone of voice because a very soft voice may lull him into a state of tranquility to such an extent that he may become unmindful of what the interrogator is saying. In fact, the interrogator may have to resort to dramatic tones and gestures. It may even become necessary at times to invoke some feigned displays of impatience.

In instances where a suspect of the type under consideration happens to be a member of a minority race or group, the interrogator must never make a derogatory remark about that race or group, even in jest. (Nor should it be assumed that a person's attitude, conduct, or even criminality are the result of skin color or nationality!) To the contrary, the interrogator should (and in good conscience always can) eulogize some outstanding member of that race or group and suggest that the suspect try to measure up to the conduct exemplified by that particular individual. Moreover, where the interrogator is personally acquainted with the individual example to whom he refers, that fact should be made known to the suspect by further emphasizing the person's commendable qualities.

Throughout the interrogation of an unintelligent, uneducated offender with a low cultural background, the interrogator must maintain a very positive attitude, without ever relenting in the display of a position of certainty regarding the suspect's guilt. It is only a matter of how, when, where, or why the offender did the act in question. With a suspect of this type, considerable emphasis should be placed upon the possible *excuses* for his conduct. In other words, in a theft case, the possibility should be emphatically stressed that the missing article may have been taken "by mistake" or without knowing he was even in possession of it. (Thereafter, of course, the interrogator should seek the truthful explanation, as was suggested earlier.)

INTERROGATION OF WITNESSES AND OTHER PROSPECTIVE INFORMANTS

The basic principles underlying the previously described techniques for interrogating suspects and offenders are, in general, equally applicable to cases involving the interrogation of witnesses and other prospective informants.

The Potentially Cooperative Witness or Informant

An illustration of the basic psychological factors involved in the interrogation of a potentially cooperative witness or informant appears in an *Accident Investigation Manual,* published by the Northwestern University Traffic Institute[1] Although this manual describes an automobile accident investigation, the principles developed are equally applicable to a murder case or any other type of offense:

> Some officers seem never to be able to find witnesses; others have little difficulty. One officer in the former category would shoulder his way through a crowd. "Did anybody see this accident?" he would shout. "How about you?" "How about you?" He would all but push the people about. Naturally, he found very few witnesses. In reporting back to his partner he would say, "There weren't any witnesses. I went through the crowd four times asking everybody, but nobody saw the accident." An adroit officer uses his head rather than his lung power. He goes about the job quietly. Perhaps he spots a talkative woman—at least one such person is to be found at most accidents. "How do you do, madam," he says. "Did I understand you to say that you saw this accident?" "Why, no, officer," she replies, probably feeling flattered that he singled her out, "I didn't see it, but that man in the straw hat over there was telling me all about it. He was right here when it happened." In approaching the man, the officer is very courteous but just a little more brisk and businesslike. He plans his question carefully. He does not say, "Did you see this accident?" but rather, "Pardon me, sir, would you mind telling me what you saw in connection with this accident?" This officer seldom has difficulty in finding witnesses.

---

[1]Pp. 171–172 (1946).

He listens carefully to their accounts of the accident. Then, if they are willing to write out a statement, he provides them with notebook and pencil and asks them to sign what they write. If they will not write the statement, he writes it, reads it to them aloud, then has them sign it. If they refuse to sign, he does not insist; they are still his witnesses and he wants their good will when they appear on the stand in the trial, if a trial follows.

In brief, the good investigator usually seeks his witnesses indirectly. He finds somebody who knows that somebody else saw the accident. Getting the witness' name if possible, he addresses him by it. He is quiet and courteous. In requesting the witness to write and sign a statement or merely to sign it, he puts his question positively, not negatively. Instead of saying, 'Won't you sign this, please?" he hands the pencil to the person and says ["Please put your name here"] It will make our investigation complete." If the witness does not want to sign, the officer [should be pleasant], not resentful.

In addition to the forgoing, the interviewer should adhere to the following general guidelines when questioning a witness:

Encourage a narrative version of the witnesses' story, and then follow up with specific questions for clarification. If the interviewer interjects too many questions *during* the narration, the flow of the witnesses' thoughts may be disrupted.

Offer the witness support and encouragement by interjecting such comments as "That's very good," "That's going to help us," or "You seem to have an excellent memory."

Protect the witness from embarrassment by separating him from the others. Do not force the witness into a position of revealing something personal (e.g., his reason for being in the area) in front of others, or of not offering information that may be accurate but contradictory to what others have said.

Avoid leading questions that suggest the information being sought (e.g., Was the car yellow with a white top?). Ask open-ended questions and use words that are compatible with the witness's ability to speak and understand.

Appear to be interested in the witness and what he has to say. Avoid sarcasm, criticism, or any display of anger or animosity.

Avoid emotionally provocative words, such as kill, murder, or rape.

Be patient. If the witness senses that the interrogator is getting impatient, the witness may stop talking.

Use sketches to establish further details.

Be careful to distinguish fact from inference.

Be aware of the verbal and nonverbal behavior symptoms that the witness displays. They may indicate an area of discussion that requires further probing, or perhaps something about which the witness has not been completely candid.

Be aware of the factors that may inhibit a witness's desire to talk, such as a fear that some previous illegal act may be exposed, or that his presence in the area will be disclosed to his embarrassment. The witness, therefore, should be reassured that the interrogator is only interested in what was seen or heard.

The Reluctant Witness or Informant

Although a criminal interrogator ordinarily will experience very little difficulty in obtaining information from witnesses to a crime or from persons in possession of information derived from some other source, there are instances when a witness or other prospective informant will attempt to withhold whatever information is known concerning another's guilt. In the interrogation of such persons, the following suggestions should be helpful in obtaining the desired information.

ASSURE THE WILLING BUT FEARFUL WITNESS OR OTHER PROSPECTIVE INFORMANT THAT HE WILL NOT BE HARMED BY THE OFFENDER OR HIS RELATIVES OR FRIENDS, AND THAT HE WILL RECEIVE POLICE PROTECTION IN THE EVENT SUCH PROTECTION BECOMES NECESSARY

It is quite natural that under certain conditions and circumstances, a witness or other prospective informant might be desirous of assisting the police but yet be restrained from doing so because of a fear of retaliation at the hands of the offender or his relatives or friends. In such instances, it is advisable to give the subject the following assurances:

1. Retaliation is an extremely rare occurrence when the witness or informant is acting in good faith and without any selfish motive, such as receiving pay for information, seeking personal revenge on the offender, etc. In this connection, it is well to ask the subject if he knows of any case where an honest court witness, or an honest police officer or prosecuting attorney, was ever subsequently harmed by the offender or by someone else acting in the offender's behalf.
2. Information will be kept confidential and, therefore, where circumstances permit, e.g., where court testimony from the witness or informant may not be necessary, the offender and others will never know of the subject's cooperation with the police.
3. If it becomes necessary for a witness to testify in court, his previous cooperation will not be disclosed by the police, because he will be subpoenaed as the witness who can always justify the act of testifying on the ground of having been ordered to do so by the court.

4. An adequate police guard will be assigned to the subject if so desired or deemed necessary.

Along with the forgoing attempts to secure the proper degree of cooperation from a person of this type, it is advisable to point out to the witness the fact that the interrogator is asking no more than would be expected of another person in the event that the witness or some member of his family were the one against whom the offense had been committed. Moreover, it is well to impress upon the subject the obligation as a citizen of the community to render such cooperation to the police.

In the event that none of the forgoing suggestions suffice to elicit the desired information, the willing but fearful witness or other prospective informant may be treated as an actual suspect in the manner described below. Ordinarily, however, resort to the latter method is unnecessary.

WHENEVER A WITNESS OR OTHER PROSPECTIVE INFORMANT REFUSES TO COOPERATE BECAUSE HE IS DELIBERATELY PROTECTING THE OFFENDER'S INTERESTS OR BECAUSE HE IS ANTISOCIAL OR ANTIPOLICE, SEEK TO BREAK THE BOND OF LOYALTY BETWEEN THE SUBJECT AND THE OFFENDER OR ACCUSE HIM OF THE OFFENSE AND PROCEED TO INTERROGATE HIM AS THOUGH HE WERE ACTUALLY CONSIDERED TO BE THE OFFENDER

Occasionally it is possible to break the bond of loyalty between a subject and the offender he is attempting to protect by convincing the subject of disloyalty on the part of the offender. For instance, in the interrogation of a subject who is the mistress of the offender, she may be told that the offender was unfaithful to her and in love with another woman (whose true or fictitious name should be given). By this method, the subject may be induced to change her attitude toward the interrogator's request for helpful information. It is also possible, on occasion, to change a subject's antisocial or antipolice attitude by patiently pointing out the unreasonableness and unsoundness of his views. Ordinarily, however, some more effective measures are necessary.

There is one consideration that a subject of this type is likely to place above all others, and that is the protection of his own interest and welfare. When all other methods have failed, therefore, the interrogator should accuse the subject of committing the crime (or of being implicated in it in some way) and proceed with an interrogation as though that person was in fact considered to be the guilty individual. A witness or other prospective informant, thus faced with the possibility of a trial or conviction for a crime he or she did not commit, will sooner or later be impelled to abandon the efforts in the offender's behalf or in support of the subject's antisocial or antipolice attitudes.

As previously stated, it is well to bear in mind that occasionally the reporter of a crime—a "witness," for instance—is actually the offender. In certain instances, therefore, or even as a rather routine procedure, the statements of important witnesses should be checked out for their accuracy and truthfulness. For instance, if a witness states that someone was with him shortly before the offense, or that he was at a certain place immediately before the offense, a check should be made on the truthfulness of that statement. Otherwise, an offender who is seeking to conceal guilt by representing himself only as a witness may well succeed in the efforts to evade detection.

SCIENTIFIC AIDS FOR INTERROGATORS

Because this text was prepared for interrogators who must rely upon tactics and techniques without the aid of any scientific instruments or procedures, no discussion has been presented respecting the value or validity of such instruments or procedures. We do suggest, however, that cautionary measures be taken by law enforcement agencies or private security units that may be contemplating their utilization. Helpful in this respect will be the summaries of the evaluations of authoritative commentators upon the various methods that have been available, such as "truth serum", hypnosis, psychological stress evaluation, and the polygraph technique.[2]

SPECIFIC RECOMMENDATIONS FOR THE BEHAVIORAL ANALYSIS INTERVIEW BY PRIVATE SECURITY OFFICERS

As discussed earlier in the text, the behavioral analysis interview is a nonaccusatory interview in which a structured set of questions is asked, some primarily for the purpose of eliciting verbal and nonverbal behavior symptoms indicative of truth or deception.

In the private security context, the principal objective of the interview procedure in cases where several employees are to be questioned is to readily eliminate from suspicion those who are in all probability innocent so as to be able to focus the interrogation on the one or more who are probably guilty.

---

[2]See MOENSSENS, INBAU, and STARRS, SCIENTIFIC EVIDENCE IN CRIMINAL CASES (3d. ed. 1986).

The basic interview format and questions can be utilized by the private security officer in either a specific issue investigation (such as the disappearance of a $4,000 deposit) or in a general loss investigation (such as a 6-month inventory shortage of several thousand dollars). The same procedure can be effectively used in the investigation of a single suspect or a large group of suspects.

When investigating a large number of employees, it is advisable to begin the interviews with those who are least likely to be involved in the issue under investigation. The purpose of this is twofold: 1) to begin the elimination early, and, at the same time, 2) to gain valuable investigative information. Due to their general tendency to be open and cooperative, truthful employees often will furnish the investigator with very helpful detailed information on the policies, procedures, and activities that prevail within their department or area, and they also may provide information pointing to the guilty person.

Earlier in the text, the authors presented a number of generally usable behavioral analysis questions and pointed out the possible truthful and deceptive answers. The following section concentrates on the ones that are of particular value in private security employee investigations. Along with the examples used, the principle underlying the suspect's verbal responses is discussed. It should be kept in mind, of course, that a suspect's nonverbal behavior must also be observed and evaluated as each question is answered. Moreover, along with the behavior-provoking questions that are listed in this section, the interviewer should ask investigative questions concerning the suspect's knowledge of the facts in the case, his relevant job functions, activities at the time of the occurrence, etc.

The following questions are appropriate, but they do not have to be asked in the order in which they are presented:

1. *Initial Contact*: "Jim, my name is _____ with the (security department, audit department, etc.). I would like to ask you a few questions, but before I begin, "Do you know why I have asked to talk to you here today?"
   (*Principle*: Innocent suspects tend readily to reveal their knowledge of some of the details respecting the issue under investigation.)

   Assuming that the specific loss or general inventory shortage that is the focus of the investigation has been discussed with the employee by the local store manager or supervisor, at least in his initial attempt to determine the circumstances of the loss, or assuming that the loss is common knowledge among the employees, the innocent suspect will usually respond to the "know why" question with some detailed response, such as "Sure, somebody stole a deposit" or "Well, I assume it's about the merchandise that we're missing from stock." On the other hand, a guilty suspect will often give a vague, unresponsive answer to the question, such as "No, I'm not sure what this is about," or "I heard something might be missing, but I don't really know."

Following the initial inquiry, the employee is given a brief summary of the events in question, and then asked if he or she was involved in the commission of the act. (To illustrate the phrasing of the interview questions, the disappearance of a $4,000 deposit from the office safe is assumed.)

2. *History*: "Jim, we are investigating the disappearance of a $4,000 deposit from the store last week. Jim, if you had anything to do with the loss of the deposit, you should tell me that now."
   (*Principle*: Truthful suspects offer spontaneous, direct, and sincere denials.)

3. *Knowledge/Suspicion*: "Jim, do you know who stole the missing deposit?" Assuming the answer is no: "Well, Jim, who do you think took the missing money? Now, let me say this: If you only have a suspicion, I want you to tell me that, even though it may be wrong. I will keep it confidential and not report it to that person. Jim, who do you think took the deposit?"
   (*Principle*: Truthful suspects will usually volunteer names.)

4. *Vouch*: "Jim, is there anyone you know well enough that you feel is above suspicion and would not do something like this?"
   (*Principle*: Truthful suspects will usually exempt some individual or individuals from suspicion.)

5. *Plausibility*: "Jim, do you think the $4,000 was stolen?"
   (*Principle*: The truthful suspect will usually acknowledge the probability of the theft.)

6. *Motive*: "Jim, why do you think someone would take a deposit like this?"
   (*Principle*: Truthful suspects usually respond without hesitation and are unafraid to discuss the motive.)

7. *Attitude*: "Jim, how do you feel about being interviewed concerning this $4,000 deposit loss?"
   (*Principle*: The truthful suspect will usually accept and understand the purpose of the interview.)

8. *Think*: "Jim, did you ever think about taking a deposit like this, even though you didn't go through with it?"
   (*Principle*: Truthful suspects tend to offer direct denials, particularly as regards a serious wrongful act.)

9. *Punishment*: "Jim, what do you think should happen to a person who took a deposit like this?"
   (*Principle*: Truthful suspects usually will suggest strong punishment.)

10. *Tell Someone*: "Jim, did you tell your wife [mother, or some close friend] about the possibility of being questioned concerning this loss?" Or, more likely the question may be asked in the following way,

in the event he has been previously questioned about it: "Did you tell your wife [mother] about your being questioned?"

(*Principle*: Truthful suspects generally discuss the issue with some member of the family or a close friend.)

11. *Polygraph Test*: "Jim, if it becomes necessary, would you be willing to take a polygraph test to verify that what you have told me about this $4,000 deposit loss is the truth?"

    (*Principle*: A truthful suspect will usually agree to take a polygraph test.) [Caution: Before asking this question and the next one, determine whether state or local law prohibits the asking of such a question. If it does (or even as a selective alternative) the suspect may be asked: "Would you be willing to be hypnotized so as to recreate for us where you were and what you were doing at the time the money disappeared?"]

12. *Polygraph Test Results*: "Jim, what do you think would be the results of the polygraph test?"

    (*Principle*: Truthful suspects usually indicate favorable test results.)

13. *Second Chance:* "Jim, if it turns out that an employee took the $4,000 deposit, do you think that person should be given a second chance with the company?"

    (*Principle*: The truthful suspect will usually reject any idea of leniency or second chance.)

14. *Opportunity:* "Jim, who do you think had the best opportunity or chance to take the deposit if he wanted to? Now, I'm not asking you to say some particular person did it—only who do you think would have had the best chance to do it if that person wanted to?"

    (*Principle*: The truthful suspect will usually name a person or group (such as "the bookkeepers") that had the best chance. Furthermore, if the innocent suspect had the best chance to commit the theft, he will usually so indicate.)

15. *Explanation of Innocence*: "Jim, tell me why you would not do something like this."

    (*Principle*: The truthful suspect usually responds in terms of himself, e.g., "Because I'm not a thief", while the deceptive person often responds in general, vague terms, perhaps using third person terminology e.g., "Well, somebody who did something like this isn't to be trusted.")

16. *Rating the Company Employer:* "Jim, how would you rate this company as a place to work on a scale of 1 to 10—1 being that it couldn't be any worse and 10 being that it couldn't be any better?"

    (*Principle*: The truthful suspect will usually offer a reasonably high rating of 7 or better, while the deceptive one will usually rate the company 6 or lower.)

    The dishonest employee often rationalizes or justifies thefts by talking about poor working conditions, poor treatment by the company or supervisor, and inadequate pay. A low rating from the suspect certainly does not mean that the suspect committed the theft; however, it could be a good indication of attitude and possible subsequent motive for having taken the money.

17. *Baiting Question*: "Jim, is there any reason why your fingerprints may have been found in that area (or on the deposit container, etc.)? Now, I'm not saying this means you took the deposit, but would there be any reason for your prints being around there?"

   (*Principle*: Truthful suspects usually spontaneously reject the implication of such a baiting question.)

   If, at the conclusion of the interview, the suspect seems truthful, he may be told: "OK, Jim, that will be all for now. Thank you for your cooperation. I'll get back to you if we need anything else."

   If a suspect seems deceptive but has agreed to take a polygraph test, such a test should be arranged. If, on the other hand, the suspect seems untruthful but refuses the polygraph examination, he should be interrogated at that time, unless there are additional suspects to be questioned. When, however, there are other suspects, the interviewer should question them before recalling the one who seemed untruthful, assuming, of course, that there will be an opportunity for a follow-up interrogation. Whenever uncertainty remains regarding a particular suspect, that person should probably be scheduled for a second interview.

The behavioral responses evoked by the procedures described can be very helpful in screening suspected persons. As with any investigative effort, however, the results of the interview should not be considered conclusive, but simply as part of the investigative process.

PART II

THE LAW ON CRIMINAL INTERROGATION AND CONFESSIONS

CHAPTER EIGHT

Interrogation Law:

"PICKING UP" A SUSPECT FOR INTERROGATION

A very crucial interrogation legal problem may arise even before an interrogator sees the suspect he is to interrogate. It concerns the procedure by which the police investigators arranged for the suspect to be available for the interrogation.

Over the years, the impression generally prevailed that the police could "pick-up" suspects for questioning. In 1979, however, the Supreme Court of the United States held, in *Dunaway v. New York*, that a confession obtained after a "pick-up" without probable cause (i.e., without reasonable grounds) to make an actual arrest could not be used as evidence.[1] In this case, the defendant, Dunaway, had been picked up as a suspect in an attempted robbery-murder upon the basis of a tip furnished by a jail inmate. Although Dunaway went along without objection or resistance, and even though he was not booked prior to interrogation, a majority of the Supreme Court observed that the trial court found from the evidence that he would have been restrained if he had refused to accompany the officers or had tried to leave, so that the circumstances were the equivalent of an arrest situation. Therefore, because probable cause for an arrest was absent, the confession, which the court considered the product (or "fruit") of Dunaway's unlawful pick-up, was tainted with illegality and, consequently, was a legal nullity. Chief Justice Burger and Justice Rehnquist dissented; they contended that because Dunaway had accompanied the police voluntarily, and because his interrogation was preceded by the proper warnings of constitutional rights, the resulting confession was also voluntary and, therefore, admissible as evidence.

Based upon an analysis of both the majority and minority opinions of the Supreme Court justices in the *Dunaway* case, the authors recommend that whenever the police desire to pick up anyone for questioning, but probable cause to arrest is lacking, they should make clear to the suspect

---

[1]442 U.S. 200 (1979).

that he is not being arrested and need not to go to the police station unless he is willing to do so, and that, once there, he will be free to leave if he wishes. In other respects too, everything feasible should be done to negate a detention in the legal sense, such as conducting the interrogation in an unbarred, unlocked room.

There will be instances, of course, when the forgoing assurances to a suspect at the time of the initial police contact will have the effect of encouraging a person to refuse to accompany the police. However, in view of the Supreme Court's decision, the only alternative to obtaining consent is for the police to follow the lead furnished by the tip and pursue their investigation of the targeted person until sufficient evidence may be developed (i.e., probable cause) to justify an actual arrest.

In the event an illegal pick-up has occurred, a lawful interrogation opportunity may present itself nevertheless. For instance, if police investigators obtain *independent evidence* that establishes probable cause *at that time* to justify an arrest of the detained suspect, an interrogation thereafter becomes legally permissible. An example of this is a case where police investigators locate a person suspected of being an accomplice and that person implicates the one in custody. Retaining custody of the original one then becomes lawful because the requirement of probable cause has now been satisfied, and a subsequent confession from him is thereby rendered admissible. Another example is a case where investigators lawfully discover bloodstained boots belonging to a murder suspect who is in illegal custody. He may then be interrogated and a confession lawfully obtained because the bloodstained boots furnish probable cause to effect his arrest thereafter and there is no linkage between the original apprehension and the finding of the boots.[2]

Obtaining a suspect's consent whenever feasible will not only avoid the pitfall illustrated by the *Dunaway* case, but, as is subsequently discussed, that practice will also render unnecessary the issuance of *Miranda* warnings; the consent of the suspect will negate the custody factor that otherwise would have required the warnings.

DELAY IN TAKING ARRESTEE BEFORE A JUDICIAL OFFICER

For reasons somewhat comparable to the legal prohibition upon police pick-ups without reasonable grounds, there are statutory restrictions upon the time the police may keep even lawfully arrested persons in custody

---

[2]The two cases to which reference has been made are People v. Rogers, 52 N.Y. 2d 527, 421 N.E. 2d 491 (1981) and State v. Barry, 86 N.J. 80, 429 A. 2d 581 (1981).

before presenting them to a judicial officer (i.e., a judge or magistrate). The statutes usually prescribe that this must occur "without unnecessary delay." Some, however, provide a specific time period for such present-ment rather than rely upon the flexibility of determining whether the delay in a particular case was or was not necessary.

The effect upon interrogations conducted beyond the statutory allow-able period of detention was first enunciated in the 1943 case of *McNabb v. United States*[3] in which the Supreme Court of the United States held inadmissible a confession federal officers had obtained in an apparent violation of the federal statute prescribing presentation of an arrestee to a judicial officer "without unnecessary delay." The Court did not hold that the confession rejection was based upon a constitutional mandate, which would have made it binding in both state and federal cases; rather, the decision was based upon the Court's supervisory power over lower federal courts, and, indirectly, therefore, upon federal law enforcement officers.

Although the federal statute used the words "without unnecessary delay," some lower federal courts after the *McNabb* case applied the statute as though this meant "immediately." That presented a severe curtailment upon the opportunities for interrogations conducted by fed-eral officers and particularly in Washington, D.C., with its street crime problems similar to many other large cities. It also augmented the initial resentment toward the *McNabb* decision in Congress as well as from other groups. Moreover, the *McNabb* rule narrowly survived a 1948 Supreme Court decision.[4] Nevertheless, the Court unanimously reaffirmed the *McNabb* rule in the 1957 case of *Mallory v. United States*.[5] Thereafter it was referred to as the *McNabb-Mallory rule*.

After repeated attempts by members of Congress to enact a bill abolish-ing the *McNabb-Mallory* rule (as it was privileged to do because the rule was not of constitutional dimension), and after a Presidential veto of one that was enacted in 1966, Congress did succeed in effecting its demise 2 years later. The life-span of the *McNabb-Mallory* rule as a federal rule was 25 years, until it was abolished in the 1968 Omnibus Crime Act.

Very few state supreme courts adopted the *McNabb-Mallory* rule; most exercised the option of rejecting it. Even some of the adopting ones diluted its effect in application. Moreover, the legislature in one of the adopting states (Maryland) nullified the rule in 1982. Thus, few of its traces remain. As one legal scholar described the fate of the *McNabb-Mallory* rule (even in 1978), it was a "grenade that fizzled."

Although the *McNabb-Mallory* rule has lost practically all its vitality,

---

[3]318 U.S. 332 (1943).
[4]Upshaw v. United States, 335 U.S. 410 (1948). In perpetuating the *McNabb* rule, the Court was divided 5 to 4.
[5]354 U.S. 449 (1957).

interrogators must be mindful of the fact that an undue detention delay, or one exceeding the specified state statutory time limitation, may be considered in determining confession voluntariness.

CONFESSION VOLUNTARINESS

The long-standing requirement that a confession must be voluntary before it may be used as evidence in a criminal case is based upon the principle of *protection of the innocent.* It was not created as prophylactic rule for keeping the police in line, or for implementing a constitutional right unrelated to the issue of guilt or innocence. There can be no valid objection, therefore, from anyone, including the police, to the continued existence of the requirement of voluntariness.

The clearest example of an interrogation practice that will void a confession is the infliction of physical force or pain upon the person under interrogation, because it is an uncontestable fact that harm of this nature may produce a confession of guilt from an innocent person. This is also true as regards indirect physical harm; for instance, an unduly prolonged, continuous interrogation, especially by two or more interrogators working in relays, or the deprivation of food, water, or access to toilet facilities for an unreasonable period of time.

A threat of physical harm may have a similar effect—the extraction of confessions from innocent persons. Similarly, an interrogator's promise to a suspect that if he confesses he will go free or receive only a lenient penalty will nullify the confession because such a promise may induce an innocent person to confess rather than to risk criminal prosecution or severe punishment. This may actually occur in the case of an innocent suspect caught in a strong web of circumstantial evidence, or one who has been identified by several witnesses as being the criminal offender. Under such circumstances, an acceptance of a promise of freedom, or of a light sentence, may be an appealing alternative, even to an innocent person.

Although the general rule is that a promise of leniency will nullify a confession, there are certain kinds of promises that are permissible. An example of this is a promise to recommend to the judge a light bail bond, or to report that the suspect cooperated in the investigation. The test that some courts use in delineating a permissible promise from an impermissible one is the test that appears in a New York statute—whether the promise presents a "substantial risk" of a false confession[6] Nevertheless, a safe practice for interrogators to follow is to avoid making any promises other than the clearly innocuous ones. In particular, a pitfall that must be avoided is one that may present itself when a suspect inquires "What will happen to me if I tell you I did this?" Whenever an interrogator encounters that question, the advisable response is: "I can't tell you. I wouldn't be fair to you if I did because I don't have the authority to make good on any promise. My advice to you is to tell the truth now, and then if you think you have a break coming, talk to the DA about it." Rarely will the inquiring suspect refrain from confessing.

In the event an interrogator is confronted with a situation where prohibited interrogation practices were used on a suspect by some other person or persons, there is the possibility that, subject to certain very restrictive conditions, a confession nevertheless may be legally obtained. The clearest example would be a case where relatives or friends of a crime victim physically abused a suspect, who may or may not have confessed, but there are substantial reasons to believe he is, in fact, the perpetrator of the crime. In such a circumstance, the suspect should be informed and also given firm assurances, substantiated by the conditions surrounding the present interrogation effort, that no further methods of that sort will be employed, and that no prior participant will be permitted even to be in the vicinity. As this is being stated, one or more impartial witnesses should be there and remain there throughout the interrogation.

Not only may a case investigation be salvaged in this manner where the abuse has been administered by a private citizen, but also when the abuser may have been a police officer, although, for understandable reasons, the difficulty presented by the latter situation may be an insurmountable one. Nevertheless, there is nothing to be lost by attempting a proper interrogation.

A less onerous task exists where a promise of leniency was previously made and the present interrogator revokes it in unmistakable terms. The difficulty lessens even further, of course, in situations where the previous impropriety consists solely of a failure to administer the prescribed warnings of constitutional rights to a custodial suspect from whom no confession had been obtained.

---

[6]Article 60.45, Criminal Procedure Law, Book 11-A, McKinney's Consolidated Laws of New York.

With respect to the aforementioned promise of light bail, and a comment that the suspect's cooperation would be reported to the prosecutor, approving cases are United States v. Ferrara, 377 F. 2d 16 (2d Cir. 1967), cert. denied, 389 U.S. 908 (promise of light bail); and, as regards reports of cooperation, United States v. Glasgow, 451 F. 2d 557 (9th Cir. 1971); People v. Hubbard, 55 Ill. 2d 142, 302 N.E. 2d 609 (1973), and Commonwealth v. Williams, 388 Mass. 846, 448 N.E. 2d Ill4 (1983).

A promise by federal agents to do what they could to see that the suspect was sent to a federal rather than a state institution on a robbery charge has been held permissible. United States v. Arcediano, 371 F. Supp. 457 (1974).

PERMISSIBLE INTERROGATION TACTICS AND TECHNIQUES

Mindful of the legal requirement that the opportunity to interrogate a suspect must be lawfully obtained; that there must be an avoidance of force, threat of force, or promise of leniency; and that there must be compliance with subsequently discussed requirements for warnings of constitutional rights to custodial suspects, an interrogator should also know, of course, about the tactics and techniques that are legally permissible. Basic to those tactics and techniques is the fact that the vast majority of criminal offenders are reluctant to confess and must be psychologically persuaded to do so, and, unavoidably, by interrogation procedures involving elements of trickery or deceit. The legality of such procedures is well established.

The Supreme Court of the United States, in its 1969 decision in *Frazier v. Cupp*, implicitly recognized the essentiality of interrogation practices involving trickery or deceit, and approved of them, even though in one of its prior decisions the impression appears that there was disapproval of such practices.[7] In *Frazier*, the Court upheld a conviction based in part upon a confession obtained by the use of a substantial piece of trickery and deceit. The defendant, while under interrogation as a murder suspect, had been told, *falsely*, that a suspected accomplice had confessed. In its opinion affirming the conviction, the Court said:

> The fact that the police misrepresented the statements that [the suspected accomplice] had made is, while relevant, insufficient in our view to make this otherwise voluntary confession inadmissible. These cases must be decided by viewing the "totality of the circumstances...."

In addition to the forgoing Supreme Court decision, there are many appellate court cases holding that a confession is admissible in evidence, even when it was obtained by trickery and deceit. There are, however, two important qualifications to that rule. The trickery or deceit must not be of such a nature as to "shock the conscience" of the court or community, nor can it be one that is apt to induce a false confession.

Examples of what may be considered as shocks to the conscience are contained in the concurring opinion of Justice Antonio Lamer of the Supreme Court of Canada in a case that otherwise approved the use of trickery and deceit.[8] He submitted hypothetical situations in which a

---

[7]The citation to Frazier v. Cupp is 394 U.S. 731 (1969). The other case to which reference was made is Miranda v. Arizona which is discussed later in this chapter.

[8]Justice Lamer's concurring opinion appears in Rothman v. the Queen, 59 C.C.C. 2d. 30 (1981), a case in which a police officer, posing as a criminal offender, obtained incriminating statements from a narcotics violator occupying the same jail cell.

police interrogator pretended to be a jail chaplain in order to procure a suspect's confession, or where the interrogator misrepresented himself as a defense attorney in order to achieve that objective. Although the United States Supreme Court has not addressed itself to the shock-the-conscience concept in the context of a criminal interrogation, the Court did apply it in a case where an arrested narcotics suspect tried to conceal two capsules by swallowing them, whereupon he was taken to a hospital for the purpose of having his stomach pumped, against his consent, in order to have him dislodge the capsules. This procedure was considered a shock to the conscience of the Court, for which reason the use of the capsules as evidence was held to be a violation of constitutional due process.[9] The same reasoning would probably be applied by the Court in an interrogation-confession case in which a police interrogator had posed as a clergyman or defense counsel.

It is of interest to point out that in contrast to its holding in the stomach-pumping case, the Supreme Court found no violation of due process in a case where, for the purpose of a chemical test for alcoholic intoxication, a blood specimen was extracted from an arrested motorist, over his objection, by a hospital physician.[10] In other words, excessiveness in the degree of police conduct is the determining factor. Therein, of course, lies the difference between an interrogator's employment of ordinary forms of trickery or deceit and the pretense of being a clergyman or defense counsel.

As for trickery or deceit that does not transgress into the shock-the-conscience concept, the test of permissibility rests primarily upon the issue of confession voluntariness, as in the previously discussed case in which the interrogator lied to the suspect about his accomplice having confessed. A guideline that an interrogator may use in any case situation where he may be in doubt as to the permissibility of any particular type of trickery or deceit, is to ask himself the following question: "Is what I am about to do, or say, apt to make an innocent person confess"? If the answer to the question is "no," the interrogator should go ahead and do or say what was contemplated. On the other hand, if the answer is "yes," the interrogator should refrain from doing or saying what he had in mind. This is the only understandable test of any practical value for interrogators to follow. Moreover, it is the only test that is fair both to the public and to the accused or suspected individual.

Measured by the suggested test, there should be judicial approval of all of the tactics and techniques involving trickery and deceit that are discussed in Part I of this text. Nevertheless, interrogators must realize that they may encounter experiences where a local trial judge, or even a

---

[9]Rochin v. California, 342 U.S. 165 (1952).

[10]Schmerber v. California, 384 U.S. 757 (1966).

prosecuting attorney, may not subscribe to the test in principle, or perhaps even may be unaware of the case law upon the subject. On such occasions, the interrogator may call to the prosecutor's attention, during a pretrial conference, the statements and supporting cases in this text or in some other source book upon the subject. He, in turn, will then be prepared to satisfy the trial judge of the propriety of the interrogation tactics and techniques that induced the confession the prosecution is submitting to the court as evidence.

In addition to the legality of employing trickery and deceit in the interrogation of criminal suspects, there is another issue that warrants consideration, although it is of relatively lesser importance to police interrogators than to private security interrogators. It relates to the "accusatory confrontation," discussed in *Step 1* of The Nine Steps to the effective interrogation of suspects whose guilt appears definite or reasonably certain.

Although the discussion of *Step 1* was accompanied by a presentation of the moral and legal justification for its usage, the authors herewith submit some further comments regarding its legality, along with appropriate legal references. They are intended as additional assurance to the interrogator and also for the purpose of enabling him to make available to prosecutors and other attorneys or judges the relevant legal authority in support of the authors' conclusion as to the validity of the accusatory confrontation constituting *Step 1*.

The law is absolutely clear that no slander or other form of defamation occurs when an interrogator directly accuses a suspect of committing a criminal offense, even though it later develops that he is completely innocent. Either of two conditions must prevail, however. First, the accusation must be made under conditions of privacy—in other words, outside the presence or hearing of a third person or persons. There can be no slander or other defamation without a "publication," which, in the legal sense, means letting another person hear or know what has been said.[11] Under the privacy setting recommended for interrogations, there will be no publication.

Second, if a third party is to be present or within hearing, there must exist what is legally known as a "qualified privilege" with respect to his awareness of what is being said. An example of this is an interrogation conducted in the presence or within the hearing of a fellow interrogator or supervisor, or of someone else who has a legitimate common interest in the subject matter of the investigation, such as the suspect's employer in an embezzlement case. Other examples are instances where the presence of a female police officer or female private security officer is considered

---

[11]Prosser and Keeton Torts §111, (5th ed. 1984).

necessary during a male's interrogation of a female suspect; or an interpreter's presence because of the language difficulty of a suspect. As to the presence of a fellow union member employee requested by the suspect, which must, by law, be honored by the interrogator, this should be considered a waiver as regards slander or other defamation.[12]

Although a suspect whom the interrogator accuses will probably be upset and incur hurt feelings if he is actually innocent, that fact alone will not provide the basis for legal action against the accuser. The general rule of law is that the First Amendment right to "free speech" renders permissive the utterance of derogatory, or even rude or insulting remarks, subject, however, to the conditions of privacy or qualified privilege. A cause of action arises only when the statements are made for the *intended purpose of inflicting severe emotional distress.*[13] That element is obviously lacking in a case situation where, in an effort to solve a criminal offense, a police interrogator, acting in the public interest, or a private security interrogator, seeking to protect an employer's legitimate interest, utilizes an accusatory confrontation during the interrogation of a suspect. There is the understandable limitation, of course, that the confrontation must not extend beyond the point where severe mental distress becomes a probability.

---

[12]The specific issue regarding interrogation situations has not been the subject of appellate court attention. However, the following references are relevant to the general law upon qualified privileges: Prosser and Keeton, *supra* Note 11, at §115; Roland v. d'Arazren, 685 F. 2d 653 (D.C. Cir. 1982); Smith v. Dist. of Colum., 399 A. 2d 213 (D.C. Ct. App. 1979) (Security guard's communication to a police officer about company employee held to be a qualified privilege that affords protection against action for slander); Lawson v. Howmet; and Alum. Co., 449 N.E. 2d 1172 (Ind. App. 1983)(Statement made by plant supervisor to plant manager about an employee vandalizing company property was held to be protected as a qualified privilege).

The legal requirement that a union member employee must be permitted to have a third person present is discussed on p. 28 of this text.

[13]Although specific case law is lacking as regards interrogation situations, the following general references are of some relevance: Prosser and Keeton, *supra* note 11, at § 12, in which the statement appears that in order for liability to result, the conduct must "exceed all bounds usually tolerated by decent society, of a nature which is especially calculated to cause, and does cause, mental distress of a very serious kind." Furthermore, say the authors, "The emotional distress must in fact exist, and it must be severe." Also see *Restatement of the Law of Torts* (2d) §§46, 312, 313, 436A, and Hall v. May Dep't., 292 Ore. 131, 637, P. 2d 126 (1982). According to Section 46 of the *Restatement*, liability is incurred only when a person "by extreme and outrageous conduct intentionally or recklessly causes severe emotional distress."

In addition to the emotional stress factor, caution must be exercised with respect to the matter of restraint, especially where the suspect is being questioned by a private security officer. Nothing should be done or said that will indicate to the suspect, as a reasonable person, that he is not at liberty to leave the room or even to leave the premises if he wishes to do so. Moreover, the physical surroundings should substantiate that fact. In other words, the interrogation room should not even have a lock on it, nor should any other normal exit from the premises be unavailable to the suspects. This, too, will afford additional protection from a claim of "false imprisonment" on the part of someone who is not already under lawful arrest. See Prosser and Keeton, *supra* Note 11, at § 11.

WARNINGS OF CONSTITUTIONAL RIGHTS AND THE ATTENDING RESPONSIBILITIES OF THE INTERROGATOR

Prescribed Warnings and the Circumstances Requiring Them

In 1966, the Supreme Court of the United States established an additional requirement for confession admissibility, one that was based upon an entirely different consideration than the protection of the innocent, which underlies the voluntariness test. It was created for the avowed purpose of assuring that *all* persons in police *custody* would know of the constitutional right not to incriminate themselves; in other words, not just those who by education or intellect would be aware of this privilege, but also the uneducated and unintelligent as well. So the Court, in its 5-to-4 decision in *Miranda v. Arizona*,[14] established the rule that before a person in police custody (or otherwise deprived of his freedom "in any significant way") could be interrogated, he must be given the following warnings:

1. That he has a right to remain silent, and that he need not answer any questions
2. That if he does answer questions, his answers can be used as evidence against him
3. That he has a right to consult with a lawyer before or during the questioning of him by the police
4. That if he cannot afford to hire a lawyer, one will be provided for him without costs

As is discussed in the next section, the Supreme Court held in a 1981 case that there is no requirement "that the contents of the Miranda warnings be a virtual incantation of the precise language contained in *Miranda*." It is sufficient if the warnings convey the basic rights to the suspect. The authors believe that the concise version of the required warnings suggested later in this chapter does precisely that.

All of the warnings must be given in such a way that the suspect clearly understands what he is being told. Also, according to *Miranda*, if the suspect indicates, at any time or in any manner whatsoever, that he does not want to talk, the interrogation must cease. The interrogator is not privileged to "talk him out of" his refusal to talk. And if the suspect says, at any time, that he wants a lawyer, the interrogation must cease until he has the opportunity to confer with one. Moreover, the interrogator cannot "talk him out of" his desire for a lawyer. The Court further stated that in instances where the suspect requests a lawyer but cannot obtain one, and

---

[14]384 U.S. 436 (1966).

no lawyer is provided for him by the police, there can be no interrogation.

The reason given by the Supreme Court for the requirement regarding the right to a lawyer at the interrogation stage was to ensure that the person to be questioned would know he had the right to remain silent; in other words, his own lawyer would tell him so. This requirement was not established because of the Constitution's Sixth Amendment provision that "in all criminal prosecutions, the accused . . . shall have the assistance of counsel for his defense," but simply to implement the self-incrimination provision of the Fifth Amendment that "no person shall be compelled in any criminal case to be a witness against himself.

The only time a police interrogation may be conducted of a suspect who is in custody or otherwise restrained of his freedom is *after* he has received the required warnings and *after* he has indicated a willingness to answer questions. Once that waiver is given, the interrogator may then proceed to conduct an interrogation. This general rule, however, is subject to the two exceptions later discussed under the titles of "The Rescue/ Lifesaving Exception to the Warning Requirement" and "Corrective Measures When Interrogation Was Not Preceded by Required Warnings."

According to the Supreme Court's mandate in *Miranda*, a confession or other statement obtained in violation of any of the Miranda requirements is inadmissible as evidence, regardless of its otherwise voluntariness.

Most police departments rely upon the oral issuance of the warnings. Their officers are supplied with printed plastic cards—on one side are the warnings to be read; on the other side are the waiver questions to be asked. Usually, the phraseology on the cards is prepared, or at least approved, by the local prosecuting attorney or other legal advisor. The warnings on a typical card have been as follows:

1. You have the right to remain silent.
2. Anything you say can and will be used against you in a court of law.
3. You have the right to talk to a lawyer and have him present with you while you are being questioned.
4. If you cannot afford to hire a lawyer, one will be appointed to represent you before any questioning, if you wish.
5. You can decide at any time to exercise these rights and not answer any questions or make any statements.

Observe the gratuitous inclusion of the fifth warning beyond the four that the Supreme Court prescribed in *Miranda*! It is not one ordered by the Court, but rather an expression the Supreme Court employed by way of an admonition to interrogators regarding their obligation in those instances where a person has already agreed to talk without an attorney being present but then has a change of mind and either wants to terminate the conversation altogether or to have an attorney present. Nowhere in the

Court's opinion is there to be found a directive to the police that this right had to be incorporated as a warning to the suspect himself. The Court merely cautioned the police that *if* the suspect, after his waiver, *had a change of mind* during the interrogation, his wishes in that respect must be honored. Since the fifth warning was not required, it should be eliminated, unless a state, by statute or court decision, specifically requires it.[15]

In June, 1984, the United States Drug Enforcement Administration revised its policy regarding *Miranda* and eliminated the fifth warning as a requirement.

In *Miranda*, the Supreme Court very clearly confined its mandate for the warnings to case situations involving suspects in *police* custody. Private security officers, therefore, are not required to issue the warnings prior to their interrogation of persons whom they have arrested pursuant to the officers' arrest privileges as private citizens.[16] The only exceptions with regard to security personnel are: 1) when they have had conferred upon them, by state statute or local ordinance, the same powers possessed by the police; 2) when they are actual police officers working part time ("moonlighting") in private security; or 3) when, in a particular case situation, they are acting in cooperation with the police, and thus functioning, more or less, as their agents.[17]

Although uncertainty had prevailed with regard to the question of whether the *Miranda* warnings are required in misdemeanor cases in which the penalty for a violation is only a fine or small jail sentence, the issue was resolved in a July, 1984, decision of the United States Supreme Court. The Court held that that even when a person is taken into custody for a traffic misdemeanor, he must receive the warnings before being interrogated.[18] The Court did state, however, that the warnings are not

---

[15]The fifth warning is required, for example, by Article 38.22 of the Texas Code of Criminal Procedure (Vernon's Stats., Vol. 4A). It is also required by the Wisconsin Supreme Court. Micale v. State, 76 Wis, 370, 251 N.W. 2d 458 (1977).

Not only is the fifth warning not generally required, but there also is no need to specifically ask, at the end of the warnings, whether the suspect is willing to talk without an attorney being present. State v. Edwards, 49 Ohio St. 2d 31, 358 N.E. 2d 1051 (1976). Nevertheless, in the *Hinckley* case, discussed in this text at pp. 225, 275, he was asked "Do you wish to answer any questions?"

[16]The leading case holding that *Miranda* does not apply to private security officers is People v. Deborah C., 30 Cal. 3d 125, 177 Cal. Rptr. 852, 635 P. 2d 446 (1981). The most recent decision was one rendered in May, 1985, by the New York Court of Appeals in People v. Ray, 65 N.Y. 2d 282, 480 N.E. 2d 1065 (1985). To the same effect are City of Grand Rapids v. Impens, 414 Mich. 667, 327 N.W. 2d 278 (1982); Metigoruk v. Municipality of Anchorage, 655 P. 2d 1317 (Alas. 1982); and People v. Raitano, 81 Ill. App. 3d 373, 401 N.E. 2d 278 (1980).

[17]With regard to the exceptions for moonlighting police officers, and for private security officers who possess general police powers, see People v. Deborah C., *supra* note 16 at pp. 140–141; 860, 454; Pratt v. State, 9 Md. App. 220, 263 A. 2d 247 (1970).

For a general discussion regarding the law affecting private security interrogations, consult INBAU, ASPEN, & SPIOTTO, PROTECTIVE SECURITY LAW (1983), Chapter 4.

[18]Berkemer v. McCarty, 103 S. Ct. 3138 (1984).

required for a temporary, brief, roadside questioning pursuant to an ordinary traffic stop, provided the stop is not prolonged in order to obtain an incriminating statement.

Questions have arisen as to whether *Miranda* warnings are required when there is a very strong presumption that the suspect is already aware of his self-incrimination privileges; for instance, when he is a judge, lawyer, police officer, or a person with prior experience as a *"Mirandized"* suspect or as a prison inmate. The answer seems clear from the Supreme Court's statement in its *Miranda* opinion that "whatever the background of the person interrogated, a warning at the time of interrogation is indispensible to overcome its pressures and to insure that the individual knows he is free to exercise the privilege at that point in time."[19]

It is of interest to note that the 1974 Louisiana Constitution, in Article 1, Section 13, requires that the warnings be given *at the time of arrest*. (The Code of Criminal Procedure, in Article 218.1, contains the same requirements.)

Preciseness of Language in the Warnings

For a number of years after *Miranda*, the misconception prevailed that the warnings must contain the exact language the Supreme Court used in stating what was required by its mandate. The pervasiveness and deleterious consequences of this misconception are well illustrated by a decision of a federal circuit court of appeals that was rendered in 1968, 2 years after *Miranda*.[20] In administering the warning to the suspect about his right to counsel, the police told him that if he was unable to hire a lawyer, "the Commissioner or the Court would appoint one for him." The Court of Appeals held this language to be defective because the suspect had not been advised that he could have an attorney present "before he uttered a syllable." The court said that "the message to him indicated only that a judge or commissioner down the line would appoint a lawyer for him if he so requested."[21] The effect of this decision prevailed for 13 years within the federal circuit that included Alabama, Florida, Georgia, Louisiana, Mississippi, Texas, and the Canal Zone. Fortunately, although belatedly, the misconception of that circuit court over the precision of the warning language was dissipated when the Supreme Court of the United States ruled, in the 1981 case of *California v. Prysock*, that there was no requirement "that the content of the *Miranda* warnings be a virtual incantation of the precise language contained in *Miranda*".[22] In other words, the requirements are fulfilled when the suspect is told simply that

---

[19]384 U.S. 436, at P. 469.

[20]*Lathers v. United States*, 396 F. 2d 524 (5th Cir. 1968).

[21]396 F. 2d at 535.

he has the right to remain silent, that anything he says may be held against him, that he has a right to a lawyer, and that if he cannot afford a lawyer, one will be provided free. (A suggested simplified set of warnings is presented later in this chapter, along with a suggestion for meeting the waiver requirement.)

Premature and Repetitious Warnings

Except in a state where the legislature or the courts specify the stage at which the warnings must be given, they should not be issued until an interrogation is about to begin. Louisiana is one such state; it has a constitutional provision (Article 1, Section 13) requiring the issuance of the warnings *at the time of arrest*. The reason for this suggestion is twofold: 1) there is a psychological disadvantage to a premature issuance; 2) in the absence of the warnings, a suspect's silence at the time of arrest or at the time an identification is made of him by the crime victim or a witness, may be usable as evidence against him (i.e., an admission by silence), at least for impeaching his credibility at trial if he takes the stand and denies committing the crime.[23] Moreover, if he fails to make an exculpatory statement (e.g., "I killed in self-defense"), that fact may be used against him if, at trial, he invokes that exculpatory explanation as a defense.[24] On the other hand, if the warnings have been issued at an earlier time than required, the suspect's silence is rendered meaningless and

---

[22]453 U.S. 355 (1981). The case that specifically overruled the *Lathers* case cited in the preceding note is United States v. Contreras, 667 F. 2d 976 (11th Cir. 1982).

The Ninth Circuit Court of Appeals, in a 2-to-1 decision in United States v. Noti, 731 F. 2d 610 (9th Cir. 1984), held that a custodial suspect must be *specifically told* that he has the right to counsel's presence during interrogation. This is at variance with the holdings of the 2nd, 7th, and 8th circuits, the citations of which are in the dissenting opinion. The dissent said "the *Miranda* warning is adequate if it conveys the substance of the defendant's constitutional rights."

A state case in accord with the viewpoint of the dissent in the *Noti* case is People v. Jones, 472 N.E. 2d 1176 (Ill. App. 1984).

[23]A case in which the general principle is extensively discussed is People v. Simmons, 28 Cal. 2d 699, 172 P. 2d 18 (1946). Also see, for textual treatment of the subject, McCORMICK, LAW OF EVIDENCE (2d Ed., 1972), § 161.

A 1982 United States Supreme Court case admitting the fact of silence (absent the warnings) for impeachment purposes is Fletcher v. Weir, 455 U.S. 603. In New York, however, evidence of silence, even in the absence of any warning, is not admissible for *any* purpose. People v. Conyers, 52 N.Y. 2d 454, 420 N.E. 2d 933 (1981). To the same effect is State v. Davis, 686 P. 2d 1143 (Wash. App. 1984), in which two of the justices rested their decision on state grounds, whereas the dissenting justice was of the opinion that the court should honor Fletcher v. Weir, and he also cited an earlier Washington case upholding the admissibility of silence.

[24]Jenkins v. Anderson, 447 U.S. 231 (1980): Fletcher v. Weir, *supra* Note 23.

unusable as evidence because one of the warnings already will have advised him of the right to remain silent.[25]

Not only are the warnings often given prematurely; they are also frequently repeated without any necessity for doing so. This practice of multiple warnings is sometimes referred to as the issuance of "fresh" *Miranda* warnings, and misconceptions prevail as to their significance and value.

An outstanding example of unnecessary as well as meaningless repetitious warnings, along with the possible loss thereby of an interrogation opportunity, is the case of John Hinckley, Jr., following his arrest for the shooting of President Ronald Reagan in Washington, D.C., on March 30, 1981. The principal motive for wanting to question him was to ascertain whether other persons were involved, as part of an assassination conspiracy.

Upon Hinckley's apprehension at the scene of the shooting, he was taken to the Washington, D.C., police headquarters in the custody of both the local police and Secret Service agents. The group arrived there at 2:40 p.m., whereupon the following events occurred. Hinckley was read the *Miranda* warnings by a Secret Service agent. (Along with the four warnings required by *Miranda*, an unnecessary fifth one was included!) Then they were read to him again by a D.C. police detective. Immediately thereafter, he was taken to the homicide squad office, where the same detective read the warnings to him a *third* time. After receiving this third set of warnings (within a *2-hour* period), Hinckley was presented with a waiver-of-rights form containing four questions. Hinckley wrote "yes" alongside the first two—"Have you read or had read to you the warnings as to your rights?" and whether he understood those rights. However, in response to the third question, "Do you wish to answer any questions?" Hinckley answered orally: "I don't know. I'm not sure. I think I ought to talk to Joe Bates," explaining that Bates was his father's lawyer in Dallas, Texas. In response to the fourth question, "Are you willing to answer questions without having an attorney present?" Hinckley verbally responded: "I want to talk to you, but first I want to talk to Joe Bates." Hinckley was advised that an effort would be made to contact Bates. No further attempt was made to interrogate Hinckley. (*Miranda*, of course, had decreed there should be none once the suspect requests an attorney.) Then, at 4:50 p.m., two FBI agents placed Hinckley under arrest for violation of the Presidential Assassination Statute. The agents were informed by the D.C. detective of all that had transpired, and they were further told that an attempt was being made to contact Joe Bates, the Dallas attorney.

---

[25]United States v. Hale, 422 U.S. 171 (1975).

The FBI agents transported Hinckley to the FBI field office. Upon arrival there, at about 5:15 p.m., Hinckley was again read the *Miranda* warnings, this being the *fourth* time. Although he signed his name to the FBI waiver form, "it was clearly understood that he did not waive his right not to answer questions before consulting counsel." Nevertheless, Hinckley did agree to answer various "background" questions, but did not talk about events that occurred after his arrival in Washington. (The "background" questions were unquestionably for the elicitation of information that would be relevant to the issue of the anticipated insanity defense, the only possible defense in view of the overwhelming evidence that Hinckley did the shooting.)

Subsequent to the filing of criminal charges against Hinckley, the D.C. District Court ruled that the "background" information obtained from him could not be used as evidence because it was, in effect, the result of an interrogation conducted after request for an attorney. The trial court ruling was affirmed by the D.C. Court of Appeals, and the government took no further appellate action.[26]

In view of the court rulings, whatever value the background information on Hinckley may have been to the prosecution in countering his insanity defense was irretrievably lost. At Hinckley's trial, psychiatrists for the prosecution testified that Hinckley was sane; those for the defense testified he was insane. The jury found him insane.

As subsequently discussed, there is the possibility that, under the particular circumstances surrounding the shooting of President Reagan, the omission of any warnings at all to Hinckley may have been considered legally permissible under the "emergency" exception to *Miranda* that the Supreme Court itself created in a case decided in July of 1984.[27] In other words, there was the urgency to ascertain whether there was a conspiracy to kill not only the President but other government officials as well. If a conspiracy had existed, Hinckley may have been induced to supply information vital to the saving of other lives. Such consideration of public interest could have been viewed as offsetting the individual rights and privileges otherwise available under the *Miranda* doctrine.

One of the factors accounting for the practice of repeating the *Miranda* warnings is the misconception that a suspect who hears the warnings as they are repeated may change his mind after having refused to talk or after having made a request for counsel. Illustrating that misconception is a

---

[26]The facts reported in the forgoing account of the *Hinckley* case appear in the opinion of the D.C. Court of Appeals in 672 F. 2d 115 (1982). For further details regarding the case and an extensive discussion of *Miranda* problems in general, see Inbau *Over-Reaction: The Mischief of Miranda v. Arizona*, 73 *J.C.L. & CRIM.* 797 (1982).

[27]The case is New York v. Quarles, 104 S. Ct. 2626 (1984) It, as well as the emergency exception principle itself, is subsequently discussed in this text in the section on "The Rescue/Lifesaving Exception to the *Miranda* Requirements at pp. 241–243."

1984 state case in which a warned suspect requested counsel and then was given several "fresh" sets of warnings by the police and by an assistant prosecuting attorney, following which the suspect confessed. The confession was used against him at trial, and a conviction resulted. However, a reviewing court reversed the decision because of the improperly admitted confession obtained after the suspect's request for a lawyer.[28]

Not only did the appellate court reverse the conviction in the above case; it also severely criticized the police and the prosecution for trying "to eucre a waiver of defendant's constitutional right to counsel." The court stated that it was obligated to ensure that criminal suspects " ...do not relinquish their constitutional rights and guarantees solely because they become matched against a more sophisticated, but uncaring law enforcement officer, or an overzealous [prosecutor]."

Another misconception regarding the repetition of *Miranda* warnings, or even a single issuance of them, is that this may rectify some illegal police procedure such as in the earlier discussed *Dunaway* "pick-up" case. An illegal arrest will not undergo a transformation into a lawful one by the issuance of *Miranda* warnings and a waiver of them by the illegally arrested person whom the police want to interrogate. The confession remains "the fruit of the poisonous tree," to use the phrase often expressed by the courts. In such instances, the police must confine themselves to further investigative efforts.

Ample case law supports the following recommendation to interrogators: Once the *Miranda* warnings have been given, followed by a waiver of rights, they should not be repeated unless there has been a considerable lapse of time since they were originally issued, for example, after a day or more.[29] There also is no need to repeat the warnings after a waiver has

---

[28]People v. Hammock, 121 Ill. App. 3d 874, 460 N.W. 2d 378 (1984).

[29]Illustrative cases are: Anderson v. State, 339 So. 2d 166 (Ala. App. 1976) (warnings the night before held sufficient); United States v. Fike, 563 F. 2d 809 (7th Cir. 1977) (9 hour lapse); State v. Russell, 261 N.W. 2d 490 (Iowa, 1978) (3 days later while hospitalized after arrest); State v. Duhaine, 29 Wash. App. 842, 631 P.2d 964 (1981) (two hour lapse).

In Smith v. State, 537 S.W.2d 158 (Ark. 1976), the suspect had been arrested for the theft of a cash register. He received the *Miranda* warnings and waived. He also signed a consent form for the search of his car, which search revealed evidence of other crimes. He was then interrogated about those offenses and confessed. Upon trial he contended that he should have been given new warnings, but the court held they were not required because no significant time had elapsed between the two interrogations and there was no indication the police had diluted the efficacy of the warnings that had been given. Also see Jennings v. Casscles, 568 F.2d 229 (2d Cir., 1977), in which the court held that since the suspect had received the warnings upon each of two occasions when arrested on rape charges, and since he said the warnings were not necessary as he was about to be questioned in the present case, *Miranda's* requirements had been satisfied.

Further, as regards repetitious warnings, consider this comment of the Illinois Supreme Court which said: "to adapt an automatic second-warning system would add a perfunctory ritual ..." People v. Hill, 39 Ill. 2d 125, 233 N.E. 2d 367 (1968), cert. denied, 398 U.S. 936. To the same effect: Gorman v. United States, 380 F.2d 158 (1st Cir. 1967).

been obtained and the interrogation shifts to another unrelated offense; nor is a repetition required where federal officers conduct an interrogation regarding the same criminal act for which the warnings had been issued a short time before by state interrogators.[30] However, if a suspect *refuses* to talk after initially receiving the warnings, and the occasion subsequently arises whereby the police want to question him about an unrelated crime, there should be a repetition of the warnings and a waiver obtained before proceeding with an interrogation.

Required Elements for Invocation of Miranda Rights

A custodial suspect who specifically states, or otherwise indicates (even by silence itself after receiving the *Miranda* warnings), that he is unwilling to be questioned, has obviously exercised his constitutional privilege against self-incrimination. This was the right of all criminal suspects even before *Miranda*, and certainly since then as well. Also, under *Miranda*, if a suspect states that he wants a lawyer, there can be no interrogation, at least until such time as he initiates a waiver of that right. Problems have arisen, however, as to what constitutes a claim of the right to a lawyer in those instances where some statement made by the suspect is later alleged to have been the "functional equivalent" of that claim.

A suspect who requests to talk to someone other than a lawyer is not considered to have asserted the *Miranda* rights. For instance, a request to talk to a parent or other relative, probation officer, or an alleged accomplice also under arrest has been held not to be the equivalent of a request for a lawyer.

There are cases where a warned suspect makes a rather ambiguous remark in which he mentions the word lawyer, such as "maybe I need a lawyer," or "I would like a lawyer, but it wouldn't do any good."[31] Although the case law has gone both ways as to the significance of such statements, it is suggested that the prudent course for an interrogator to follow is to say to the suspect, "It's up to you; do you want a lawyer or not?" If the suspect responds with a "yes," that will preclude any interview; if he says "no," and also acknowledges a willingness to talk, the interrogator may proceed to inquire about the matter under investigation.[32]

---

[30]See State v. Ture, 353 N.W. 2d 518 (Minn. 1984); and United States v. Hopkins, 433 F. 2d 1041 (7th Cir. 1970).

[31]See, for example, United States v. Lame, 716 F. 2d 515 (8th Cir. 1983) (the latter statement was not a request for a lawyer, but rather a waiver).

[32]A case illustrative of the need for clarification of an equivocal statement is Thompson v. Wainwright, 601 F. 2d 768 (5th Cir. 1979). Also see State v. Moulds, 105 Idaho 880, 673, P. 2d 1074 (1983).

The Nature, Form, and Other Requirements of Waiver of Rights

The Supreme Court in *Miranda* stated that after a suspect has received the warnings of constitutional rights, he may "knowingly and intelligently waive those rights and agree to answer questions or make a statement." As regards the mental frame of mind for the making of a legal waiver, the Supreme Court, in a 1979 case, held that a 16-year-old murder suspect was capable of waiving his *Miranda* rights, the test being "consideration of age, experience, and intelligence."[33]

In *Miranda*, the Court did not specify the kind or form of waiver that was required; it did, however, settle a major issue in the subsequent case of *North Carolina v. Butler*, in which the Court held that the waiver does not have to be a written one. In that case, the suspect orally waived his rights to silence and to have an attorney present, but he refused to sign a written waiver to that effect. The Supreme Court ruled that despite his refusal, the oral waiver was sufficient.[34]

Common sense, along with the rulings of the Supreme Court in *California v. Prysock*, discussed earlier, and in the above case of *North Carolina v. Butler*, as well as what the Court said in the *Miranda* opinion itself, warrants a simplification of the required warnings and waiver. It is recommended, therefore, that the warnings be issued orally as follows: "You have a right to remain silent; anything you say may be used against you; you have a right to a lawyer; and if you cannot afford a lawyer one will be provided free." After an appropriate pause to permit the suspect to respond, he should be told: "I would like for you to talk to me about this matter [specifying the case under investigation]. OK?"[35] If the suspect expresses or otherwise indicates a willingness to talk, even by an affirmative

---

[33]Fare v. Michael C., 442 U.S. 707 (1979).

[34]441 U.S. 369 (1979). For a state case to the same effect see State v. Clark, 592 S.W. 2d 709 (Mo. 1979).

A good example of the inadvisability of employing written waivers, especially when elaborately phrased, is United States v. Montgomery, 714 F. 2d 201 (1983). Agents of the Bureau of Alcohol, Tobacco, and Firearms arrested a suspect for violation of federal firearms laws. After *Miranda* warnings were issued, he was shown an ATF form entitled "Waiver of Rights to Remain Silent and of Right to Advice of Counsel." He initialed each of the warnings in the "Statement of Rights" but refused to sign the waiver portion until he conferred with an attorney. He then asked "Am I being charged with each gun?" His question was answered. He proceeded to ask other questions, and in the course of the exchange he made incriminating statements. They were held inadmissible as evidence.

Another example is United States v. Heldt, 745 F. 2d 1275 (9th Cir. 1984), in which the court held that a suspect's refusal to sign a written waiver may be viewed as the equivalent of an exercise of the right to counsel. The court stated that when the interrogator presented the written waiver form, he created, at best, "an ambiguous situation," because the suspect "could reasonably have believed he waived nothing because he had refused to sign." This case should be evaluated in the light of the Supreme Court's holding in *Butler* that the refusal to sign a written waiver did not negate the oral waiver.

[35]Unless the crime is identified, the argument may be made to the effect that there can be no

nod of his head, the interrogator may proceed with the interrogation.[36] On the other hand, of course, if the suspect states or nonverbally indicates an unwillingness to do so, as by a negative shake of his head, or if he requests a lawyer, no interrogation is permissible.

In suggesting the forgoing type of oral warnings and waiver, the authors believe that it is not only supportable by what the Supreme Court has held and said, but that it also comports with the element of fairness. Although *Miranda* prohibits talking a suspect out of a claim of silence or the assistance of counsel, it does not require that a suspect be *talked into* the exercise of those rights, which may be the practical effect of the ritualistic warnings and written waiver procedures that have been so frequently used.[37]

In June 1984, the United States Drug Enforcement Administration, in its revised policy regarding *Miranda* warnings, dispensed with the procedure of obtaining signed waivers. However, the fact that the warnings had been given and a waiver made is incorporated in the introductory part of any written confession submitted to a confessor for his approval and signature.

As stated in the preceding section, there are instances where an apparent waiver will be ambiguous or indecisive. When this occurs, the interrogator should ask for a clarification of what the suspect means or intends to do; however, caution must be exercised to avoid crossing the line into an interrogation, which, of course, is impermissible until a waiver of *Miranda* rights becomes obvious or can reasonably be implied.[38]

---

waiver unless the suspect knows of the particular crime about which the police seek to interrogate him. A case to the effect that this is a factor for consideration, but not solely determinative, in deciding whether there has been an effective waiver, is State v. Condon, 468 A. 2d 1348 (Me. 1983), Cert. denied. 104 S. Ct. 2385.

In United States v. Mc Crary, 643 F. 2d 323 (5th Cir. 1981), the court expressed the view that the crime should be specified, although the failure to do so was harmless error, in view of other certain circumstances of the case.

[36]In one "nod of the head" case, the Colorado Supreme Court stated: "In law, as in life generally, there are cases where actions speak louder than words, and this, in our opinion, is such a case." People v. Ferran, 196 Colo. 513, 591 P. 2d 1013 (1978). Also see Bliss v. United States, 445 A. 2d 625 (D.C. App. 1982). In People v. Williams, 464 N.E. 2d 1176 (Ill. App. 1984), the warnings were issued to a group of four suspects. The nods of their heads were considered adequate waivers.

[37]"Investigating officers are not required to convince a defendant that he needs an attorney." Delap v. State, 440 So. 2d 1242, at 1248 (Fla. 1983), cert. denied, 104 S. Ct. 3554. In a federal case, United States v. Duke, 409 F. 2d 669, 670–671 (4th Cir. 1969), the court said: "*Miranda* does not require law enforcement officials to insist upon or to suggest the refusal of cooperation. As long as the suspect is clearly told and clearly understands that he need not talk, that he may consult a lawyer, before deciding whether or not to talk, and that he may have one present when he talks, if he decides to talk, all of the requirements of *Miranda* are met."

[38]See, for examples, the following cases: Kennedy v. Fairman, 618 F. 2d 1242 (7th Cir. 1980); United States v. Charlton, 565 F. 2d 86 (6th Cir. 1977); State v. Monroe, 101 Idaho 251, 611 P. 2d 1036 (1980); State v. Weinacht, 203 Nebr. 124, 277 S.W. 2d 567 (1979).

Not only may a suspect waive his *Miranda* rights prior to any attempted interrogation; he also may exercise a waiver at any time thereafter, even after expressing a right to silence or a right to a lawyer. In other words, the suspect is privileged to a change of mind, even when he already has a lawyer, either one appointed without costs or retained on a fee basis. The Supreme Court has so held, and there are state cases to the same effect;[39] moreover, there are cases upholding this principle even though the arrestee's lawyer has instructed the police to refrain from questioning his client.[40] New York's highest court, however, has ruled that once an arrestee has a lawyer, there can be no waiver without the lawyer being present,[41] which in effect, will almost invariably foreclose any interrogation.[42]

The important qualification to the rule regarding waivers *after an initial invocation of constitutional rights* is that the willingness to talk must be *initiated by the arrestee*.[43] This, of course, is in conformity with the Supreme Court's mandate in *Miranda* to the effect that the police are not permitted to talk a suspect out of his initial refusal or after he has requested or has obtained a lawyer.

Although an oral waiver is sufficient, if a written form is preferred, it, too, should be a simple one, such as this: "I have been advised that I have a right to remain silent; that anything I say may be used against me; that I have a right to a lawyer; and if I cannot afford a lawyer, one will be provided free. Nevertheless, I am willing to talk to you." There need be no embellishments. Furthermore, as earlier discussed, there is no requirement for the fifth warning that often has been added to the basic four. This

---

[39]Edwards v. Arizona, 451 U.S. 477 (1981); Oregon v. Bradshaw, 103 S. Ct. 2830 (1984); State v. Norgaard, 653 P. 2d 483 (Mont. 1982).

In State v. Jackson, 205 Nebr. 806, 290 N.W. 2d 458 (1980), the court specifically held there was no need to notify counsel of the suspect's intention to waive.

[40]See Brewer v. Williams, 430 U.S. 387 (1977), in which the Supreme Court said that the suspect had the right to effect a waiver despite his attorney's admonition to the police to refrain from talking to his client. The Court found, however, that upon the particular facts of the case there was no such waiver. Also see Shreeves v. United States, 395 A. 2d 774 (D.C. Ct. App. 1978); Watson v. State, 282 Md. 73, 382 A. 2d 574 (1978), in which the court pointed out, at 580, that the Sixth Amendment is "a right of the client and not the lawyer."

Another state case upholding the right to waiver is: Commonwealth v. Currie, 388 Mass. 776, 448 N.E. 2d 740 (1983). A case rejecting a confession because of a disregard of counsel's admonition is State v. Weedon, 342 S. 2d 642 (La. 1977) (2 dissents).

[41]People v. Hobson, 39 N.Y. 2d 479, 348 N. E. 2d 894 (1976); People v. Cunningham, 49 N.Y. 2d 203, 400 N. E. 2d 360 (1980).

A West Virginia case that established a similar rule to the basic one in New York is State v. McNeal, 251 S. E. 2d 484 (W.Va. 1979).

[42]The late Justice Robert Jackson of the United States Supreme Court made the following statement in the 1949 case of Watts v. Indiana, 338 U. S. 49, at 59: "Under our adversary system . . . any lawyer worth his salt will tell the suspect to make no statement to the police under any circumstances."

[43]Edwards v. Arizona and Oregon v. Bradshaw, *supra* note 39.

is the one in which the suspect is told: "If you want to answer questions now without a lawyer present, you will still have the right to stop answering at any time. You also have the right to stop answering at any time until you talk to a lawyer."[44]

In the utilization of written, rather than oral, waivers, law enforcement agencies overlook a very important psychological factor. Individuals in general have an understandable reluctance to sign *any* written document. They may have personally encountered an unfavorable experience, such as being persuaded to sign a contract calling for installment payments far beyond their ability to pay. Most certainly, they will have heard or read about individuals being fleeced as a result of signing papers of one sort or another. Consequently, most persons will talk much more freely than they will sign their name to a document. An excellent example of this in a criminal interrogation setting is the previously discussed waiver case of *North Carolina v. Butler*, in which the suspect orally waived his *Miranda* rights but then balked at signing his name to a written one.[45]

The Meaning of "Custody" as a Basis for the Requirement of *Miranda* Warnings

In *Miranda*, the Supreme Court clearly indicated that the warnings were required only in custodial situations. Nevertheless, a few state appellate courts and one federal circuit court of appeals interpreted *Miranda* to mean that the police had to give the warnings to every person *upon whom suspicion had focused*. The Supreme Court removed this misconception in a 1976 case, which held that focus of suspicion was not the test; the warnings are required only when the suspect is in police *custody*.[46] A state court, however, is privileged to apply the focus test if it wishes to do so under its own constitution.[47]

The meaning of custody (and of the auxiliary phrase from *Miranda*, "deprivation of freedom in any significant way") is illustrated by the

---

[44]This is the fifth warning contained in the District of Columbia Police Department regulations which was given to John W. Hinckley, Jr. at the time when he was questioned about his attempted assassination of President Ronald Reagan on March 30, 1981. References to this as well as other details of the *Hinckley* case were presented in note 26.

[45]Case discussed in text, *supra* p. 231.

[46]Beckwith v. United States, 425 U.S. 341, 347 (1976). This was a case in which agents from the criminal division of the IRS interrogated a taxpayer suspected of filing a false return. He was questioned in his home as well as in his office, without benefit of the proper *Miranda* warnings. The Supreme Court held that since he was not in custody, even though suspicion had focused upon him, the warnings were not required.

[47]A United States Supreme Court case regarding the basic right of the states to impose stricter requirements under their *own* constitutions is Oregon v. Hass, 420 U.S. 714 (1975). Some of the state cases to the same effect are State v. Santiago, 53 Hawaii 254, 492 P. 2d 657 (1971) and People v. Disbrow, 127 Cal. Rptr. 360, 545 P. 2d 272 (1976).

Supreme Court case of *Orozco v. Texas*,[48] in which a suspect was questioned at 4 a.m. in his boarding house bedroom by four police officers, one of whom testified, in effect, that the suspect was under arrest. The Court held that the suspect was the subject of a custodial interrogation, even though the questioning was brief and took place in his own bedroom.

In determining whether an interrogation *within a police facility* constitutes a custodial situation, a case of considerable significance to police interrogators is *Oregon v. Mathiason*,[49] decided by the Supreme Court in 1977. During the course of a burglary investigation, the police learned that the woman whose home had been burglarized expressed a suspicion about one of her son's close associates, who had been a visitor in the home. Furthermore, he was a parolee, presumably because of a conviction for burglary.

The suspect, Mathiason, lived about 2 blocks from a state police patrol office, located in a building that housed several state agencies. The police tried to contact him upon several occasions, but without success. Finally, an officer, who was known to the suspect, left a note at his apartment asking him to call because "I'd like to discuss something with you." The next afternoon, Mathiason phoned, and the officer asked where it would be convenient to meet. They agreed upon the state patrol office about 5 p.m. The two met in the hallway, shook hands, and entered an office. Mathiason was told he was not under arrest. The door was closed and the officer informed him that the matter to be discussed was a burglary. Within 5 minutes, Mathiason confessed, without having received *Miranda* warnings.

Although the Oregon Supreme Court held that the confession should have been rejected by the trial court because the "coercive environment" required the issuance of the warnings, a sizable majority of the United States Supreme Court reversed that ruling. The Court did not consider the interrogation to be a custodial one. The comments of the Court are sufficiently important to warrant a full quotation:

Any interview of one suspected of a crime by a police officer will have coercive aspects to it, simply by virtue of the fact that the police officer is part of a law enforcement system which may ultimately cause the suspect to be charged with a crime. But police officers are not required to administer *Miranda* warnings to everyone whom they question. Nor is the requirement of warnings to be imposed simply because the questioning takes place in the station house, or because the questioned person is one whom the police suspect. *Miranda* warnings are required only where there has been such a restriction on a person's

---

[48]394 U. S. 324 (1969).
[49]429 U. S. 492 (1977).

freedom as to render him "in custody". It was *that* sort of coercive environment to which *Miranda* by its terms was made applicable, and to which it is limited.[50]

The principle of the forgoing *Mathiason* case was reaffirmed in 1983 by the Supreme Court,[51] and it has been applied by a number of state courts.[52]

Mathiason is an excellent illustration of the advisability of arranging, whenever feasible, for an interrogation opportunity based upon a consensual situation. A suspect who has willingly consented to come to or be taken to the place of interrogation, even a police facility, is not in custody; consequently, the police are under no obligation to issue the *Miranda* warnings. In such circumstances, the police may further ensure the consent element by specifically informing the suspect, as was done in *Mathiason*, that he is not under arrest. Furthermore, the interrogation should be conducted in a room that is unlocked and without bars on the door or windows, so as to minimize any suggestion of detention.

In addition to the advantage of rendering *Miranda* warnings unnecessary, the consent of a suspect to come to or be brought to a police facility will afford protection from the pitfall encountered in the *Dunaway* "pick-up" case discussed at the outset of this chapter. In *Dunaway*, a confession was nullified solely because the suspect had been picked up by the police without the reasonable grounds required for a lawful arrest. Had the suspect been requested, and voluntarily consented, to accompany the police, his presence in the police station, as well as his interrogation there, would have been lawful, thereby rendering his otherwise voluntary confession admissible as evidence.[53]

---

[50]429 U. S. 492, at p. 495. There were two aspects of *Mathiason* that the Court was not called upon to decide. One was the false statement made by the interrogator that Mathiason's fingerprints were found at the scene of the burglary, a tactic held permissible in the previously discussed Supreme Court case of Frazier v. Cupp *supra* Note 7. The other was the interrogator's statement that "truthfulness would possibly be considered by the district attorney or judge." The latter comment should be avoided, however, because it may be viewed as a promise of leniency that might nullify the confession.

[51]California v. Beheler, 463 U.S. 1121 (1983).

[52]For example: People v. Wipfler, 68 Ill. 2d 158, 368 N.E. 2d 870 (1977); State v. Fields, 291 Ore. 872, 635 P. 2d 376 (1981); State v. Cruz-Mata, 138 Ariz. 370, 674 P. 2d 1368 (1983); State v. McQuillan, 345 N.W. 2d 867 (S.D. 1984).

Of particular interest to private security officers is the case of United States v. Dockery, 736 F. 2d 1232 (8th Cir. 1984), which involved the interrogation of a bank employee who was suspected of embezzlement. The interrogation was conducted in a small room by government agents, at the request of her employer. The court held it was not custodial; that the employee's freedom of movement was not restricted by governmental agents but rather by her voluntary obligation to her employer.

[53]The value of obtaining a suspect's consent also applies to many other police investigative procedures, such as the seizure of physical evidence from a suspect's person, car, and even residence. Once he consents to the search, the seizure becomes lawful and the seized material admissible as evidence. There must, however, be convincing proof that the consent was voluntarily given.

During the course of interrogation of a noncustodial suspect (for whom *Miranda* warnings are not required), a question may arise as to whether a noncustodial situation may develop into a custodial one that requires the issuance of the warnings. For instance, suppose a suspect makes an incriminating statement or says that he will reveal how he committed the crime, must the interrogator interrupt him in order to issue the *Miranda* warnings? The present case law does not provide a definitive answer (and there is no Supreme Court decision specifically in point), but an analysis of the Court's opinion in *Miranda* rather clearly indicates that once a noncustodial suspect has made an incriminating statement or has expressed a willingness to confess, he should be permitted without interruption to continue to make a full confession. Moreover, there should be no legal impediment to the interrogator asking questions at that time relating to the details of the crime.

Foremost among the reasons in support of the forgoing conclusion is the fact that the *Miranda* decision was based upon the Fifth Amendment provision that no person shall be *compelled* to incriminate himself. The opinion of the Court in *Miranda* clearly revealed that its concern was over the interrogation of a suspect *after* he has been *taken into custody* (or otherwise deprived of his freedom). The Court was of the view that in order to dispel the aura of compulsion created by such taking into custody, the suspect has to be advised of his right to remain silent.[54]

At the time a *noncustodial* suspect is interrogated, he is not under the compulsion the Court attributed to an arrest situation. When the suspect makes an incriminating statement, or expresses a willingness to confess, the mere fact that the interrogator at that time determines an arrest will be made does not give rise to the compulsion factor to which the Court addressed itself in *Miranda*. The situation is comparable to two other circumstances under which various appellate courts have held that the warnings are not required. One is where a suspect enters a police station or approaches a police officer and states that he wants to confess a crime.

---

[54]The following quotations from the Supreme Court's opinion in *Miranda*, 384 U.S. at 478, are particularly relevant: "To summarize, we hold that when an individual is *taken* into custody or otherwise deprived of his freedom ... in any significant way [as in Orozco v. Texas, *supra* Note 48] *and* is subjected to questioning, the privilege against self-incrimination is jeopardized." [Emphasis added by authors] "In dealing with statements obtained through interrogation, we do not purport to find all confessions inadmissible. Confessions remain a proper element in law enforcement. Any statement given freely and voluntarily *without any compelling influences*, is of course, admissible in evidence. The fundamental import of the privilege while an individual is in custody is not whether he is allowed to talk to the police without the benefit of warnings and counsel, but whether he can be interrogated. There is no requirement that police stop a person who enters a police station and states he wishes to confess to a crime, or a person who calls the police to offer a confession or any other statement he desires to make. Volunteered statements of any kind are not barred by the Fifth Amendment and their admissibility is not affected by our holding today. [Emphasis added.]"

The *Miranda* warning flag need not be raised; the police may listen to the suspect's confession and ask questions about the details of the offense without prefacing them with the warnings. The compulsion factor is not present. Another similar circumstance is one in which the police seek to question a person upon whom suspicion has merely focused and there is no taking into custody. The Supreme Court itself, as already stated, has specifically ruled that focus of suspicion is not the test as to whether the warnings are required; the test is custody. This differentiation between focus and custody would be practically meaningless if the courts were to hold that a noncustodial suspect who started to confess, or stated he wanted to confess, had to be interrupted with the administration of the *Miranda* warnings; the cases holding that focus is not the test are usually ones involving confessions made without benefit of the warnings.

Even if the analysis presented might be considered unacceptable by a particular trial or appellate court, the adverse consequences of an unfavorable ruling would be confined to a rejection of the suspect's statement *after* the time when "custody" was deemed to have begun. The initial incriminating statements obviously would have to be considered admissible as evidence. The risk is minimal, therefore, when police interrogators permit a noncustodial suspect to fully confess a crime without interrupting him with an issuance of *Miranda* warnings, even though at some early point, the interrogator has already determined that an arrest will be made.

Although there need be no interruption for the issuance of the warnings as a noncustodial suspect proceeds with the oral confession, it is suggested that in the preparation of the written confession, a statement should be inserted at its beginning, somewhat as follows:

> I have been advised that I have a right to remain silent; that anything I say may be used against me; that I have a right to a lawyer; and if I cannot afford a lawyer, one will be provided free. Nevertheless, I am willing to give this written statement.

The Meaning of "Interrogation" as a Basis for the Requirement of the Warnings

A definitional statement of "interrogation" for purposes of the requirement of *Miranda* warnings appears in a 1980 decision of the United States Supreme Court in *Rhode Island v. Innes*, discussed later in this chapter. The view was expressed in *Innes* that interrogation encompasses not only "express questioning, but also any words or actions on the part of the police (other than those normally attendant to arrest and custody) that the police know are reasonably likely to elicit an incriminating response."

Asking a question specifically related to the suspect's guilt or innocence is clearly interrogation; nevertheless, there are certain conditions and circumstances under which even they do not come within the prohibition of *Miranda*. An illustration is the case of a man who comes into a police station and announces that he just killed his wife. He is asked where and how, and he responds by saying: "at my home, with an ax". He is then asked where he lives and the police take him there, where they indeed find his wife's body. Questions of that nature, as well as ones asked as part of the booking procedure, are generally referred to as "threshold quest-ions."[55] They are to be contrasted, however, with questions asked of a custodial suspect, such as "Do you know why you're here?" or "Do you know why I'm here?" which are considered to be interrogational in nature.[56] On the other hand, it has been held that if the suspect himself inquires about the reason for his arrest and the officer says "you know why," which is followed by a confession, the interchange is not viewed as involving interrogation.[57]

In determining whether police comments or actions in certain case situations involving custodial suspects constitute *Miranda*-prohibited in-terrogation, the United States Supreme Court has applied a "functional equivalent" test. The outstanding example of its application is the 1977 case of *Brewer v. Williams*.[58] This was a child abduction (suspected

---

[55]People v. Savage, 102 Ill. App. 2d 477, 242 N.E. 2d 446 (1968), the ax-killing case; United State v. Hackley 636 F. 2d 493 (D.C. Cir. 1980); State v. Branch 298 N.W. 2d 173 (S.D. 1980); United States v. Downing, 665 F. 2d 404 (1st Cir. 1981). But see People v Rucker, 26 Cal. Rptr. 3d 162, 605 P. 2d 843 (1980), barring admission of *any* responses to routine booking questions.

A 1984 decision of the United States Supreme Court vacated an unpublished opinion of a California Court of Appeals in People v. Howard, which had held that *Miranda* warnings should have been administered to a suspect who had appeared to a police station to confess a crime. 36 Cr. L. 4001 (1984).

[56]An example of such a "know why" question being considered as interrogation is People v. Lowe, 200 Colo. 470, 616 P. 2d 118 (1980).

Prior to *Miranda*, a "know why" question was an effective start of an interrogation of a suspect, whether custodial or not, and it was suggested as a technique in the 1962 pre-*Miranda* edition of INBAU and REID, CRIMINAL INTERROGATION and CONFESSIONS (p. 91). At that time, it was legally proper because there was no requirement for the issuance of any warnings. After the 1966 *Miranda* mandate, however, it was no longer, useable on custodial suspects, and readers of the 1967 second edition of the authors' book were cautioned to that effect (p. 94).

[57]State v. Ladd, 308 N.C. 272, 302 S.E. 2d 164 (1983). Also, to the same effect is United States v. Guido, 704 F. 2d 675 (2nd Cir. 1983), in which the suspect asked for and was given the details of the crime.

In addition to answering the suspect Guido's question that the arrest was for narcotics, he was also told that he should consider cooperating with the authorities, and that he should discuss the possibility of cooperation with his attorney. He had requested one earlier, while in his apartment where his arrest had occurred. Although the court thought that the agents had been slow in letting the suspect call his attorney (about 1½ hours after his arrest), the delay was not considered an egregious one. His confession had already been obtained.

[58]430 U. S. 387 (1977).

murder) case in which a police officer, while in a police car with a custodial suspect who had exercised his *Miranda* rights and already had an attorney, was told that the police hoped they could find the child's body before it became covered with an impending snowfall. The arrestee revealed the body's location. His statement was considered by the Supreme Court to be the functional equivalent of an interrogation; consequently, neither it nor the fact of finding the body was admissible as evidence. (Williams's later conviction was subsequently sustained, in 1983, on the ground that the child's body would have been found, even if he had not disclosed its location.)

In a case situation somewhat similar to *Brewer v. Williams*, the Supreme Court held, in *Rhode Island v. Innes*,[59] that there was no functional equivalent to interrogation when a police officer commented *to another officer*, while in a police car with an armed robbery arrestee, that he hoped that the suspect's discarded weapon could be found before some children in a neighborhood school came across it, whereupon the arrestee disclosed its location. The arrestee's statement, as well as the finding of the gun, was held admissible as evidence. The essential factual difference between *Innes* and *Williams* was, of course, that in the latter, the comment was made to the suspect; whereas in *Innes*, it was made to a fellow officer.

Illustrative of the varying results that may be reached in the application of the functional equivalent test are two cases decided by the same federal circuit court of appeals. In one, decided after *Innes* by a three-judge panel of that circuit court's 24 judges, a police officer had commented to an arrestee that a gun was in his car, and his acknowledgment of its ownership was held admissible as evidence in a prosecution for the interstate transportation of a prohibited firearm. The officer's comment was held not to be the equivalent of interrogation. On the other hand, many members of the full composition of all the judges of the same court, who considered a case decided shortly before *Innes*, had expressed the view that interrogation was implicit in the question "What is this?" with regard to a powdered substance discovered during the search of an arrestee suspected of dealing in drugs.[60]

An exhortation to "tell the truth" and "be honest" obviously constitutes interrogation;[61] likewise, a request of a custodial suspect to take a polygraph test, without his having received the *Miranda* warnings and having

---

[59]446 U. S. 291 (1980). This is the case to which reference was made at the outset of this section.

[60]The three-judge panel case is United States v. Bennett, 626 F. 2d 1309 (5th Cir. 1980). The latter one, the full-panel case, is Harryman v. Estelle, 616 F. 2d 870 (5th Cir. 1980), in which the court decided, however, that the admission of the suspect's statement was harmless error because there was ample other proof to sustain his conviction for heroin possession.

[61]Such expressions, as explained in Part I of this text, are often used in the interrogator's effort to obtain a confession.

waived those rights, has been held to constitute interrogation and is, thus, impermissible.[62]

A number of cases have involved the issue as to whether or not a display to a custodial suspect of crime-scene evidence or of police investigative reports constitutes the functional equivalent of an interrogation. Some have held that the display is not the equivalent of interrogation, but a 1984 decision of the New York Court of Appeals held that it does amount to interrogation.[63]

The Massachusetts Supreme Judicial Court upheld a robbery-murder confession that resulted from the bringing into the interrogation room a suspected accomplice who, while seated 20 to 25 feet away, asserted his innocence and requested to talk to the first suspect, which he was permitted to do. The first one then confessed, although he had earlier invoked his right to silence. This was held not to involve police interrogation.[64]

The issue surrounding the display of evidence or police reports only arises in case situations where a custodial suspect either had not been given the required warnings or else had exercised his right to silence or to see a lawyer. No display restriction is applicable of course, regarding noncustodial suspects or those custodial ones who had made a waiver following the issuance of the warnings.

The "Rescue"/"Lifesaving" Exception to the Warning Requirement

A classic illustration of the application of this exception to the *Miranda* warning requirement is a case in which the police are attempting to locate a kidnapped person and are about to interrogate a suspect whom they reasonably believe to have committed the kidnapping or else knows the location of the victim. Time, obviously, is a critical factor. The suspect's refusal to talk, provoked by the *Miranda* warnings and request for a waiver, and the attending delay thereby occasioned in locating the victim, could account for a loss of life, particularly where the victim is a child.

California is the first state in which this issue has arisen. Its courts have reasoned that the underlying principle of *Miranda* contemplates case situations in which the critical time factor is not present. According to the

---

[62]People v. Johnson, 671 P. 2d 958 (Colo. 1983), 681 P. 2d 524 (Colo. 1984).

[63]People v. Ferro, 63 N.Y. 2d 316, 472 N.E. 2d 13 (1984), cert. denied, 37 Cr. L. 4082 (1985). Accord: In the Interest of Durand, 206 Neb. 415, 293 N.W. 2d 383 (1980).

Among the cases holding that a display is not the functional equivalent of interrogation are: State v. Grisby, 97 Wash. 2d 493, 647 P. 2d 6 (1982); State v. McLean, 242 S.E. 2d 814 (N.C. 1978); Vines v. State, 285 Md. 369, 402 A. 2d 900 (1979).

[64]Commonwealth v. Williams, 388 Mass. 846, 448 N.E. 2d 1114 (1983).

reasoning of the California courts, the requirement for the issuance of warnings of constitutional rights "assumes the possibility of substantial delay" before, for instance, the element of the right to counsel be satisfied, whereas that allowance cannot be tolerated in cases such as a kidnapping. In one of the California cases, the court stated that an emergency sufficient to excuse the *Miranda* requirements contains the following elements:

"1. Urgency of need in that no other course of action promises relief;
2. The possibility of saving human life by rescuing a person whose life is in danger;
3. Rescue is the primary purpose and motive of the interrogators"[65]

Since this exception to the requirement for the issuance of the *Miranda* warnings is founded upon the existence of an emergency situation, it has been held to be inapplicable in a case in which the police were investigating the 3½-month disappearance of a child.[66]

In addition to kidnapping cases, there are others in which the lifesaving concept has been applied. For instance, a police officer, upon arresting a suspect who was known to have had a gun, inquires, "Where is the gun?" May the argument be advanced that the primary purpose was to learn of its location for the protection of the officer or other persons, and, therefore, time and circumstances did not permit the issuance of *Miranda* warnings? A 1983 Kansas Supreme Court held that the lifesaving exception dispensed with the need for *Miranda* warnings, but the opposite conclusion was reached in a 1983 decision of the Arizona Supreme Court.[67] However, in a 5-4 decision of the United States Supreme Court in the 1984 case of *New York v. Quarles*,[68] the Court ruled that a "public safety" exception to *Miranda* applied to the interrogation of a rape suspect regarding the location of a pistol the victim said he had. The interrogation occurred after the suspect was apprehended by the police and handcuffed outside a grocery store into which he had fled. A frisk revealed an empty shoulder holster, and when the suspect was asked, without being given the *Miranda* warnings, what he had done with the gun, he revealed its location within the store. The majority of the Court held that because of the urgency to find the weapon in order to protect the public from its misuse (and also the

---

[65]People v. Riddle, 83 Cal. App. 3d 563, 148 Cal. Rptr. 170, 177 (1978), cert. denied 440 U.S. 937. This case contains an analysis of a prior California Supreme Court case and also of a California appellate court case.

[66]People v. Manning, 672 P. 2d 499 (Colo. 1983). In this case, the police also made a promise of leniency to the suspect in return for her disclosure of the location of the child. She did reveal where the child's body was.

[67]State v. Roadenbaugh, 234 Kans. 474, 673 P. 2d 1166 (1983), and State v. Hein, 138 Ariz. 360, 674 P. 2d 1358 (1983). Another state decision that applied the emergency exception is State v. Lane, 77 Wash. 2d 860, 467 P. 2d 304 (1970).

[68]104 S. Ct. 2626 (1984).

police in the event someone might use it to assist the suspect), "overriding considerations of public safety justified the officer's failure to provide *Miranda* warnings before asking questions devoted to locating the abandoned weapon." Three of the four dissenting justices expressed the view that by its "public safety" exception, the Court practically abandoned *Miranda*.

As previously suggested by the authors, the exception announced in *Quarles* might have been applied in the John Hinckley, Jr. case in view of the possibility of Hinckley's involvement in a conspiracy to kill not only the President but other government officials as well.

Corrective Measures When Warnings Do Not Precede Initial Interrogation

In instances where an interrogator has failed to administer the *Miranda* warnings in the mistaken belief that, under the circumstances of the particular case, the warnings were not required, there are corrective measures that may be employed to salvage an interrogation opportunity. Some other interrogator at a different place and time may issue the warnings and, after a waiver has been made by the suspect, proceed to interrogate him. Several federal circuit and state court cases have held that such warnings and waivers remove the "taint" occasioned by the failure to issue the warnings initially, provided the earlier police questioning was not accompanied by coercion. The Supreme Court of the United States made a similar ruling, by a 6-to-3 decision in the 1985 cases of *Oregon v. Elstad*.[69] Because of the considerable importance of this case to law enforcement, the facts as well as the specific holding of the Court are worthy of attention.

In *Elstad*, police officers went to the residence of his parents with a warrant for his arrest in connection with a burglary. After being admitted to the defendant's home by his mother and directed to his bedroom where they waited for him to dress, he was taken to the living room by one of the officers while the other one went to the kitchen with defendant's mother. The officer sat down with the defendant on a sofa and asked him if he knew why the officers were there. The defendant said he did not. The officer inquired whether the defendant knew the victim of the crime. The defendant said he did. The defendant also said that he had heard about the crime. The officer replied that he thought the defendant was involved in the burglary, and asked him what he knew about it. The defendant responded, "I was there." The officer did not ask any further questions of the defendant at that time, nor did he otherwise attempt to clarify the nature or extent of the defendant's participation in the crime, if any.

---

[69]105 S. Ct. 1285 (1985).

The defendant was then taken to a police station, where he was advised of his rights by a reading from a standard *Miranda* rights card. This was administered by one of the two officers who went to his home to arrest him, but not by the one who interviewed him. The officer asked the defendant if he understood the rights, and he answered affirmatively, signed the *Miranda* waiver form and gave a written confession.

No threats or promises were made to the defendant either at his home or at the police station when he gave his statement. The trial court found, in denying his motion to suppress the written confession, that the confession was freely and voluntarily given. The trial court also found that the pre-*Miranda* warning admission did not taint the subsequent confession. However, the Oregon Court of Appeals held that the trial court erred in refusing to suppress the defendant's written confession. The court concluded, as a matter of law, that the police action in obtaining an admission from the defendant in violation of *Miranda* exerted a coercive impact on his later confession, despite the fact that the subsequent confession was preceded by *Miranda* advice and a waiver of rights. A review of that decision was granted by the United States Supreme Court. In reversing the ruling of the Oregon court, Justice Sandra O'Connor, expressing the opinion of the six-justice majority of the Court, stated:

> We find that the dictates of *Miranda* and the goals of the Fifth Amendment proscription against use of compelled testimony are fully satisfied in the circumstances of this case by barring use of the unwarned statement in the case in chief. No further purpose is served by imputing "taint" to subsequent statements obtained pursuant to a voluntary and knowing waiver. We hold today that a suspect who has once responded to unwarned yet uncoercive questioning is not thereby disabled from waiving his rights and confessing after he has been given the requisite *Miranda* warnings.

With regard to the argument by the Oregon court that Elsted's ultimate confession should be excluded because it was the result of the initial illegal questioning and should be treated in the same way as evidence derived from illegally seized physical evidence, Justice O'Connor said: "The Fourth Amendment exclusionary rule is to deter unreasonable searches, no matter how probative their fruits," whereas "the Fifth Amendment prohibits ... only *compelled* testimony," and "does not require that the statements and their fruits be discarded as inherently coercive."

One of the three dissenting justices in *Elstad*, Justice Stevens, in his separate dissenting opinion, stated that although he found "nothing objectionable" in the majority holding, he was apprehensive that the decision "will breed confusion and uncertainty in the administration of criminal justice." He also expressed the view that "it denegrates the importance of one of the core constitutional rights that protects every American citizen from the kind of tyranny that has flourished in other countries."

THE INTERROGATION OF YOUTHFUL (JUVENILE) SUSPECTS

Confession Voluntariness

In the absence of a statutory provision regarding the interrogation of youthful (juvenile) suspects, the same basic legal rules usually apply to them as to adults. Immaturity is obviously a factor, but it is only one of several for determining whether the interrogation produced an inadmissible confession.

The issue of confession voluntariness in any particular youthful suspect case is determined on the basis of what the courts term the "totality of the circumstances." This means that all factors must be considered—the youth's intelligence, education, background, and the interrogation setting—to determine his vulnerability to possible suggestions and subtle pressures on the part of his interrogator. Applying this standard, but also illustrative of the thin line that may be drawn in some cases, is a 1982 federal circuit decision in which, by a 2-to-1 margin, the murder confession of a 15-year-old youth who had an I.Q. of 62 and a mental age of 9, was held to be voluntary and admissible as evidence.[70]

In another federal case, the confession of an 18-year-old was ruled valid, despite the interrogator's lies to him that he had been positively identified and that his fingerprints were found in the victim's purse.[71] Nevertheless, the "inherent coercion" atmosphere of a police station may be a substantial factor with respect to the issue of voluntariness of the confession of a youthful suspect.[72]

Miranda Warnings

Youthful suspects who are in custody are entitled to receive the *Miranda* warnings, but, as with adults, they may, as a general rule, waive those rights. A United States Supreme Court case with respect to such waivers is the 1979 one of *Fare v. Michael C.*[73] The defendant, who was 16 years old when questioned as a suspect, had received the warnings, whereupon he asked to talk to his probation officer who had been assigned to him for a prior offense. At no time, however, did he ask for a lawyer. A majority of the Court held that the request for a probation officer was not the

---

[70]Vance v. Bordenkircher, 692 F. 2d 978 (4th Cir. 1982). The Supreme Court decline review.

[71]In re D.A.S., 391 A. 2d 255 (D. C. Ct. App. 1978).

[72]See In re William L., 287 N.Y. S. 2d 218 (App. Div. 1968), and People v. Johnson, 74 Cal. Rptr. 3d 889, 450 P. 2d 265–71 (1969). Also see dissent in Vance v. Bordenkircher supra Note 70.

[73]442 U.S. 707 (1979).

equivalent of a request for a lawyer, and the majority further found that there was adequate evidence in support of a waiver of the right to a lawyer. In addition to its specific holding, *Michael C.* is of general value to police interrogators of youthful suspects. In its opinion, a majority of the Court made the following comments, after stating that the "totality of circumstances" approach was the one to use in such cases:

> We discern no persuasive reasons why any other approach is required where the question is whether a juvenile has waived his rights, as opposed to whether an adult has done so. The totality approach permits—indeed, it mandates—inquiry into all the circumstances surrounding the interrogation. This includes evaluation of the juvenile's age, experience, education, background, and intelligence, and into whether he has the capacity to understand the warnings given him, the nature of his Fifth Amendment rights, and the consequences of waiving those rights[74]

A test comparable to the forgoing one was set forth by Massachusetts's highest court in a case involving the validity of a waiver by a 17 year old. It stated that the issue was to be determined by "the totality of all the surroundings—both the characteristics of the accused and the details of the interrogation."[75] In other words, youthful age is not the sole determining factor.

Most courts have declined to adopt a fixed rule that renders youthful suspects incapable of waiving *Miranda* rights.[76] Some courts, however, have applied what is referred to as the "interested adult rule," which prescribes that there can be no waiver by a youth under a certain age (16, 17, or 18) unless he has been afforded consultation with "an interested, informed, and independent adult."[77] Although the Pennsylvania Supreme

---

[74]P. 725.

[75]Commonwealth v. Williams, supra, Note 64.

[76]Quick v. State, 599 P. 2d 712 (Alas. 1979); State v. Hunt, 607 P. 2d 297 (Utah, 1980); Dutil v. State, 93 Wash. 2d 84, 606 P. 2d 269 (1980).

[77]Lewis v. State, 259 Ind. 431, 288 N.E. 2d 138 (1972). In another Indiana case, it was held that although the confessor was under the statutory age when the crime was committed, his being over that age at the time of the interrogation rendered the confession valid. 371 N.E. 2d 703 (Ind. 1978).

Another case example is In re E.T.C. 141 Vt. 375, 449 A. 2d 937 (1982). In a subsequent case, however, the Vermont Court rejected as "untenable" a contention that the warning requirement rule should be extended to cover all situations (noncustodial as well as custodial), in which minors are questioned by the police. The reason given for rejection was "that a requirement to produce an adult" could cause prejudicial delay in investigatory situations when time is of the essence." State v. Piper, 143 Vt. 468, 468 A. 2d. 554 (1983).

In their dissents to a denial of Supreme Court review of State v. Little, 261 Ark, 859, 554 S.W.2d 312 (1978), which involved a youth about 15 years of age, Justices Brennan and Marshall disapproved of the Arkansas decision that the youth's waiver was valid despite the absence of an adult adviser who did not have a "significant conflict of interest," as did the

Court had at one time applied such a rule, it came around full circle in the 1984 case of *Commonwealth v. Williams* and returned to the totality of circumstances test for the validity of a juvenile's waiver and the voluntariness of his confession.[78]

Several state legislatures have been more definitive with respect to the interested adult requirement. They have prohibited any waiver without consultation with a parent or lawyer, and have also declared invalid any confession obtained during an interrogation outside the presence of a parent (or other guardian) or lawyer.[79]

One state supreme court has held that not only are *Miranda* warnings required for a custodial youthful offender, but he also must be told of the possibility that the case may be transferred from the juvenile court to the adult criminal court. The general rule, however, is to the contrary.[80]

Apart from the statutory requirements prescribed in a few states, and except for particular rules established by a few state courts, such as the statutes and decisions discussed, the interrogation of youthful (juvenile) suspects may be conducted in essentially the same way as for adults. The basic guideline in all cases should be that nothing shall be said or done that is apt to make an innocent person confess.

---

youth's mother who was herself a suspect in the killing of the husband/father. 435 U.S. 957 (1978).

Also, upon the subject generally, In re E.T.C., 144 Vt. 375, 449 A. 2d 937 (1982).

[78] 470 A.2d 1376 (Pa. 1984).

[79] See for example, Colo. Rev. Stat. Ann. § 19-2-102(3)(c)(I) (1974) and also Conn. Gen. Stat. Ann. § 17-66d (West Supp. 1976).

In one Colorado case, the murder conviction of a 16 year old was reversed because his confession had been obtained when his parents were not present, even though they had been present earlier when the warnings were issued and a waiver made, and they had consented to the son's taking a polygraph test. People v. Saiz, 620 P.2d 15 (1980).

[80] A case holding that such a warning must be given is State v. Pike, 516 S.W.2d 505 (Mo. 1984). Contra: People v. Prude, 66 Ill.2d 470, 363 N.E.2d 371 (1977), cert. denied, 434 U.S. 930.

CHAPTER NINE

Confession Law

HISTORICAL REVIEW OF THE TESTS OF CONFESSION ADMISSIBILITY

The cruelty and injustice that were involved in the early practices of extorting confessions from accused persons (tearing their bodies apart on a rack or inflicting other forms of torture) eventually led to the development of certain precautionary rules regarding the admissibility of confessions.[1] The basic rules declared that before a confession could be used against an accused person, it must have been shown to represent a *voluntary* acknowledgment of guilt, or else it must have been obtained under conditions or circumstances that could not reasonably be considered as rendering it *untrustworthy*.

Legal scholars have differed as to which of the two tests–voluntariness or trustworthiness–was the historically accurate one. Some of the scholars were of the view that a kinship existed between the confession rule and the early concept of the self-incrimination privilege.[2] Wigmore pointed out, however, that the privilege antedated the confession rule by about 100 years, and that the sole purpose of the confession rule was to ensure reliability. Moreover, he contended that the privilege covered only statements made in court under a compulsory process, whereas the confession rule applied to both in-court and out-of-court statements.[3] For all practical purposes at the present time, the issue is one of academic interest only, especially in view of the current concept of excluding illegally obtained

---

[1]WIGMORE, EVIDENCE §§ 822, 865, 2266 (3d ed., 1940).

[2]McCormick, *Some Problems and Developments in the Admissibility of Confessions*, 24 TEX. L. REV. 239 (1946), and Morgan, *The Privilege Against Self-Incrimination*, 34 MINN. L. REV. 1 (1949).

[3]WIGMORE, §§ 823, 827, 2266.

A discussion of the relative merits of the two differing viewpoints appears in McCormick, *The Scope of Privilege in the Law of Evidence*, 16 TEX. L. REV. 447, pp. 452–457 (1938).

Upon the general subject, see also Culombe v. Connecticut, 367 U.S. 568 (1961), in which the Court stated, in Footnote 25, that although the fear of false confession played a large part

evidence. In this chapter's historical review, therefore, the test of confession admissibility is broadly referred to as a voluntary-trustworthy one, which is the way to which it was referred in earlier cases that are discussed.

The voluntary-trustworthy test of confession admissibility prevailed in both federal and state courts until 1943–1944, at which time the United States Supreme Court laid down a much more restrictive test in federal cases, and also modified the conventional test in state cases.[4]

Tests in Federal Cases

By reason of its supervisory power over lower federal courts, the United States Supreme Court has always had the privilege of imposing whatever standards it desired regarding confession admissibility in federal cases. It exercised this power in the 1943 case of *McNabb v. United States*,[5] in which the Court held that not only must a confession be voluntary and trustworthy, but it must also have been obtained by "civilized" interrogation procedures. Specifically, the Court held that where federal officers interrogated an arrested person, instead of taking him without unnecessary delay before a United States commissioner or a federal judge, as required by law, any confession obtained during the period of delay was inadmissible in evidence, regardless of its voluntariness or trustworthiness.

McNabb reached the United States Supreme Court shortly after the Court had reversed several state court convictions based on confessions obtained by interrogation procedures that could well have induced confessions from innocent persons.[6] The Court apparently had assumed that

---

in the rule of admissibility, "it is equally clear that there soon mingled with this ... the conception that the use of extorted confessions set at naught the underlying tenet of the accusatorial system, that men might not be compelled to speak what would convict them." "Quite apart from testimonial unreliability," the Court added "where it appeared that coercion had been applied ... the Courts refused to be a party to such proceedings."

[4]Prior to 1943, the Supreme Court, in both federal and state cases determined from trial court records whether the judge had acted reasonably in holding that the defendant's confession had not been "forced" out of him or, stated somewhat differently, "had not been obtained in a manner which rendered it untrustworthy." If the Supreme Court decided that the evidence clearly indicated force, and therefore untrustworthiness, the due process clause of either the Fifth Amendment (in federal cases) or the Fourteenth Amendment (in state cases) would be invoked and the case reversed. On the other hand, if the record did not clearly disclose coercion or untrustworthiness, the Court would accept as final the trial court's finding that the confession was voluntary or trustworthy. Wilson v. United States, 162 U.S. 613 (1896); and Brown v. Mississippi, 297 U.S. 278 (1936), which was the first state court confession case to be decided by the United States Supreme Court.

[5]318 U.S. 332 (1943).

[6]Chambers v. Florida, 309 U.S. 227 (1940); White v. Texas, 310 U.S. 530 (1940); Ward v. Texas, 316 U.S. 547 (1942). →

such practices were universally employed by all or most law enforcement officers, federal as well as state, and in *McNabb*, embarked upon its crusade to end such practices.

The *McNabb* case involved an investigation into the killing of an agent of the Alcohol Tax Unit of the Bureau of Internal Revenue. Five members of the McNabb family were arrested as suspects and questioned regarding the killing. Several hours after the last McNabb was arrested, he confessed upon being told that his brothers had accused him of firing the fatal shot. Later, two others confessed their implication in the crime. A federal court trial resulted in a verdict of guilty, and the defendants ultimately appealed to the United States Supreme Court, alleging that the confessions were improperly admitted into evidence. The government contended that the confessions had been voluntarily given and therefore had been properly admitted.

Ordinarily, an issue of the sort raised in the *McNabb* appeal would have been resolved on the basis of a "due process" inquiry as to whether the confessions were voluntary or trustworthy. Here, however, the Court conceded that because the defendants had not been threatened, abused, or otherwise coerced, there was no problem of constitutional law respecting the confessions and their admissibility; but the Court then stated that its reviewing power in federal cases was not confined to the ascertainment of constitutional validity. Justice Frankfurter, speaking for the majority of the Court, said that: "Judicial supervision of the administration of criminal justice in the federal courts implies the duty of establishing and maintaining civilized standards of procedure and evidence," and that such standards "are not satisfied merely by observance of those minimal historic safeguards ... summarized as 'due process of law.'"[7] Justice Frankfurter

---

In *Chambers*, the defendants were kept in jail for a week and interrogated every day for many hours—to such an extent that the sheriff, according to his own testimony, was too tired to continue at night—and then an all-night session was finally held, during which time the subjects were interrogated in the presence of a number of persons, including police officers and several private citizens. The first written confession obtained that night was rejected by the prosecuting attorney, who thereupon informed the interrogators not to call him from his home again until they had secured "something worthwhile." Subsequently, the interrogators obtained confessions that were considered satisfactory. At their trial, the defendants were convicted, and the convictions were sustained by the Supreme Court of Florida. When the case reached the United States Supreme Court, however, it was reversed on the ground that the use of the confessions thus obtained had deprived the defendants of due process of law.

In *White*, a farmhand who had been arrested on a rape charge had been confined to jail for about a week and had been taken into the woods on several nights and interrogated there "because the jail was too crowded," and then, just prior to his confession, had been interrogated in a locked elevator for 4 hours. On the basis of these facts, the United States Supreme Court held that the defendant had been deprived of the due process of law guaranteed by the Constitution of the United States, and, therefore, the Texas Court of Criminal Appeals was held to be in error in upholding the admissibility of the confession. Similar physical and psychological abuses were involved in *Ward*.

[7]318 U.S. 332 at p. 340 (1943).

then proceeded to state that the McNabb brothers had been put in "barren cells" and had been kept there for many hours of "unremitting questioning" instead of being taken "before a United States commissioner or a judicial officer, as the law requires, in order to determine the sufficiency of the justification for their detention."[8] Because of this supposed infraction of the law by federal agents, the Court held that the confessions obtained during the delay in arraignment (i.e., "preliminary hearing") should not have been admitted in evidence and accordingly the convictions were set aside. The Court considered the interrogators' conduct a "flagrant disregard" of federal laws and expressed the view that if the convictions were upheld, the Court would become an accomplice to the willful disobedience of the law; and that although Congress had not explicitly forbidden the use of evidence so procured, if the courts permitted such evidence to stand, they would be stultifying the policy that Congress had enacted into law. In opposition to this view, Justice Reed objected to "broadening the possibilities of defendants escaping punishment by these more vigorous technical requirements in the administration of justice." "If these confessions are otherwise voluntary," said Justice Reed, "civilized standards ... are not advanced by setting aside these judgments because of acts of omission which are not shown to have tended toward coercing the admission."[9]

A rather amazing feature of the *McNabb* case is the fact that the defendants actually had been arraigned promptly, but the trial court record had not disclosed the arraignment and the Supreme Court erroneously had assumed that no arraignment had occurred until after the confessions had been obtained.[10] Moreover, the fact of actual arraignment had even been called to the Court's attention in the government's petition for a rehearing, but to no avail.[11] A retrial of the case resulted in a second conviction which was affirmed by the Circuit Court of Appeals and the case ended there.[12]

In addition to the Court's mistaken interpretation of the factual situation in the *McNabb* case, the federal statute itself, which was viewed by Justice Frankfurter, who wrote the Court's opinion, as embodying a policy that an affirmance of the case would "stultify," was actually enacted for entirely different reasons. Its legislative history reveals that the sole purpose of the legislation (passed in 1893 as *an amendment to an appropriation bill*) was to suppress a widespread practice whereby federal commissioners and marshals were cheating the government in the matter of fees and

---

[8]318 U.S. 332 at pp. 344–345 (1943).

[9]318 U.S. 332 at p. 349 (1943).

[10]See Circuit Court of Appeals' decision affirming the conviction of the McNabbs upon their second trial 142 F.2d 904 (6th Cir. 1944).

[11]319 U.S. 784 (1942); also, *supra* Note 9 and 90 Cong. Rec. 9199 (1944).

[12]*Supra* Note 10.

mileage expense charges. The issue of interrogation practices and confessions was entirely without congressional consideration.[13]

Regardless of the Court's misinterpretation in the *McNabb* case of the pertinent statutory provisions and of the case facts themselves, there is no doubt but that the Supreme Court possessed the inherent power to establish such a test of confession admissibility for use in federal cases. The Court did not need the *McNabb* case, nor even the breach of any federal statute; it could have prescribed a similar rule in any other federal confession case where federal law enforcement officers had employed what the Court considered to be "uncivilized" interrogation procedures.

The new rule was immediately subjected to considerable criticism. Very soon after the *McNabb* decision, the American Bar Association (ABA) voted overwhelmingly against a proposal that had been made to incorporate the rule of that case into the Federal Rules of Criminal Procedure. The proposed rule was deleted from the draft of rules finally presented to the Supreme Court by the drafting committee.[14] The Court's approval of the final draft without the *McNabb* rule in it did not, of course, remove the effect of the decision itself.

In addition to the ABA's action on the *McNabb* rule, Congress soon embarked upon a series of attempts to nullify it, which Congress was privileged to do, because the rule was not of constitutional dimension but only a rule established by the Court in the exercise of its supervisory power over lower federal courts. The first bill to be introduced was known as the Hobbs bill. This bill was passed by the House of Representatives at three successive sessions and received favorable action by a senate judiciary subcommittee.[15] The bill progressed no further, however, because some of its supporters thought that legislation was no longer necessary after a 1944 Supreme Court decision[16] that was erroneously interpreted as representing a substantial modification of the extreme position the Court had taken in the *McNabb* case. As a matter of fact, the rule actually experienced a close call from the Supreme Court itself in

---

[13]For a detailed discussion of the legislative history of this act as well as of similar federal legislation, see Inbau, *The Confession Dilemma in the United States Supreme Court*, 43 ILL. L. REV. 442, 455–459 (1948).

[14]A Statement by the Committee on Bill of Rights of the American Bar Association on H.R. 3690, 42 (1944); 90 CONG. REC. 9366, 9368 (1944). See also Waite, *Police Regulation by Rules of Evidence*, 42 MICH. L. REV. 679, 688–692 (1944).

The senior author of this text (Inbau) attended the 1944 meeting of the ABA at which the rule was considered. He was prepared to express his views in opposition to the proposal, but there was such vigorous opposition voiced by lower federal judges and others in government that he remained silent and listened with much satisfaction to what was being said.

[15]Hearings Before Subcommittee 2 of the Committee on the Judiciary, House of Representatives, 78 Cong., 1st Sess., on H.R. 3690, 11–17 (1944).

[16]Mitchell v. United States, 322 U.S. 65 (1944).

1948. In the case of *Upshaw v. United States*,[17] the rule survived by the narrow margin of a 5-to-4 decision. However, in the 1957 case of *Mallory v. United States*, the Supreme Court unanimously reaffirmed the *McNabb* rule; thereafter, it was generally referred to as the McNabb-Mallory rule.[18]

The circumstances of *Mallory*, the defendant's subsequent criminal history, and the unanimity of the decision renewed congressional activity.[19] Another factor was the extremes taken by the courts in the District of Columbia in applying the *McNabb-Mallory* rule. They had interpreted the statutory requirement of "unnecessary delay" to be the equivalent of "immediately." This practically amounted to a deprivation of the opportunity for federal officers to interrogate arrested persons; a confession obtained during even a slight delay in taking an arrestee before a judicial officer would be suppressed as evidence, irrespective of its voluntary nature. Illustrative of the stringency that was being encountered is a case in which FBI agents, assisted by two local D.C. police officers, arrested a bank robbery suspect about 9 p.m., pursuant to a federal arrest warrant. The arrestee was placed in a police car and, a few blocks away, the driver of the car parked it under a street lamp. The agents then advised the arrestee of his option to remain silent (even though no warnings were required in this pre-*Miranda* era) and proceeded to interview him concerning the robbery. Within a few minutes he confessed. He told where he had hidden the loot ($2,083) and the pistol he had used in the robbery. He took them to his parents' home, where the money and the pistol were recovered. The arrestee was then taken to police headquarters, where he signed a confession. The conviction was reversed because the arrestee had

---

[17]335 U.S. 410 (1948).

[18]354 U.S. 449 (1957).

[19]The facts of *Mallory* are as follows: A woman who lived in an apartment house in Washington, D.C., had gone to the basement about 6:00 p.m. to do some laundry. Having encountered difficulty with the water system, she sought the help of the building's janitor, who lived in a basement apartment with his wife, three children, and a 19-year-old half-brother, Andrew Mallory. Only Mallory was in the janitor's apartment at the time. Mallory rendered the needed assistance. Soon thereafter, the woman was raped by a masked man, whose general features were later described to the police as resembling those of Mallory, as well as of two of the janitor's sons. Shortly after the rape, Andrew Mallory and one of his brother's sons disappeared from the apartment building. Mallory was apprehended the following afternoon about 2 p.m. and was taken, along with his brother's two sons, to police headquarters. They were questioned for approximately 30 minutes, and were then asked to take polygraph tests, to which they agreed. The polygraph examiner was not then available, but, at about 8:00 p.m., Mallory was tested after polygraph tests were administered to the two sons. A half hour later Mallory confessed. He was tried and convicted, but the conviction was reversed by the Supreme Court because of a violation of the statutory prohibition against "unreasonable delay" in presenting him to a judicial officer. The government abandoned any further prosecution. (Mallory was convicted 4 years later in Washington, D.C., for assaulting a female, and 2 years later he was convicted in Philadelphia on a charge of rape and burglary, for which he received a long sentence. He had also been indicted for three other burglaries.)

not been brought before a magistrate "as quickly as possible." The delay rendered inadmissible the confession as well as the seized evidence.[20]

In 1958, 1 year after the *Mallory* decision, a new bill was introduced in Congress providing essentially that no statement or confession would be held inadmissible as evidence in a federal case solely because of a delay in taking an arrestee before a federal commissioner or judge.[21] It passed the House by a substantial majority. The Senate, however, by a 41-to-39 vote, amended it by the addition of one very crucial word. Whereas the House bill provided that no confession was to be excluded "solely because of delay" in arraignment, the Senate amendment inserted the word "reasonable," so that the Senate version would have required that no confession was to be excluded "solely because of reasonable delay." The bill, as thus amended, was referred to a House-Senate conference committee. Some of the House conferees, apparently realizing that the word "reasonable" just about emasculated the bill, resorted to the ingenious device of adding a rather cumbersome proviso, which appears in the italicized portion of the bill as reported by the committee:

> Evidence, including statements and confessions otherwise admissible, shall not be inadmissible solely because of reasonable delay in taking an arrested person before a commissioner or other officer empowered to commit persons charged with offenses against the laws of the United States; *Provided, that such delay is to be considered as an element in determining the voluntary or involuntary nature of such statements or confessions.*

Congress was in its last day of session when the bill reached the Senate floor. A strong supporter of the *McNabb-Mallory* rule raised a point of order, claiming that the conference committee had added "new matter' to the bill in violation of Senate rules. His point of order was sustained, and no vote was taken on the bill.[22]

In 1963, the House passed another anti-*McNabb-Mallory* bill, but it, too,

---

[20]Greenwell v. United States, 336 F.2d 962 (D.C. Cir. 1964).

Another case illustration of the deleterious consequences of the McNabb-Mallory rule in the District of Columbia is the 1962 case of Killough v. United States, 315 F.2d 241, in which the police were investigating the disappearance of the defendant's wife, who had disappeared under suspicious circumstances following an argument between the two. The defendant was questioned while in police custody, and he admitted killing his wife. He led the police to the garbage dump in which he had buried her body. He was tried and convicted, but the Court of Appeals, in a 5-to-4 decision of the full court, held the confession inadmissible and reversed the conviction because the police had neglected to take the defendant before a commissioner or judge "without unnecessary delay."

[21]H.R. 11477, 85th Cong. 2nd Sess.; offered again in 1966 as H.R. 5688.

[22]For a detailed account of the congressional activities regarding this bill, as well as a report on other bills dealing with the same subject, see Hogan and Snee, *The McNabb-Mallory Rule: Its Rise, Rationale and Rescue*, 47 GEO. L. J. 1 (1958).

failed to pass the Senate. Of considerable interest, in view of what the Supreme Court subsequently held in its 1966 case of *Miranda v. Arizona*, which mandated the warnings of constitutional rights as a prerequisite to the interrogation of custodial suspects, the 1963 bill not only would have abolished the *McNabb-Mallory* rule, but one of its provisions would also have required that custodial suspects be advised of their self-incrimination privilege. The same bill was finally enacted by Congress in 1966, but it was vetoed by President Lyndon B. Johnson on the grounds of "unconstitutionality." Had the bill become law, it may have forestalled the Supreme Court's *Miranda* mandate because the basis for that decision was the Court's objective that custodial suspects be made aware of their self-incrimination privilege, which is precisely what the vetoed bill would have accomplished. The bill did not contain, of course, any reference to a suspect's right to a lawyer at the time of interrogation but, in *Miranda*, the Court announced that the only purpose underlying the right to a lawyer was to further assure that the suspect would be made aware of his self-incrimination privilege.

After all of its attempts to abolish the *McNabb-Mallory* rule, Congress finally succeeded, with the passage of the 1968 Omnibus Crime Act. One of the provisions stated that no confession shall be declared inadmissible in a federal court because it had been obtained during a delay in taking the arrestee before a judicial officer, *unless the delay was over 6 hours*. Even if the delay exceeded that period, the confession could still be used as evidence, provided the extended delay was a reasonable one, considering the means of transportation and the distance to be traveled to the nearest judicial officer.[23] Ironically, the Omnibus Crime Act also contains a provision purporting to nullify *Miranda's* requirement for the issuance of warnings of constitutional rights; it provided that the test of confession admissibility was voluntariness, and that the failure to administer any of the warnings would not categorically nullify a confession but could only be considered along with the totality of circumstances in determining whether the confession was voluntary. The constitutionality of this latter provision of the Omnibus Crime Act has not been tested thus far; moreover, the courts, both federal and state, still consider themselves bound by the *Miranda* mandate. That provision, along with *Miranda* and its various ramifications, will be the subject of later discussion in this text.

Until the enactment of the provision of the 1968 Omnibus Crime Act that abolished the *McNabb-Mallory* rule, if federal law enforcement officers delayed in bringing an arrested person before a federal commissioner or judge for arraignment (i.e., the equivalent of a "preliminary hearing" in state courts), any confession obtained during the period of delay was

---

[23] 18 U.S.C. § 3501.

inadmissible in evidence. This was true on the local federal level (e.g., the Washington, D.C., police) as well as on the national level (e.g., the FBI), and the exclusion applied, regardless of the confession's independent quality of voluntariness or trustworthiness.

Despite the abolition of the *McNabb-Mallory* rule within the federal system, the states themselves were and still are privileged to adopt a similar rule either by statute or by the invocation of the state supreme courts' inherent power over lower state courts with respect to the evidence they may admit. The experimentation of several states respecting that rule is discussed later in this chapter.

Long before the Supreme Court's adoption of the *McNabb-Mallory* rule, as well as after its abolition by Congress, the federal courts consistently applied admissibility requirements to safeguard against the use of involuntary (or untrustworthy) confessions as evidence. The standards that were used are reflected in this chapter's review of state confession cases based upon constitutional considerations.

The following section traces the historical developments of the tests of confession admissibility in state cases that ultimately came within the scrutiny of the Supreme Court. The vascillations that occurred may have been the result of the Court's fascination with the "civilized standards" concept it had embraced in the federal case of *McNabb v. United States*.

Tests in State Cases

One year after the United States Supreme Court promulgated its "civilized standards" doctrine for federal cases, a somewhat similar attempt was made to impose a higher ("civilized") standard of investigative practices on state law enforcement officers. Lacking the supervisory power that it could exercise in federal matters, the Supreme Court invoked the seemingly simple expedient of enlarging its concept of the "due process" requirement of the Fourteenth Amendment. Instead of merely requiring that confessions be voluntary or trustworthy, the Court now insisted that they should be free of any "inherent coercion." It laid down that rule in the 1944 case of *Ashcraft v. Tennessee*.[24]

In *Ashcraft*, the defendant had been taken late one afternoon to a morgue, where he identified as his wife the body of a woman who had been beaten to death. From the morgue, Ashcraft was escorted to the county jail and questioned for several hours, after which he was released without having been placed under formal arrest. Nine days later, he was arrested and taken to jail for further questioning. He was interrogated intermittently for 28 hours, whereupon he told the officers that a man

---

[24]322 U.S. 143 (1944).

named Ware had killed his wife. Ware, who had not been suspected previously, was arrested and promptly admitted the killing, stating further that Ashcraft had hired him to do it. Ashcraft was confronted with Ware's confession, and the interrogation continued for another 8 hours, at the end of which Ashcraft admitted his guilt but refused to sign a written confession. He repeated his admission of guilt to two businessmen and to his own family physician, who were called in to witness the confession. The doctor also examined Ashcraft and found him free from any signs of physical abuse. His oral confession was admitted in evidence, and his conviction in the trial court was affirmed by the Supreme Court of Tennessee. Upon appeal to the United States Supreme Court, however, that Court, in a 6-to-3 decision, reversed the conviction on the ground that the holding of Ashcraft incommunicado, without sleep or rest, for 36 hours of interrogation, was "inherently coercive" and a violation of "due process."

In its consideration of *Ashcraft*, the majority of the Court made what seems to be an abstract psychological appraisal of a 36-hour interrogation and decided that an interrogation of that duration was "inherently coercive." For this reason, the confession would be held inadmissible, regardless of the effect of the police practices upon the particular defendant and regardless of the otherwise trustworthiness of the confession.

The principal objection to *Ashcraft* has been directed not so much to the result reached in the case itself, but rather to the general rule laid down in the majority opinion. For instance, in his dissenting opinion, Justice Jackson severely criticized the majority opinion for excluding a confession "on an irrebuttable presumption that custody and examination 'are inherently coercive' if of some unspecified duration within 36 hours." In his analysis of the case, Justice Jackson expressed the view that "despite the 'inherent coerciveness' of the circumstances of Ashcraft's examination, the confession when made was delivered free, and voluntary in the sense in which that term is used in criminal law."

In further criticism of the majority opinion in the *Ashcraft* case, Justice Jackson said:

> The Court bases its decision on the premise that custody and examination of a prisoner for thirty-six hours is "inherently coercive." Of course it is. And so is custody and examination for one hour. Arrest itself is inherently coercive, and so is detention. When not justified, infliction of such indignities upon the person is actionable as a tort. Of course such acts put pressure upon the prisoner to answer questions, to answer them truthfully, and to confess if guilty .... If the constitutional admissibility of a confession is no longer to be measured by the mental state of the individual confessor but by a general doctrine dependent on the clock, it should be capable of statement in definite terms. If thirty-six hours is more than is permissible, what about 24?; or 12?; 6?; or 1? All are "inherently coercive."

For several years following *Ashcraft*, it seemed that the growing restrictions on state interrogation practices would soon eliminate the opportunity for effective interrogation of criminal suspects. This possibility seemed quite imminent after the Supreme Court's 5-to-4 decision in *Haley v. Ohio*,[25] a 1948 case in which a reversal was ordered of the conviction of a 15-year-old boy who had been questioned, without the use of force, threats, or promises, for 5 hours by several police officers "in relays of one or two each." His interrogation was considered "inherently coercive." The majority opinion stated that in any case where the undisputed evidence "*suggested*" that coercion was used, the conviction would be reversed "*even though without the confession there might have been sufficient evidence for submission to the jury* [emphasis added]."

The author of the majority opinion in *Haley*, Justice Douglas, soon thereafter expressed himself as favoring the outlawing of any confession, however freely given, if it was obtained during the period between the arrest and the preliminary hearing before a judicial officer.[26] In answer to this suggestion, another member of the Court, Justice Jackson, pointed out that an opportunity to interrogate criminal suspects was an absolute necessity, because many crimes are solvable only by that process. He also added that there were only two alternatives regarding this issue of whether or not police interrogations should be permitted: "to close the books on crime and forget it," or "to take suspects into custody for questioning . . . ." He further commented that if the Constitution required the Supreme Court to hold that a state may not take into custody and question a person suspected reasonably of an unwitnessed murder, "the people of this country must discipline themselves to seeing their police stand by helplessly while those suspected of murder prowl about unmolested."[27]

Four of the Supreme Court justices who dissented in *Haley* rather clearly committed themselves, in three state cases that were decided in 1949, to abandoning *Ashcraft*'s "inherent coercion" test in favor of the original voluntary-trustworthy test of state court confession admissibility.[28] Within a couple of years thereafter, a majority of the Court justices did revert to the voluntary-trustworthy test. This was done in the

---

[25]332 U.S. 596 (1948).

[26]Watts v. Indiana, 338 U.S. 49 at p. 57 (1949). Also see Justice Jackson's reference to Justice Douglas's concurring opinion. Justice Jackson said: "A concurring opinion . . . goes to the very limit and seems to declare for outlawing any confession, however freely given, if obtained during a period of custody between arrest and arraignment—which, in practice, means all of them." (338 U.S. at p. 58.)

[27]338 U.S. 49 at pp. 58 and 61 (1949).

[28]Watts v. Indiana, 338 U.S. 49 (1949); Turner v. Pennsylvania, 338 U.S. 62 (1949); and Harris v. South Carolina, 338 U.S. 68 (1949).

1951–1952 cases of *Gallegos v. Nebraska*[29] and *Stroble v. California*,[30] both of which had only two dissenters (Justices Douglas and Black). The majority of the Court in *Gallegos* said that, "So far as due process affects admissions before trial . . ., the accepted test is their voluntariness." The opinion further stated that the voluntariness issue in any case requires an appraisal of the particular facts of that case. In other words, the inherent coercion test of *Ashcraft* was no longer applicable.

The majority of the Court in *Gallegos* and *Stroble* also unequivocally rejected defense counsel proposals to categorically outlaw confessions obtained by state law enforcement officers during a period of "unnecessary delay" in taking an arrested person before a committing magistrate for a preliminary hearing. The Court held that in state cases, such a delay was only one factor to be considered along with all the other evidence in determining the voluntariness of the confession.

In addition to its return in *Gallegos* and *Stroble* to the voluntary-trustworthy test of state court confession admissibility, a majority of the Supreme Court soon thereafter also repudiated what had been said in *Haley* and in several other cases about the inherent invalidity of any conviction in which a coerced confession had been used as evidence. In a 6-to-3 decision in the 1953 case of *Stein v. New York*,[31] the Court held that a state court conviction that was supportable by other evidence would stand, even when a coerced confession had been used as evidence in the trial. The majority opinion pointed out that in confession cases, the Fourteenth Amendment is not a rigid exclusionary rule of evidence, but only a guarantee against convictions based upon untrustworthy evidence. The opinion also clearly revealed, as did the opinions in *Gallegos* and *Stroble*, that in determining a confession's admissibility in state cases, the Court would no longer make a psychological appraisal of the facts and circumstances involved in the interrogation of the accused (as was done in *Ashcraft*) but that it would examine the confession and events leading up to it and determine whether or not the interrogation had a coercive effect on the particular person making the confession. In utilizing that test of admissibility, the Court, in a 6-to-3 decision in the 1957 case of *Fikes v. Alabama*,[32] held inadmissible a confession made by an uneducated man of low mentality, who had been questioned intermittently over a 10-day period of detention, during which time he had been isolated from other prisoners and denied visits from his father and a lawyer who had tried to see him. The majority of the Court held that the "totality of these

---

[29]342 U.S. 55 (1951).
[30]343 U.S. 181 (1952).
[31]346 U.S. 156 (1953).
[32]352 U.S. 191 (1957).

circumstances" went beyond allowable limits. The three dissenting justices were of the view that the interrogation had not involved police brutality or psychological coercion, which are usually associated with a due process violation. They also expressed the opinion that the Court should have "due regard for the division between state and federal functions in the administration of criminal justice."

The "totality of circumstances" approach in the *Fikes* case was also utilized in the 1958 case of *Payne v. Arkansas*[33] to reverse the conviction of a 19-year-old male accused of robbery-murder. He had been held incommunicado for 3 days, had been denied food "for long periods of time," and had been told that a mob was outside the jail to "get him." The Court decided that even though there was other evidence of guilt, "no one can say what credit and weight the jury gave the confession," and, consequently, the conviction would have to be reversed because of a violation of due process. Justice Clark, however, dissented on the ground that there was sufficient other evidence, apart from the confession, to sustain the conviction on the authority of the Court's 1953 decision on this point in *Stein v. New York*.

In the 1959 case of *Spano v. New York*,[34] the Supreme Court seems to have brushed aside all that it had been saying and holding in several of its cases during the preceding 8 years, for now the Court began to talk once more about factors other than voluntariness or trustworthiness in determining a confession's admissibility in the state courts. It expressed itself as though it was about ready to impose upon the states, as a due process requirement, the same kind of "civilized standards" rule it had imposed on lower federal courts and federal officers in *McNabb* and *Mallory*. Here is what the Court said in *Spano*:

> The abhorrence of society to the use of involuntary confessions does not turn alone on their inherent trustworthiness. It also turns on the deep rooted feeling that the police must obey the law while enforcing the law; that in the end life and liberty can be as much endangered from illegal methods used to convict those thought to be criminals as from the actual criminals themselves.

The Court found fault with the fact that the defendant, a foreign-born man, 25 years of age, with only one-half year of high school, was questioned by a number of persons for about 8 hours. It also mentioned that the interrogation had not been conducted "during normal business hours." Emphasis was also placed upon the fact that the defendant had been denied the right to contact his attorney. This denial was considered all the more serious by

---

[33]356 U.S. 560 (1958).
[34]360 U.S. 315 (1959).

reason of its coming after the defendant had been indicted—in other words, after the criminal prosecution had been initiated.

Perhaps because the "totality of circumstances" may have been considered sufficient to warrant a reversal anyway, there was no dissent in *Spano*. On the other hand, four of the justices (Warren, Black, Brennan, and Douglas) made it perfectly clear that they viewed the denial of counsel factor sufficient, in itself, to constitute a violation of due process, and in their opinion, it mattered not whether the denial came before or after the judicial process had begun. In two earlier 5-to-4 decisions, however, the Court had held that a denial of counsel prior to the beginning of the judicial process (e.g., indictment) did not constitute a due process violation, and consequently, a confession obtained thereafter was admissible as evidence.[35]

The clearest expression to emanate from the United States Supreme Court regarding a "general test" of state court confession admissibility was the 6-to-2 majority opinion in the 1961 case of *Rogers v. Richmond*.[36] In this case, the Court said that a confession's admissibility in a state court should be determined on the basis of "whether the behavior of the State's law enforcement officials was such as to overbear [the suspected person's] will to resist and bring about confessions not freely determined." The Court also stated that this question was to be answered "with complete disregard of whether or not [the accused] in fact spoke the truth."

Three months after *Rogers*, the Supreme Court decided another state court confession case, *Culombe v. Connecticut*,[37] in which the majority opinion stated that "the ultimate test" of confession admissibility in the state courts "remains that which has been the only clearly established test in Anglo-American courts for two hundred years: the test of voluntariness." The majority opinion then went on to outline the following criteria in determining voluntariness:

Is the confession the product of an essentially free and unconstrained choice by its maker? If it is, if he has willed to confess, it may be used against him. If it is not, if his will has been overborne and his capacity for self-determination critically impaired, the use of the confession offends due process . . . . The line of distinction is that at which governing self-direction is lost and compulsion, of

---

[35]See Crooker v. California, 357 U.S. 433 (1958); and Cicenia v. La Gay, 357 U.S. 504 (1958).

[36]365 U.S. 534 (1961).

[37]367 U.S. 568 (1961). Between the *Rogers* and the *Culombe* decisions, the Court had reversed, 7 to 2, the case of Reck v. Pate, 367 U.S. 433 (1961), because the majority found that a "totality of coercive circumstances" surrounded the defendant's confession. The minority of the Court was of the view that the Supreme Court should not set aside the trial court findings of facts that had been accepted by the previous reviewing courts.

whatever nature or however infused, propels or helps to propel the confession.[38]

Even assuming that the above-stated general test is clear and understandable, the various concurring opinions of Justices Warren, Black,
Brennan, and Douglas cast considerable doubt as to the qualifications that
would be attached to this test in future cases. Indeed, Chief Justice Warren
actually castigated Justice Frankfurter, who authored the *Culombe* case
opinion, for speaking out in such general terms. Chief Justice Warren said
that although Justice Frankfurter's opinion had been unquestionably written with the intention of clarifying the law regarding confession admissibility, "it is doubtful that such will be the result, for while three members
of the Court agree to the general principles enunciated by the opinion, they
construe those principles as requiring a result in this case exactly the
opposite from that reached by the author of the opinion." The Chief
Justice said he "would prefer not to write on many of the difficult
questions which the opinion discusses until the facts of a particular case
make such writing necessary." But in the Court's 1966 case of *Miranda v.
Arizona*,[39] Chief Justice Warren did precisely what he so severely criticized Justice Frankfurter of doing in *Culombe*.

Evidence of the fact that the *Culombe* opinion did not represent much of
a clarification of a general test of confession admissibility is to be found in
the following excerpt from the majority opinion of the Court:

It is impossible for this Court, in enforcing the Fourteenth Amendment, to
attempt precisely to delimit, or to surround with specific, all-inclusive restrictions, the power of interrogation allowed to state law enforcement officers in
obtaining confessions. No single litmus paper test for constitutionally impermissible interrogation has been evolved: neither extensive cross-questioning—
deprecated by the English judges; nor undue delay in arraignment—proscribed
by McNabb; nor failure to caution a prisoner—enjoined by the Judges' Rules;
nor refusal to permit communication with friends and legal counsel at stages in
the proceeding when the prisoner is still only a suspect—prohibited by several
state statutes.

---

[38]367 U.S. 568 at p. 602. Justice Frankfurter, who authored the test, offered an explanation of it
in the following terms which may well not help much: "The inquiry whether, in a particular
case, a confession was voluntarily or involuntarily made involves, at the least, a three-phased
process. First, there is the business of finding the crude historical facts, the external,
'phenomenological' occurrences and events surrounding the confession. Second, because the
concept of 'voluntariness' is one which concerns a mental state, there is the imaginative
recreation, largely inferential, of internal, 'psychological' fact. Third, there is the application
to this psychological fact of standards for judgment informed by the larger legal conceptions
ordinarily characterized as rules of law but which, also, comprehend both induction from,
and anticipation of, factual circumstances" (p. 603).

[39]384 U.S. 436 (1966).

The next confession case decided by the Supreme Court was in 1962, *Gallegos v. Colorado*,[40] which reversed (in a 4-to-3 decision involving only seven of the nine justices) the murder conviction of a 14-year-old boy because the trial court had admitted a confession that had been obtained while the boy was being questioned alone. According to the majority of the Court, he had "no way of knowing what the consequences of his confession were without advice regarding his constitutional rights from someone concerned with securing him those rights—and without the aid of more mature judgment as to the steps he should take in the predicament in which he found himself." "Adult advice," said the majority, "would have put him on a less unequal footing with his interrogators."

The language of the majority opinion seemed to lay down a general rule protecting persons of the approximate age of the defendant from any interrogation conducted outside the presence of counsel or other "friendly adult advisor." The dissenting justices were very critical of the majority view. They referred to "the hop, skip, and jump fashion" in which the majority concluded that "the totality of circumstances" of this case constituted a violation of due process, and they expressed their "regret" that the conviction was reversed "without support from prior cases and on the basis of inference and conjecture not supported in the record." They found no significant factors of coercion or even impropriety in the questioning of the defendant. To them, the written confession, and more particularly the one made by the defendant immediately after he was apprehended, was completely voluntary.

In the 1963 case of *Lynumn v. Illinois*,[41] the Court, in a unanimous opinion, reversed a woman's conviction for the possession and sale of marijuana because of the use of a confession obtained after the police interrogators had told her that if she did not "cooperate" she would be deprived of state financial aid and her children would be taken away from her. Quite understandably, the Court considered the confession to have been obtained by coercion.

The unanimity of the Court in *Lynumn* was only a fleeting one. Two months later, the Court split 5-to-4 in *Haynes v. Washington*,[42] which involved the following facts: The defendant had been observed walking along the street near the place of a nighttime gas station robbery shortly after its commission. As the police car approached him, the defendant went into the yard of a home. When questioned, he told the police he lived there. He then walked onto the porch of the home and began fumbling with the screen door, as if to unlock it. An officer remained at the sidewalk

---

[40]370 U.S. 49 (1962). (This is a different case from Gallegos v. Nebraska in Note 29.)
[41]372 U.S. 528 (1963).
[42]373 U.S. 503 (1963).

curb observing the defendant. Within a few moments, the defendant came down from the porch and told the officers: "You got me, let's go." He was placed in a police car and he then admitted the robbery. As the police drove to the scene of the robbery, the defendant identified the filling station where the robbery had occurred. He was then taken to the police station, where he arrived 20 minutes after his arrest, and there he made a second oral confession to a police lieutenant. Both confessions were within 1 hour and 20 minutes after his arrest. On the following morning, a written confession was obtained by the police, and later on he made another confession to a deputy prosecutor, but this one he refused to sign. Thereafter the defendant was held incommunicado for a week.

The defendant (who had a prior criminal record as a burglar) challenged the admissibility of the written confession on the ground that it was obtained after he had requested and had been denied permission to call his wife and an attorney, and after he had been told that he could call after a written confession was obtained. The police testimony, according to the majority of the Court, did not refute the defendant's claims. The majority reversed because they found that what the police did amounted to coercion.

Four members of the Court (Justices Clark, Harlan, Stewart, and White) considered the issue of what had actually occurred to be a disputed one, and they also referred to the Court's previous decisions in which the Court found no coercion or inducement in confessions obtained after the arrestees had actually been denied counsel and not just merely the opportunity to contact one.

As is obvious from the forgoing historical review, considerable uncertainty prevailed over the years in the Supreme Court opinions regarding the precise test to be employed by the lower courts in determining confession voluntariness. Professor Joseph Grano has made the following proposal:

> .... The law of confessions should revert to a new due process voluntariness test, one that preserves a certain degree of mental freedom, protects against fundamental unfairness, and prevents interrogation practices that create a risk of untrustworthy confessions.[43]

This proposal is analyzed later in this chapter when trickery and deceit as interrogation techniques are discussed.

Among the general legal principles of criminal interrogation and confessions that have attributes of certainty are the prohibitions upon the actual

---

[43]Grano, *Voluntariness, Free Will and the Law of Confessions*, 65 VA. L. REV. 859–945 at 865 (1979).

use of physical force and the threat of such force in an effort to obtain a confession. Less certainty exists, however, when indirect force is invoked, such as the deprivation of rest, sleep, food, water, or access to toilet facilities. In such instances, there is no generic rule to be applied; the degree of the resulting pressures must be assessed on a case-by-case basis.

Whenever actual physical force or the threat of force is used, a resulting confession is categorically nullified, and evidence derived therefrom is also subject to exclusion. The only possible exception would be a case where such a tactic might be employed to save the life of a kidnapped person, or another innocent person whose whereabouts must immediately be ascertained. Case law squarely in point is lacking. The closest case occurred in 1982. In this case, the threat of force and the actual use of force were used to locate a kidnapped person; and the appellate court there held the resulting statement (which the prosecution did not offer as evidence) had not tainted and thereby rendered inadmissible a confession that was later made under different circumstances.[44]

Less certainty prevails with respect to the effect of promises upon a resulting confession's validity than is true regarding the use of force or the threat of force. Here, too, the determination of voluntariness depends upon the nature of the promise made. Some are permissible; others will clearly nullify a confession. The law generally upon that subject is treated later in this chapter. Also explored are other categories, such as the effect of the use of trickery and deceit on confession admissibility.

LEGAL OBLIGATIONS OF THE POLICE WHEN PROCURING THE OPPORTUNITY TO CONDUCT AN INTERROGATION

The Initial Police-Suspect Contact—"Pick-Up," Arrest, Consent?

As discussed in Chapter 8 of this text, unless the police have probable cause for actual arrest, they have no legal right to resort to a "pick-up" in order to interrogate a suspect. Lacking probable cause for an arrest, the police have the alternative either to obtain the suspect's consent to accompany them to the place of interrogation, or to await the procurement of evidence—physical, circumstantial, or direct (as from witnesses, etc.)—to establish probable cause for an actual arrest.

In the event lawful procedures are not followed in obtaining the interrogation opportunity, a confession obtained from the suspect will be

---

[44]Leon v. State, 410 So. 2d 201 (Fla. App. 1982).

suppressed, regardless of its otherwise voluntary nature. A principal case to that effect is *Dunaway v. New York,* decided by the Supreme Court in 1979.[45] The defendant Dunaway had been "picked up" on the basis of a mere tip from a jail inmate that Dunaway had attempted a robbery-murder. Although Dunaway went along without objection or resistance, a majority of the Supreme Court concluded from the trial court record that he would have been restrained if he had refused; consequently, he had, in effect, been arrested. Since the jail inmate's tip did not constitute probable cause, the police action was illegal; therefore, the confession Dunaway made, although voluntary in other respects, was to be rejected as the product or "fruit" of the unlawful pick-up. Two of the justices dissented on the ground that the evidence at trial had established that Dunaway had voluntarily accompanied the police.

Two state cases, both decided in 1981, one by the New York Court of Appeals and the other by the Supreme Court of New Jersey, established an important exception to the application of the *Dunaway* exclusionary rule. They each held that if *independent* incriminating evidence is lawfully obtained against the person in illegal custody, a confession *obtained thereafter* would be admissible.

In the New York case,[46] the unlawfully held murder suspect's bloody boots were found and were lawfully seized by other officers. That fact established probable cause for the detainee's arrest and therefore rendered lawful his custody thereafter. The same conclusion was reached in the New Jersey case,[47] in which an accomplice of the illegally detained person confessed and implicated both of them. The accomplice also revealed the location of the guns used in the crime. The only admissibility requirement in both cases was that the probable cause evidence (i.e., the bloody boots, the accomplice's confession, and the guns) was not a derivative of the illegal pick-up and detention; in other words, the evidence must have been procured independently of the unlawful arrest. The rationale of the courts in these two cases, as well as that in others to the same effect, was that the intervening circumstance of the independently

---

[45]442 U.S. 200 (1979). A case to the same effect is Taylor v. Alabama, 457 U.S. 687 (1982), in which four justices dissented on the ground that the taint of the illegal arrest had been removed by a combination of the following circumstances: 1) the arrestee had spent most of the preconfession 6-hour detention alone, 2) his girlfriend and her companion had been permitted to visit him, and 3) he had received the *Miranda* warnings three times.

The doctrine of *Dunaway* and *Taylor* was originally established by the Supreme Court in Brown v. Illinois, 422 U.S. 590 (1975).

[46]People v. Rogers, 52 N.Y.2d 527, 421 N.E.2d 491 (1981).

[47]State v. Barry, 86 N.J. 80, 429 A.2d 581 (1981). United States Supreme Court Justices White, Brennan, and Marshall dissented from denial of cert. 454 U.S. 1017.

obtained evidence severed any causal connection between the illegal arrest and the subsequent confession.[48]

As suggested in Chapter 8, the entire *Dunaway* problem may be avoided in many cases by obtaining the suspect's consent to accompany the officers rather than resorting to a pick-up.[49]

The Requirement of Taking Arrestees To a Judicial Officer "Without Unnecessary Delay"

Federal law enforcement officers are required by a federal rule of criminal procedure to take arrestees before a judicial officer "without unnecessary delay."[50] Practically every state system has a rule of criminal procedure or a statute with the same or comparable requirement;[51] some states, however, specify a particular time period, which may last as long as 12 or 48 hours.[52]

The early statutory provisions in England regarding the preliminary examination of arrested persons by justices of the peace were to provide

---

[48]Among other cases in accord with *Rogers* and *Barry* are: McCall v. People, 623 P. 2d 397 (Colo. 1981); In Interest of R.S., 93 Ill. App. 3d 941, 418 N.E. 2d 195 (1981); People v. Washington, 99 Mich. App. 330, 297 N.W. 2d 915 (1980).

Upon the general issue of the kind of intervening circumstances that will remove the taint of an illegal arrest, see the dissenting opinion to a denial of cert in *Barry, supra* Note 47. As subsequently discussed, the taint will not be removed only by the issuance of *Miranda* warnings.

It has been held that the *Dunaway* exclusionary rule is not applicable in a case where an arrest was made in good faith reliance upon an invalid warrant United States v. Mahoney, 712 F.2d 956 (5th Cir. 1983). Also see United States v. Lame, 716 F.2d 515 (1983) in which the court referred to the statement the Supreme Court made in Brown v. Illinois, *supra* Note 45, that an "accused's presentation before a magistrate for a determination of probable cause" purges the taint of an illegal arrest.

[49]See *Chapter 8*, at p. 214. A good appellate court illustration of pursuing the consent procedure is State v. Morgan, 261 S.E.2d 827 (N.C. 1980). On the issue of whether consent is to be determined by an objective or subjective test, see Barber v. State, 93 Ill. App. 3d 911, 419 N.E.2d 439 (1981). In People v. Townes, 91 Ill. 2d 32, 435 N.E.2d 103 (1982), cert. denied, 459 U.S. 87, the Illinois Supreme Court divided 5 to 2 as to whether the suspect had consented to accompany the police to the station for questioning in a rape case. The justice who wrote the dissent made the following observation: "When one of... [two persons] resembles a general description by the victim and has a record of similar offenses, I would think good police practice would dictate that an officer with no more specific clues should attempt, in a reasonable manner, to interview him even though probable cause, as such, does not exist. Too, no constitutional guarantee known to me bans asking that individual if he is willing to talk to the officers at the station where, as here, there is not the slightest hint of coercion."

[50]Rule 5 (a), Federal Rules of Criminal Procedure.

[51]Virginia, for example, requires that the arrestee be taken "forthwith" before a judicial officer in a warrantless arrest situation, but where the arrest is upon a warrant it must be done "without unnecessary delay." Va. Code,§§ 19.2-82 and 19.2-80.

[52]In Kentucky, the period is 12 hours, but in "exceptional cases," the period becomes one of "without unnecessary delay." Ky. R. Crim. P., 3.02(2). In the following states, the period is 24 hours: Alaska (Alaska Stats.,§ 12.25.150 (a)); Arizona (Ariz. R. Crim. P., 4.1 (a)); Delaware

the prosecution with a means for obtaining further evidence against the arrestee.[53] The primary purpose of the present-day statutory provisions, however, is to determine whether the known evidence against the arrestee is sufficient to justify further proceedings against him. It is intended to obviate the unfairness, annoyance, and expense of a defense in any further proceeding unless there is sufficient evidence to indicate at least the probability that the arrestee is guilty. If the examining magistrate concludes that there is insufficient evidence to justify further proceedings, the accused is released from custody. On the other hand, if the evidence disclosed by the prosecution indicates that a conviction might reasonably result, the accused can be held in jail for trial or temporarily released on bond.

Until the United States Supreme Court decision in the 1943 case of *McNabb v. United States*,[54] there was no doubt of the admissibility of voluntary confessions that had been obtained during a period of delay in taking arrestees before a committing magistrate for a preliminary hearing.[55] At most, the delay, in violation of a statutory provision regarding an early hearing before a committing magistrate, was only one factor to be considered in determining the voluntariness or trustworthiness of the confession.[56] The only direct consequence of the violation was a possible civil action against the arresting officer or perhaps disciplinary action against him by his commanding officer.[57] In *McNabb*, however, the Supreme Court held that a confession obtained by federal officers during a period of "unnecessary delay" in arraignment (i.e., "a preliminary hearing") was inadmissible as evidence in a federal case, regardless of its voluntariness or trustworthiness; the Court specifically stated that it was establishing this rule in the exercise of its supervisory power over lower federal courts (and, thereby, indirectly over federal officers), rather than by reason of the Court's constitutional power to safeguard "due process."

Since the Supreme Court has no supervisory power over state courts, and the *McNabb* rule was not of constitutional dimension, the states were at liberty to either adopt or reject the rule. That rule later became known

---

(Del. Code, Tit. 11,§ 1909; Florida (Fla. R. Crim. P., 3130); and Indiana (Ind. Code,§ 18-1-11-8. Minnesota (Minn. R. Crim. P., 4.02(5) (1)), and Georgia (Ga. Code,§ 48. 27-212 prescribe 36 hours, Nebraska allows one night or longer "as the occasion may require so as to answer the purposes of the arrest" (Neb. Stat.,§ 29.410). Oregon limits the delay to 36 hours, or to 96 hours "for good cause shown" (Ore. Rev. State.§ 135.010).

[53]Orfield, Criminal Procedure from Arrest to Appeal 53–59, 72–75 (1947).

[54]318 U.S. 332 (1943).

[55]State v. Alex, 265 N.Y. 192, 192 N.E. 289 (1934). Also see Cahill v. People, 111 Colo. 29, 137 P.2d 673 (1943), which was decided a few days after *McNabb*, but apparently without knowledge of the Supreme Court decision; and People v. Devine, 46 Cal. 46 (1873).

[56]People v. Mummiani, 258 N.Y. 394, 180 N.E. 94 (1932).

[57]Madsen v. Hutchison, 49 Idaho 358, 290 Pac. 208 (1930).

as the *McNabb-Mallory* rule, following the Supreme Court's reaffirmation of the *McNabb* case principle in the 1957 case of *Mallory v. United States* (see previous section in this chapter).

When defense counsel in an early state case urged the adoption of the *McNabb-Mallory* rule, the Supreme Court of Oregon expressed the view that "adherence to such a rule would place unnecessary obstacles in the way of the detection of crime and result in the acquittal of many a guilty man."[58] In another case, the Supreme Court of Connecticut said is was not unmindful of the judicial and ethical standards involved in *McNabb*, but it considered that "society, as well as the defendant, is entitled to equal protection of the law and to due process of law."[59] Similar views have been expressed, or are implicit, in the numerous state court decisions rejecting the *McNabb* case principle.[60]

Very few state appellate courts adopted, or professed to adopt the *McNabb-Mallory* rule, even in modified form. It is of some interest and value, however, to briefly trace the course taken by the Michigan Supreme Court, the first one to experiment with the rule. In the 1960 case of *People v. Hamilton*,[61] that court's opinion contained language suggestive of adoption, but there were other factors in the case, such as denial of counsel, that may have warranted a reversal on the basis of the "totality of circumstances." Nevertheless, in the 1962 case of *People v. Harper*,[62] the Michigan court refused to hold a confession inadmissible because of the arraignment (i.e., preliminary hearing) delay factor alone. The court stated that there were no circumstances suggestive of involuntariness as was true in the original Michigan case. However, in a third Michigan case, *People v. McCager*,[63] decided shortly after the preceding one, the court stated that in its first case, *People v. Hamilton*, Michigan would become "the first state to adopt the exclusionary rule principle announced in *McNabb v. United States*." (In *McCager*, the confession was made *4 days* after the defendant's arrest.)

Despite the unequivocal statement in *McCager* that Michigan had adopted the *McNabb-Mallory* rule, four of its eight justices declined to rely upon it in

---

[58]State v. Folkes, 174 Ore. 568, 150 P.2d 17 (1944).

[59]State v. Zukanskas, 132 Conn. 450, 45 A.2d 289 (1945).

[60]A list of the various cases and their citations, arranged in state alphabetical order may be found in the previous edition of the present text. INBAU AND REID, CRIMINAL INTERROGATION AND CONFESSIONS (2d ed 1967) at pp. 165–166. Although the right of the states to reject the *McNabb-Mallory* rule was obvious from the fact that it was not founded upon a constitutional law basis, the Supreme Court specifically stated that to be so in Stroble v. California, 343 U.S. 181 (1952).

[61]359 Mich. 410, 102 N.W.2d 738 (1960).

[62]365 Mich. 494, 113 N.W.2d 808 (1962).

[63]367 Mich. 116, 116 N.W.2d 205 (1962).

their "remand" of the 1965 case of *People v. Ubbes*.[64] They, or three of them anyway (since one of the four concurred "in result" only), were of the view that "time of detention alone, without arraignment is not the test of confession admissibility"; in their view, "the lapse of 16-1/2 hours *per se* is not conclusive." The other four justices wanted to "reverse and remand" solely because of the delay in arraignment.

Following a 1968 decision in *People v. Farmer*,[65] which did not contribute to a clarification of the Michigan rule, its supreme court held, in the 1974 case of *People v. White*,[66] that the defendant's confession given after a 34-hour delay "was not the product of a police interrogation." The court stated that the exclusionary rule of its first case, *People v. Hamilton*,[67] applied "only where the delay has been used as a tool to extract a statement." "This formulation," as one commentator observed, "is so conceptually similar to the voluntariness test that, in effect, Michigan is back where it started."[68]

Six years after Michigan had begun its experimentation, the Wisconsin Supreme Court embarked upon its own adventure[69] and encountered similar difficulties. Then, in 1975, the court acknowledged the basic inconsistencies in its series of cases, and the experiment was terminated. The court reached the conclusion in *Klonowski v. State*[70] that although some of its cases indicated that any confession made during an unreasonably long detention is inadmissible, others had held that the real purpose of its exclusionary rule was "to prevent an accused from having his resistance weakened by the psychological coercion of being detained and 'worked upon' by the police to secure evidence." In effect, therefore, no confession was to be excluded because of a period of delay unless it was also excludable under the voluntariness test.

Summarizing the experimentation of the Michigan and Wisconsin Supreme Courts, one writer upon the general subject of the *McNabb-Mallory* rule concluded:

In both Michigan and Wisconsin, the introduction of a causal requirement diluted their versions of *McNabb-Mallory* to meaningless dicta. A reading of the cases suggests that the primary corrosive force was judicial reluctance to

---

[64]374 Mich. 571, 132 N.W.2d 669 (1965). There was an intervening case between *McCager* and *Ubbes*, but it only augmented the prevailing uncertainty. That case was People v. Walker, 371 Mich. 599, 124 N.W.2d 761 (1963).

[65]380 Mich. 198, 156 N.W.2d 504 (1968).

[66]392 Mich. 404, 221 N.W.2d 357, *cert. denied*, 420 U.S. 912 (1974).

[67]*Supra* Note 61.

[68]Keene, *infra* Note 71.

[69]Phillips v. State, 29 Wis. 2d 521, 139 N.W.2d 41 (1966).

[70]68 Wis. 2d 604, 229 N.W.2d 637 (1975).

exclude voluntary confessions. Whether this was based on a concern for public or legislative response, or for effective law enforcement, at base the price was simply too high when it came time to reverse the convictions of confessed criminals. Courts considering adoption of this form of *McNabb-Mallory* should note the probability of its erosion. A causation-based rule invites confusion with the voluntariness test. It promotes contradictory appellate decisions. If the Michigan-Wisconsin experience is any guide, adoption results in little, if any, additional protection for an arrestee over the voluntariness test. It is a waste of judicial time.[71]

In 1965, Delaware's Supreme Court adopted a *per se* exclusionary rule with respect to confessions obtained after the 24-hour delay provided by the state's preliminary hearing statute. The rationale of the court was that such automatic exclusion was "the most practical and effective means" of enforcing the statutory provision.[72] With respect to confessions obtained during the allowable 24-hour period, the Delaware court ruled that they, too, may be excluded if the delay is an unreasonable one. The court acknowledged that there are "no clear-cut standards of reasonableness," and that "the question was strictly evidentiary, to be decided solely by the trial judge in each case."[73]

In 1978, Maryland's Court of Appeals also adopted a *per se* exclusionary rule, identical to Delaware's, for confessions obtained beyond the allowable period of delay. It considered any deference to a voluntariness standard as a "hopelessly inadequate means of safeguarding a defendant's right to prompt presentment."[74] In a dissenting opinion in that case, one of the judges stated:

The *most effective* protection of a nonconstitutional right of an accused is not the sole goal of criminal justice. There is also to be considered the protection of the right of society to have a person who has committed offenses against it answer for his acts according to the law of the land.

Maryland's lower courts were reluctant to apply the *per se* rule that had been established. They held it inapplicable to confessions that were 1) used for impeachment purposes, 2) made by a person already under legal detention for another crime, and 3) where the arrestee signed a "waiver of rights" form. Some of the courts evaded the court of appeals' rule by

---

[71]Keene, *The Ill-Advised State Court Revival of the McNabb-Mallory Rule*, 72 J. C. L. & CRIM. 204, at 217–218 (1981).

[72]Norhauer v. State, 59 Del. 35, 212 A.2d 886 (1965).

[73]Webster v. State, 59 Del. 54, 213 A. 2d 298 (1965).

[74]Johnson v. State, 282 Md. 314, 384 A.2d 709 (1978). (The quotation is from the dissenting opinion of Judge Orth, at 384 A.2d p. 724.)

formulating a precise and restrictive definition of arrest in order to toll the delay time clock.[75]

The dissatisfaction of the Maryland legislature with the *per se* exclusionary rule resulted in its abolition with the passage of the following statutory provisions in 1981:

> (a) A confession may not be excluded from evidence solely because the defendant was not taken before a judicial officer after arrest within the prescribed time of 24 hours.
>
> (b) Failure to strictly comply with the prescribed rule pertaining to taking a defendant before a judicial officer after arrest is only one factor, among others, to be considered by the court in deciding the voluntariness and admissibility of a confession.[76]

Pennsylvania, which had no specific time limit, but only the "unnecessary delay" prohibition, encountered an interesting experience with the *McNabb-Mallory* principle. In the first Pennsylvania Supreme Court case upon the general subject, which involved a lineup identification rather than a confession, the court banned all evidence obtained after an unnecessary delay, except where no reasonable relationship existed between the delay and the evidence.[77] Subsequent cases had to decide what constituted "unnecessary delay" as well as what comprised a "reasonable relationship." In one of those cases, the court declared that "prearraignment delay will always be unnecessary unless justified by administrative processing—fingerprinting, photographing and the like."[78] That test opened the floodgate for litigation seeking judicial examination of the necessariness of prearraignment detentions; there were approximately 14 cases that had to be decided within 2 years.[79] In an effort to better administer its exclusionary rule, the court in a 1977 case ruled that all confessions obtained after a prearraignment delay of 6 hours would be automatically excluded.[80] Shorter delays would not result in confession rejection "except as may be relevant to constitutional standards of admissibility." The court then went on to state that the significant period to measure was that between arrest and arraignment, rather than between

---

[75]Keene, *supra* Note 71 at p. 221.

[76]§ 10-912, Cts. & Jud. Proc., Md. Code Ann.

[77]Commonwealth v. Futch, 447 Pa. 389, 290 A.2d 417 (1972).

[78]Commonwealth v. Williams, 455 Pa. 569, 319 A.2d 419 (1974).

[79]Commonwealth v. Davenport, 471 Pa. 278, 286, n.7, 370 A.2d 301, 306 n.7 (1977).

[80]Commonwealth v. Davenport, *supra* Note 79. In selecting 6 hours as the time limit, the court cited a standard of the Standards and Goals of the National Advisory Commission on Criminal Justice (1973) and § 103.2 of the ALI Model Code on Prearraignment Procedure. The court neglected to mention, however, that Congress had set a similar time limit in the 1968 Omnibus Crime Act of 1968, subsequently quoted in the text at Note 83.

arrest and confession. Under that unique standard, therefore, even confessions well within a reasonable period, such as for administrative processing, are excluded if the total prearraignment period exceeds 6 hours!

The Montana Supreme Court relied heavily upon the first of the Pennsylvania cases in deciding that it, too, would adopt the *McNabb-Mallory* principle; however, it declined to promulgate a particular time standard, and the Montana delay statute did not prescribe one.[81]

Several other states, either by court decisions or legislative provisions, have at least intimated an inclination to follow the *McNabb-Mallory* principle. They are discussed in a very scholarly article written by Jerald P. Keene while a student at Northwestern University School of Law.[82] Keene's article is recommended to any jurist or legislator contemplating the adoption of the rule that was established by the United States Supreme Court in *McNabb* and *Mallory*.

It was earlier stated that Congress was privileged to abolish the *McNabb-Mallory* rule because the rule was not of constitutional dimension, but rather one established by the Supreme Court in the exercise of its supervisory power over lower federal courts.[83] Congress did abolish the rule in the following provision of the 1968 Omnibus Crime Act (18 U.S.C. § 3501):

> In any criminal prosecution by the United States or by the District of Columbia, a confession made or given by a person who is a defendant therein, while such person was under arrest or other detention in the custody of any law-enforcement officer or law-enforcement agency, shall not be inadmissible solely because of delay in bringing such person before a magistrate or other officer empowered to commit persons charged with offenses against the laws of the United States or of the District of Columbia if such confession is found by the trial judge to have been made voluntarily and if the weight to be given the confession is left to the jury and if such confession was made or given by such person within six hours immediately following his arrest or other detention: *Provided*, That the time limitation contained in this subsection shall not apply in any case in which the delay in bringing such person before such magistrates or other officer beyond such six-hour period is found by the trial judge to be reasonable considering the means of transportation and the distance to be traveled to the nearest available such magistrate or other officer.

---

[81]State v. Benbo, 174 Mont. 252, 570 P.2d 894 (1977).

More recently, the Supreme Court of West Virginia held that a delay of 2 hours and 25 minutes between arrest and presentment to a magistrate rendered a confession involuntary. State v. Guthrie, 315 S.E.2d 397 (W. Va. 1984).

[82]*Supra* Note 71.

[83]For a discussion of the congressional authority to supercede the Supreme Court's evidentiary powers, see S. Rep. No. 1097, 90th Cong., 2d Sess. 63–63, reprinted in [1968] U.S. Code Cong. and Ad. News, 2112, 2139-50.

This demise of the *McNabb-Mallory* rule within the federal system and the feeble degree of reception it had received by the states prompted one legal scholar, Professor Yale Kamisar, to label the rule as a "grenade that fizzled."[84]

WARNINGS OF CONSTITUTIONAL RIGHTS TO CUSTODIAL SUSPECTS—THE SUPREME COURT'S MANDATE IN *MIRANDA V. ARIZONA*

Prescribed Warnings, Their History, and the Practical Considerations Attending Compliance

The constitutional provision that no person shall be compelled to be a witness against himself always has been considered of such force and effect as to require a judicial tribunal to advise accused persons who are unrepresented by counsel of their privilege against self-incrimination before their testimony could be heard; and the rule was extended to apply not only to trial court proceedings but also to pretrial proceedings, such as preliminary hearings and coroner's inquests.[85] However, in the absence of a statutory provision, police interrogators, until the Supreme Court's 5-to-4 decision in the 1966 case of *Miranda v. United States*,[86] were not obligated to warn a suspect of the right to remain silent. Decisions to that effect had been rendered by the highest courts of more than 30 states[87] and

---

[84]Kamisar, Police Interrogation and Confessions (1980) 98.

[85]Maki v. State, 18 Wyo. 481, 112 Pac. 334 (1911); McDonald v. State, 70 Fla. 250, 70 So. 24 (1915); State v. Meyer, 181 Iowa 440, 164 N.W. 794 (1917); Wood v. United States, 128 F.2d 265 (D.C. 1942). See also cases collected and discussed at 79 A.L.R.2d 643 (1961). The underlying reason for the warning requirements in judicial proceedings, as stated in the early case of State v. Gilman, 51 Me. 206 at p. 223 (1862), were: "The impressiveness of obligation and the solemnity of the occasion would have a tendency to wring from the party thus situated facts and circumstances which he is not bound to disclose, and therefore can in no just sense be said to be voluntary. As a general proposition this may be true, especially if the party is uninformed with regard to his rights." In Bram v. United States, 168 U.S. 532 at p. 550 (1897), the United States Supreme Court stated: "The reason upon which this rule rested undoubtedly was that the mere fact of the magistrate's taking the statement, even though unaccompanied with an oath, might, unless he was cautioned, operate upon the mind of the prisoner to impel him involuntarily to speak."

[86]384 U.S. 436 (1966).

[87]The previous (1967) edition of the present text, at 169–171, contains an alphabetical listing of state cases. Included, until 1965, were the decisions of the California and Oregon Supreme Courts, both of which changed their rulings and prescribed the warning because of their broad interpretation of Escobedo v. Illinois, 378 U.S. 478 (1964), and an accurate anticipation of what was forthcoming in *Miranda* in 1966. The only other pre-1965 requirements for the

by a federal circuit court of appeals.[88] *Miranda* changed all this by declaring that the constitutional privilege against self-incrimination mandated the issuance of the warning to all persons who are interrogated while in police custody or who are otherwise deprived of their freedom "in any significant way." The Supreme Court also decreed that in addition to the self-incrimination warning itself, the suspect must be advised that he had a right to counsel before and during the interrogation. Only after a "knowing and intelligent" waiver of those rights could there be any interrogation at all. Moreover, a failure to administer the warnings would render inadmissible as evidence any statement the suspect might make.

The Court in *Miranda* specifically stated that the suspect must be told:

> That he had the right to remain silent, and that he need not answer any questions. That if he does answer questions his answers can be used as evidence against him. That he has a right to consult with a lawyer before or during the questioning of him by the police. That if he cannot afford to hire a lawyer, one will be provided for him without costs.[89]

Justice Clark, in his dissenting opinion in *Miranda*, described its impact by stating that it represented "one full sweep changing [of] the traditional rules of custodial interrogation which this Court has for so long recognized as a justifiable and proper tool in balancing individual rights against the rights of society."[90] Justice Harlan also dissented, along with Justices Stewart and White. He accentuated their viewpoint with the following observation and prediction (which preceded the embellishments that were later engrafted upon the original warnings by subsequent administrative directives to the police and by court decisions):

> There can be little doubt that the Court's new code would markedly decrease the number of confessions. To warn the suspect that he may remain silent and remind him that his confession may be used in court are minor obstructions. To

---

warning about the self-incrimination privilege appeared in the Texas Criminal Code (Art. 727) and in the Code of Military Justice (Art. 3).

[88]United States v. Wilson, 264 F.2d 104 (2d Cir. 1959); Heitner v. United States, 149 F.2d 105 (2d Cir. 1945).

Also relevant are two 1958 decisions of the United States Supreme Court about which Justice Clark had this to say in his dissenting opinion in *Miranda*: "To require all [the warnings and rights prescribed by *Miranda*] at one gulp should cause the Court to choke over more cases than Crooker v. California, 357 U.S. 433 (1958), and Cicenia v. LaGay, 357 U.S. 504 (1958), which it expressly overrules today." Miranda v. Arizona, 384 U.S. at 502.

[89]As is discussed later in this chapter, the Supreme Court, in the 1981 case of California v. Prysock, 453 U.S. 355 (1981), ruled that there was no requirement "that the contents of the *Miranda* warnings be a virtual incantation of the precise language contained in *Miranda*." It is sufficient if the warnings convey the basic rights to the suspect.

[90]*Supra* Note 86, p. 503.

require also an express waiver by the suspect and an end to questioning whenever he demures must heavily handicap questioning. And to suggest or provide counsel for the suspect simply invites the end of the interrogation.[91]

The motivation of the five-justice majority for the *Miranda* mandate was based on a consideration entirely different from the protection of the innocent, which underlays the voluntariness test of confession admissibility. *Miranda* was the product of the Warren Court's pursuit of its egalitarian philosophy. Toward that objective, the basic consideration was this: The rich, the educated, or the intelligent suspect very probably knows from the outset that he has the privilege of silence, whereas the poor, the uneducated, or the unintelligent suspect is unaware of that privilege. Consequently, *all* persons in custody or otherwise deprived of their freedom, must be advised of their right to remain silent and, moreover, in order to ensure that they be made aware of that privilege, they should also be told that they have a right to have a lawyer present before and during the interrogation. Contrary to the generally prevailing impression, even within the legal profession itself, the right to a lawyer during the interrogation process was not based upon the *Sixth* Amendment provision: "In all criminal *prosecutions*, the accused shall enjoy the right ... to have the assistance of counsel *for his defense*."[92] Rather, the inclusion of the right to a lawyer as part of the *Miranda* warnings was only to supplement the *Fifth* Amendment's privilege against self-incrimination.

Many persons, particularly those in the area of law enforcement, view the warning about the right to a lawyer before or during an interrogation of a custodial suspect to be the most damaging feature of *Miranda*'s mandate, and, as previously noted, that view was even shared by one of the dissenting justices in *Miranda*.[93] It was also clearly implicit in the comment of a former Supreme Court justice in a much earlier case. In his dissent in the 1949 case of *Watts v. Indiana*, which was discussed earlier in this chapter, Justice Robert Jackson stated that "under our adversary

---

[91]*Supra* note 86 pp. 516–17. In a footnote, Justice Harlan stated that the Court's "vision of a lawyer 'mitigating the dangers of untrustworthiness' ... by witnessing coercion and assisting accuracy in the confession is largely a fancy; for if counsel arrives, there is rarely going to be a police station confession." *Id.* at 516 n.12.

[92]U.S. Const. Amend, VI. (Emphasis added.) In other decisions unrelated to the subject matter of the present text, the Supreme Court has interpreted "criminal prosecution" to extend to the very beginning of the judicial process, such as preliminary hearing or indictment. Even in *Miranda*, however, the Court did not rule that the Sixth Amendment right was invoked by a custodial interrogation; the right to counsel in that setting, as has already been stated, was considered only an implementation of the Fifth Amendment right to silence.

[93]*Supra* Note 91.

system ... any lawyer worth his salt will tell the suspect in no uncertain terms to make no statement to police under any circumstances."[94]

As a prelude to a discussion of the most recurring troublesome *Miranda* issues that prosecutors encounter, the authors wish to present, as was done in the preceding Chapter 8, an overview of the basic fundamental problems created by *Miranda*. They resulted in large measure from an overreaction to it, and an understandable one, on the part of lower federal and state courts, prosecuting attorneys and other police legal advisors, and, finally, on the part of the police themselves. The overreaction by the police is due in large measure to the prescribed administrative rules under which they must function in the interrogation process. What follows has been adopted from an article published by the senior author under the title of "Over-Reaction — The Mischief of *Miranda v. Arizona*."[95] He began with the effect of *Miranda* on the investigation into the attempted assassination of President Ronald Reagan in Washington, D.C., on the afternoon of March 30, 1981.

Immediately after the shooting of the President, John W. Hinckley, Jr., was arrested by Secret Service agents and the Washington, D.C., police. He was taken to local police headquarters, arriving there at 2:40 p.m. The police wanted not only to question Hinckley about his motive but also about the possible involvement of accomplices. Before doing so, however, they dutifully read to him the warnings of constitutional rights that the Supreme Court had mandated in its *Miranda* decision. The warnings given to Hinckley contained embellishments of the ones specified in *Miranda*, and they were read to him on *three separate occasions* within a *2-hour period*. The first set of warnings was read by a Secret Service agent; it was read again by a Washington, D.C., detective; and, after Hinckley was taken to the homicide squad office, the same detective issued the warnings a third time. After receiving the third set of warnings, Hinckley was presented with a "waiver of rights" form on which he responded "yes" to the questions regarding whether he had read his rights and had understood

---

[94]338 U.S. 49, 59 (1949).

It is of interest to note that in a 1983 robbery-murder case, the defendant (with a new lawyer) convinced the trial judge that his confession should be suppressed because his original lawyer had advised him to talk to the police following his arrest as a suspect, even though the prosecutor had told the suspect's lawyer that there was insufficient evidence at that time to charge him with the crime. The trial judge ruled that this demonstrated lawyer incompetence because of his surrender of the defendant's constitutional rights. The judge's suppression ruling was reversed on appeal on the ground that at the time of the interrogation, no prosecution stage had been reached and consequently, there was no Sixth Amendment right to counsel. The New York Court of Appeals stated: "Unless the Constitution is read to require counsel for *all* persons—innocent or guilty—at the moment when a crime is committed, a line must be drawn at some point. The commencement of criminal prosecutions is the logical choice." People v. Claudio, 59 N.Y.2d 556, 453 N.E.2d 500 (1983).

[95]Inbau, 73 J. Crim. L & C. 797-810 (1982). An updated version of the article appears in *The Prosecutor*, the official publication of the National District Attorneys Association (Winter, 1985 issue, p. 7).

them. Then he was asked whether he "wished to answer any questions." At this point, Hinckley answered, "I don't know. I'm not sure; I think I ought to talk to Joe Bates (his father's lawyer in Dallas)." Hinckley added: "I want to talk to you, but first I want to talk to Joe Bates."[96] Under *Miranda*, this ended the interrogation opportunity; there could be no further questioning about the crime, because Hinckley had asked for a lawyer.

Following the D.C. police "booking procedure" (identification data and fingerprints), and while the police were attempting to contact Joe Bates, two FBI agents arrived and arrested Hinckley for violation of the Presidential Assassination Statute.[97] They were informed of all that had transpired and then took Hinckley to the FBI field office at approximately 5:15 p.m. There he received the *Miranda* warnings for the *fourth time*. He was also presented with another waiver form, supplied by the FBI. Hinckley signed his name to it; however, "it was clearly understood that he did not waive his right not to answer questions before consulting counsel." Nevertheless, he did answer various "background" questions asked by FBI agents.

The "background" information was suppressed by the District of Columbia trial court. It reasoned that the information was elicited from Hinckley in violation of *Miranda*, which prohibits the interrogation of a custodial suspect after he announces or indicates he wants to have a lawyer present.[98] As already quoted, Hinckley had said he wanted one, although he had done so rather hesitatingly.

The District Court ruling was affirmed by the court of appeals for the D.C. Circuit.[99] Both courts rejected the government's contention that the questioning of Hinckley at the FBI office was merely "standard processing procedure" of an "essentially administrative nature." The courts concluded that Hinckley had, in fact, been interrogated and that the purpose of the questioning was to obtain personal background information from Hinckley that would negate an anticipated insanity plea at the time of trial. It was obvious that Hinckley could not deny he had done the shooting, so the only conceivable defense would be that of insanity. That was, in fact, the plea at his trial, which began April 26, 1982.

In view of the court rulings declaring the "background information" inadmissible at trial, whatever value that information may have been to the prosecution was irretrievably lost. The government decided not to seek

---

[96]The above quotations, and the ones that follow, as well as all the case facts reported in this discussion, are from the published opinion of the Court of Appeals for the District of Columbia, which affirmed the district court's decision suppressing all the statements made by Hinckley during the interrogation subsequent to his expression of interest in talking to his father's lawyer. United States v. Hinckley, 672 F.2d 115 (1982), *aff'g* 525 F. Supp. 1342 (1981).

[97]Presidential Assasination Statute, 18 U.S.C.§ 1751 (1970).

[98]United States v. Hinckley, 525 F. Supp. 1342 (1981).

[99]United States v. Hinckley, 672 F.2d 115 (1982) (per curium).

Supreme Court review of the appellate court's decision. At trial, therefore, reliance had to be placed upon other evidence of Hinckley's sanity. The government presented the testimony of psychiatrists that Hinckley was sane at the time of the shooting; the defense psychiatrists testified he was insane. The jury returned a verdict of insanity.[100]

As earlier discussed, after Hinckley's arrest and as he was about to be questioned in the police station, he received the prescribed warnings *3* times within a *2-hour* interval, and that a signed waiver was sought from him at the Washington, D.C., police station when he was asked if he wished to answer any questions. Nowhere in the *Miranda* opinion is there anything requiring such a repetition of the warnings, or the need for a signed statement, or the ascertainment of any other kind of waiver than an indicated willingness to be questioned.

The events in the *Hinckley* case resulted from an understandable concern on the part of law enforcement officers that whatever they say to a suspect by way of *Miranda* requirements might later be considered inadequate by a prosecutor, a trial judge, or an appellate court. Hence, they overreact. Every time someone wants to talk to the suspect, or the same interrogator wants to resume his interrogation, the warnings are repeated. The repetitive warnings are then followed by a request to sign a legalistically shrouded waiver form. The police want to be absolutely sure the suspect has been properly "Mirandized," an expression often used in police parlance. In such cases, when officers overreact, suspects who might otherwise have been willing to talk are far less apt to do so.

Another illustration of overreaction to *Miranda* appears in an appellate court case within the District of Columbia, which was decided only 1 month prior to the interrogation of Hinckley. In that case, *United States v. Alexander*,[101] a suspected murderer received the following warnings, as prescribed in a D.C. police department regulation:

You are under arrest. Before we ask any questions, you must understand what your rights are.

You have the right to remain silent. You are not required to say anything to us at any time or to answer questions. Anything you say can be used against you in court.

You have the right to talk to a lawyer for advice before we question you and to have him with you during questioning.

If you cannot afford a lawyer and want one, a lawyer will be provided for you.

$\longrightarrow$

---

[100] As later discussed in the text, at pages 281–284 the warnings to Hinckley might not have been needed at all on the basis of the "lifesaving" exception to *Miranda's* requirement. Apparently that argument was not presented to the court.

[101] 428 A.2d 42 (D.C. 1981).

If you want to answer questions now without a lawyer present, you will still have the right to stop answering at any time until you talk to a lawyer.

Following a reading of the warnings to the suspect, she was presented with a printed waiver form, on which the first three questions were:

1. Have you read or had read to you the warnings as to your rights?
2. Do you understand these rights?
3. Do you wish to answer any questions?

Alongside each of the forgoing questions, the suspect wrote "yes." The next question was:

4. Are you willing to answer questions without having an attorney present?

To this fourth question, the suspect wrote "No." Despite the suspect's "no" to the fourth question, she was told "We know you are responsible for the stabbing," whereupon she confessed and agreed to give a written statement. At this point, the officer issued "fresh *Miranda* warnings."

The trial court in *Alexander* suppressed the resulting confession for the same reason stated in the *Hinckley* case: the questioning of a custodial suspect after an indication of an interest in having a lawyer present. The suppression order was affirmed by the appellate court. Consequently, the confession could not be used as evidence at trial.

The warnings that were used in *Alexander* were the same ones that were given by the D.C. police department to Hinckley. In those warnings and in the waiver forms, the drafters of the documents went far beyond what the Supreme Court mandated in *Miranda*, or in any of its subsequent decisions prior to (or since) the interrogations of Alexander and Hinckley. What the Court stated in *Miranda* was that before a custodial suspect could be interrogated:

> . . . . He must be warned prior to any questioning that he has the right to remain silent, that anything he says can be used against him in a court of law, that he has the right to the presence of an attorney, and that if he cannot afford an attorney one will be appointed for him prior to any questioning if he so desires.

Following this specification of the required four warnings, the Court proceeded to admonish interrogators that the suspect's "opportunity to exercise these rights must be afforded to him throughout the interrogation," meaning that if he changed his mind and decided to remain silent or wanted an attorney present, he should be accorded that privilege. But this was only a *warning to interrogators*, not something for incorporation into the required warnings to the suspects themselves, as was embodied in the fifth warning contained among those issued in *Alexander* and in *Hinckley*. Nowhere in the Supreme Court's opinion in *Miranda* did it state that interrogators had to tell *the suspect* of the right to change his mind. All that the Court said was that if the suspect exercised that right, it would have to be honored by the interrogator.

Most police departments, instead of utilizing written waivers, as in *Alexander* and *Hinckley*, rely upon the oral issuance of both the warnings and the waiver questions. The practice of embellishing the warnings prevails, nevertheless, and so does the ritualization of the waivers. Departmental instructions are on plastic cards issued to all police officers. One side of the card contains the warnings that must be read to the suspect; the other side contains the waiver questions. The phraseology appearing on both sides of the card has been prepared, or at least approved, by a prosecutor or some other police legal advisor.

The warnings on a typical card are as follows:

1. You have the right to remain silent.
2. Anything you say can and will be used against you in a court of law.
3. You have the right to talk to a lawyer and have him present with you while you are being questioned.
4. If you cannot afford to hire a lawyer, one will be appointed to represent you before any questioning, if you wish.
5. You can decide at any time to exercise these rights and not answer any questions or make any statements.

The waiver questions sometimes are:

1. Do you understand each of these rights?
2. Having these rights in mind, do you wish to talk to us now?

Observe, again, the gratuitous inclusion of the fifth warning. As earlier stated, this is not a warning required by *Miranda*, but rather an expression the Supreme Court employed by way of an *admonition to interrogators* regarding their obligation in those instances where a person has already agreed to talk without an attorney being present.[102]

Although for many years law enforcement agencies, both federal and state, have prescribed the issuance of the fifth warning, in June, 1984, the United States Drug Enforcement Administration deleted it as a requirement. (The validity of DEA's omission of the fifth warning was sustained by a U.S.

---

[102]There are two states, however, that require the fifth warning. Texas does so by a provision in its general Code of Criminal Procedure on the admissibility of statements (Art. 38.22, § 2 (a) (5)) and Wisconsin by decision law, Micale v. State, 76 Wis. 370, 251 N.W.2d 458 (1977).

District Court for the District of Colorado in *U.S. v. Ignatius*, Case # 85–CR–10.)

In addition to overreaction with regard to the language of the warnings and waivers, difficulties result from the frequently followed police practice of issuing "fresh" *Miranda* warnings every time an interrogation has been renewed by the original interrogator, or when a different interrogator becomes involved. This occurs even after the suspect waived his rights upon the first occasion, and even though only a short time has elapsed since the first set of warnings were given.[103]

Implicit in what has already been stated, prosecuting attorneys (and other legal advisors to the police) also participate in the overreaction process. Prosecutors are concerned, and understandably so, about trial court rejection of confessions or appellate court reversals of convictions because of some presumed flaw in the *Miranda* warnings or in the waiver. Even more damaging, however, are the supercautious warnings and waiver forms that are prepared or approved for police usage, such as the ones already discussed. Prosecutors and other legal advisors to the police seem to have exercised as much meticulous care with the warnings and waivers as prosecutors do in the drafting of jury instructions for the presiding judge. Nothing must be omitted!

Not only have the police and prosecutors overreacted to *Miranda*; the same has been true of lower federal courts and of the state courts at all levels. An early overreaction by a federal circuit court of appeals concerned the phraseology of the warning about the right to appointed counsel. When the appellant in *Lathers v. United States*[104] was to be questioned while a custodial suspect, the *Miranda* warnings he received included the statement that "if he was unable to hire an attorney, the Commissioner or the Court would appoint one for him." This was held by the Fifth Circuit Court of Appeals to be defective because the suspect "was not advised that he could have an attorney present with him before he uttered a syllable." The court said, "[t]he message to him indicated only that a judge or commissioner somewhere down the line would appoint a lawyer for him if he so requested."[105] This ruling prevailed for *13 years* in that circuit, which prescribed the law for the lower federal courts (and indirectly, therefore, for federal law enforcement officers) within a six-state area.

A subsequent decision overruled *Lathers*. The court in *United States v. Contreras*[106] expressed its reluctance to overturn a prior decision in its

---

[103]With regard to the lack of necessity to repeat the warnings, as well as the adverse effect they may have, see Chapter 8.

[104]396 F.2d 524 (5th Cir. 1968).

[105]*Id.* at 535.

[106]667 F.2d 976 (11th Cir. 1982). This appears as a decision of the eleventh circuit court of appeals, which was split off from the fifth circuit by Congressional action due to the

own circuit, but felt impelled to do so because of the 1981 Supreme Court decision in *California v. Prysock*.[107] In that case, the Supreme Court held there was no requirement "that the contents of the *Miranda* warnings be a virtual incantation of the precise language contained in *Miranda*." Instead, it is sufficient if the warnings convey the basic rights to the suspect. According to the *Contreras* court, this meant, therefore, that the warnings about the right to counsel "need not," as the earlier *Lathers* case had indicated, "explicitly convey to the accused his right to counsel 'here and now'" Ultimately, therefore, the 13 years of mischief that was created within the fifth circuit was finally dissipated. In addition to overreaction to *Miranda* by police, prosecutors, and courts, one state (Louisiana), by a constitutional provision, requires that the warnings be given *at the time of arrest*, rather than only prior to a custodial interrogation.[108]

The "Rescue"/"Lifesaving" Exception to the Requirement for Warnings

In the law on searches and seizures, an exception to the exclusionary rule has been widely accepted where "exigent circumstance" required police actions that would otherwise be violative of the suspect's Fourth Amendment protection against unreasonable searches and seizures and thereby result in the suppression of the seized evidence. A simple illustration is where a police officer hears someone screaming in a private residence; he may immediately enter because of a possible life-endangering situation.[109] The principle was even extended, in the California case of *People v. Sirhan*, to justify entry into a private home to conduct an exploratory search because of the possibility that the shooting of

---

excessive case load in the original fifth circuit. Nevertheless, in the *Contreas* opinion, the court referred to the *Lathers* decision as one of its own. The present eleventh circuit encompasses Alabama, Florida, and Georgia; the fifth circuit, Louisiana, Mississippi, Texas, and the Canal Zone.

[107]453 U.S. 355 (1981).

[108]Art. 1, 13.

Where, as in all states except Louisiana, the warnings are only required as a precondition to an interrogation, it is inadvisable to give the warnings prematurely. If, for instance, an arrestee fails to tell the police that he killed in self-defense or if he fails to offer some other exculpatory explanation for the conduct that occasioned his arrest, and he had not previously received the warnings, he may be cross-examined upon his failure to offer at the time of arrest the explanation he gave at the trial. Jenkins v. Anderson, 447 U.S. 231 (1980); Fletcher v. Weir, 445 U.S. 603 (1982). The same would be true of a failure to make a denial to an accusation by a crime victim or witness. On the other hand, of course, a failure to make an exculpatory statement or remaining silent after receipt of the warnings are of no significance, and unfairness would obviously result from any usage of such fact in view of the warnings themselves as to the right to remain silent. United States v. Hale, 422 U.S. 171 (1975); Doyle v. Ohio. 426 U.S. 610 (1976). A Louisiana case to the same effect is State v. Sam, 412 So. 2d 1082 (La. 1982).

[109]United States v. Barone, 330 F.2d 543 (2d Cir. 1964); State v. Hills, 283 So. 2d 220 (La. 1973).

Senator Robert Kennedy might have been the first in a conspiracy to kill other national figures.[110] Prompt action by the police to learn whatever they could from a search was deemed proper possibly to save the lives of other intended victims. If such actions warrant exceptions to the protection of the Fourth Amendment, there should be no doubt as to the justification for a relaxation of the Fifth Amendment self-incrimination privilege by withholding the *Miranda* warnings when the police are about to question a suspect in a case situation where he may be able to furnish information that could save the life or lives of innocent persons from imminent danger. Fortunately, there is case law that allows for a "rescue"/ "lifesaving" exception to the requirement of *Miranda*.

A classic illustration of the application of this exception to the requirement of *Miranda* warnings is where the police are attempting to locate a kidnapped child, and they have in custody a suspect reasonably believed to be one of the kidnappers. Time, obviously, is a critical factor. The suspect's refusal to talk, provoked by the *Miranda* warnings and request for a waiver, or the attending delay in procuring counsel if requested, could result in loss of life.

California is the first state in which this issue has arisen. Its court reasoned that the *Miranda* principle contemplates case situations in which time is *not* a critical factor. According to the reasoning of the California courts, the requirement for the issuance of warnings of constitutional rights "assumes the possibility of substantial delay" before, for instance, the element of the right to counsel can be satisfied, whereas that allowance cannot be tolerated in cases such as a kidnapping. In one of the California cases, the court stated:

> An emergency sufficient to excuse the *Miranda* requirements contains the following elements: 1. Urgency of need in that no other course of action promises relief, 2. The possibility of saving human life by rescuing a person whose life is in danger, and 3. Rescue is the primary purpose and motive of the interrogators.[111]

Since the rationale for the exception is the urgent need for action to save a life, the Colorado Supreme Court held that the exception was inapplicable in a case in which the police were investigating the 3-1/2-month disappearance of a child.[112]

---

[110]7 Cal. 3d 710, 497 P.2d 1121 (1972).

[111]People v. Riddle, 83 Cal. App. 3d 563, 148 Cal. Rptr. 170 (1978). This case contains an analysis of a prior California Supreme Court case and also of an appellate court case.

[112]People v. Manning, 672 P.2d 499 (Colo. 1983). In this case, the police also made a promise of leniency to the suspect in return for her disclosure of the location of the child. She did reveal where the child's body was.

The lifesaving concept has been applied in instances other than kidnapping cases. For example, if a police officer, upon arresting a suspect who was known to have had a gun, inquires "Where's the gun?" may the argument be advanced that the primary purpose was to learn of its location for the protection of the officer or of other persons? A 1983 Kansas Supreme Court held that the lifesaving exception dispensed with the need for *Miranda* warnings, but the opposite conclusion was reached in a 1983 decision of the Arizona Supreme Court.[113] The most recent and most important decision in point is the 1984 case of *New York v. Quarles*,[114] in which the United States Supreme Court applied what it labeled a "public safety" exception to *Miranda* with respect to the interrogation of a rape suspect regarding the location of a pistol the victim said he had at the time of the crime. In this case, the suspect had been apprehended by the police and handcuffed outside a grocery store into which he had fled. A frisk revealed an empty shoulder holster, and when the suspect was asked, without being given the *Miranda* warnings, what he had done with the pistol, he revealed its location within the store. A majority of the Court held that the warnings were not required because of the urgency to find the weapon in order to protect the public, and also the police, from its misuse by the person who might come into possession of it. This "overriding consideration," said the Court, "justified the officer's failure to provide *Miranda* warnings before asking questions devoted to locating the abandoned weapon." Three of the four dissenting justices expressed the view that by applying this exception, the Court practically abandoned *Miranda*.

The same public safety exception that was invoked in *Quarles* might have been applicable with respect to the attempted interrogation of John Hinckley, Jr., following the shooting of President Reagan, provided the police had not given him the *Miranda* warnings. There, obviously, was the urgency of trying to ascertain from Hinckley whether the shooting was part of a conspiracy to kill not only the President but other government officials as well. The concern at that time was comparable to that which existed immediately after the shooting of Senator Robert Kennedy, which was held to justify the immediate warrantless search of the home of the assassin Sirhan.[115]

---

[113]State v. Roadenbaugh, 234 Kans. 474, 673 P.2d 1166 (1983), and State v. Hein, 138 Ariz. 360, 674 P.2d 1358 (1983). Another state decision that adopted the emergency exception shortly after *Miranda* was decided is State v. Lane, 77 Wash. 2d 860, 467 P.2d 304 (1970).

[114]104 S. Ct. 2626.

[115]In another case, Innes v. Rhode Island, 446 U.S. 291 (1980), later to be discussed in the section on "The Meaning of Interrogation," the public safety rationale would have been a more acceptable one than that expressed by the Court. In *Innes* the police apprehended a suspect for robbery in which a sawed-off shotgun had been the weapon. After receiving the *Miranda* warnings, the suspect asked for a lawyer. While driving the suspect to the police

Inapplicability of *Miranda* to Private Security Officers and Probation/Parole Officers

The law is clear, from the *Miranda* opinion itself as well as from subsequent cases, that the warnings of constitutional rights are only required when the person to be interrogated is in *police* custody (or otherwise deprived by them of his freedom "in any significant way"). Nevertheless, a widespread misconception has prevailed among private security officers (and their legal advisors) that they, too, must comply with the *Miranda* mandate. The authors of this text are familiar with many illustrations of this misconception, the following two of which also demonstrate its absurd extension. In the first case, a woman was the victim of a theft of money from her purse while shopping in a nationwide chain drugstore. She reported it to the manager and the matter was referred to a security officer. He escorted the shopper to a room for questioning, and immediately proceeded to read the *Miranda* warnings to her, whereupon she advised him that she was the victim rather than a suspect. The officer responded: "We give the warnings to everybody; here, sign this waiver form." She obligingly did so, even though, by virtue of a professional position she held, she knew fully well the absurdity of the practice.

In the second case, three girls, ages 11, 11, and 12, were arrested for shoplifting by a private security officer in an Illinois branch of a nationwide chain of department stores. One of the girls had been observed placing a small, inexpensive item of merchandise in her pocket and attempting to pass the checkout counter without paying for it. After the girls had been escorted into the security office room, and as all three were crying as a result of being arrested, the security officer proceeded to read from the warning form prepared by the company. Ninety-three words were used for the warnings and 73 more were used to tell the girls of their legal rights as juveniles. These included a statement about the possibility of their case being transferred from the juvenile court to the adult criminal court. One of the girls was later asked whether she and the other girls had understood what they had been told. She responded: "We were all crying and had no idea at all what the woman was telling us."

Private security officers in practically every state and municipality possess only the arrest powers of a private citizen. Most of them can only make "citizen arrests" for offenses committed in their presence. They function, therefore, in a nonpolice capacity, and they were not targets of

---

station, one officer said to another, as they passed a school in the vicinity of the robbery, that he would like to find the gun before some schoolchildren found it. The suspect interrupted the conversation and told where the gun was. This was not considered to be an interrogation in violation of *Miranda*. Here, however, the Court might have relied upon the public safety exception it later used in the *Quarles* case.

the Supreme Court's *Miranda* mandate. Among the cases holding that security officers do not have to give the warnings to arrested persons whom they wish to interrogate, the leading one is *People v. Deborah C.*,[116] a case that involved a juvenile arrested for shoplifting.

The only occasions when private security officers are required to administer the *Miranda* warnings are when: 1) they have had conferred upon them, by statute or local ordinance, the same powers possessed by the police; 2) they are actual police officers working part time ("moonlighting") in private security; or 3) in a particular case situation, they are acting in cooperation with the police, and thus functioning, more or less, as their agents.[117] Except for any such circumstance, private security officers do not have to issue the warnings, even though they have made an arrest pursuant to their rights as private citizens. This is also true even with respect to detentions or arrests specifically authorized under state shoplifting statutes.[118]

In a 1984 decision, *Minnesota v. Murphy*,[119] the United States Supreme Court held that a probation officer was not required to issue *Miranda* warnings to a probationer who was called in for questioning after he had abandoned a treatment program for sexual offenders and after a treatment counselor had informed the probation officer that the probationer had admitted a rape-murder prior to the offense for which he had been convicted. His admission of the rape-murder to the probation officer was held admissible at trial. The Court ruled that the probationer was not in custody "for purposes of receiving *Miranda* protection." The same reasoning is obviously applicable to a parolee-parole officer situation.

Permissible Interrogation Regarding Unrelated Offense after Initial Invocation of Rights

There are cases in which a prosecutor is confronted with a situation where a particular crime suspect exercised his right to remain silent, the right was respected, but then he was interrogated about an unrelated

---

[116]177 Cal. Rptr. 852, 635 P.2d 446 (1981). To the same effect: City of Grand Rapids v. Impens, 414 Mich. 667, 327 N.W.2d 278 (1982); and People v. Raitano, 84 Ill. App. 3d 373, 401 N.E.2d 278 (1980). The most recent decision is one rendered in May, 1985, by the New York Court of Appeals in People v. Ray, 65 N.Y. 2d 282, 480 N.E. 2d 1065 (1985).

[117]With regard to moonlighting police officers and private security officers who possess general police powers, see People v. Deborah C., *supra* note 116 at pp. 860, 454; and also Pratt v. State, 9 Md. App. 220, 263 A.2d 247 (1970).

[118]For an extensive documented discussion of the law governing the various aspects of private security operations, consult INBAU, ASPEN, AND SPIOTTO, POTECTIVE SECURITY LAW (1983). Chapter 4 covers "The Interrogation of Suspected Persons." Also, as to the right of a suspected employee to have a fellow union member present at an interrogation, see Chapter 3 of the present text, in the section on "Privacy," at pp. 24–29.

[119]104 S. Ct. 1136 (1984).

crime under investigation by other officers within the same police department or from another department. If the warnings are again given to the suspect, and he makes a waiver, followed by a confession to the second offense, is the confession outlawed by the *Miranda* doctrine?

In the 1975 case of *Michigan v. Mosley*,[120] the United States Supreme Court upheld the admissibility of a suspect's confession that had been made under the following circumstances: A police detective sought to interrogate the defendant, who was under arrest as a robbery suspect. The detective issued the required *Miranda* warnings, after which the arrestee stated that he did not want to talk. There was no interrogation. More than 2 hours later, another detective wanted to question the arrestee about an unrelated crime—a murder. This time, following a second advisement of the *Miranda* warnings and waiver, the arrestee first denied his involvement but then, after being told an accomplice had named him as the killer, implicated himself in the murder. At no time during the interrogation did he state that he did not want to talk or that he wanted to consult with a lawyer. A majority of the Court, with two justices dissenting, held there was no *Miranda* violation because the interrogation was only about the murder, and the defendant's right "to cut off questioning" had been "scrupulously honored."

Although there are state cases following the principle established in *Mosley*,[121] a more restrictive rule has been applied by some courts when the original case was one in which the suspect had specifically claimed the right to counsel, or where the suspect already had counsel in that case. The supportive rationale for the differentiation is the attribution of a higher value to the right to counsel than to the right to silence.[122] Professor Yale Kamisar, a strong supporter of *Miranda*, found the differentiation to be "baffling" in that, as he correctly pointed out, the basic concern of the Supreme Court in *Miranda* was the protection of the Fifth Amendment self-incrimination privilege, with only a secondary or auxiliary consideration being accorded the right to counsel.[123]

---

[120]423 U.S. 96 (1975).

[121]For example, Commonwealth v. McFadden, 225 Va. 103, 300 S.E.2d 924 (1983).

[122]One of the cases placing a higher value upon the warning or claim of the right to counsel than the right to silence is Shreeves v. United States, 395 A.2d 774 (D.C. Ct. App. 1978), cert. denied, 441 U.S. 943. Also see State v. Routhier, 137 Ariz. 90, 669 P.2d 68 (1983), cert. denied, 104 S. Ct. 985. On two occasions, Supreme Court Justice Marshall stated in dissenting opinions that potential waivers of the right to counsel should be subjected to greater scrutiny than the right to silence. See Wyrick v. Fields, 459 U.S. 42, 53–55 (1982), and his dissent from a denial of cert. in Fields v. Wyrick, 104 S. Ct. 556, at 557 (1983).

In People v. Martin, 102 Ill. 2d 412, 466 N.E.2d 228 (1984), a majority of the Illinois Supreme Court upheld the admissibility of the confession a murder suspect had made after having received *Miranda* warnings and upon a waiver of his rights, even though he was in custody on an unrelated rape charge and had had counsel for it at a preliminary hearing.

[123]Kamisar, Yale, 34 *Cr. L.* 2101 (1983). (Comment made during Symposium on "Supreme Court Review and Constitutional Law").

Requirements for Waiver of *Miranda* Rights

WAIVER IMMEDIATELY AFTER WARNINGS

The Supreme Court in *Miranda* established the rule that there could be no interrogation of a custodial suspect following the issuance of the warnings unless he "knowingly and intelligently" waived those rights and agreed "to answer questions or make a statement." The Court did not explain what it meant by the phrase "knowingly and intelligently." One thing is clearly apparent, however. The word "intelligently" is rather meaningless, or at least superfluous, as is exemplified by the following hypothetical case situation: A custodial suspect did in fact commit the crime about which the police sought to question him. He received the warnings and was asked whether he wished to answer questions without counsel, or else sign a written waiver form to that effect. If he consented to be questioned and declined his right to counsel, would not that fact alone evidence a lack of intelligence necessary to make an intelligent waiver? Intelligent action would warrant an avoidance of the risk of lying and of having his statements established to be false and provable as such. In view of his commission of the act, silence or a request for a lawyer would be the intelligent course to follow. Presumably, the Court's usage of the word "intelligently" was merely to signify, if anything, that the suspect must be aware of what he has been told and also has voluntarily agreed to be questioned without benefit of counsel.

The factors that are to be weighed in determining the mental qualifications of a suspect to make a valid waiver are contained in the Supreme Court's majority opinion in a 1979 case involving the interrogation of a 16-year-old juvenile in custody as a murder suspect. In that case, *Fare v. Michael C.*,[124] the Court upheld the juvenile's waiver of *Miranda* rights by applying a "totality of circumstances" test that included "consideration of age, experience, background, and intelligence."[125]

The Supreme Court did not specify in *Miranda* whether waivers had to

---

[124]439 U.S. 1310 (1979). This case and the general subject of interrogating juveniles are discussed in Chapter 8 at pp. 245–248.

[125]According to the New York Court of Appeals in People v. Williams, 62 N.Y.2d 285, 465 N.E.2d 327 (1984), "an effective waiver of *Miranda* rights may be made by an accused of subnormal intelligence so long as it is established that he or she understood the immediate meaning of the warnings." The court added that "an inability to comprehend the import of the *Miranda* warnings in the larger context of criminal law generally does not itself vitiate the validity of the waiver."

For references to other cases, federal and state, regarding waivers by juveniles and by adults who are mentally retarded or insane, or in an intoxicated or drugged condition, see INBAU, THOMPSON, HADDAD, ZAGEL, AND STARKMAN, CASES AND COMMENTS ON CRIMINAL PROCEDURE, (3rd ed. 1980) at p. 136. The same casebook contains references to numerous cases involving other aspects of *Miranda* waivers (pp. 134–139).

be in writing and signed. However, in one of its subsequent decisions, the Court held that signed written waivers are not required. In *North Carolina v. Butler*,[126] the defendant, while a custodial suspect, received the *Miranda* warnings from FBI agents. He was then asked whether he had understood them and he replied that he had but he refused to sign a written waiver form. He was told that he did not have to sign it, but that the agents would like for him to talk to them, whereupon he said: "I will talk to you, but I am not signing any form." Six of the nine members of the Court considered this to be an adequate waiver. Three of the justices dissented on the ground that Butler did not make an "affirmative waiver" in the nature of an "express written or oral statement." Upon one issue, however, there was no disagreement among the justices—a written waiver is not required; an oral one is sufficient.

Although oral waivers are judicially approved, some law enforcement agencies continue the practice of using written ones. An outstanding exception is the United States Drug Enforcement Administration. In June, 1984, it dispensed with the practice of procuring signed waivers. However, the fact that the four required warnings had been given and a waiver made is incorporated in the introductory part of any written confession submitted to a confessor for his approval and signature. Written waivers do possess, of course, the advantage of providing more convincing evidence of the fact of waiver, but they also entail some practical disadvantages, one of which has already been illustrated by the facts of *Butler*. A suspect is much more likely to waive his rights orally than to sign a written waiver form. This is due to the natural reluctance of many persons to sign *any* document, irrespective of the nature of its consequence.

Whenever an orally waiving suspect refuses to sign a written waiver form, a prosecutor may encounter two problems with respect to the confession that may follow: 1) the trial judge or jury might consider implausible the testimony of the police that the suspect did in fact make an oral waiver, in light of his refusal to sign a written one; and more important, 2) defense counsel might successfully argue that the refusal to sign the written waiver evidenced the suspect's *change of mind* after having orally waived, a privilege that was definitely available to him under *Miranda*. As a consequence, the suspect's subsequent confession might be ruled inadmissible.

In consideration of all of the forgoing factors, the interrogator should rely upon an oral waiver and, moreover, a very simplified one. Following is an example, along with the simplified set of warnings that were recommended in Chapter 8:

---

[126]441 U.S. 369 (1979). This case should be considered along with the text discussion at Note 34 (and the cases there cited) in Chapter 8.

"You have a right to remain silent; anything you say may be used against you; you have a right to a lawyer; and if you cannot afford a lawyer one will be provided free." After an appropriate pause to permit the suspect to make his response, he should be told: "I would like for you to talk to me about this matter [the case under investigation] OK?" If the suspect expresses *or otherwise indicates a willingness to talk*, perhaps even by an affirmative nod of the head, the interrogator may proceed with the interrogation.[127] In other words, an explicit waiver is not required.[128]

In suggesting this simplified version of the required warnings and acknowledgment of waiver, it is helpful to recall a point made in Chapter 8 of this text: Although *Miranda* prohibits talking a suspect out of his claim of silence or the assistance of counsel, it does not require that a suspect be *talked into* the exercise of those rights, which may be the practical effect of the ritualistic warnings and waiver procedures that have been so frequently used.

Sometimes a suspect's response to the warnings will be indecisive or

---

[127]In one "nod of the head" case, the Colorado Supreme Court stated: "In law, as in life generally, there are cases where actions speak louder than words, and this, in our opinion, is such a case." People v. Ferran, 196 Colo. 513, 591 P.2d 1013 (1978). To the same effect: Bliss v. United States, 445 A.2d 625 (D.C. App. 1982).

In People v. Williams, 464 N.E.2d 1176 (Ill. App. 1984), the warnings were issued to four suspects as a group, and the nods of their heads were considered adequate waivers. That practice, however, may not be generally acceptable.

[128]The following statement appears in the majority opinion of North Carolina v. Butler, *supra* note 126: "Ten of the 11 United States Courts of Appeals and the courts of at least 17 states have held that an explicit statement of waiver is not invariably necessary to support a finding that the defendant waived the right to remain silent or the right to counsel." The case citations are in note 5 of the opinion.

Some examples of implied waiver are in State v. Gilbert, 650 P. 2d 814 (N.M. 1982), where the suspect said that calling a lawyer would do no good because he would "just tell me not to talk"; United States v. Lame, 716 F.2d 515 (8th Cir. 1983), the statement "Maybe I should get a lawyer," which was followed by a resumption of a statement he started to make, was deemed to be a waiver. In State v. Cannady, 427 So. 2d 723 (Fla. 1983), the suspect said, after making several admissions following the warnings, "I think I should call my lawyer," whereupon the police gave him a telephone, but he continued to make incriminating statements. After several minutes, the officer asked him if he wanted "to talk about it," and he proceeded to confess. The court held that the remark was not an invocation of a right to counsel, but that even if it were the suspect waived it.

A suspect's repeated request for information about the case has been held to constitute a waiver. Howard v. United States, 452 A. 2d 966 (D.C. Ct. App. 1982), cert. denied, 460 U.S. 1087 (1983).

In State v. Rogers, 674 S.W.2d 608 (Mo. App. 1984), after the arrestee expressed an unwillingness to talk, stating that he would "take his chances with a jury," a detective asked him, 2 hours later, while taking him to jail, if he wanted to know what he was up against and he said "yes," whereupon the detective read a portion of the state's capital offense statute. He was again given the warnings, after which he confessed. It was ruled admissible; the court found that his rights had been "scrupulously honored.".

However, see State v. Billings, 110 Wis. 2d 661, 329 N.W.2d 192 (1983), and also Mc Donald v. Lucas, 677 P.2d 518 (5th Cir. 1982), in which the court held that merely talking to the police after refusing to sign a waiver was not, in itself, evidence of an implied waiver.

ambiguous, in which event the cases generally hold that the interrogator is privileged to ask for a clarification.[129] Clarification may not be used, however, as an excuse for eliciting a waiver of the right to silence or the right to counsel.[130]

With respect to the evidentiary proof required to establish that *Miranda* warnings were given and orally waived, the courts generally hold that the testimony of the interrogator or of another police officer will suffice. It need not be corroborated, even if contradicted by the defendant.[131] One court has ruled, however, that where the defendant denies the waiver, the prosecution is obligated to call as a witness some other person who may have been present at the time of the alleged waiver.[132] Another court has held that a waiver must be established beyond a reasonable doubt, and that the trial court also must enter a specific finding to that effect.[133] In a 1983 case, decided by the Supreme Judicial Court of Massachusetts, the court stated that the administration of justice would be facilitated by requiring that a "knowing and intelligent" waiver be proved beyond a reasonable doubt; the court added, however, that its announced rule was not "constitutionally mandated."[134]

Any requirement for proof of a waiver beyond a reasonable doubt seems totally unwarranted. *Miranda* itself was not a due process case; moreover, the United States Supreme Court held, in the 1972 case of *Lego v. Twomey*, that a *confession* need not be proved beyond a reasonable doubt; a preponderance of the evidence is sufficient.[135]

---

[129]State v. Weinacht, 203 Nebr. 124, 227 N.W.2d 567 (1979); State v. Moulds, 105 Idaho 880, 673 P.2d 1077 (1982).

[130]Nash v. Estelle, 597 P.2d 513 (5th Cir. 1979); State v. Robtoy, 98 Wash. 2d 30, 653 P.2d 284 (1982). Both cases held that the clarification did not exceed the proper limitation, but they issued the caution that the police may not use the "guise of clarification" to elicit a waiver. But see Anderson v. Snurth, 36 Cr. L. 2289 (1985), in which the Second Circuit Court of Appeals held that the questions were not of a clarification nature.

In the 1984 case of Smith v. Illinois, 105 S. Ct. 490 (1984), the Supreme Court, in a 6-to-3 decision, voided a confession following this exchange between the interrogator (I) and suspect (S): I: "Do you wish to talk to me at this time without a lawyer being present?" S: "Yeah and no, uh, I don't know what's what, really." I: "Well, you either have to talk to me this time without a lawyer being present and if you do agree to talk with me without a lawyer being present, you can stop at any time you want to." S: "All right. I'll talk to you then."

[131]Illustrative cases are: Neitz v. People, 170 Colo. 428, 462 P. 2d 498 (1969); State v. Briggs, 81 N.M. 581, 469 P.2d 730 (1970); and Bridges v. State, 255 Ind. 201, 263 N.E.2d 368 (1970).

[132]Williams v. State, 220 So. 2d 325 (Miss. 1969).

[133]State v. Gullick, 118 N.H. 912, 396 A.2d 554 (1978).

[134]Commonwealth v. Day, 387 Miss. 915, 444 N.E.2d 384 (1983).

[135]404 U.S. 477 (1972).

VALIDITY OF SUSPECT'S REVOCATION OF ASSERTED *MIRANDA* RIGHTS

A prerequisite to the validity of any waiver that may follow an initial exercise of *Miranda* rights is that the suspect himself must initiate a willingness to talk. The Supreme Court established this requirement in the 1981 case of *Edwards v. Arizona*.[136] The problem posed by that condition is the determination in any particular case whether there was in fact an initiation by the suspect, or whether he was induced by the police to speak out with reference to the matter under investigation.

The uncertainty in the law, and the dilemma the uncertainty has created for the police with regard to waivers following an initial exercise of *Miranda* rights, is well illustrated by the 1983 Supreme Court case of *Oregon v. Bradshaw*.[137] In *Bradshaw*, the defendant, while under arrest in a fatal traffic accident investigation, received the warnings and asked for a lawyer. As he was being transported from the police station to a jail, about 10 miles away, the defendant inquired of the police, "Well, what is going to happen to me now?" The officer responded by saying, "You do not have to talk to me. You have requested an attorney and I don't want you talking to me unless you so desire.... It has to be at your own free will." The defendant stated that he understood. The two discussed their destination and the charge that would be placed against him. The officer then suggested that the defendant take a polygraph test, and he agreed to do so. The next day, the *Miranda* warnings were again given and a test was administered. After the test, the defendant made incriminating admissions that were used against him at trial.

In a 5-to-4 decision, the Supreme Court sustained the defendant's conviction. Justice Rehnquist, in an opinion joined by three other justices, stated that although Bradshaw's question as to what was going to happen to him was ambiguous, it "evidenced a willingness and a desire for a generalized discussion about the investigation." According to Justice

---

[136]451 U.S. 477 (1981). Also see Brewer v. Williams, 430 U.S. 387 (1977).

In *Edwards*, the Court stated that after the arrestee has asserted his right to counsel, there can be no interrogation "unless the accused himself initiates further communication, exchanges, or conversations with the police." According to the Court's opinion, initiation occurs only when the suspect makes inquiries that can be "fairly said to represent a desire on the part of the accused to open up a more generalized discussion relating directly or indirectly to the investigation." Three justices concurred in the result reached in *Edwards*, but two of them stated that the opinion written on behalf of the Court by Justice White "appears to be an undue, and undefined emphasis on a single element: 'initiation'." They were of the view that "initiation" was only "a single element of fact" among others that may be relevant to determining whether there had been a valid waiver."

[137]103 S. Ct. 2830 (1983).

Rehnquist, the defendant's question "could reasonably have been interpreted by the officer as relating generally to the investigation."

Justice Marshall, joined by three other members of the Court, dissented on the ground that Bradshaw's question did not relate to "the subject matter of the criminal investigation." It only represented a desire "to find out where the police were going to take him."[138] Justice Powell, the remaining justice, concurred in the decision reached by Rehnquist and the three other justices, but Powell commented that both of the two separate opinions in the case "reflect the ambiguity of some of the [language in the earlier case of *Edwards v. Arizona*], particularly on the meaning of 'initiation.'" He noted, however, that the opinions written by Rehnquist and by Marshall were in agreement in one respect; that the "initiation" question is "the first step of a two-step analysis, the second step being the application [of the standard] that requires examination of the 'totality of circumstances.'" This "two-step analysis," Powell urged, "could confound the confusion ... evidenced by the conflicting reading of [the opinion in *Edwards v. Arizona*] by Justices Marshall and Rehnquist." According to Powell, courts "should engage in more substantive inquiries than 'who said what first.'" He was of the view that the issue should be resolved on the basis of the "totality of circumstances." By that standard, he concluded that the defendant Bradshaw had "knowingly and intelligently waived his right to counsel."[139]

Here, then, is a decision in which four justices concluded that the waiver had been valid, four concluded that it had not been valid, and a ninth justice agreed with the result reached by the first four but found fault with the reasoning underlining their determination of its validity. This uncertainty among the Supreme Court justices themselves renders difficult the task of police academy instructors and of other police legal advisors to provide guidelines for the police to follow in cases involving factual situations upon which they, as nonlawyers, must make on-the-spot determinations as to whether a suspect has initiated a valid waiver.[140] The only course available to them, presumably, is to assume that anything resembling a suspect's willingness to talk about some seemingly relevant aspect

---

[138]103 S. Ct. 2830 at 2840.

[139]103 S. Ct. 2830 at 2837, 2838.

[140]Two other cases illustrate the uncertainty confronting the police and their legal advisors. In Stumes v. Solem, 671 F.2d 1150 (8th Cir. 1982), the court held that an interrogation after a waiver following a 10-hour transportation to a jail facility destination in a police car did not revoke a suspect's waiver of his initial request for counsel. In United States v. Montgomery, 714 F.2d 201 (1st Cir. 1983), after demanding counsel, the suspect asked two questions about the charges against him, to which the officer responded "Why do you want to know?," and the suspect incriminated himself. The court believed there might have been an initiation but found there was no waiver. It suggested, however, that the result might have been different had new warnings been given.

of the case should be treated as the initiation of a waiver. As the next case demonstrates, however, they may be adjudged to have erred even when the suspect asks a question that simply cannot be shrugged off without an affirmative answer that may be productive of an incriminating statement.

In *People v. Braeske*,[141] decided by the California Supreme Court in 1979, the police issued the *Miranda* warnings to a suspect in custody for a triple murder. Although the suspect had initially waived his rights, once the interrogation began and the police had pointed out some incriminating evidence, Braeske refused to talk without having a lawyer present. The interrogation ceased, but as Braeske was being booked he requested to speak "off the record." He then proceeded to admit the commission of the offense and told of the location of the gun he had used in the killings. The California Supreme Court, in a 4-to-3 decision, held that the "off the record" request did not constitute a waiver. The confession and the evidence derived from it were held inadmissible as evidence.[142]

REVOCATION BY SUSPECT OF RIGHT TO CONTINUED ASSISTANCE OF COUNSEL

A suspect may not only waive the initial right to counsel, as well as revoke a claim to that right once it has been waived, but he may also waive his right to *continued assistance* of counsel appointed for or retained by him. This is in conformity with the traditionally recognized right of a suspected or accused person to waive any other constitutional rights or privileges. For instance, a defendent in a criminal case may decide to waive his Fifth Amendment self-incrimination privilege and may testify as a witness, despite his lawyer's disapproval. The defendant may even dismiss the lawyer altogether and proceed to trial without one—thereby completely disregarding the Sixth Amendment right to counsel "for his defense."

Although a number of state and lower federal court decisions uphold the

---

[141]159 Cal. Rptr. 684, 602 P.2d 384 (1979).

[142]After the grant of review by the Supreme Court of the United States, the case was remanded to the California Supreme Court "to consider whether its judgement was based on federal or state grounds, or both." California v. Braeske, 446 U.S. 932 (1980). The California court certified that its judgment was "based upon *Miranda v. Arizona* ... and the Fifth Amendment to the United States Constitution." It added, "we reiterate [our opinion] in its entirety." 168 Cal. Rptr. 603, 618 P.2d 149 (1980). Further review was denied by the United States Supreme Court. 451 U.S. 1021 (1981). The defendant Braeske was retried and convicted. The prosecution used as evidence incriminating statements Braeske made while in jail after his first conviction, during a television interview with Mike Wallace on CBS's "60 Minutes." Braeske's defense at his second trial was influence of an hallucinogenic drug ("angel dust") at the time of the killings. "Without the tape", said prosecutor Michael Cordozo, "Braeske would be a free man." *San Francisco Chronicle*, February 25, 1982, p. 4. This second conviction is on appeal.

right of a suspect to dispense with the continued assistance of counsel and to agree to be interrogated by the police,[143] a contrary rule has been established by New York's highest court. The New York Court of Appeals held that once a suspect has a lawyer, there can be no waiver without the lawyer being present.[144] Moreover, the rule has been extended to include situations where the suspect has a lawyer in a totally unrelated criminal case.[145] The dissenting judges in the case that made this extension criticized the rule on the ground that it conferred an unnecessary benefit on repeat offenders. One qualification to New York's extended rule was made in a case where the state police had no knowledge that the waiving suspect already had an attorney in a case for which he had been arrested by a local police agency.[146]

Relevant to the issue of a suspect's right to revoke the continued assistance of counsel are cases in which a suspect requests counsel at the time of arraignment, but later, after making a waiver following *Miranda* warnings, submits to a police interrogation. One federal court of appeals case held that a suspect's request for counsel at arraignment had indicated a desire for counsel in the Sixth Amendment sense—in other words, for representation at trial—but that it had not indicated a desire to take advantage of his Fifth Amendment right to silence, with the auxiliary right to counsel, at a police interrogation.[147] An Oregon case, coming to a similar conclusion, referred to a request for counsel at arraignment as a "merely routine" procedure that would not be viewed, without an additional explicit statement, as a request for counsel at a subsequent interrogation.[148]

Prosecuting attorneys must be mindful of the legal profession's code of ethics whereby an attorney is not privileged to communicate with another attorney's client except through that attorney or with his permission. However, even though a breach of this ethical principle may result in a reprimand of the prosecutor, it will not nullify an incriminating statement made by a suspect who did not have the guidance of an attorney.[149]

---

[143]United States v. Bentley, 726 F.2d 1124 (6th Cir. 1984); State v. Norgaad, 653 P.2d 483 (Mont. 1982); State v. Jackson, 205 Nebr. 806, 290 N.W.2d 458 (1980); Kennedy v. Fairman, 618 F.2d 1242 (7th Cir. 1980); Shreeves v. United States, 395 A.2d 774 (D.C. Ct. App. 1978).

[144]People v. Hobson, 39 N.Y.2d 479, 348 N.E.2d 894 (1976); People v. Marrero, 51 N.Y.2d 56, 409 N.E.2d 980 (1980). A similar rule prevails in West Virginia. State v. McNeal, 251 S.E.2d 484 (W.Va. 1979). Also see the cases cited in State v. Burbine, 451 A. 2d 22, at 29, a case rejecting the New York rule. *Burbine* itself is discussed *infra* at Note 152.

[145]People v. Bartholomeo, 53 N.Y.2d 225, 423 N.E.2d 371 (1981).

[146]People v. Fuschino, 59 N.Y.2d 91, 450 N.E.2d 200 (1983).

[147]Collins v. Francis, 728 F.2d 1322 (11th Cir. 1984).

[148]State v. Sparklin, 672 P. 1182 (Ore. 1983). The Oregon court specifically rejected the rule espoused by the New York Court of Appeals, *supra* Note 144—that representation by an attorney on one charge insulates a person from questioning regarding other crimes.

[149]People v. Green, 405 Mich. 273, 274 N.W.2d 448 (1979).

EFFECT OF DEFENSE COUNSEL'S INSTRUCTION TO POLICE TO
REFRAIN FROM INTERROGATING CLIENT/SUSPECT, AND EFFECT
OF UNSUCCESSFUL ATTEMPT TO CONTACT CLIENT/SUSPECT

The case law is divided as to the admissibility of confessions obtained
after the suspect's lawyer already has instructed the police to refrain from
interrogating the client. Some of the cases, however, have upheld the
admissibility of confessions procured even after the police had breached
an agreement with counsel to comply with the lawyer's instruction.[150] In
any event, admissibility is contingent upon the suspect's waiver of silence
and right to counsel.

The Supreme Court dealt tangentially with this issue in the 1977 case of
Brewer v. Williams.[151] In *Williams,* where the suspect's lawyer had
telephoned the police not to question his client, the Court found that the
facts did not establish a waiver of the continued assistance of counsel, but
it specifically disclaimed that it was holding that a suspect "could not,
without notice to counsel, have waived his right."

Some cases have held that there can be no waiver of right to counsel
where, although unknown to the suspect, an attorney was trying to contact
him at the police station or by telephone.[152] In any consideration of this
issue, however, the fact should not be overlooked that no impediment to
waiver exists by reason of the Supreme Court's decision in *Escobedo v.
Illinois,*[153] the precursor of *Miranda. Escobedo* is not controlling because,
in it, the suspect had requested a lawyer and, in fact, the lawyer he retained

---

[150]Watson v. State, 282 Md. 73, 382 A.2d 574 (1978) (approved waiver despite agreement not
to question—three dissenters); McPherson v. State, 562 S.W.2d 210 (Tenn. Cr. App. 1977)
(attorney requested no questioning, but police did not agree to comply—court said the police
"tread on thin ice" when they question suspect in face of request of counsel not to do so);
State v. Jones, 19 Wash. App. 850, 578 P.2d 71 (1978) (suspect may be questioned but must be
told his attorney called and instructed police not to do so); Commonwealth v. Currie, 388
Mass. 776, 448 N.E.2d 740 (1983) (attorney cannot stop interrogation where fully advised and
waiving suspect was aware his attorney had telephoned police and had told them not to
question his client.) Contra: State v. Weedon, 342 So.2d 642 (La. 1977) (improper to violate
agreement—three dissenters); Stone v. State, 280 Ark. 167, 655 S.W.2d 448 (1983); State v.
Duerr, 8 Ohio App. 3d 396, 457 N.E.2d 834 (1982) (one of questions presented, apart from
voluntariness issue, was whether attorney may invoke privilege against self-incrimination on
behalf of client by telephoning police during her statement to cease further questioning).
[151]430 U.S. 387 (1977).
[152]The core issue will be considered by the United States Supreme Court in the October, 1985,
term in Moran v. Burbine. In this case, as State v. Burbine, 451 A. 2d 22 (1982), the Rhode
Island Supreme Court had held that the defendants' waivers prior to three confessions were
valid, but that holding was reversed by the First Circuit Court of Appeals, 753 F. 2d 178
(1985). In Weber v. State, 487 A. 2d 674 (Del. 1983), such a waiver was invalidated, but the
court stated that a waiver would be approved if the suspect is first advised of the attorney's
interest. The opinion contains a discussion of a number of other relevant cases.
[153]378 U.S. 478 (1964).

was at the police station but was denied the opportunity to confer with him. The subsequent confession was held inadmissible on the basis of a denial of the right to counsel guaranteed by the Sixth Amendment. The waiver issue under *Miranda*, as previously discussed, rests upon Fifth Amendment considerations.

EFFECT OF INDICTMENT OR OTHER FORMAL CHARGE UPON VALIDITY OF ACCUSED PERSON'S WAIVER OF RIGHTS

In the 1964 Supreme Court case of *Massiah v. United States*,[154] and the 1980 one of *United States v. Henry*,[155] the Court held that after a suspect has been indicted (or otherwise formally charged with a crime), the prosecution cannot become involved in "deliberately eliciting" information by surreptitious means (e.g., through a government informant). To do so is violative of the Sixth Amendment right to counsel.

Neither *Massiah* nor *Henry* dealt with the issue of whether, after indictment or other formal charge, there could be any overt interrogation of the accused—following a legally valid waiver, of course. Applying the previously discussed reasoning based upon the extensive power of waiver—e.g., the rights of a defendant to waive his self-incrimination privilege and testify at his own trial and to have the case tried without any assistance of counsel—there should be no ban upon waiver by the accused person of any pretrial rights after indictment or upon the filing of any other formal charge. With respect to an interrogation, however, some courts have held that the accused must be advised of the fact of indictment in addition to receiving the *Miranda* warnings.[156] If, of course, the suspect claims *Miranda* rights, there can be no interrogation. However, an individual may, at any time, revoke those rights, provided he initiates a waiver. In such a case situation, the issuance of *Miranda* warnings is advisable prior to the start of the statements of the accused, even though at that time he may be represented by counsel. This may seem paradoxical in view of the authors' previous suggestion to avoid unnecessary or repetitious warnings, but the issuance of the warnings, in the context of the commencement of the judicial process, is nevertheless an advisable precaution. Furthermore, as a practical matter, after the accused has initiated the

---

[154]377 U.S. 201 (1964).

[155]477 U.S. 264 (1980).

[156]United States v. Clements, 728 F.2d 654 (4th Cir. 1984); United States v. Karr, 742 F.2d 493 (9th Cir. 1984); Parnell v. State, 664 S.W.2d 96 (Tex. Cr. 1984).

Compare, however, the New York Court of Appeals case of People v. Lopez, 28 N.Y.2d 23, 268 N.E.2d 628 (1971), cert. denied, 404 U.S. 840, in which the court in a 4-to-3 decision held that failure to advise the suspect of his indictment had not been fatal to waiver and had not barred the use of his incriminating statement.

waiver, it is unlikely that the issuance of the warnings will deter him from confessing.[157]

Corrective Measures When Warnings Do Not Precede Initial Interrogation

In instances where an interrogator has failed to administer the *Miranda* warnings in the mistaken belief that, under the particular circumstances of the case, the warnings were not required, there are corrective measures that may be employed to salvage an interrogation opportunity. Some other interrogator at a different place and at a later time may issue the warnings and, after a waiver by the suspect, proceed to interrogate him. Several federal circuit and state court cases have held that such warnings and waivers remove the "taint" occasioned by the failure to issue the warnings initially, provided the earlier police questioning was not accompanied by coercion. The Supreme Court of the United States made a similar ruling, by a 6-to-3 decision, in the 1985 case of *Oregon v. Elstad.*[158] The facts of the case and the details of the Court's opinion appear in the preceding chapter under the same section heading as the above one.

Upon occasion, prosecuting attorneys may be confronted with case situations of this nature. When they are, they may arrange for a utilization of the forgoing procedure and thereby salvage a case in which an accused person's own admissions or confession are indispensable to a successful prosecution.

The Meaning of "Custody"

In *Miranda*, the Supreme Court clearly indicated that the warnings are required only in custodial situations. Nevertheless, for several years thereafter, one federal circuit court of appeals (the Seventh Circuit) interpreted the *Miranda* mandate to mean that the police had to give the warnings prior to the interrogation of anyone *upon whom suspicion had focused.* A few state appellate courts also adopted, or else viewed with favor, the focus of suspicion test.

---

[157]Some other cases relevant to the issue of formally accused persons are: Estelle v. Smith, 451 U.S. 454 (1981); Shreeves v. United States, 395 A.2d 774 (D.C. Ct. App. 1978); State v. Carter, 412 A.2d 52 (Me. 1980); State v. Norgaard, 653 P.2d 483 (Mont. 1982); State v. Sparklin, 296 Ore. 85, 672 P.2d 1182 (1983).

On May 28, 1985, the Supreme Court granted certiorari in Michigan v. Jackson and Michigan v. Bladel to review the issue of postindictment interrogations and the relationship between First Amendment and Sixth Amendment waivers.

[158]105 S. Ct. 1285 (1985). Details of the cases are in Chapter 8, at pp. 241–243.

Among the other cases referred to in the above text are: United States v. Knight, 395 F.2d 971 (2d Cir. 1968); Knott v. Howard, 511 F.2d 1060 (1st Cir. 1975); United States v. Toral, 536 F.2d 893 (9th Cir. 1976), and People v. Tanner, 30 N.Y.2d 102, 282 N.E.2d 98 (1972).

The rationale for the interpretation expressed by the Seventh Circuit Court of Appeals was the perception that focus of suspicion constituted "psychological compulsion" and was, therefore, "tantamount to the deprivation of the suspect's 'freedom of action in any significant way,' repeatedly referred to in *Miranda*."[159] This perception, however, was not acceptable to the Supreme Court. In its 1976 decision in *Beckwith v. United States*, the Court unequivocally declared, with only one justice dissenting, that "focus of suspicion" was not the test for determining whether the *Miranda* warnings were required; the test was, rather, whether a custodial situation existed.[160] Nevertheless, the "focus of suspicion" rule prevailed within the Seventh Circuit (which encompasses three large central states) from the time of its imposition in 1969 until the 1976 Supreme Court decision in *Beckwith*—a span of 7 years. After *Beckwith*, of course, the issue was resolved for all federal courts and for all federal officers. "Custody," not "focus of suspicion," now definitely prevails as the test throughout the federal system. It also prevails among the states, although two of them (Minnesota and Michigan) had adopted the focus test prior to *Beckwith*, and a third one (Colorado) had given an indication to that effect.

The Supreme Court of Minnesota adopted the focus of suspicion test in 1970 and reaffirmed it in 1975,[161] but two years later the court, without specifically overruling those cases, held that focus was no longer the test for *Mirandas'* applications.[162]

Michigan's courts had adopted the focus test, rejected it after *Beckwith*, and now apply the custody test.[163] The Colorado Supreme Court referred to the "focus test" in a case decided shortly after *Miranda*, but the case actually involved a custodial situation.[164] Since then, and even before *Beckwith*, custody was declared by the Colorado court to be the proper standard for the police to follow.[165]

---

[159]United States v. Oliver, 505 F.2d 301 (7th Cir. 1974). Also see the original Seventh Circuit case of United States v. Dickerson, 413 F.2d 1111 (7th Cir. 1969).

[160]425 U.S. 341, 347 (1976). Justice Stevens, who authored the opinion in *Oliver* while on the Seventh Circuit Court, took no part in *Beckwith*.

[161]State v. Kinn, 288 Minn. 31, 178 N.W.2d 888 (1970); State v. Raymond, 305 Minn. 160, 232 N.W.2d 879 (1975).

[162]State v. Kusley, 254 N.W. 2D 73 (1977). This apparently has been discontinued.

[163]In People v. Martin, 78 Mich. App. 518, 521, 260 N.W. 2d 869, 870 (1977), the court stated that "at first blush, it would seem we are bound to follow the mandate of People v. Reed" [393 Mich. 342, 224 N.W.2d 867 (1975)], which had used the "focus" test, but it followed *Beckwith*, as did the 1980 Michigan appellate court case in People v. Schram, 98 Mich. App. 292, 296 N.W.2d 840.

[164]People v. Orf, 172 Colo. 253, 472 P.2d 123 (1970).

[165]*See, e.g.*, People v. Conner, 195 Colo. 525, 579 P.2d 1160 (1978).

The meaning of "custody," and particularly of the auxiliary phrase "deprivation of freedom in any significant way," is illustrated by the 1969 case of *Orozco v. Texas*.[166] In *Orozco*, a suspect was questioned at 4 a.m. in his boarding house bedroom by four officers, one of whom testified, in effect, that the suspect had been under arrest. The Court held that even though the questioning was brief and took place in his own bedroom, the suspect had been the subject of custodial interrogation. A failure to give the suspect the warnings rendered his confession inadmissible as evidence.

In determining what constitutes a custodial interrogation within a police facility, consideration should be given to the 1977 decision of the Supreme Court in *Oregon v. Mathiason*.[167] Mathiason was a parolee and a close associate of the son of a woman whose residence had been burglarized. The victim told the police she suspected Mathiason, who lived about 2 blocks from the patrol office of the state police, which was located in a building that housed several state agencies. The police tried to contact Mathiason upon several occasions, but without success. An officer finally left a note for him to telephone the officer who would like to "discuss something with him." When Mathiason called, he was asked where it would be convenient for the two to meet. Not receiving an expression of a preference, the officer suggested the state patrol office. The two met in the hallway of the office building. They shook hands, entered a room, and the door was closed. Mathiason was told he was not under arrest, but that the officer wanted to talk to him about a burglary that the police believed he had committed. About 5 minutes later, he confessed, without having received the *Miranda* warnings.

After Mathiason's trial and conviction for the burglary, an appeal to the Oregon Supreme Court resulted in a reversal, the court holding, by a divided vote, that the interrogation had taken place in a "coercive environment," thereby requiring the *Miranda* warnings. However, that holding of the Oregon court was reversed by the United States Supreme Court, which did not deem the interrogation to be a custodial one.[168]

The principle embodied in *Mathiason*—that consent will negate custody, even regarding station house interrogations—was reaffirmed by the

---

[166]394 U.S. 324 (1969).

[167]429 U.S. 492 (1977).

[168]There were two aspects of *Mathiason* that the court was not called upon to decide. One was the false statement the interrogator made to the suspect that his fingerprints were found at the scene; the second was the interrogator's remark that "truthfulness would possibly be considered by the district attorney or judge." The legal effect of those two statements is discussed later in this chapter.

United States Supreme Court in the 1983 case of *California v. Beheler*,[169] and also has been applied by a number of state courts.[170]

In the 1984 case of *Berkemer v. Mc Carthy*, the Supreme Court made a custody delineation between on-the-scene questioning of a detained suspect in a minor misdemeanor (traffic violation) case and the questioning of him in the police station. The Court held that although *Miranda* applied to minor misdemeanor custody cases, custody for *Miranda* warning purposes did not exist during the brief on-the-scene questioning.[171]

Another on-the-scene restraint case involving the custody issue is one in which two bank robbery suspects were handcuffed during an investigatory stop. The cuffs were put on them as one of two investigating officers left the scene momentarily to interview a possible witness nearby. The questioning of each suspect separately, while still handcuffed, elicited several inconsistent and contradictory statements as to the reason and circumstances of their being at the scene near the robbery, including the reason one of them had related to a nearby resident. Upon appeal from their conviction, the defendants argued that once they were handcuffed, they were not free to leave and, consequently, in the absence of the *Miranda* warnings, their statements were not usable as evidence. The federal circuit court of appeals affirmed the district court's admission of the incriminating statements. According to the appellate court, the handcuffed suspects had not been confronted with any evidence of their guilt when questioned, and "neither the physical surroundings of the interrogation, nor the duration of the detention could be considered to be coercive as that term was used in *Miranda*." There was, therefore, no custody so as to require the warnings.[172]

There are many instances where the police unnecessarily give *Miranda* warnings in noncustodial case situations. That fact, however, does not transform the situation into a custodial one. An interrogator's misconception that issuance of the warnings was required is irrelevant to a custody

---

[169]463 U.S. 1121 (1983).

[170]For example: People v. Wipfler, 68 Ill. 2d 158, 68 N.E.2d 870 (1977); Smith v. Commonwealth, 219 Va. 455, 248 S.E.2d 135 (1978); State v. Cruz-Mata, 138 Ariz. 370, 674 P.2d 1368 (1983); State v. Mc Quillen, 345 N.W.2d 867 (S.D. 1984).

In United States v. Dockery, 736 F.2d 1232 (8th Cir. 1984), which involved the interrogation of a bank employee who was suspected of embezzlement, the interrogation was conducted in a small room by government agents, at the request of her employer. The court held it was not custodial; that the employee's freedom of movement was not restricted by governmental agents but rather by her voluntary obligation to her employer.

[171]103 Ct. 3138 (1985). The rule is subject to the qualification that the traffic stop must not be prolonged for the purpose of obtaining an incriminating statement.

[172]United States v. Bautista, 684 F.2d 1286 (1982).

issue determination.[173] Also, the undisclosed intention of an officer to make an arrest is not a controlling factor. The generally applicable rule with respect to the test for custody is the objective, "reasonable person" one, based upon the "totality of the circumstances."[174]

The Meaning of "Interrogation"

More troublesome than the meaning of "custody" under *Miranda* has been the meaning of "interrogation." Moreover, both issues may arise in the same case, as occurred in *United States v. Mesa,*[175] a 1980 decision of the third circuit court of appeals. In this case, a suspect for whom the FBI had obtained an arrest warrant on a charge of shooting both his common-law wife and his daughter barricaded himself, while armed, in a motel room. The agents called repeatedly on a bullhorn, urging him to come out. He refused, but agreed to talk on a mobile phone to an FBI negotiator. Their conversation was recorded and, in it, the suspect made some incriminating statements, after which he peacefully surrendered. The district court suppressed the statements on the ground that they were made in a custodial situation, without the suspect having received the *Miranda* warnings. Upon appeal, the circuit court of appeals reversed by a 2-1 majority. The chief judge concluded that "where an armed suspect who possibly has hostages barricades himself away from the police, he is not in custody [within] the meaning of the *Miranda* rule." Another judge was of the view that the agent's conversation with the suspect had not constituted an interrogation. The third judge dissented because he concluded that there had been *both* custody and interrogation.[176]

Various attempts have been made by the courts to develop a test for satisfactorily determining when a case situation involves an interrogation within the context of *Miranda*. According to one stated by the Supreme

---

[173]People v. Wipfler, *supra* Note 170.

[174]An excellent, extensive discussion of the objective, reasonable person test appears in Hunter v. State, 590 P.2d 888 (Alas. 1979).

Among the many cases that have considered this issue are United States v. Hall, 421 F.2d 540 (2d Cir. 1969), cert. denied, 397 U.S. 990; State v. Roberti, 293 Ore. 59, 644 P.2d 1104 (1982); Yount v. Patton, 710 F.2d 956 (3d Cir. 1983); and United States v. Woods, 720 F.2d 1022 (9th Cir. 1983).

[175]638 F.2d 582 (3d Cir. 1980).

[176]Rather than quibbling over the custody-interrogation issue in this case, the court might have invoked the rescue/lifesaving (emergency) exception to the requirement for *Miranda* warnings, discussed earlier in this text at page 283. Any conclusion based upon that concept would have been more palatable than the divergent views expressed by the three judges. In fact, the emergency alternative was intimated by a judge on the third circuit's full panel, who dissented from a denial of the petition for review (638 F.2d at 598).

Court, in the 1980 case of *Rhode Island v. Innes*,[177] interrogation encompasses not only "express questioning, but also any words or actions on the part of the police (other than those normally attendant to arrest and custody) that the police should know are reasonably likely to elicit an incriminating response . . . ." A differently worded test was submitted by a number of the judges on the full panel of the fifth circuit court of appeals in a case prior to *Innes*. *Miranda*, according to them, applied only to "investigative custodial questioning, aimed at eliciting evidence of a crime," and did not apply to "routine police functions bearing no resemblance to traditional station house investigation."[178]

Although asking a question that directly bears on a suspect's guilt or innocence is clearly interrogation, there are certain conditions and circumstances under which specific questioning does not come within the coverage of *Miranda*. An illustration is the actual case of a man who voluntarily came into a police station and announced "I done it; arrest me," whereupon he was asked what he had done. He replied: "I killed my wife." He was then asked "What did you kill her with?" Reply: "With an ax; that's all I had." His statements were held properly admitted at his trial for murder.[179] The appellate court quoted from the *Miranda* opinion in which the Court stated:

> There is no requirement that police stop a person who enters a police station and states that he wishes to confess to a crime, or a person who calls the police to offer a confession or any other statement he desires to make.[180]

Such occurrences are generally referred to as "threshold questioning." Also within that general category are questions asked during the police booking procedure of an arrestee; they, too, are usually deemed noninterrogative.[181]

A variety of case situations have arisen in which the courts have had to determine whether seemingly routine questions that are asked of a *custodial* suspect constitute interrogation so as to come within the coverage of *Miranda*. For instance, is interrogation involved when an arrested suspect is asked by a police officer "Do you know why you're here?" or "Do you know why I'm here?" As a rule, such questions are viewed by the courts as likely to elicit incriminating answers, and therefore, they are, considered

---

[177]446 U.S. 291, at 301 (1980). The facts of *Innes* are discussed in this text, *infra*, p. 306.

[178]Harryman v. Estelle, *infra* Note 189, at p. 881.

[179]People v. Savage, 102 Ill. App.2d 477, 242 N.E.2d 446 (1968).

[180]384 U.S. 436, 478 (1966). This, however, is an issue apart from the waiver one that arose in the California case of People v. Braeske, *supra* Note 142.

[181]United States v. Downing, 665 F.2d 404 (1st Cir. 1981). But see People v. Rucker, 26 Cal. Rptr. 3d 162, 605 P.2d 843 (1980), barring *any* response to routine booking questions.

to fall within the prohibition of *Miranda* when asked of a custodial suspect and when they were not preceded by the warnings and a waiver.[182] On the other hand, it has been held that there was no interrogation when, after an arrested suspect inquired about the reason for his arrest, the officer replied "you know why," which was followed by an incriminating statement.[183] A similar conclusion was reached in a case where a suspect arrested for murder told an officer "It was like a bad dream," and the officer asked: "What's like a bad dream?" whereupon the suspect made the incriminating statement: "To shoot a man six times and see him still try to get up."[184]

In distinguishing permissible from unpermissible comments and actions, the Supreme Court has applied the test of whether they represent the "functional equivalent" of interrogation. The outstanding example is the 1977 case of *Brewer v. Williams*.[185] This was a child abduction (suspected murder) case in which a police officer, while in a police car with a custodial suspect who had exercised his *Miranda* rights and already had an attorney, was told that the police hoped they could find the child's body before it became covered with an impending snowfall. The arrestee revealed the body's location. His statement was considered to be the functional equivalent of an interrogation, in consequence of which neither it nor the fact of finding the body was admissible as evidence.[186]

---

[182]An example of such implicit interrogation is People v. Lowe, 200 Colo. 470, 616 P.2d 118 (Colo. 1980).

Prior to *Miranda*, a "know why" question was an effective and legally permissive way to start some interrogations, and it was presented as a technique in the 1962 edition of CRIMINAL INTERROGATION AND CONFESSIONS. The 1967 post-*Miranda* edition cautioned that the question no longer could be used on custodial suspects and should be restricted to those who were not in custody. That caution is repeated in the present test in the discussion of "Initial Interview Procedures" in Chapter 5.

[183]State v. Ladd, 308 N.C. 272, 302 S.E.2d 164 (1983). In State v. Guido, 704 F.2d 675 (2d Cir. 1983), the court held that *Miranda* was not violated when, in response to the suspect's own question, the interrogator had given details of the crime, after which the suspect confessed.

[184]People v. Guichici, 118 Mich. App. 252, 324 N.W.2d 592 (1982).

[185]430 U.S. 387 (1977).

[186]There were four dissenters. They were of the view that Williams had waived his right to counsel and that, therefore, his statement was admissible.

Upon Williams' second trial the fact of finding the child's body was admitted as evidence on the basis of the "inevitable discovery" doctrine—in other words, the body would inevitably have been discovered. However, a federal circuit court vacated the second conviction because the prosecution had not proved the absence of police bad faith, which the court considered an essential element of the inevitable discovery doctrine. Williams v. Nix, 700 F.2d 1164 (8th Cir. 1983). The Supreme Court reversed that holding as an unwarranted qualification to the inevitable discovery rule. Nix v. Williams, 106 S. Ct. 2501 (1984). In its opinion in the latter case the Court used the commendable expression about the "enormous societal cost of excluding truth in search for truth in the administration of justice."

Williams is discussed elsewhere in this text with respect to the issue of the waiver of the right to continued assistance of counsel.

In a case situation somewhat similar to *Brewer v. Williams*, the Supreme Court held, in *Rhode Island v. Innes*,[187] that there was no functional equivalent to interrogation in a comment made by one police officer *to another officer* while in a police car with an armed robbery arrestee. The officer had expressed the hope that his discarded weapon could be found before some children in a neighborhood school came across it, whereupon the arrestee disclosed its location. The arrestee's statement, as well as the finding of the gun, was held admissible as evidence; the statement was not considered the functional equivalent of interrogation. The essential factual difference between *Innes* and *Williams* was, of course, that in the latter case, the comment was made to the suspect, whereas in *Innes*, it was made to a fellow officer, although the Court itself did not base its holding on that particular distinction. Rather, the Court, in a footnote to its *Innes* opinion, pointed out that the *Williams* decision rested on the Sixth Amendment right to counsel, whereas *Innes* was a Fifth Amendment case and that "the two constitutional protections are quite distinct."

Illustrative of the varying results that may be reached in the application of the functional equivalent test are two cases decided by the same federal circuit court of appeals. In one, decided after *Innes* by a three-judge panel, a police officer had commented to an arrestee that a gun was in his car, and his acknowledgment of its ownership was held admissible as evidence in a prosecution for the interstate transportation of a prohibited firearm. The officer's comment was held not to be the equivalent of interrogation.[188] On the other hand, many members of the full panel of the same court, in a case decided shortly before *Innes*, had expressed the view that interrogation was implicit in the question "What is this?" with regard to a powdered substance discovered during the search of an arrestee suspected of dealing in drugs.[189]

The problem has arisen in some cases as to whether the interrogation factor is present with respect to a *third person's comments* to the police within the hearing of the suspect. In the case of *Haire v. Server*,[190] a murder suspect, whose wife had already confessed to the crime, was taken along with her to a rural area where she had said the two of them had disposed of the body. No questions were asked of the husband, who had not received the *Miranda* warnings; however, after his wife said the

---

[187]446 U.S. 291 (1980).

[188]United States v. Bennett, 626 F.2d 1309 (5th Cir. 1980). Compare, however, United States v. Jordan, 557 F.2d 1081 (5th Cir. 1977), in which the court held that an officer's accusation that the suspect was in possession of a sawed-off shotgun was held to constitute interrogation.

[189]Harryman v. Estelle, 616 F.2d 870 (5th Cir. 1980). (The admission in evidence of the arrestee's statement was considered harmless error, however, in view of other proof of his possession of heroin.)

[190]437 F.2d 1262 (8th Cir. 1971).

body was on the right side of the road, he stated, "No, honey, on the left side," which is where the body was found. The wife was then asked about the gun that had been used in the killing. When she said it was home under the bed, the husband corrected her by saying it was hidden in the fireplace, where it actually was found. A federal circuit court of appeals, with one of three judges dissenting, ruled that the occurrence did not involve an interrogation of the husband, and consequently no warnings were required. The Supreme Court declined to review the case.[191] What the Court might have held in a similar case that did receive its close scrutiny is a matter of speculation, although the Court's holding in *Innes* may be considered supportive of the circuit court's decision in *Haire*.

Another illustration of the *Innes* concept is a case in which the police were investigating the burglary of a post office. Upon his arrest, a suspect was given the *Miranda* warnings. He responded by saying that questions could be asked but that he would only respond to the ones he chose to answer. Equipped with a search warrant, the police accompanied the suspect to his apartment where they found a large roll of postage stamps and also equipment for use in credit card frauds. After federal agents arrived on the scene, the suspect again received the warnings. He then told them he would talk, but not about the credit card fraud. He was told that the investigators wanted to locate over $100,000 in money orders that had been stolen. When the suspect was told that his girlfriend would be questioned about them, he said that he would turn them over the next morning after he had talked to his attorney, whereupon one investigator said to another: "That's it, let's go talk to the girl." The location of the money orders was then revealed. In holding that the investigator's comment did not constitute interrogation, a federal circuit court of appeals, in a 2-to-1 decision, stated: "There is nothing in the record to compel a finding that the police conversation was more evocative than the one used in *Innes*."[192]

An exhortation to "tell the truth" or "be honest" has been held to constitute interrogation,[193] and a request of a custodial suspect to take a polygraph test has also considered by one court to be of an interrogative nature.[194]

Several cases have involved the issue as to whether or not a display to a

---

[191]404 U.S. 910.

[192]United States v. Thierman, 678 F.2d 1331 (9th Cir. 1982).

In State v. Thomas, 312 S.E.2d 458 (N.C. 1984), after the suspect had invoked his right to counsel, a police officer's comment "Be sure to tell your attorney that you had an opportunity to help yourself and you didn't" was held not likely to elicit an incriminatory statement and, therefore, was not interrogative in nature.

[193]State v. Finehout, 136 Ariz. 226, 665 P.2d 570 (1983).

[194]People v. Johnson, 671 P.2d 958 (Colo. 1983), 681 P.2d 524 (1984).

custodial suspect of crime-scene evidence constitutes the functional equivalent of an interrogation. The courts are divided, although the latest one, decided by the New York Court of Appeals in 1984, held that it was the functional equivalent.[195]

The Massachusetts Supreme Judicial Court upheld a robbery-murder confession that resulted from the bringing into an interrogation room a suspected accomplice who, while seated 20 to 25 feet away, asserted his innocence and requested to talk to the first suspect, which he was permitted to do. The first one then confessed, although he had earlier invoked his right to silence. This was held not to involve police interrogation.[196]

The issue surrounding the display of evidence or police reports only arises, of course, in case situations where a *custodial* suspect had not been given the required warnings or else had exercised his right to silence or to see a lawyer. The restriction is not applicable regarding noncustodial suspects or custodial ones who had made a waiver following the issuance of the warnings.

Limited Use of *Miranda*-Flawed Confession

Two years after *Miranda*, three of the four justices who were in dissent in that case (the fourth one having retired) dissented in another case—*Mathis v. United States*—and expressed the view that *Miranda* should be overruled.[197] Then, in less than 3 years thereafter the same three justices, along with two others, held, in *Harris v. New York*,[198] that a confession obtained without the required *Miranda* warnings could nevertheless be used to impeach the confessor after he had taken the stand and had denied the commission of the offense. Chief Justice Burger, who authored the majority opinion, stated that the privilege of a defendant to testify or not testify "cannot be construed to include the right to commit perjury," and

---

[195]People v. Ferro, 63 N.Y.2d 316, 472 N.E.2d 13 (1984) cert. denied 37 Cr. L. 4082 (1985); In the Interest of Durand, 206 Nebr. 415 293 N.W.2d 383 (1980).

Among the cases holding that a display is not the functional equivalent of interrogation are: State v. Grisby, 97 Wash. 2d 493, 647 P.2d 6 (Wash. 1982); State v. McLean, 242 S.E.2d 814 (N.C. 1978), and Vines v. State, 285 Md. 369, 402 A.2d 900 (1979). In the *Ferro* case, a dissenting justice stated that: "the prophylactic safeguards do not preclude . . . nonverbal, noncoercive, nonthreatening, nonbothersome police conduct."

[196]Commonwealth v. Williams, 388 Mass. 846, 448 N.E.2d 1114 (1983). This case and some of the forgoing ones were referred to in Chapter 8.

[197]Justices Stewart, White, and Harlan expressed that view in Mathis v. United States, 391 U.S. 1 (1968), a case which held, in a 5-3 decision, that a person incarcerated in a penitentiary for one offense was in custody for purposes of interrogation regarding another offense. (Justice Clark, who had also dissented in *Miranda*, had retired at the time of this decision; he was succeeded by Justice Abe Fortas.)

[198]401 U.S. 222 (1971).

that "the shield provided by *Miranda* cannot be perverted into a license to use perjury by way of defense, free from the risk of confrontation with prior inconsistent utterances."

In another Supreme Court case shortly after *Harris*, a majority of the Court, in *Oregon v. Hass*,[199] once again approved the use for impeachment purposes of a *Miranda*-flawed incriminating statement. In *Hass*, an interrogator had continued to interrogate the suspect after he had indicated a desire to consult with counsel.[200] A few state courts, in the exercise of their option to adopt a stricter standard than the federal one, have rejected the *Harris* and *Hass* concepts.[201]

For a reason that should be readily apparent, the federal rule regarding the use of a *Miranda*-flawed confession for impeachment purposes is inapplicable with regard to a coerced confession.[202] The latter presents the risk of utilizing a completely false statement against an innocent person, whereas the former involves only a prophylactic rule unrelated to the issue of trustworthiness.

In addition to permitting *Miranda*-flawed statements to be used for impeachment purposes, the Supreme Court has sanctioned the derivative use of such statements. In *Michigan v. Tucker*,[203] evidence was held admissible, even though it had been obtained as the result of a disclosure made by a custodial suspect who had not received the proper *Miranda* warnings. (The interrogator had neglected to advise the suspect of his right to counsel in the event he could not afford one.) The Court upheld the prosecution's use as a witness an individual whose name was given to the police in a false alibi statement made by the improperly warned suspect.

The state of Texas has provided, by statute, for the admissibility of evidence derivatively obtained from a *Miranda*-flawed confession. After providing that no statement of a custodial suspect shall be received in evidence without the required warnings, it specified that the prohibition "shall not apply to any statement which contains assertions of facts or circumstances that are found to be true and which conduce to establish the guilt of the accused, such as the finding of secreted or stolen property or the instrument with which he states the offense was committed."[204]

---

[199]420 U.S. 714 (1975).

[200]In his dissent, Justice Brennan referred to the majority's decision as a "fundamental erosion of the Fifth and Sixth Amendments."

[201]State v. Santiago, 53 Hawaii 254, 492 P.2d. 657 (1971); People v. Disbrow, 127 Cal. Rptr. 360, 545 P.2d 272 (1976) (a 4-3 decision of the California Supreme Court).

[202]Mincey v. Arizona, 437 U.S. 385 (1978).

[203]417 U.S. 433 (1974).

[204]Article 38.22 Sec. 3(c), Texas Stats. Ann. (Vernon's Code of Criminal Procedure).

CONFESSION VOLUNTARINESS

The Coercive Factors of Physical Force and Threats

A basic fact that must be considered with respect to the legal requirement of confession voluntariness as a prerequisite to admissibility as evidence is the inevitability of some degree of perceived "coercion" in any police interrogation of a criminal suspect. As stated in a per curiam opinion of the United States Supreme Court in the 1977 case of *Oregon v. Mathiason*, "Any interview of one suspected of crime by a police officer will have coercive aspects to it, simply by virtue of the fact that the police officer is part of the law enforcement system which may ultimately cause the suspect to be charged with crime."[205] There can be no legal test, therefore, that will provide complete freedom from a suspect's perceived coercion during the course of a police interrogation. That could only be achieved by an absolute prohibition upon all police interrogations—an unaffordable societal protection. One jurist did, however, offer such a proposal some years ago, but he conditioned it upon a trade-off with the self-incrimination privilege to the extent that accused persons could be required to take the witness stand and be cross-examined.[206] No attempt was ever made to implement this proposal.

Although the responsibility for establishing rules of confession admissibility has been a traditional judicial function, a few state legislatures have attempted to establish their own tests. Most tests have proved to be unsatisfactory, and some have only served to confuse the issue. A notable exception has been the New York statute, which is worthy of presentation here in its entirety. After declaring confessions inadmissible that are "involuntarily made," the statute provides that a confession is involuntary when obtained:

> (a) By any person by the use or threatened use of physical force upon the defendant or another person, or by means of any other improper conduct or undue pressure which impaired the defendant's physical or mental condition to the extent of undermining his ability to make a choice whether or not to make a statement; or

---

[205]424 U.S. 492 (1977). In this case, which was discussed in an earlier part of the text on the meaning of "custody" for *Miranda* purposes, the Court granted a writ of certiorari, summarily reversed the Oregon Supreme Court, and remanded the case for proceedings not inconsistent with the Court's opinion regarding the custody issue. Justice Brennan agreed to the granting of the writ but dissented from the summary disposition of the case; he wanted it set for oral argument. Justices Marshall and Stevens also dissented.

[206]This suggestion was submitted by a former justice of the Illinois Supreme Court, Walter v. Schaefer. See Schaefer, *Police Interrogation and the Privilege Against Self-Incrimination*, 61 *Nw. U. L Rev.* 506 (1966). Justice Schaefer had also been a Professor of Law at Northwestern University.

(b) By a public servant engaged in law enforcement activity or by a person acting under his direction or in cooperation with him:
(i) by means of any promise or statement of fact, which promise or statement creates a substantial risk that the defendant might falsely incriminate himself; or
(ii) in violation of such rights as the defendant may derive from the constitution of this state or the United States.[207]

Among the many appellate court cases decided upon the issue of confession voluntariness, the easiest to resolve are those in which there has been an infliction of direct physical harm upon the suspect, such as a blow from a fist or some physical object. Confessions following such occurrences are categorically rejected. Although most decisions to that effect are founded upon the realization that the conduct may produce a confession from an innocent person, some courts also invoke the concept that an admission into evidence of a confession obtained by such means would be an affront to the integrity of the judicial system.

Uncertainty does prevail, however, with respect to confessions obtained after the suspect has encountered force of an indirect nature, such as a lengthy interrogation by two or more interrogators, or the deprivation of food, water, sleep, or access to toilet facilities. Here, of course, there are many variables, primarily with respect to the suspect's tolerability or sensitivity to what has occurred. Then, too, consideration must be given to the extent or degree of any such deprivations.

Illustrative of the task confronting the courts in any particular case situation involving indirect force is the 1944 case of *Ashcraft v. Tennessee*, discussed earlier in this chapter.[208] In this case, the defendant, while under suspicion for the murder of his wife, had been interrogated "intermittently" over a 28-hour period during a total detention time of 36 hours. He confessed 8 hours after being confronted with the confession of the person who had stated that Ashcraft had hired him to do the killing. He repeated his confession in the presence of two businessmen and his own physician. Moreover, the physician physically examined Ashcraft and observed no signs of abuse.

Upon Ashcraft's appeal from his conviction, a six-member majority of the United States Supreme Court ruled that the confession was erroneously admitted in evidence because the lengthy interrogation had been "inherently coercive." Justice Jackson, in a dissenting opinion in which he was joined by Justices Frankfurter and Roberts, opposed the adoption of such an irrefutable presumption. Each case, according to them, should be

---

[207] Article 60.45, Criminal Procedure Law, Book 11-A, McKinney's Consolidated Laws of New York.
[208] *Supra* at Note 24.

decided upon its own particular set of facts. They contended that *any* interrogation, even one of an hour's duration, might be considered "inherently coercive," an observation that comports with the viewpoint expressed 40 years later in the case of *Oregon v. Mathiason*, discussed at the beginning of this section, that any police interrogation will unavoidably involve some element of coercion.[209]

Of the various forms of indirect force, the one that most suggests confession coercion is the participation of multiple interrogators over a lengthy time period. Ironically, one phase of the practice, that of multiple interrogators, will at times psychologically deter a guilty person from confessing. In Part 1 of this text, a number of case situations illustrated the advisability of having only one person conduct an interrogation, or at most two, working separately and under conditions of privacy. Moreover, as to the time factor, rarely will a competent interrogator require more than approximately 4 hours to obtain a confession from an offender, even in cases of a very serious nature. Moreover, an interrogation within the suggested 4-hour period is less likely to be viewed by a court or jury as unreasonable than one that has extended over a longer period.[210] Nevertheless, there should be no hard and fast rule in this respect because in exceptional situations, there may be a need for a somewhat longer period. Most cases, of course, require considerably fewer than 4 hours.

In addition to psychological considerations, there is a very pragmatic reason for the avoidance of multiple interrogators—the difficulty it presents to a prosecutor in establishing proof of the confession's voluntariness. Some courts have held that whenever the defense of coercion is raised, the prosecution must offer as a witness, whenever practicable, each and every person who participated in the interrogation or witnessed the actual act of confession.[211] This, obviously, places a considerable burden on the prosecuting attorney and may constitute a very real danger to the

---

[209]Another Supreme Court expression to the same effect appears in Stein v. New York, 346 U.S. 156, at 186 (1952). Referring to the issue of the voluntaries of the confessions made to a murder by the three defendants, the Court said, "Of course, these confessions were not voluntary in the sense . . . that they were completely spontaneous, like a confession to a priest, a lawyer, or a psychiatrist. But in this sense no criminal confession is voluntary."

[210]Many courts have held, however, that although the number of interrogators is a factor in determining a confession's voluntariness, the participation of several interrogators, as well as the length of the interrogation, does not necessarily render a confession inadmissible. State v. Wallace, 59 Wis.2d 66, 207 N.W.2d 855 (1973); State v. Morgan, 294 N.C. 151, 261 S.E.2d 427, 832 (1980).

[211]There are several Illinois Supreme Court cases to this effect, one of the earliest being People v. Ardenarczyk, 367 Ill. 534, 12 N.E.2d 2 (1937). Another example is People v. Sloss, 412 Ill. 61, 104 N.E.2d 807 (1982), and one of the latest is People v. Lumpp, 113 Ill. App. 3d 694, 447 N.E.2d 963 (1983). The court held that the prosecution's obligation was not relieved by the fact that, of the several officers who participated in the interrogation of the defendants, one was no longer on the police force and another was on furlough. See, however, the exception

entire prosecution effort where perhaps five, 10, or more witnesses may have to be produced to establish the voluntary character of a confession. First, considerable time and expense will be consumed in producing the testimony of all persons who were present. Second, the more witnesses there are, the more likely will be a certain amount of inconsistency in their testimonies as to the various details surrounding the confession—even though all of them may be attempting to tell the absolute truth—and this inconsistency is apt to lend credence to unfounded allegations of duress.

With regard to the threat factor of coercion, the most obvious example of conduct that will invalidate a confession is when an interrogator leads a suspect to believe that unless he confesses, he will be subjected to loss of life or other bodily harm. The belief does not require a specific expression from anyone to that effect; for example, it may result from an act of physical abuse to some other presumed suspect within sight or hearing of the one under interrogation.[212]

A threat to send the suspect to the penitentiary for a more serious offense unless he confesses to the present one will nullify the confession.[213] Another form of an invalidating threat is illustrated in a case where a female narcotics violator suspect is told that if she does not "cooperate," she will be deprived of state financial aid and her children will be taken from her custody.[214]

Not only may a threat to the suspect himself nullify a confession; the same consequence may result from a threat to arrest the suspect's wife or

---

to the general rule in People v. Jankowski, 391 Ill. 298, 63 N.E.2d 362 (1945), where the defendant testified that he did not remember making a confession and did not know what he had signed, but claimed that a particular officer, whom he named, was the only one who had beaten him. That officer was produced as a witness for the prosecution and denied any abuse. The court held that under the circumstances, it had been unnecessary to call the other officers as witnesses.

The Illinois Criminal Code, §114-11(d), provides that "Objection to the failure of the state to call all material witnesses on the issue of whether the confession is voluntary must be made in the trial court."

Some decisions in other state courts similar to the Illinois ones are State v. Scarborough, 167 La. 484, 119 So. 523 (1929); State v. Lord, 42 N.M. 638, 84 P.2d 80 (1938); Holmes v. State, 211 Miss. 436, 51 So.2d 755 (1951). However, the New York Court of Appeals has held, in People v. Buckler, 39 N.Y.2d 895, 352 N.E.2d 583 (1976), that it was unnecessary for the prosecution to produce as witnesses the two detectives who had witnessed the confession. The court also commented that it is not incumbent upon the prosecution to call at trial a witness to a crime or to make a complete and detailed accounting to the defense of all law enforcement investigative work.

[212]People v. Flores, 15 Cal. App.2d 385, 59 P.2d 517 (1936).

[213]State v. Harvey, 145 Wash. 161, 259 P. 21 (1927). See, also, Roger E. G. v. Kirkpatrick, 125 Cal. Rptr. 625 (Cal. App. 1975), in which a juvenile was threatened with prosecution in the adult criminal court.

[214]Lynum v. Illinois, 372 U.S. 528 (1963). A similar case situation was present in United States v. Tingle, 658 F.2d 1332 (9th Cir. 1981), which reached a result of confession rejection based upon *Lynum*.

another member of the family, especially in one case, where a threat was made to bring the suspect's wife, who was an invalid, into the police station for questioning.[215]

It has been held permissible for an interrogator to ask a question rather roughly,[216] to assume in his various questions that the suspect is guilty,[217] to express impatience with the suspect's alleged lying,[218] or to tell a suspect that the investigators will secure or have already secured the necessary proof to convict him anyway.[219] Also, the "friendly-unfriendly" tactic described in Part 1 (*Step 3*) is not violative of the voluntariness test of confession admissibility provided, of course, the "unfriendly" one of the two interrogators does not tarnish it with force or threat of force. The comments must be confined to derogatory remarks and expressions of impatience. Although the majority of the Supreme Court in *Miranda* referred to this tactic as the "Mutt and Jeff" act (which some interrogators themselves had called it), the quotation from one of the books the Court cited reveals that the author (O'Hare) was in fact recommending more than mere derogatory remarks or expressions of impatience.[220] The correct judicial view upon the subject is the one embodied in a 1983 decision

---

[215]Rogers v. Richmond, 365 U.S. 534 (1961), in which the court stated that admissibility was to be determined on the basis of whether the police conduct "was such as to overbear . . . the will to resist and bring about confessions not freely determined."

In regard to a confession to protect a girlfriend, see United States v. McShane, 462 F.2d 5 (9th Cir. 1972).

[216]Anderson v. State, 133 Wis. 601, 114 N.W. 112 (1907).

[217]People v. Fitzgerald, 322 Ill. 54, 152 N.E. 542 (1926).

[218]Dame v. State, 191 Ark. 1107, 89 S.W.2d 610 (1936). The interrogator's impatience even to the extent of swearing at the subject has been held insufficient to nullify a confession. State v. Dehart, 242 Wis. 562, 8 N.W.2d 360 (1943). Also, upon this point, see Buschy v. People, 73 Colo. 472, 216 Pac. 519 (1923); the second *McNabb* case, 142 F.2d 904 (6th Cir. 1944); and State v. Henderson, 182 Ore. 147, 184 P.2d 392 (1947).

[219]State v. Johnson, 137 S.C. 7, 133 S.E. 823 (1926); People v. Castello, 194 Cal. 595, 229 Pac. 855 (1924).

[220]O'HARE, FUNDAMENTALS OF CRIMINAL INVESTIGATION (1956), quoted in *Miranda* at p. 452. The opinion also referred to O'Hare's recommendations of reliance upon "an oppressive atmosphere of dogged persistence;" and his recommendation that the interrogator "must interrogate steadily and without relent, leaving the subject no prospect of surcease," and also "dominate . . . and overwhelm him with his inexorable will to obtain the truth."

Along with the quotations from O'Hare, the Court quoted from Inbau and Reid's 1962 edition of CRIMINAL INTERROGATION AND CONFESSIONS regarding their recommendation of privacy during an interrogation, the use of excuses and sympathy for the suspect's conduct, and talking a suspect out of his interest in remaining silent. What the Court neglected to mention, however, was the number of times throughout Inbau and Reid's book where they cautioned the avoidance of any tactic or technique that was apt to induce an innocent person to confess. Moreover, with regard to the "friendly-unfriendly" tactic itself, the authors urged that the unfriendly interrogator "should resort only to verbal condemnation" and "under no circumstances should he ever employ physical abuse or threats of abuse or other mistreatment" (p. 59). The same admonition appears in Part I of the present text.

The O'Hare book also recommends a "reverse lineup" tactic by which a suspect is placed in a lineup where he would be "identified" by fictitious victims or witnesses.

of the Colorado Supreme Court.[221] In it, the court took into consideration the *totality* of what had occurred during the interrogation. Although it found that, in the particular case before it, the "totality of the circumstances" revealed coercion sufficient to nullify the confession, the court specifically stated that neither the friendly-unfriendly tactic nor any of the others used in the interrogation, considered separately, would have produced that result.

There remains another issue regarding threats to which some attention is warranted, although it involves primarily a semantics problem rather than a matter of substance. It pertains to the interrogator's usage of comments containing the word "better" when trying to persuade a suspect to confess. Although merely advising or imploring a suspect to confess will not adversely affect a confession,[222] difficulties have arisen when the suspect is told "You had better confess," or "It would be better for you to confess." Some courts have considered such expressions to constitute threats, and one has reached the same conclusion where the interrogator had told the suspect "It would be better to tell the *truth*."[223] There are many cases, however, that have held that expressions of the forgoing nature are permissible.[224]

The resolution of the issue with respect to cases wherein the word "better" is used should be made on the basis of the circumstances surrounding each particular case. For instance, if the word "better" had been accented by the interrogator, or if he clenched his fist or made some other gesture of a similar nature as he spoke, the reasonable inference could be one of a threat. Mere words themselves, however, do not warrant the same conclusion. Nevertheless, the prudent course for interrogators to follow is to completely avoid expressions containing the word "better". At best their value for eliciting the truth is very limited anyway.[225]

Along with the Court's association of the Inbau and Reid text with the one by O'Hare, they were identified as police officers on the staff of the Chicago Police Scientific Crime Detection Laboratory. In fact, Inbau had been director of that laboratory in a civilian capacity from 1938 to 1941, and from 1945 until 1978, he was a professor of law at Northwestern University. Also, Reid had been on the laboratory's staff from 1940 until 1947; thereafter he had no connection with it. *Miranda* was decided in 1966.

[221]People v. Freeman, 668 P.2d 1371 (Colo. 1983), subsequently discussed in the section on *Totality of Circumstances Test of Voluntariness* at page 327.

[222]People v. Davis, 10 Ill.2d 430, 140 N.E.2d 675 (1957); State v. Statler, 331 S.W.2d 526 (Mo. 1960); State v. Morgan, *supra* note 210. Also see Lynum v. Illinois, 372 U.S. 528 (1963).

An approving case is People v. Jimenez, 147 Cal. Rptr. 172, 580 P.2d 672 (1978), in which the suspect was not only exhorted to tell the truth but also told that people would think better of him if he did tell the truth.

[223]For example, Edwards v. State, 194 Md. 387, 71 A.2d 487 (1950).

[224]See, for example, People v. Pugh, 409 Ill. 584, 100 N.E.2d 909 (1951).

[225]In the next section, consideration is given to the issue of whether such expressions may be subject to interpretation as promises.

Promises

Expressions of the type discussed at the conclusion of the preceding section, such as "It would be better to confess," not only have been the subject of allegations that they constitute threats, but they also have been challenged in a number of cases on the ground that they amounted to promises of *leniency* and therefore nullified the confessions that followed. As with threats, although to a lesser degree, a promise of leniency may have the effect of inducing an innocent person to confess. This is a risk, particularly in case situations where there is strong circumstantial evidence or perhaps even positive eyewitness identification pointing to the suspect as the offender. Under such circumstances, a promise of a lighter sentence than the one that seems probable may be an appealing alternative to the risk of incurring a much greater punishment.

The case law regarding confessions following expressions containing the word "better" has been divided on the issue of whether a promise of leniency is to be inferred. The majority of such decisions has declined to assume that the word itself necessarily implies leniency; there must be additional factors to support such a conclusion.[226]

As stated in the preceding section, the tone of the interrogator's voice and his behavior when uttering the word "better" can be very meaningful to the suspect. For instance, if "better" is stated in a very friendly tone, and perhaps even accompanied by a pat on the shoulder or some other comparable gesture, an inference of favorable disposition of the case on the part of prosecutor or judge is not an unreasonable one. The mere word itself, therefore, should not be the determining fact; all the surrounding circumstances are deserving of consideration. As one court stated, "even if a suspect ... influenced perhaps by wishful thinking ... assumed he would get more lenient treatment ... [this] would not, as a matter of law, make the confession inadmissible ...." "It is not every inducement," added the court, "that vitiates a confession, but only such inducement as involves any fair risk of a false confession."[227]

To be contrasted with expressions containing the word "better" are exhortations "to tell the truth,"[228] or advice to the suspect that he will "feel

---

[226]Examples of leniency inferred: State v. Linn, 179 Ore. 499, 173 P.2d 305 (1946); Kier v. State, 213 Md. 556, 132 A.2d 494 (1957). Examples of no inference of leniency: People v. Klyaczek, 305 Ill. 150, 138 N.E. 275 (1923); People v. McGuire, 39 Ill.2d 244, 234 N.E.2d 772 (1968); Frazier v. State, 107 So.2d 16 (Fla. 1958).

[227]State v. Nunn, 212 Ore. 546, 321 P.2d 356 (1958).

[228]People v. Hill, 58 Cal. Rptr. 340, 426 P.2d 908 (1967). The innocuous nature of the exhortation will be dissipated, however, by the addition of comments that the suspect (in a murder case) could get the police "working for him" and he would also "get the people on his side."

better" for doing so.[229] Both have been considered permissible because they have been considered free from the influence of stimulating false confessions.

An interrogator's statement that he will "go to bat" for the suspect will nullify a confession.[230] This also is true as to a specific statement that the interrogator will do whatever can be done to persuade the proper authorities to grant immunity or a reduced sentence.[231] As to the latter, some interrogators have raised the question as to the difference between making that commitment, at least when they genuinely believe the recommendation will be approved, and the practice whereby an accused person may enter into a plea bargain upon appearance in court, in other words, when there is an agreement to plead guilty in return for a light sentence or probation. The answer, of course, is that before and at the time of the plea bargaining the accused person will have had the advice and assistance of counsel.

The courts have rather uniformly held that a confession's validity is not adversely affected by the interrogator's statement that a report will be made to the prosecutor or judge that the suspect did "cooperate." In a 1983 case, the Supreme Judicial Court of Massachusetts approved the making of such a statement. "What is prohibited," said the court, "is not a statement about the value of cooperation, but a promise that cooperation . . . will aid the defense or result in a lesser sentence being imposed."[232]

---

[229]People v. Jackson, 168 Cal. Rptr. 603, 618 P.2d 149 (1980).

[230]Hillard v. State, 406 A.2d 415 (Md. Ct. App. 1979). See also State v. Tardiff, 374 A.2d 598 (Me. 1977), in which exhortations to tell the truth were considered proper, but not a promise that if the suspect told the truth, the number of charged offenses would be reduced.

The Arkansas Supreme Court adopted a very strict rule regarding promises of the type under discussion. In Tatum v. State, 585 S.W.2d 957 (Ark. 1979), an interrogator's statement that he would "do all he could to help" nullified the confession and resulted in an aggravated robbery conviction reversal, even though, said the court, there was sufficient evidence to otherwise sustain the conviction. And in Freeman v. State, 527 S.W.2d 909 (Ark. 1975), the court stated that "the burden is upon the state to show the statement [of the accused murderer] to have been voluntarily, freely, and understandably made, without hope of reward or fear of punishment."

[231]People v. Martorano, 359 Ill. 258, 194 N.E. 505 (1935). In fact, an intimation of such assistance will also nullify a resulting confession. See Edwards v. State, 194 Md. 387, 72 A.2d 487 (1950), where the interrogator showed the accused a letter from a convict which stated: "Next time you get a smart guy . . . show him this letter, from other wise guy, and don't forget to tell him what it cost me for not listening to you."

Telling an 18 year old who was beyond the state's statutory age for juveniles that he might receive juvenile court treatment, or that the murder charge against him might be reduced to a lesser offense, rendered his confession involuntary. State v. Biron, 266 Minn. 272, 123 N.W.2d 392 (1963).

[232]Commonwealth v. Williams, 388 Mass. 846, 448 N.E.2d 1114 (1983). The court referred to an earlier Massachusetts case in which the statement was made that the interrogator may state in general terms that "cooperation has been considered favorably by the courts in the past."

$\rightarrow$

Whenever an interrogator tells the suspect that the authorities will be advised of his cooperation, it is advisable to couple the statement with the comment: "I can't promise you anything, of course, but I will report that you did cooperate." At least one court attached a favorable significance to that appendage.[233]

During the course of an interrogation, a suspect may ask: "What will happen to me if I told you I did this?"or "What will happen if I told you the truth?" The advisable response, as suggested in Part 1 of this text, is to say: "I can't tell you. It is not within my power to make any promise, and it wouldn't be fair for me to tell you anything as to what may happen to you. My advice to you is to tell the truth now, and if you think you have a break coming, you talk to the prosecutor or the judge."

If a suspect inquires: "What is the maximum penalty I could receive for this?," the interrogator may tell him in the event he knows for a fact what it is.[234] Even then, however, the safer practice is to advise the suspect to address his inquiry to the prosecuting attorney, because once such a question is asked, the suspect is beginning a confession anyway, and there is no reason to entangle the interrogation procedure in an unnecessary legal controversy at a later time.

One promise that is generally recognized as permissible is the promise of secrecy.[235] Here, of course, the very fact of the suspect's interest in having an incriminating statement kept secret is an added assurance of its truthfulness. The clearest example of a case situation when the secrecy promise is apt to occur is one where the suspect asks: "If I tell you about this, will you not tell my mother [or some other relative or friend]"? This, of course, is a promise that the interrogator can conscientiously make, for there obviously is no need to tell anyone other than the authorities about the matter until courtroom testimony is required.

A promise to recommend light bail will not render a confession in-

---

Also see, with respect to approval of a report of cooperation: People v. Eckles, 470 N.E.2d 623 (Ill. App. 1984), citing People v. Hubbard, 55 Ill.2d 142, 302 N.E.2d 603 (1973); State v. Finehout, 136 Ariz. 226, 665 P.2d 570 (1983).

[233]People v. Bulger, 382 N.Y. Supp.2d 133 (App. Div. 1976).

[234]A case in which an answer was considered proper, even when accompanied by a statement of the possibility of lenience in return for his cooperation, is United States v. Reynolds, 532 F.2d 1150 (7th Cir. 1976). Also see United States v. Guido, 706 F.2d 675 (2d Cir. 1983).

[235]Commonwealth v. Edwards, 318 Pa. 1, 178 Atl. 20 (1935); Markley v. State, 173 Md.2d 309, 196 Atl. 95 (1938); People v. Stadnick, 207 Cal. App.2d 767, 25 Cal. Rptr. 30 (1962). Also see Commonwealth v. Fournier, 361 N.E.2d 1294 (Mass. 1977). One early case held that a promise not to tell anyone was impermissible because it implied a promise not to prosecute. White v. State, 70 Ark. 24, 65 S.W. 937 (1901).

It is of interest to note that a Georgia statute specifically provides that a confession shall not be excluded because of a promise of secrecy. See *infra* Note 243.

admissible,[236] nor will a promise to seek psychiatric treatment for the suspect after his incarceration.[237]

Inconsequential to the admissibility of a confession is the promise the interrogator may have made to the suspect to afford him a gratification of a personal desire or comfort, for instance refreshments of one sort or another.[238] One court drew the line, however, when a promise was made to place a homosexual suspect in a "gay cell." This was held to invalidate his incriminating statement regarding the offense about which he was being quostionod.[239]

There are cases that have tolerated the promise of a benefit to a third person on the theory that it was not likely to have rendered a confession involuntary, especially when the suspect presented the idea, or offered to make a deal to confess if leniency would be accorded a third person.[240] Less likely is this to be allowed, however, if the third person is a close relative.[241]

The forgoing discussion was devoted to the general case law upon the subject of promises. There arc, however, a few state statutes that must be borne in mind by police interrogators in their respective states. The provisions in two of the statutes also should be of particular interest.

A Georgia statute provides that "To make a confession admissible, it must be made voluntarily, without being induced by another, by the slightest hope of benefit or remotest fear of injury."[242] Along with that provision is another one which states: "The fact a confession shall have been made under spiritual exhortation, or a promise of secrecy, or a promise of collateral benefit, shall not exclude it."[243] The Georgia Court of Appeals held that the statute prohibited a promise that a suspect could be

---

[236]United States v. Ferrar, 377 F.2d 16 (2d Cir. 1967)

[237]People v. Moe, 86 Ill. App. 3d 762, 408 N.E.2d 483 (1980) (The interrogator testified she had used the same tactic to elicit the truth from other sex offenders); State v. Beck, 390 So.2d 748 (Fla. App. 1980) (Comments about psychiatric assistance "do not result in the exclusion of a confession, so long as aid is not offered in return for a consequent statement," citing a number of cases from Florida as well as other jurisdictions).

[238]State v. Blair, 118 Vt. 81, 99 A.2d 677 (1953).

[239]State v. Greene, 588 P.2d 548 (N.M. 1978).

[240]State v. Torres, 121 Ariz. App. 110, 588 P.2d 852 (1979). In United States v. Reese, 351 F. Supp. 719 (D.C. Pa. 1972), a promise of benefit to suspect's live-in girlfriend was held to be "merely collateral." Also see State v. Anderson, 298 N.W.2d 63 (Minn. 1980).

[241]People v. Trout, 6 Cal. Rptr. 759, 354 P.2d 231 (1961) (promise to release wife from custody); Hammer v. Commonwealth, 207 Va. 135, 148 S.E.2d 878 (1966) (promise not to arrest other members of defendant's family). Where no express promise, or threat, is made, a suspect's belief that his cooperation will benefit a relative will not invalidate a confession. People v. Steger, 128 Cal. Rptr. 161, 546 P.2d 665 (1976); Roberts v. State, 545 S.W.2d 157 (Tex. Cr. 157) (1977).

[242]Ga. Code, Ch. 38, § 411.

[243]Ga. Code, Ch. 37, § 412.

released on bail.[244] In another case, the trial court suggested that spiritual exhortations should be left to the clergy.

Louisiana's statute requires the prosecution to prove that a confession was not made under the influence of "fear, duress, menaces, threats, inducements or promises."[245] Although no promises seem permissible under this statute, in a case where a deputy sheriff had obtained a confession after telling a suspect it would be "easier for him," the Louisiana Supreme Court attached favorable consideration to the fact that the statement had been preceded by an admonition that the suspect should not confess unless he was guilty.[246] Also, in another case, the court found that the statute had not been violated by the interrogator's comment that the suspect would be better off if he cooperated because "rather than being promises or inducements designed to extract a confession," statements of that sort are "more likely musings not much beyond what defendants might have concluded for himself."[247]

Accusatory Confrontation, Trickery, and Deceit

ACCUSATORY CONFRONTATION

In the course of a competently conducted interrogation of *a suspect whose guilt appears definite or reasonably certain*, the interrogator should confront the suspect with a direct statement that he is considered to be the person who committed the offense. The sense in which the word "guilt" is used in this context is entirely different from guilt in the legal sense, as explained in the beginning of Chapter 6 of this text. That chapter also contains a detailed discussion of the precise manner in which the accusatory confrontation should be conducted, and it also includes a presentation of the moral as well as the legal justification for its utilization. In further support of that justification is an excerpt from the opinion of three of the four justices who dissented in *Miranda*:

---

[244]Hickox v. State, 138 Ga. App. 882, 227 S.E.2d 829 (1976).

[245]La. Cr. Proc., § 451.

[246]State v. Richards, 223 La. 674, 66 So.2d 589 (1953).

[247]State v. Petterway, 403 So.2d 1157 (La. 1981).

Among the few other states with statutory provisions regarding confession admissibility is the following one in the code of the state of Washington (Rev. Code Section 10.58.030): "The confession of a defendant made under inducement, with all the circumstances, may be given as evidence against him, except when made under the influence of fear produced by threats; but a confession made under inducement is not sufficient to warrant a correction without corroborating testimony."

Interrogation is no doubt often inconvenient and unpleasant for the suspect. However, it is no less so for a man to be arrested and jailed, to have his house searched, or to stand trial in court, yet all this may properly happen to the most innocent given probable cause, a warrant, or an indictment. Society has always paid a stiff price for law and order, and peaceful interrogation is not one of the dark moments of the law.[248]

The fourth one of the dissenting justices referred to interrogation as "the nerve center of crime detection."[249] That statement deserves consideration not only in regard to the need for such tactics as the accusatory confrontation, but also with respect to the utilization of trickery and deceit in the course of criminal interrogations. Moreover, none of those tactics presents inducements for false confessions.

TRICKERY AND DECEIT

The Introduction and Chapter 8 of this text presented reasons for supporting the position that trickery and deceit are at times indispensable to the criminal interrogation process. It also was stressed that they do not present the risk of false confessions. Case law in support of trickery and deceit was also discussed. The objective in the present section is to offer an expanded presentation on the law for prosecuting attorneys and other members of the legal profession who may need additional information and case references.

Not only has the United States Supreme Court sanctioned the use of interrogation trickery and deceit, but so has the Supreme Court of Canada. There are also many state appellate court decisions to the same effect.

In the 1969 United States Supreme Court case of *Frazier v. Cupp*, the Court upheld a conviction based in part on a substantial piece of trickery.[250] The defendant, while under interrogation as a murder suspect, was told *falsely* that a suspected accomplice had confessed. In the Supreme Court's opinion affirming the conviction, Justice Thurgood Marshall, writing for the Court, stated that although the misrepresentation about the accomplice's confession had been relevant, it had not rendered the otherwise voluntary confession inadmissible as evidence. He then stated that cases of this nature were to be decided upon "the totality of the circumstances."

The Supreme Court of Canada, in the 1981 case of *Rothman v. the Queen*,[251] was confronted with the question of the admissibility of

---

[248]384 U.S. 436, at 517 (1966).

[249]*Supra* at p. 501.

[250]394 U.S. 731 (1969).

[251]59 C.C.C.2d 30 (1981).

incriminating statements by a narcotics violator to a police officer who had posed as a criminal offender. The Court ruled that this deception had not rendered inadmissible what had been revealed to the officer. In a concurring opinion, Justice Antonio Lamer stated:

> There is nothing inherently wrong in outsmarting criminals into admitting their guilt or into jeopardizing the liberty they might be tempted to take with the truth in the course of their trial.... It must also be borne in mind ... that the investigation of crime and the detection of criminals is not a game to be governed by the Marquess of Queensbury rules.[252]

Justice Lamer recognized the fact that the police "must sometimes of necessity resort to tricks or other forms of deceit." He did caution, however, that the trickery and deceit must not be of such nature as to "shock the community," and he gave two illustrations: a police officer posing as a chaplain to hear a suspect's confession, or one pretending to be a legal aid lawyer in order to elicit incriminating statements.[253] He stated, however, what would also shock the community would be preventing the police from using the vitally necessary tactics and techniques based upon trickery and deceit, particularly in a case such as this one that involved a trafficker in drugs.

In addition to the leading case of *Frazier v. Cupp*, many other cases, state and federal, have upheld the legal validity of trickery and deceit in the interrogation process. They encompass decisions sustaining the practice with respect to fingerprints;[254] playing one accomplice against another;[255] placing blame upon, and condemning the victim;[256] lying to a murder suspect that the victim was still alive; and other similar tactics.[257]

---

[252]*Supra* Note 251 at 72.

[253]*Supra* Note 251 at 74–75.

[254]State v. Cobb, 115 Ariz. 484, 566 P.2d 85 (1977); People v. Lira, 174 Cal. Rptr. 207 (Cal. App. 1980).

[255]Ward v. State, 408 N.E.2d 140 (Ind. App. 1980); State v. Flowers, 592 S.W.2d 167 (Mo. 1979); U.S. ex rel Hall v. Director of Corrections, 578 F.2d 194 (7th Cir. 1978).

[256]Rowe v. State, 41 Md. App. 641, 398 A.2d 485 (1979). In this case the interrogator referred to the murder victim as a "no good son-of-a-bitch," and the interrogator said he would like to shake the hand of the person who killed him, whereupon the suspect held out his hand to the interrogator. "Deception," said the court, "short of an overbearing inducement," is a "valid weapon of the police arsenal."

In Frazier v. Cupp itself (*supra* Note 250), the Supreme Court referred to the interrogator having "sympathetically suggested that the victim had started a fight by making homosexual advances," at which point, said the Court, the suspect "began to spill out his story."

[257]State v. Cooper, 217 N.W.2d 589 (Iowa 1974); For example: People v. Crowson, 124 Cal. App. 3d 198, 177 Cal. Rptr. 352 (1981); U.S. ex rel Caminito v. Murphy, 222 F.2d 698 (2d Cir. 1955), but see Edwards v. State, 412, N.E.2d 223 (Ind. 1980).

Generally rejected has been a per se rule of inadmissibility due to trickery and deceit.[258] One outstanding aberration is a 1984 decision of an Illinois appellate court, which exhibited a gross misconception of judicial precedent as well as the judicial rationale for the allowance of trickery and deceit. It, along with the dissenting opinions of three of the seven justices of the Illinois Supreme Court in another case, warrants analysis.

In the Illinois appellate court case, *People v. Payton*,[259] decided in 1984, the police interrogator had falsely told the suspect: 1) that his fingerprints had been found at the scene of a residential burglary, and 2) that he had been positively identified by the victim. In reversing the conviction, the appellate court erroneously stated that such trickery was disallowed by both the United States Supreme Court and the Illinois Supreme Court. It cited *Miranda v. Arizona*, which made no such ruling, and the appellate court opinion did not even mention *Frazier v. Cupp*. It also cited an Illinois Supreme Court case that had not involved that issue. The decision drew severe criticism from an Illinois trial court judge, Judge Robert J. Steigmann of the sixth judicial circuit, although he had not been personally involved in the case itself. Judge Steigmann's criticism appeared in the *Chicago Daily Law Bulletin*.[260] In it, he called attention to the court's erroneous statements regarding the holdings of both the United States Supreme Court and the Illinois Supreme Court and also directed attention to the faulty reasoning with respect to interrogation trickery. The appellate court had stated that "a suspect grossly and intentionally misled as to the amount and strength of the evidence against him might well be induced to confess as a direct result of those misrepresentations." Of that statement, Judge Steigmann submitted the following analysis, which should be considered by any court confronted with this issue:

> Assume that the police officer accurately, instead of falsely, represented to the defendant that he was seen leaving the scene of the burglary and that the police had recovered his fingerprints at the scene. Under those circumstances, could it be seriously argued that the defendant's subsequent confession should be suppressed because the police revealed too much about the strength of their case against him? Or assume that the police officer made the same representations to the defendant about his identification and fingerprints but that the police officer was mistaken despite his honest belief that the information he was

---

[258]With regard to the basic principle underlying the deception issue, see State v. Oliver, 341 N.W.2d 25 (Iowa, 1983), in which the court points out that the American Law Institute, in its Model Penal Code of Pre-Arraignment Procedure, §140.4 and the commentary on p. 357, merely requires that it be considered along with other circumstances in determining whether there was coercion. A per se rule of rejection of a confession due to deception is not part of the code.

[259]122 Ill. App. 3d 1030, 462 N.E.2d 543 (5th Dist. 1984).

[260]CHICAGO DAILY LAW BULLETIN, July 6, 1984.

relaying to the defendant was accurate. Under these circumstances, should the court conclude that the statements of the defendant ought to be suppressed because of police "trickery?"

The only difference between those two hypotheticals and the fact of [the case under discussion] is the state of mind of the police officer, not the defendant. However, it is the defendant's state of mind which ought to be the focus of an inquiry into whether the waiver of his rights and his subsequent statements were voluntarily given. The effect upon the defendant of the representations by the police officer concerning the strength of the state's case is precisely the same whether those representations are true, whether they are lies, or whether the police officer believes them to be true and is mistaken.[261]

In another trickery-deceit case, *People v. Martin*,[262] decided by the Illinois Supreme Court about the same time as the forgoing decision of the Illinois appellate court, three of the supreme court's justices were as far off target as were the three appellate court judges in the forgoing case. It involved a situation where a suspect in a murder case had been falsely told that his accomplice had named him as the "trigger man." Although four members of the supreme court were of the view that the interrogator's lie had not rendered the resulting confession inadmissible, three members of the court dissented. The almost incredible statement was made by the dissenting justices that "There is no difference in principle between the withholding of evidence favorable to a defendant and the willful, knowing falsehood which tricked defendant into making the statement."

Once again, Judge Steigmann, who only 3 months earlier had applied his analytical skills to the appellate court case of *People v. Payton*, stated in his second article[263] that the primary problem with the dissent in *People v. Martin* is that it "focuses upon the mental state of the police officer, not the defendant," whereas the mental state of the officer is irrelevant to the question of "whether the defendant's statement was involuntarily induced by police conduct...." He stated that this improper focus could be demonstrated, as he had suggested in his first article, by presenting two questions: "1) What if the police representations to the defendant were true, and 2) If the defendant believes the police representations to be true,

---

[261]Judge Steigmann also made the following comment in his article: "No court in this state ought to arrogate to itself the supervision of the investigative tactics of police officers according to some arbitrary rule book authored by the court after the fact. The concern of the police ought not be to avoid offending the court's sensibilities, but rather to obtain trustworthy statements from suspects.

"The investigation of crime is not a game, and the Appellate Court disserves the public when it treats it as if it were. Requiring the police to pander to the aesthetic values of the courts has its costs."

[262]102 Ill. 2d 412, 466 N.E.2d 228, cert. denied, 105 S.Ct. 334.(1984).

[263]CHICAGO DAILY LAW BULLETIN, October 16, 1984.

how logically can it matter whether those representations were true or not when a court determines whether the defendant's admissions were voluntarily made?" As to the first question, Judge Steigmann stated he knew of no case where a defendant's confession was suppressed "because the police *truthfully* told him about the strength of the evidence against him." In answer to the second question, Judge Steigmann posed another one: If the interrogator was lying, how would the suspect's confession be rendered involuntary by what was in the *interrogator's* mind?

With regard to the claim of the dissenting justices in the *Martin* case that the admission into evidence of a confession obtained as a result of an interrogator's lie would "serve to denigrate and demean the judicial process," Judge Steigmann pointed out that the defendant in the case, sentenced to 75 years in prison for murder did not deny his guilt in the appeal or even allege that his confession had been beaten or forced out of him. Upon a new trial, without the confession being available to the prosecution, Judge Steigmann stated that there would be an acquittal. Presumably, therefore, "the release of this murderer under these circumstances would not 'serve to denigrate and demean the judicial process.' "[264]

Youthfulness and Mental/Physical Impairment as Affecting Voluntariness

A legal determination of voluntariness does not depend upon youthfulness alone but rather upon the totality of all the circumstances, including experience, education, background, and intelligence of the suspect.[265]

---

[264]Also of interest are two Arizona appellate court decisions regarding interrogation trickery. One involved the misrepresentation to a woman suspected of killing her husband that he was still alive when, in fact, he was dead; in the other case a false statement was made to the suspect that his fingerprints were found at the crime scene. In the former, State v. Denny, 27 Ariz. App. 354, 555 P.2d 111 (1976), the suspect's confession was rejected, whereas in the latter, decided shortly thereafter, State v. Winters, 27 Ariz. App. 508, 556 P.2d 809 (1976), the confession was considered acceptable by the same court. The distinction the court made between the two was that in the latter case, the suspect's will was "not overborne by police deception to a degree sufficient to render the statement false or unreliable." In a case note in 19 ARIZ., L. REV. at 576 (1977), the earlier opinion was viewed as "somewhat puzzling."

Regarding the general subject of interrogation trickery, consider the following comments by Professor Welsh S. White in *Police Trickery in Inducing Confessions*, 127 U. PA. L. REV. 581 (1979) at 627–629: ". . . the use by law enforcement officers of any tactic that challenges a suspect's honor or dignity raises a fundamental question for our judicial system . . . . Interrogation tactics that are calculated to make the suspect feel that he is not a decent or honorable person unless he confesses constitute direct assaults upon that dignity." Professor White recommended that practically all forms of trickery "should be absolutely prohibited."

In addition to the Illinois cases cited in notes 259 and 262, there is another Illinois appellate court decision exhibiting the same degree of unawareness of the case law and the various other considerations involved in the trickery and deceit issue. People v. Lee, 128 Ill. App. 3d 774, 471 N.E. 2d 567 (Dec. 1984).

[265]Chapter 8 of this text contains a discussion of the various issues concerning the interrogation of youthful offenders, at page 243.

The fact that a suspect is mentally deficient or mentally ill will not necessarily render him incapable of making a confession that will meet the requirement of admissibility. The same is true of such conditions as intoxication, drug addiction, and other disabilities. The degree and extent to which they have affected the mental processes relevant to a suspect's capacity to understand his present predicament and to relate with reliability the happening of an event will depend upon a court's consideration of the totality of the circumstances rather than upon any particular factor. Based upon this limitation, there is little to be gained by references to the decided cases, except for the viewpoint expressed in one wherein the court stated:

> As with other mental faculties, the presence of intellect or volition are questions of degree. Just as the ability to assist counsel with a "modicum of intelligence" is sufficient for capacity to stand trial, so, too, the presence of minimal intelligence and free will should suffice for a finding of competency to confess.[266]

Effect of Polygraph Examination

Despite the general rule of inadmissibility of polygraph examination results, if a suspect agrees to submit to it (and, if in custody, has waived *Miranda* rights), incriminating statements made by him prior to, during, or after a test, are admissible as evidence. This is subject to the condition, of course, that neither the pretest interview nor a posttest interrogation involved any force, threats, or promises of leniency.

In laying the foundation for the admissibility of a polygraph subject's incriminating statements, the prosecuting attorney should avoid any reference to the fact that a polygraph examination was conducted, or even that the witness is a polygraph examiner; otherwise, the inference may be drawn that the test results indicated deception, which would be tantamount to direct testimony to that effect, in violation of the general inadmissibility rule. The procedure that should be followed, therefore, is for the prosecutor to present the examiner as a witness, without identifying him as an examiner, and have the examiner relate that he had questioned the suspect, who then made the incriminating statements, and that they were obtained without any force, threats, or promises of leniency. The decision will then have to be made by defense counsel whether the polygraph issue should be injected into the case for the purpose of showing that polygraph experience was a coercive factor behind the confession.[267]

---

[266]People v. Brown, 380 N.Y.S.2d 476 (App. Div. 1985).

[267]A discussion of the polygraph technique itself is contained in REID AND INBAU, TRUTH AND

Totality of Circumstances Test for Confession Voluntariness

There are numerous appellate court decisions that have held that a confession was either admissible or inadmissible as evidence on the basis of whether the "totality of circumstances" during an interrogation rendered the confession voluntary or involuntary. One of the most incisive appellate court opinions on this issue was that of Chief Justice William Erickson of the Colorado Supreme Court in the 1983 case of *People v. Freeman*.[268] In the interrogation of the defendant as a kidnap-murder suspect, the police indulged in several tactics found by the court to be objectionable, such as a threat of prosecuting the suspect's stepbrother, a veiled promise of a lesser sentence in return for revealing the location of the victim's body, and the employment of the so-called "Mutt and Jeff" routine performed by two interrogators. The court concluded that although none of those factors, considered alone, would have rendered a confession involuntary, the "totality of the circumstances" had compelled that result. Other cases applying that test reached results of voluntariness;[269] some, however, discussed the issue in terms of whether the interrogator's conduct had an "overbearing effect upon the suspect's will," or else that phrase was used along with "totality of circumstances."[270]

In concluding this discussion of the issue of confession voluntariness, the authors suggest that the courts should bear in mind the fact that being coaxed into confessing is not the equivalent of being coerced.

DECEPTION: THE POLYGRAPH ("LIE-DETECTOR") TECHNIQUE (2nd ed. 1977). The confession issue appears on pp. 372–373, and reference is there made to the following relevant cases: Johnson v. State, 355 A.2d 504 (Md. App. 1976); State v. Green, 271 Ore. 153, 531 P.2d 245 (1975); Leeks v. State, 95 Okla. Cr. 326, 245 P.2d 764 (1952); Stack v. State, 234 Ga. 19, 214 S.E.2d 514 (Ga. 1975). One of the very few confession cases where a conviction was sustained, even though the testifying examiner revealed the polygraph test results is Tyler v. United States, 193 F.2d 24 (D.C. Cir. 1951). In that case, however, the court placed heavy emphasis upon the fact that the trial judge had issued a "clear and positive instruction to the jury" that the examiner's testimony was to be considered only upon the voluntariness issue. Also, the following cases have held that the mere identification of the witness as an examiner was not improper in and of itself: State v. Carey, 288 N.C. 254, 218 S.E.2d 387 (1975); People v. Sammons, 17 Ill.2d 316, 161 N.E.2d 322 (1959).

The attorney or judge who is confronted with the legal problems in cases where suspects or witnesses have undergone tests for deception by means of "truth serum," hypnosis, or voice stress evaluation will find helpful information in MOENSSENS, INBAU and STARRS, SCIENTIFIC EVIDENCE IN CRIMINAL CASES (3rd ed., scheduled for publication in early 1986).

[268]668 P.2d 1371 (Colo. 1983). Another 1983 case, in which a confession was held inadmissible on the basis of totality of circumstance but under the label of "brainwashing," is People v. Sickley, 448 N. E.2d 612 (Ill. App. 1983). The trial court had reached that result with some difficulty, having twice denied a motion to suppress the confession but, after "much soul searching" granted it, which the appellate court found to have been the proper ruling.

[269]Among the many cases, and one in which the "totality of circumstances" test is fully discussed, is State v. Edwards, 49 Ohio St.2d 31, 358 N.E.2d 1051 (1976).

[270]Miller v. Fenton, 741 F.2d 1456 (3rd Cir. 1984), a 2 to 1 decision in a habeas corpus case,

---

also explores the issue, particularly in the dissenting opinion, of whether federal review involves a "mixed question of law and fact."

On the broad issue of confession voluntariness, see the scholarly article by Professor Joseph D. Grano of Wayne State University, 65 VA. L. REV. 859–945 (1979), "Voluntariness, Free Will and the Law of Confessions."

APPENDIX

THE PSYCHOLOGICAL PRINCIPLES OF CRIMINAL INTERROGATION

Brian C. Jayne[1]

The nine steps of interrogation that were discussed in this text were developed primarily through insightful observations of successful interrogations coupled with information obtained through interviews of criminal suspects following their confessions. It is often observed in science that the explanation follows the discovery. So it is with *the nine steps* of interrogation. This appendix outlines a psychological model applicable to interrogations and confessions. The Reid model provides a rationale, built on psychological theories and principles, to describe why *the nine steps* of interrogation are successful in eliciting the truth. The purpose for constructing psychological models is that they permit generalizations and predictions without supporting empirical data. To this end, a successful interrogator should have a good grasp of the psychological principles and theories underlying interrogations and confessions.

Psychologically, interrogation can be thought of as the undoing of deception. Therefore, to understand the psychology of confessions requires a fundamental understanding of the psychology of deception. For the purposes of criminal interrogation, deception can be defined as: "a selected behavior of distorting or denying the truth for the purpose of benefit to the individual." The significant portion of this definition is "for the purpose of benefit to the individual" because it provides that all criminal deception shares a common motivation.

Not only can it be stated that all criminal deception shares a common motivation but, furthermore, that the motivation of deception is avoidance—avoiding the consequences of telling the truth. The consequences being avoided through deception fall into one or both of two categories: *real* or *personal* consequences.

[1]Director of Reid College of Detection of Deception, John E. Reid and Associates, Chicago, Illinois.

Real consequences generally involve loss of freedom (going to jail, having a probation revoked) or loss of income (being fired, paying restitution or civil damages). Personal consequences, on the other hand, affect the individual's self-concept. Loss of self-esteem, pride, or integrity can be very significant personal consequences to avoid through deception. The mere embarrassment of having to admit an act of wrongdoing can pose a formidable barrier to overcome during an interrogation.

An irony presents itself in view of the fact that criminal deception is motivated through avoiding the consequences of telling the truth. The irony is that it is society that places these consequences on the criminal directly through laws and indirectly through social learning. Because of such consequences, society actually encourages successful deception through what is called operant conditioning. Operant conditioning describes a method of controlling or changing behavior by adding or taking away punishments or reinforcements. If a suspect is being questioned about a robbery he committed and tells the truth about his involvement, society punishes that behavior (telling the truth) by prosecuting and imprisoning the individual. On the other hand, if the suspect lies about his involvement in the robbery, and lies convincingly, the societal consequences associated with robbery have been avoided. In addition, the suspect is able to reap the rewards of the criminal behavior by spending the stolen money, and has thereby established confidence that he could commit another robbery and again lie successfully.

It is important to note that rewards are only present during successful deception. If the suspect initially lies about a robbery and later confesses, all is lost. Therefore, while society does not encourage deception, it indirectly rewards successful deception.

If operant conditioning were the only force influencing truth or deception, no suspect would ever tell the truth about any crime involving negative real or personal consequences. Interrogation and confessions would be a nonexistent phenomenon within our criminal justice system. However, interrogations do result in countless criminal confessions; therefore, there exists a counteracting force that combats or minimizes the effects of operant conditioning.

A social paradox exists in understanding and describing deception. On the one hand, successful deception is reinforced by society when a person evades punishment by successfully lying; but, conversely, through parents, churches, schools, and other social institutions, the teaching is that it is always best to tell the truth. Generally accepted is the principle that individuals want to live in a society of honest, truthful members whom they can trust and hold responsible. Thus, although an individual may escape the consequences of telling the truth through successful deception, he does so at the cost of inner conflict resulting from internalized beliefs that it is wrong to lie.

Psychologically, the results of the inner conflict produced by lying are frustration and anxiety. Anxiety is an ambiguous state of apprehensive uneasiness, generally not associated with a specific cause. It exists when there is a conflict or cognitive dissonance between what the individual perceives as desirable and what in fact is real. As the distance between the desirable goal and reality becomes greater, cognitive dissonance increases, resulting in greater anxiety. It is this increase of anxiety that explains, in part, why suspects confess during an interrogation. Although the suspect desires to avoid the consequences of telling the truth, he does not want to do this at the cost of increasing the internal anxiety associated with the deception. The potency of anxiety as a confession inducement is evident when considering the number of false confessions volunteered following a well-publicized crime. Through confessing, these individuals are often relieving pent-up anxiety that is in no way related to the precipitating criminal offense.

Anxiety is an integral part of each person's life. Although probably unavoidable, anxiety can be substantially controlled through behavior and various psychological processes. Controlling anxiety, in fact, is such a natural process that most individuals are unaware of the mechanisms by which this goal is accomplished.

As an undesirable state, anxiety ranks very high in the hierarchy of most individuals' consciousness. In fact, this axiom could be stated about anxiety reduction: "The mind and body will work together to reduce anxiety even at the cost of the psychological well-being or physical health to the individual." In its extreme states, an individual's attempt to deal with anxiety can cause neuroses, including somatic illnesses, such as blindness or paralysis. Although the anxiety associated with deception is rarely this dramatic, a trained observer can identify the individual's behavioral and cognitive attempts to relieve anxiety during deception by observing verbal and nonverbal behavior symptoms.

GENERAL PSYCHOLOGICAL FACTORS

Reducing Anxiety through Behavior

At the verbal level, a suspect chooses the degree of anxiety associated with deception through the words he uses in verbalizing a deceptive answer. For simplification, three categories of deception are evaluated with respect to their influences on anxiety (see Figure A.1). Note that as the answer accepts less responsibility, anxiety increases. The following examples illustrate the differences among the illustrated levels of deception.

Joe stole $500 from yesterday's deposit at work, and is asked by his employer, "Did you steal that $500?" If Joe merely shakes his head and says nothing, he has engaged in omission. The nonverbal behavior implies denial, but Joe technically has not lied. On the other hand, Joe may reply: "No I didn't, but I did borrow $500 from that deposit and was going to repay it." Again, this is omission. The answer involves accepting responsibility for taking the $500 but it is not a truthful one because Joe would not have repaid the money had he not been confronted with the implied accusation. During omission, the individual may accept responsibility for the act, but in such a way as to minimize the consequences. Assume that the deposit was $50 short to begin with, so that Joe only had stolen $450. If he replies, "I did not steal that $500," he again is implying that he did not steal any money from the deposit by this very specific denial.

Evasion involves less responsibility than omission, but it causes more anxiety. If Joe replies with an objection, "Why would I steal money from you? I like my job too much," he has engaged in evasion. Similarly, Joe may simply state in feigned disbelief, "You think I stole $500?" Or he may qualify his answer with "I don't believe I removed any money from that deposit." Evasion does not represent a denial and often leaves an opening for a future omission if deception is suspected. A denial would take the form of a definitive statement like: "No I didn't"! It, of course, is accompanied by the greatest amount of anxiety.

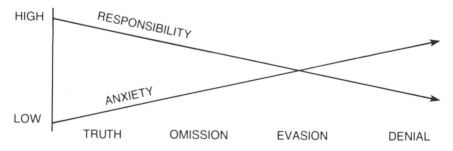

Figure A.1. If the guilty suspect tells the truth when questioned, full responsibility is accepted for the offense and no cognitive dissonance is experienced; thus, anxiety has been avoided. Omission involves an implied truth, although it produces some anxiety for the individual. Evasion often leaves a potential escape route for psychological retreat if the deception is discovered. Finally, denial accepts no responsibility for the offense, but at the cost of maximum anxiety to the individual.

Nonverbally, anxiety can be reduced through body movements or somatic (physical) activities. Generally, nonverbal behavior reduces anxiety by displacement or distraction. If a suspect shifts position in his chair at the moment he lies, anxiety is being displaced by muscle movements. On the other hand, if a suspect starts picking lint from his clothing or plays with his glasses while lying, the person is directing attention to something other than the deceptive verbal response.

Behavior symptoms of guilt or deception that the astute interviewer observes are efforts on the suspect's part to reduce the anxiety associated with deception. It is important to realize that there is no overt behavior or internal change occurring within an individual that is unique to deception. Deception can be inferred with a degree of statistical accuracy by not only observing the behavior of anxiety reduction, but also by paying close attention to the timing and consistency of the behavior.

Reducing Anxiety Cognitively

In addition to the reduction of anxiety through body movements and somatic activity, the mind attempts to reduce anxiety through a series of hypothetical constructs called defense mechanisms. A defense mechanism is an adjustive reaction typically employed to reduce anxiety, guilt, or loss of self-esteem. Defense mechanisms operate within the individual by distorting or denying reality. For the purposes of this discussion, two defense mechanisms will be analyzed.

The first of the defense mechanisms is *rationalization*. This is the act of redescribing what a person does in such a way as to avoid any responsibility for the consequences of his behavior. If a customer removes lipstick from a display stand and puts it in her purse, at the time the lipstick is found during a search, the customer may claim that she absent-mindedly put the lipstick in her purse believing that it was hers. By rationalizing the theft, she has sought to avoid responsibility or "intent" for doing the act, thus reducing anxiety. The employee who has been embezzling funds from a bank may rationalize the thefts by stating that the money was only being borrowed, and that eventually it would have been repaid.

The second defense mechanism is *projection*. During projection, an individual shifts the blame for his own thoughts or actions onto another person, place, or thing. A rape suspect who accuses the victim of wearing revealing clothing and engaging in promiscuous, teasing behavior is projecting the crime back onto the victim. Likewise, an employee may reduce anxiety associated with theft by blaming the employer for not paying him overtime. In the employee's mind no theft occurred; he simply was taking what was due to him.

An important concept with respect to defense mechanisms is that although they function through distorting or denying reality, this does not mean that the individual loses touch with reality; reality has merely been redefined. An analogous situation exists in describing the proverbial optimist's and the pessimist's description of water in a glass. The optimist views the glass as half-full, whereas the pessimist perceives the glass as being half-empty. Both individuals are acknowledging the same amount of water in the glass (reality), but they view reality differently.

In summary, all criminal deception is motivated through the hope of avoiding the consequences of telling the truth. Whether these consequences are real or personal, they represent a perceived threat to the individual. Because of social learning, avoidance occurs concomitantly with anxiety during deception. Anxiety is reduced simultaneously through physical behavior and defense mechanisms to the point that many individuals are able to tolerate the internal anxiety associated with their deception.

THE PSYCHOLOGY OF THE NINE STEPS TO EFFECTIVE INTERROGATION

If interrogation is the undoing of deception, what are the elements of deception that can be undone or influenced? To answer this question it is useful to evaluate why a person chooses to confess. An individual will confess (tell the truth) when he perceives the consequences of a confession as more desirable than the continued anxiety of deception. If, on the other hand, the consequences of the confession are perceived as less desirable than the anxiety associated with deception, the individual will continue to lie. The variables contained within these two conditions are perceived consequences and perceived anxiety; both of these variables can be affected psychologically during an interrogation. The goal of interrogation, therefore, is to decrease the suspect's perception of the consequences of confessing, while at the same time increasing the suspect's internal anxiety associated with his deception, as illustrated in Figure A.2.

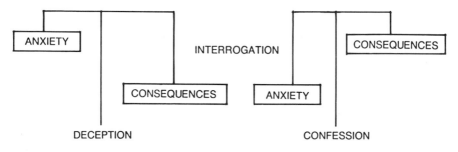

Figure A.2.

References to influencing anxiety during an interrogation do not mean, or imply, use of any threats, coercion, or abuse to the suspect. Anxiety, as used in this discussion, refers only to the suspect's internal feelings of uneasiness as a result of his own cognitive dissonance. Similarly, in reference to decreasing the suspect's perception of the consequences, no promises should be made of leniency.

There are four basic concepts involved in the relationship between consequences and anxiety and how they can be influenced to elicit a desired behavior. Apart from confessions, the concepts apply to other elicited behavioral actions, such as purchasing a particular product, voting for a certain political candidate, or abstaining from alcoholic consumption. These concepts are expressed in Figure A.3.

EXPECTANCY + PERSUASION $\xrightarrow{\text{belief}}$ BEHAVIOR (CONFESSION)

Figure A.3.

The concept of *expectancy* refers to a want or goal perceived as desirable or inevitable. The deceptive suspect's expectancy at the onset of the interrogation is that if he confesses, the consequences (as he perceives them at that time) are inevitable, and that the most desirable goal would be not to confess.

The concept of *persuasion* is a form of communication wherein the listener's attitudes, beliefs, or perceptions are changed. Expectancies are changed through persuasion. If one person can change what another person believes to be desirable or inevitable, a change of expectancy will result.

The concept of *belief* is the vehicle of persuasion; beliefs are not fact and therefore are subject to interpretation and external influences. The catalyst of belief is important in another way, too. During a legal interrogation, reality cannot be changed. A confession will be inadmissible as evidence if the interrogator takes away the consequences of the confession (promises), or physically adds anxiety (threats, abuse) during the interrogation. However, the interrogator can legally change the suspect's *perception* of the consequences of confessing or the suspect's *perception* of the anxiety associated with deception through influencing the suspect's beliefs.

It should be made very clear at this point that the authors are talking about beliefs in the structure of internal messages that tend to support or refute an expectancy. The interrogation procedures and tactics expressed in this text in no way are intended to lead an innocent person into believing he is guilty.

Persuasion

On a daily basis, the average person is bombarded with persuasion in the media through advertisements, in stores through sales clerks, and on television when a politician addresses his constituents. Because of its prevalence and effectiveness at changing expectancies, persuasion is a much researched psychological phenomenon. After studying persuasion under different conditions and testing different variables, psychologists have identified four essential criteria for changing a listener's expectancies: credibility, awareness of a listener's attitudes, ability to have the message internalized, and feedback.

CREDIBILITY

The persuader must be perceived by the listener as a credible source of information. Credibility is constructed on sincerity, knowledge, and demeanor. Sincerity, real or feigned, as a desirable quality of a good interrogator cannot be overstated because it lends credibility to the interrogator's image, words, and actions. Sincerity can be displayed behaviorally through good eye contact, the use of open-hand gestures, a forward posture in the chair, and open facial expressions. Conversely, sincerity is lost behaviorally by not facing the listener, keeping the arms in a defensive, folded position, or displaying facial expressions reflecting disgust or degradation. On a verbal level, sincerity is enhanced by talking slowly and using careful, deliberate statements. The fast-talking, fast-walking used car salesperson is the epitomy of an insincere source of information.

The interrogator's knowledge is portrayed during an interrogation through familiarization with the investigation and with the suspect's background. Few occurrences during an interrogation are more destructive than the interrogator who is confused about names, places, dates, and events. The deceptive suspect can use the interrogator's ignorance to fortify his own denials.

It has been said of expert witnesses that it does not matter so much what the expert says in court, but rather how he says it. This is also true of the interrogator to some degree. On occasion, the interrogator must bluff or deceive the suspect. The demeanor of the interrogator will dictate whether or not the suspect can tell when the interrogator is on factual or fictitious ground. From the clothes worn to the confidence in his voice, the interrogator must instill an image of unquestionable credibility.

PERSUADER'S AWARENESS OF LISTENER'S ATTITUDES

As a person enters an auto dealership, the salesperson usually "sizes up" that person to identify probable attitudes with respect to likes and dislikes in a car. An older, conservative male customer accompanied by his wife will be interested in a particular model, options, and price range different from the young single man who strides in with a young woman on each arm. To use the same salespitch on both customers almost guarantees that one of them will not buy a car.

Two specific factors are important for the interrogator to assess. The interrogator should have a fairly good idea of first, what consequences the suspect is avoiding through deception, and second, what level of anxiety the suspect will accept through denial (anxiety tolerance). Since the goal of the interrogation is to affect perceived consequences and anxiety, this information directs the selection of themes, the timing of alternatives, and the identification of the most appropriate anxiety-enhancing statements.

Identifying the consequences being avoided during deception may be simple, as in the case of a young employee suspected of theft who does not want to lose his job, or it may be more involved, such as in the case of a rape suspect who has been to prison before and is presently engaged to be married. Does the second suspect fear most returning to prison (real consequence) or having to face his fiancée with his crime (personal consequence)? Case facts and background information may provide accurate information about the consequences the suspect is avoiding through deception. However, the best source of information is the suspect himself. During the behavioral analysis interview, the suspect may be asked introspective questions about the crime, the answers to which might reveal the consequences weighing most heavily on his mind. Some examples of these types of questions would be, "How do you think the person who did this feels right now?"; "What do you think should happen to the person who did this?"; or, "What considerations do you think should be evaluated in deciding what will happen to the person who did this?"

The degree of anxiety a suspect will accept will be evident during the behavioral pause following the direct, positive confrontation. A suspect who retorts with a definitive denial, "You're crazy. I didn't break into that store!" is indicating a much higher level of anxiety tolerance than the suspect who responds with a weak objection, " .... But sir, why would I want to jeopardize my good record by doing something like that?" The suspect's physical demeanor during the interrogation will also provide clues to anxiety tolerance. A suspect who is able to maintain direct eye contact, sit erect in the chair, and lean toward the interrogator in a challenging posture is indicating a greater anxiety tolerance than the suspect who slumps in the chair with his eyes vacantly staring at the floor.

INTERNALIZING THE PERSUADER'S MESSAGE

The Reid model describes the metamorphosis of a deceptive suspect's expectancy through altered beliefs. Psychologically, the process of transforming expectancies is quite involved and beyond the scope of this text. On a very fundamental level, an expectancy will be changed if the individual can be led to internalize a message. Before internalization occurs, the individual must be capable of comprehending new ideas against which to compare his present beliefs. Comprehension requires some degree of intelligence, understanding, and volition. The paranoid schizophrenic is an example of someone upon whom persuasion is ineffective, largely because his mind does not comprehend or process new ideas in the same manner an unaffected individual does.

Internalizing a concept or message involves more than simple comprehension; it is a three-stage process; as shown in Figure A.4.

RELATING ⟶ ACCEPTING ⟶ BELIEVING

Figure A.4.

Relating implies understanding, acknowledging, or comprehending a thought or idea. If A wants B to donate money to a foreign country to feed the starving population, B could relate to the message in that B acknowledges that the country's population probably is starving. However, that by itself will not be sufficient for B to donate money. As A keeps talking and reminds B that the life-style of the average American is 90 percent better than that of the rest of the world and that all Americans have a responsibility to foreign countries because of their good fortune, B may begin to accept the arguments. Accepting involves agreement and concurrence. B is not only relating to the idea that people are starving, but B has also accepted the concept that it is his duty to send money to feed them. However, B has not written out a check. Before B does that, he must believe that his check is really needed. B can relate to and accept the message, but he has not internalized it because he still has no personal incentive to give money to that country.

Beliefs are realized through an impetus. To internalize a message requires an incentive. As A overcomes B's objections and sees B's head nodding in agreement, A pulls out his donation tablet with the names and addresses of donors conspicuously displayed. B sees some of his neighbor's contributions and now has a reason to believe the message that he should donate money. A is going to go to B's other neighbors and B doesn't want them to see "no contribution" (probably in capital letters written in red) after his name. So, B writes out a check for an amount $1 more than his neighbor's contributions and A shakes his hand warmly.

Initially, an interrogation theme must deliver a purpose for the suspect to tell the truth. Whether this message is introduced through the concept that it is expected of every responsible citizen to tell the truth, impressing the idea of the futility of continued denials, or that the actual truth may not be as serious as that which is now believed to be true, the suspect must be able to relate to this aspect of the theme. The suspect must also accept the supporting arguments to tell the truth. The reinforcing arguments and statements contained in the theme material must be credible and plausible to the suspect. If a theme is developed around the message that everyone at a warehouse steals merchandise, the suspect must mentally acknowledge that, in fact, most of the employees working at the warehouse do, or probably do, steal.

Finally, the suspect must internalize or believe the message, which again requires an impetus. This incentive is typically provided through the use of an alternative. The alternative should be perceived as a natural extension of the theme and represent a choice wherein the suspect is offered the opportunity to confess with minimum anxiety or maximum anxiety. Table A.1 illustrates the process of internalizing a message.

Table A.1. The process of internalizing a message

Joe, the reason that I want to get this clarified is that at this time all I can prove is that you were the person who took that money from the gas station; that's not good enough for me. When I resolve a case I always try to report the whole truth, and the whole truth goes way beyond just proving who did something. The whole truth includes the reason why he did it. It has been my experience that people don't judge another person nearly as much by what he did, but rather why he did it. I'm sure you found that to be true also. If someone shoplifts a steak, don't you think its important to find out if the person was just plain dishonest and wanted to cheat the store out of money or, on the other hand, if the person was down on his luck and trying to make ends meet but just couldn't. With a family to feed and other responsibilities he took the steak out of sheer desperation. At least I think there's a big difference between those two people.	**Statement of purpose** **Supporting analogy**

Your case is different. I know, with times as they are, everyone is short of

Table A.1 Continued

money. Prices go up on food, clothes, and
gas while at the same time people are
getting paid less for the same amount of
work, not getting deserved raises, and
being laid off work completely. I've never   **Relating**
seen anytime in history where jobs are so
hard to get. What we're seeing is a lot of
guys who have tried for months to find
work, while at the same time borrowing
money just to keep alive. At some point in
time, their credit runs out and their
savings are spent. What choice does a man
have? He still has to eat and clothe his
family. He is forced to take things just to
survive.

In talking with some people who
know you well, all of them seem to say
the same thing—"Joe is a responsible,
hard-working man who thinks of
others before himself." I wish I could
say that about half the guys I work
with! And that's one of the reasons I
took the time to talk to you today. I   **Anxiety enhancement**
asked myself: How can a guy who is
well liked and respected by his friends,
a guy who probably never took a
penny in his life from anyone, how can
a guy like that hold up a gas station?
Well, I guess the truth of it is that the
very things that I respect in you are
probably responsible for what happened. It's because of your responsibilities and tendency to think of others
first that this thing happened. You tried
and tried to get a job, but no one would
give you one. You wanted to earn an
honest living, but how can someone do
that if he isn't given a chance to work!

Joe, if everything I've heard about you
is true, I'm convinced that you didn't
take that money for selfish reasons.

I'll bet it was for your family, who
needed money just to pay rent, buy
food, and keep shoes on your son's
feet. I'll bet that if someone had given
you a job, this, never would have hap-
pened at all! If even one employer   **Accepting**
were as generous as you are, I
wouldn't even be talking to you today.
But we can't change history. You didn't
get offered a job, you didn't have
money to provide for your family. In a
desperate moment, because of the fact
that you are so responsible and caring,
this thing happened.

Joe, this is important. If this money
wasn't spent on your family, if they
didn't see a penny of it and you spent it
all on booze or a girlfriend, never giving
a second thought to your poor family,
well, as far as I'm concerned, you can
leave this room right now!   **Internalization**
But Joe, if you didn't do this for your-
self — if it was your family's welfare
you had in mind, that's what I want to
put in my report because that's the
whole truth. Did you spend this
money on booze and things for yourself, or was it spent on things for
your family? It was for your family,
wasn't it?

In dissecting the interrogation in Table A.1, the first paragraph states a
purpose for telling the truth with a supporting analogy about shoplifting.
The second paragraph is the relating portion of the theme, made up of
statements the suspect can basically acknowledge to be true. The third
and fourth paragraphs are the accepting phase of the interrogation.
Anxiety-enhancing messages emphasizing Joe's desirable traits are introduced and reinforced. Finally, the fifth and last paragraph contain the
alternative question that provides the incentive for the confession. Although an actual interrogation will not have these concise, well-defined
delineations, this example contains the basic components that are present
in successful interrogations.

PERSUADER'S RESPONSE TO LISTENER'S FEEDBACK

Regardless of the thoroughness of a background investigation, or how skilled the interrogator is in identifying motives, consequences, or anxiety tolerance, it is unlikely that the interrogator's actions and statements will be effective in persuasion by predictable design. The interrogator must constantly monitor suspect feedback to determine whether or not the suspect is accepting the theme, whether he needs more anxiety enhancement, or if the timing of the alternative is right. Persuasion is a dynamic process that requires constant adjustments and alterations to keep the momentum on the side of the persuader.

Some of the specific behavioral cues relating to suspect feedback are discussed under "Psychodynamics of Interrogation." Prior to that discussion, however, it should be emphasized that before an interrogator can respond to suspect feedback, the suspect must give feedback. Whether this feedback is acceptance, rejection, aggression, or withdrawal, the suspect must provide information to the interrogator.

The two most difficult types of suspects from whom to elicit confessions are those with extremely high levels of anxiety tolerance (no guilt, remorse, constant challenges, and aggression), and those who are emotionally neutral. In the extreme form, the latter type of suspect will be impossible to offend and will accept challenges or degradation without the slightest rebuttal. Similar to the first type of suspect, symptoms of guilt, remorse, or regret are absent in the behaviorally neutral suspect. The interrogator could be down on his knees with tears flowing from his eyes in expressed sincerity, and this suspect would look on with a vacant, emotionless expression. Most suspect personalities fall somewhere between these two extremes. If the suspect has a tendency to be emotionally neutral, the interrogator must employ some emotion-inducing techniques. Hypothetical questions, challenging statements, and attention-getting tactics are each productive in eliciting suspect feedback.

Reducing Perceived Consequences

Perceived consequences are generally reduced through themes that employ rationalization or projection. As defense mechanisms, rationalization and projection reduce anxiety through redefining the reality of the consequences. Because reducing anxiety is a desirable goal within the suspect being interrogated, most suspects are very willing to rationalize or project their criminal behavior. Lillyquist[1] identified five "techniques of neutralization," which Sykes and Matza theorized are used by criminals to

---

[1] LILLYQUIST, UNDERSTANDING AND CHANGING CRIMINAL BEHAVIOR (1980).

reduce perceived consequences of their behavior.[2] This list is hardly exhaustive but provides a sample of the types of beliefs that reduce perceived consequences of criminal behavior.

1. Denial of responsibility (blame alcohol, drugs, amnesia, stress)
2. Denial of injury (the victim wasn't really hurt; the company won't go bankrupt)
3. Denial of victim (He deserved to be robbed; she wanted to have sex)
4. Condemnation of the condemner (everyone else steals)
5. Appeal to higher loyalties (suspect did not do it for himself)

Sympathy and compassion are effective consequence-decreasing tactics as well. As a general rule, real consequences of a confession are most effectively decreased through rationalization or projection, whereas personal consequences seem to be more susceptible to reduction through sympathy or rational logic. The reason this may be true is that if the suspect who is concerned about avoiding personal consequences believes that the interrogator can understand and seems to forgive the offense or suspect, he may believe that others will also be sympathetic and forgiving.

The alternatives that naturally grow from a theme should present a situation of choosing between maximum consequences (high anxiety) and minimum consequences (low anxiety). Some examples of these alternatives are:

1. Have you done this many times, or was this the first time?
2. Did you take $5,000, or just $1,000?
3. Did you plan to do this, or was it a spur of the moment decision?
4. Did you do this on purpose, or was it accidental?
5. Was this your idea, or were you just going along with the other guys?

At the time the alternative questions are presented to the suspect, it is important that the interrogator build up a strong enough case for the negative consequence so the suspect believes that if he does not confess to the one alternative, silence will mean the other one will be believed.

Just as there are statements that diminish perceived consequences of a confession, there are statements and actions that augment perceived consequences and are obviously detrimental to the interrogation process. Examples of statements that tend to increase perceived consequences are reminding the suspect how long he will be in jail or how his loved ones will feel toward him once they find out what he did. Especially when dealing

---

[2]Sykes and Matza, *Techniques of Neutralization: A Theory of Delinquency*, 22 Amer. Soc. Rev. (1957) 664-670.

with a suspect facing personal consequences, a demeaning or judgmental attitude is not conducive to eliciting confessions. Descriptive words such as murder, rape, rob, or steal should be avoided until after the suspect has confessed because of the consequence-stigma these words represent. Similarly, interrogators who wear badges, guns, or other authority paraphernalia are indirectly increasing the consequences perceived by the suspect when he tells the truth, for they are symbolic reminders of what will happen after he confesses.

Increasing Perceived Anxiety

Perceived consequences and perceived anxiety are not mutually exclusive phenomena, and their symbiotic nature can create a problem during an interrogation. If the interrogator only decreases perceived consequences, the anxiety associated with reduced consequences is also less. The effect of only reducing perceived consequences is shown in Figure A.5, which illustrates that at the outset of the interrogation perceived consequences outweigh perceived anxiety (X). If during the interrogation only the perceived consequences are minimized, without proper attention to the anxiety factor, the perceived consequences will still outweigh the perceived anxiety (Y). In other words, anxiety must be independently increased without increasing perceived consequences.

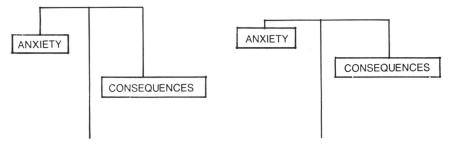

Figure A.5.

Anxiety is an illusive concept to understand or clearly define. Although anxiety is considered the precursor to guilt, remorse, shame, and many other emotional states, it must not be confused with its predicate results. The clearest distinction between anxiety as an antecedent and the subsequent emotional states derived from anxiety is that anxiety is directed inward, toward the individual. Many other emotional states (fear, anger, hate, etc.) are generally expressed away from the individual. This distinction is of paramount importance in utilizing anxiety-enhancing techniques or statements during an interrogation.

Statements or actions that are intended to increase anxiety must be directed at the suspect's perception of himself within the interrogation environment. For a suspect to be told that he is a "low-down, scheming, irresponsible thief" will naturally arouse a defensive emotional state. However, for the suspect to discover this himself through implication, insight, or suggestion will yield internally directed anxiety states. To identify which beliefs tend to enhance anxiety, consider what values and traits everyone nurtures and protects. Examples of some typical desirable human characteristics are:

1. Loyalty
2. Responsibility
3. Integrity
4. Religious beliefs
5. Love, compassion
6. Intelligence
7. Accomplishments
8. Respect

Statements such as, "You obviously don't care about this," or "You must not love your kids," serve as reminders of desirable human traits that have been violated through deception. However, the interrogator must be careful in his condemnations; the suspect should experience anxiety not because of the crime committed, but rather because he is lying about it.

Anxiety can be influenced independently from perceived consequences. However, a statement like "Someone who takes money from an employer is obviously not the type of responsible individual this company wants to employ," which increases anxiety as well as consequences, is nonproductive for interrogation purposes. Changing the statement to "Someone who is responsible and conscientious, the type of individual this company wants to employ, should be man enough to admit when he's made a mistake," increases perceived anxiety without increasing perceived consequences.

Anxiety-enhancing statements need not be as challenging as "Joe, if you were as smart as your IQ indicates, you would see that what I'm saying makes sense!"; in fact, sometimes a more effective approach is, "Joe, you obviously are an intelligent, bright person. Hell, you've got to be—just to have the responsible position you earned in this company. But just because you have a higher IQ than most of the people here doesn't mean that you don't have your weak moments like the rest of us . . . ." In addition, the anxiety-enhancing statements generally must be expanded upon within the theme and reinforced with examples and testimony. If an interrogator passively mentions that the suspects seems to be a good Christian (in response to a religious remark by the suspect), it is a token comment. However, if the theme develops around *how* religious he is, with recollections of his past good deeds, anxiety will be enhanced as the suspect perceives his own reality (lying) being a great distance from the immediately desirable goal (avoiding the consequences of telling the truth).

Some suspects have such well-developed defense systems established against opposing arguments that more direct anxiety-enhancing techniques must be utilized, such as a challenge: "Joe, if you don't want to get this straightened out, fine, you can leave. But if you stay, let's get this straightened out now." However, this type of challenge should only be made to a suspect who is no longer denying the accusation and is in a passive relating state. When issuing the challenge, the interrogator should remain seated, thereby making the suspect's departure not only difficult psychologically but socially as well. The challenge increases anxiety because the suspect realizes that the interrogator does not have endless patience. Moreover, by staying in the room, he has nonverbally confessed.

Other anxiety-enhancing efforts would fall under the category of attention-getting tactics. Feigned anger or impatience on the interrogator's part tends to make the suspect realize that the decision of whether or not to confess is becoming more imminent. These techniques are generally only successful, however, after the interrogator has established a working rapport with the suspect. The suspect prefers the interrogator's "other" demeanor and thereby experiences increased anxiety because he realizes that it is his persistent lying that caused the interrogator's emotional flare-up.

Nonverbally, anxiety can be increased through proximics. As the interrogator moves closer and closer to the suspect's chair, the suspect's nonverbal network of anxiety-reducing behavior greatly diminishes, and the suspect is now in a position where the intensity and sincerity of the interrogator's message is difficult to psychologically ignore; again, a decision between telling the truth and continued lying is becoming more imminent. Other nonverbal techniques that increase anxiety are maintaining mutual gaze above 80 percent (staring), sitting forward in the chair, and hand gestures referring to a thick investigative folder.

Anxiety conversely is nonproductively reduced during an interrogation by allowing the suspect to verbalize his denials, move around in the room, smoke, or substitute a more object-oriented emotional state for anxiety, such as anger or hostility. Anger can be vented much easier than anxiety because it is directed away from the individual. If a suspect becomes angry, he can use that anger for self-fulfilling purposes by blaming the interrogator for getting him angry. The interrogator must not invite this trap by insulting or degrading the suspect and must not fall into the trap of the suspect generating his own anger.

Again, the term "anxiety" is used here in a purely psychological sense.

Any behavior or statement that threatens the suspect's physical well-being, or his perception of it is not advocated legally or psychologically for interrogation purposes.

The Psychodynamics of Interrogation

For a suspect to pass from an expectancy of believing that the worst thing he could do is to confess to an expectancy of believing that a confession is acceptable, and perhaps even desirable, involves a dramatic change. This process occurs in steps or stages, one leading to the other. Although not every step applies to each interrogation or every suspect, through experience, the following stages are frequently observed:

The *direct positive confrontation*, from a psychological perspective, may produce two seemingly contradictory results. On the one hand, it provides valuable behavioral information with respect to the suspect's truthfulness and anxiety tolerance, as well as an exhibition of the interrogator's confidence of the suspect's guilt. Conversely, the nature of the direct positive confrontation tends to shatter the well-developed network of defense mechanisms the suspect has established since committing the crime. The neutralization techniques that permitted the suspect to live with the anxiety associated with his act prior to being confronted are now abolished. After the direct positive confrontation, the suspect finds himself in undeniable reality, with his mind focused primarily on the negative consequences of telling the truth.

During *active rejection*, the suspect may intellectually or emotionally attempt to persuade the interrogator that the results of the investigation are in error. This is generally accomplished through denials or objections. If the suspect cannot tolerate the anxiety associated with verbal rejections, he may psychologically withdraw and place a sound barrier between himself and the interrogator. Because the interrogator's persuasive statements are falling on deaf ears, the suspect will seem behaviorally neutral.

Few interrogations are successful unless the suspect can be moved beyond the active rejection stage. During active rejection, the suspect would like to destroy the interrogator's confidence, encourage an argument, become angry, or make an enemy of the interrogator so that the suspect will have something tangible to attack besides his own anxiety. If each of these defenses can be shut down, the suspect must rely on his own willpower and inner determination to keep from confessing. The suspect has then entered the state of passive relating.

During *passive relating*, the interrogator's themes are reintroducing latent defense mechanisms that have been cast aside because of the reality-invoking positive confrontation. In the beginning, themes should be general and perhaps not specifically address the suspect's crime. Statements with which the suspect can agree or acknowledge to be true make up the bulk of the introductory theme material. Psychologically, the suspect is agreeing with the interrogator's concepts, but still not believing that the reasonable thing for him to do is to confess. Behaviorally, the suspect is quiet, although he may still assume a forward, aggressive posture. Eye contact is maintained at normal levels, and there may even be some nonverbal expression of agreement. One of the reasons the suspect is passively relating is that the themes do not direc.ly apply to his case; the suspect can relate to them without sacrificing his own determination to resist. In other words, it is easy to relate to the message that jobs are hard to find, but it is quite another thing to accept the fact that the suspect held up a gas station because he did not have a job.

After a period of time during which the suspect has been passively relating to the interrogator's theme, a rapport and trust develops. The interrogator is perceived as a credible, sympathetic individual whom the suspect does not want to offend or challenge. Behaviorally, the suspect may seem almost relaxed in the chair. The forward posture is gone, and the eyes become warmer with no threatening stare. As the interrogator moves his chair closer to the suspect's, there is no attempt on the suspect's part to physically or psychologically retreat from the more intimate proximics. The interrogator's theme is becoming condensed as the interrogator talks slower and more deliberately. Sympathy and expression abound from the interrogator's voice. The suspect has moved into a state of acceptance.

During *acceptance*, the suspect is mentally weighing the consequences of confessing against the anxiety associated with his deception. Some of the anxiety-enhancing statements have registered with the suspect and his head and shoulders fall into a resigned slump. Posture in the chair has seemingly collapsed and his eyes seem glued to the floor; the suspect is ashamed to look at the interrogator. He still needs an impetus to confess; the suspect must still internalize the message.

During the alternatives, the suspect is searching for a way to admit the offense with minimal anxiety and in the fewest words. As the alternatives are developed and the negative alternative becomes a real possibility in the suspect's mind, he is anxious to prove that the negative choice is incorrect, finally believing and internalizing the positive choice. After the suspect nods his head in agreement to the lesser alternative, it becomes easier to relate the details of the confession as the pent-up anxiety is finally released.

As the diagram in Figure A.6 illustrates, the psychodynamics of interrogation describes the course of altering expectancies through decreasing perceived consequences of a confession and increasing perceived anxiety associated with deception. The suspect's perceptions of consequences and anxiety are only slightly affected during passive relating. However, a dynamic change is realized at the point of acceptance. It is this stage of the interrogation that the suspect is most susceptible to confessing. The transient nature of the altered expectancy achieved through the process of interrogation requires that the impetus of the confession be strategically timed. The garrulous interrogator may see the juncture between consequences and anxiety come and go before the alternative is presented. On the other hand, the interrogator who presents alternatives too early may lose the tactical effectiveness of the impetus. Even if the alternative question is later repeated at a more appropriate stage of the interrogation, the premature exposure of this vehicle of incentive may permit the suspect to perceive the presented choices as offering a no-win situation.

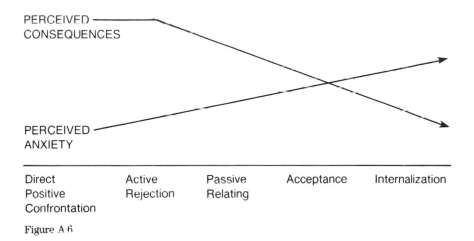

PERCEIVED
CONSEQUENCES

PERCEIVED
ANXIETY

Direct Positive Confrontation	Active Rejection	Passive Relating	Acceptance	Internalization

Figure A 6

In conclusion, The Nine Steps of interrogation describe an approach of changing a suspect's expectancy toward telling the truth. The technique is not broken down into steps merely because it simplifies understanding, but because expectancies are altered in stages. The psychodynamics of interrogation are important for recognizing the different stages of interrogation as well as identifying the time to use broad themes, anxiety-enhancement tactics, condensed themes, portrayals of sympathy, and alternatives.

INDEX

PRINCIPAL INTERROGATION/CONFESSION CASES